COMPUTER PERFORMANCE MODELING HANDBOOK

Notes and Reports
in
Computer Science and Applied Mathematics

Editor
Werner Rheinboldt
University of Pittsburgh

COMPUTER PERFORMANCE MODELING HANDBOOK

Edited by

STEPHEN S. LAVENBERG

IBM Thomas J. Watson Research Center
Yorktown Heights, New York

ACADEMIC PRESS, INC.
Harcourt Brace Jovanovich, Publishers
Orlando   San Diego   New York
Austin   Boston   London   Sydney
Tokyo   Toronto

ACADEMIC PRESS, INC.
Orlando, Florida 32887

United Kingdom Edition published by
ACADEMIC PRESS, INC. (LONDON) LTD.
24/28 Oval Road, London NW1 7DX

Library of Congress Cataloging in Publication Data
Main entry under title:

Computer performance modeling handbook.

   (Notes and reports in computer science and applied
mathematics ; no. 4)
   Includes bibliographical references and index.
   1. Electronic digital computers--Evaluation.
2. Digital computer simulation. I. Lavenberg, Stephen S.
II. Series.
QA76.9.E94C66   1983   001.64'028'7   82-8840
ISBN 0-12-438720-9   AACR2

To J

Contents

8 Extended Queueing Network Models

Charles H. Sauer and Edward A. MacNair

Preface

Computer systems have become so complex that intuition alone is not sufficient to predict their performance, and mathematical modeling has come to play an important role. Mathematical models of system performance range from relatively simple ones, whose solution can be obtained analytically, to very complex ones that must be simulated. This *Computer Performance Modeling Handbook* is a state-of-the-art reference manual for computer performance modeling practitioners. It is intended to help practitioners formulate and apply performance models by providing (1) analytical results for a wide variety of performance models, (2) guidance in the simulation of performance models, and (3) numerous application examples. It differs from a textbook in that mathematical derivations are not presented; rather, the emphasis is on easy-to-apply analytical results and simulation procedures. Anyone working in the area of computer performance evaluation should find the handbook indispensable. In addition, it is a useful source of material for performance evaluation courses at the senior or graduate level.

Chapter 1 ("Introduction to Performance Modeling" by Stephen S. Lavenberg) provides an introduction to the analysis, simulation, and validation of computer performance models. Chapter 2 ("Mathematical Prerequisites" by Stephen S. Lavenberg) contains basic material on probability, random variables, and the Poisson process to aid a modeler in understanding the assumptions made about a model and the results obtained from the analysis or simulation of the model. Little's formula, an important formula relating performance measures, is also discussed.

The models that play the most important role in performance evaluation are queueing models, in particular, queueing networks. Chapter 3 ("Analytical Results for Queueing Models" by Stephen S. Lavenberg and Charles H. Sauer) contains the most extensive collection of analytical results for queueing models currently available in the literature. The results are either formulas for performance measures or, as is typically the case for queueing networks, algorithms that can be used to compute performance measures. Over thirty examples are presented. Chapter 4 ("Approximate Analysis of Queueing Networks" by Stephen S. Lavenberg and Charles H. Sauer) presents approximate analysis methods for queueing networks for which either exact analytical results are not available or, if they are available, the computational expense is prohibitive. This is an area of continuing research activity. However, several methods that have practical uses are presented.

Chapters 5 and 6 deal with statistical aspects of simulation. Chapter 5 ("Generation Methods for Discrete Event Simulation" by Gerald S. Shedler) describes methods for generation of the random inputs that drive a simulation. General methods for random number generation are discussed and specific algorithms are provided for generation of samples from a variety of distributions. Chapter 6 ("The Statistical Analysis of Simulation Results" by Peter D. Welch) discusses the statistical analysis of the random outputs produced by a simulation. The purpose of the analysis is to produce an estimate of a performance measure and a meaningful statement about the accuracy of the estimate. The estimation of both transient and steady-state performance measures is considered.

Chapter 7 ("Simulator Design and Programming" by Harry M. Markowitz) discusses aspects of the designing, coding, and debugging of simulation programs. Simulation programming is illustrated first using SIMSCRIPT, a language specifically designed for simulation programming, and then a general-purpose programming language such as Fortran or PL/I.

Chapter 8 ("Extended Queueing Network Models" by Charles H. Sauer and Edward A. MacNair) describes a set of powerful modeling elements that can be used to define queueing networks that represent complex system features. The resulting class of queueing networks is far broader than the class of networks considered in Chapters 3 and 4, so typically these networks must be simulated. A series of examples is provided illustrating the usefulness of these networks.

Each chapter is largely self-contained. However, Chapters 1 and 2 contain basic material that is useful for understanding the remaining chapters, and the material on queueing networks in Chapter 3 is useful for understanding Chapter 4.

All of the authors are members of the IBM Research Division, and all except one are at the IBM Thomas J. Watson Research Center in Yorktown Heights, New York. Gerald Shedler is at the IBM Research Laboratory in San Jose, California. I am grateful to the Research Division for the time and facilities provided for the preparation of the handbook. In addition, financial support was provided by a grant from the IBM Group Technical Assignment System Structure Technology program. I wish to thank Hisashi Kobayashi for his participation in the conception of the handbook. The inspiration for the handbook was provided by the success of the IBM manual, *Analysis of Some Queueing Models in Real-Time*

Systems, Second Edition, GF20-0007-1, written by Philip H. Seaman and published in 1971. That manual is no longer up-to-date. In particular, it does not cover important results for queueing networks, and it does not contain any material on simulation.

I wish to thank Marylou Dietrich for her careful typing of major portions of the manuscript and for her cheerful cooperation with several authors and their many revisions. The careful typing and other assistance given by Betty A. Smalley during the early stages of preparation of the handbook is also gratefully acknowledged.

1

Introduction to Performance Modeling

Stephen S. Lavenberg

1.1 The Role of Performance Modeling

This handbook deals with the use of models in computer performance evaluation and is intended to be a state-of-the-art reference manual for performance modeling practitioners. While the evaluation of a computer system may involve such factors as cost, availability, reliability, serviceability, and security, we shall be concerned only with computer system performance, where performance is measured by such quantities as throughput, utilization, and response time. Performance is one of the key factors that must be taken into account in the design, development, configuration, and tuning of a computer system. Of course the overall system performance is affected by the performance characteristics of the various subsystems and ultimately the individual hardware and software components that constitute the system. Hence, the design of new hardware and software components has system performance implications that should not be ignored.

Once a particular computer system has been built and is running, the performance of the system can be evaluated via measurements, using hardware and/or software monitors, either in a user environment or under controlled benchmark conditions. However, in order to evaluate the performance of a system, subsystem, or component that cannot be measured, for example, during the design and development phases, it is necessary either to make performance predictions based on educated guesses or to use models as an aid in making performance predictions. The interactions in present-day computer systems are so complex that some form of modeling is necessary in order to be able to predict and understand computer system performance.

Performance modeling is widely used, not only during design and development, but also for configuration, tuning, and capacity planning purposes. One of the principal benefits of performance modeling, in addition to the quantitative predictions obtained, is the insight into the structure and behavior of the system that is obtained in the course of developing a model. This is particularly true during system design. The modeler must abstract the essential features of the design and this process leads to increased understanding and may result in the early discovery and correction of design flaws.

Many performance models can be mathematically analyzed to obtain such performance measures as utilizations, throughputs, and average response times. Such models are the subject of Chapters 3 and 4 of the handbook. Other performance models are so complex that they must be simulated in order to estimate performance measures. The simulation of performance models is the subject of Chapters 5–8. It is assumed that the reader has a basic familiarity with the complexities of present-day computer systems and a strong interest in their performance. Mathematical prerequisites are covered in Chapter 2. The remainder of this chapter contains introductory sections on the analysis and simulation of performance models as well as a discussion of model validation.

1.2 Analysis of Performance Models

A computer system can be viewed as a collection of interconnected hardware and software resources that provides service to a community of users. Figure 1.1 shows in a simplified way some of the resources that may comprise a computer system and the flow of work through the system. The work to be performed consists of transaction processing for interactive users at terminals and processing of a batch job stream. The hardware resources shown are terminals, main memory, processors, channels, and I/O devices. The software resources shown are the terminal access method, the batch job entry system, the scheduler (which swaps jobs and transactions in and out of main memory), the dispatcher (which schedules work on the processors), and the I/O supervisor (which schedules I/O requests). Important functions of the software are (1) to allow the hardware to be used in an efficient manner, e.g., by allowing as much sharing of the hardware among the users as possible and (2) to schedule work on the hardware to provide quick response to users, particularly to interactive users. In order to achieve efficient usage of the hardware, several jobs (we use the term jobs to refer to transactions or batch jobs) can simultaneously contend for such resources as main memory, processors, and the I/O subsystem. The figure shows the queues that form for these resources as a result of contention. The time spent waiting in these queues can have a

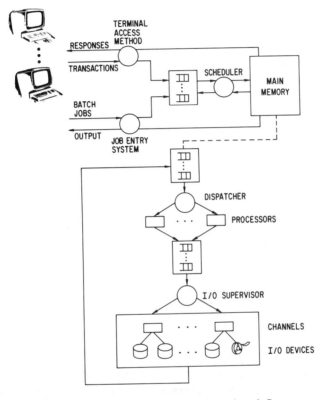

Fig. 1.1   Computer system resources and work flow.

substantial impact on the performance of the system. Perhaps the major reason models are needed in performance evaluation is to predict the effect of contention for resources on performance. The kinds of performance models that play the most important role in this regard are queueing models. The resource requirements of jobs are specified as inputs to a queueing model, and the model explicitly represents the queueing delays that occur. Examples of resource requirements of jobs are the number of instructions to be executed on a processor, the number of bits to be transmitted over a communication line, the amount of main memory required to store a program, the number of instructions executed while holding a serially reusable piece of software, and the length of a record to be read from a disk drive.

Queueing models began to be analyzed around the turn of the century in connection with performance problems in telephone systems. They have since given rise to a mathematical discipline known as queueing theory, a topic in applied probability. Queueing theory employs a variety of mathematical techniques to analyze queueing models. Many queueing models that represent the contention for a single resource have been analyzed. Chapter 3 presents analytical results for single resource queueing models that are useful in predicting the performance of individual components, such as communication lines, processors, and I/O devices.

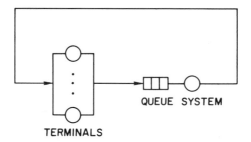

Fig. 1.2 Queueing model with system represented as a single resource.

One of the earliest successful applications of queueing models to problems in computer performance occurred in the late 1960s during the development of IBM's OS/360 Time Sharing Option (TSO). A simple queueing model was used to predict the performance of TSO running a single partition in main memory (see Lassettre and Scherr, 1972). This model is shown in Fig. 1.2 and described in detail in Chapter 3. It is assumed in the model that there are a fixed number of interactive users at terminals. A user thinks, enters input at the terminal, waits for the computer to provide service in response to the input (during which time the keyboard is locked), and receives output at the terminal. This process continues indefinitely. The time it takes to receive output, to think, and to enter input is specified as an input to the model and assumed to be a random variable having a known distribution. The service provided by the system consists of swapping a user's program in and out of main memory and executing the program. The time it takes to perform this service is also specified as an input to the model and assumed to be a random variable having a known distribution. Since there is only a single partition, service for one user cannot go on in parallel with service for another user. Thus, the system is represented as a single resource which can serve at most one user at any one time, and a queue is shown in front of this resource. If there were more than one partition so that service for different users could go on in parallel, a different representation of the system would be required. The model was primarily used to determine the number of interactive users the system could support without exceeding a specified average response time.

In a multiprogramming system several user programs simultaneously reside in main memory so that the processing activity of one program can go on in parallel with the I/O activity of other programs. Furthermore, contention can occur for the processing and I/O resources. What is needed in such a situation is a model that explicitly represents the contention for the multiple resources that comprise a system. Starting in the late 1950s such queueing models, which were developed to represent job shop systems, were analyzed in the operations research literature. Analytical results were obtained for a fairly broad class of models. Independent of this work, multiple resource queueing models were used to predict computer performance as early as the mid-1960s. However, it was not until the 1970s, when the results in the operations research literature began to be applied, that the use of multiple resource queueing models to predict computer performance became widespread. One such

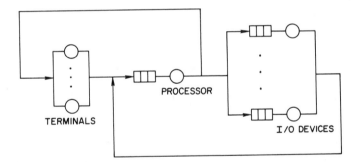

Fig. 1.3 Queueing model with system represented as a network of resources.

multiple resource queueing model is shown in Fig. 1.3. In comparison with Fig. 1.2 the system is no longer represented as a single resource, but as a network of resources, each resource having its own queue of requests. The application of queueing networks to computer performance modeling has led to further progress in developing and analyzing such models. For example, queueing network models that explicitly represent different types of jobs, e.g., batch jobs and TSO transactions, were analyzed. Chapter 3 presents analytical results for a broad class of queueing network models and examples of their application. These models are now widely used in performance evaluation. Several program packages, some of which are commercially available, have been developed to allow users to define and solve queueing network models of computer performance. For a survey of such program packages see Sauer and MacNair (1979).

Although the class of queueing network models that have been exactly analyzed has grown in recent years, many system features cannot be explicitly represented in such models. One important feature that is not represented in the queueing network in Fig. 1.3 is contention for main memory space. The model in Fig. 1.4 differs from that in Fig. 1.3 in that a queue for memory is

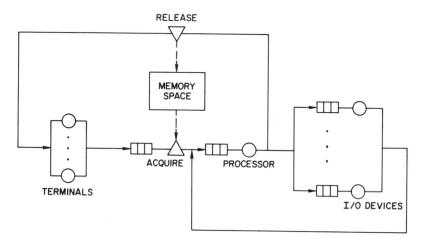

Fig. 1.4   Queueing model with contention for memory space represented.

shown. A job cannot get access to the processing and I/O resources of the system until it has acquired a portion of memory. When the job completes its processing and I/O services, it releases its portion of memory. Queueing networks in which jobs must possess a limited resource (such as memory space) in order to get service from another resource (such as a processor) have not been exactly analyzed. Chapter 4 presents an important technique, based on decomposing a model into a hierarchy of submodels, which can be used to approximately analyze such networks. Other useful approximate analysis techniques, e.g., for networks that explicitly represent processor dispatching based on priorities, are discussed in Chapter 4.

1.3   Simulation of Performance Models

Many performance models are so complex that an exact mathematical analysis is not possible and no reasonable approximate analysis techniques exist. For example, this is usually the case with queueing network models that explicitly represent complex resource scheduling algorithms. In such cases it is necessary to simulate the model. The kind of simulation we refer to is discrete event simulation on a digital computer. Once a model has been formulated a simulation program is written that keeps track of the evolution in time of the model as determined by the occurrence of events at discrete time instants. An event might be the arrival of a transaction or the completion of a service. The simulation program is run in order to obtain estimates of performance measures. Since most performance models incorporate some form of randomness in their inputs, e.g., to determine the times at which jobs arrive or to determine the resource requirements of a job, the outputs produced by such models, e.g., a resource utilization or an average response time, are also random quantities. Thus, the simulation of a model that incorporates randomness has statistical aspects that should not be ignored. Statistical aspects of simulation are discussed in Chapters 5 and 6.

Chapter 5 describes methods for generation of the random inputs that drive the simulation. Typically, the inputs to a model are independent samples from specified distributions. Although simulation programming languages provide some facilities for sampling from common distributions, the methods used do not always represent the state-of-the-art in terms of computational efficiency or appearance of randomness. Chapter 5 provides specific algorithms for generation of independent samples from a number of standard distributions, as well as a discussion of general methods for random number generation and considerations in the use of random number streams. This material will help the practitioner who has to program a procedure to generate samples from a distribution. In addition, Chapter 5 gives some methods for generating event times (e.g., times at which jobs arrive) as inputs to a model when the times between events are not independent samples from the same distribution.

Chapter 6 discusses the statistical analysis of the random outputs produced by the simulation. This is an important aspect of simulation that, if ignored, can result in erroneous conclusions being drawn from a model. The basic problem is that an unknown deterministic quantity in the model is estimated by a random quantity generated by the simulation. The purpose of the statistical analysis is to produce a meaningful statement about the accuracy of the estimate. Both the estimation of transient performance measures and the estimation of steady-state performance measures are considered.

In a trace-driven simulation the inputs that drive the simulation, e.g., the arrival times of jobs and their sequences of resources requirements, are not random quantities obtained by sampling from distributions, but are deterministic quantities usually obtained from tracing the jobs on a running system. Unless randomness is introduced elsewhere in the model a trace-driven simulation will be purely deterministic. Trace-driven simulation is discussed in review articles by Sherman and Browne (1973) and by Sherman (1976).

The design, coding, and debugging of a simulation program is often a very time consuming task. Simulation has the advantage that it can be applied to very detailed performance models, but this is also one of its major pitfalls. Some simulation projects have failed because the model was so detailed that the programming was not completed in a timely manner or because the model required more detailed input data than was available. Thus, it is often good practice to start with a fairly simple model and add detail if the simple model proves to be inadequate. Although it is difficult to say in general how detailed a performance model should be, the level of detail should be chosen based upon the purpose for which the model is intended, the information available about the system design, the kind of input data available, and the time and resources available to code, debug, and run the simulation program. Chapter 7 discusses aspects of the design, coding, and debugging of simulation programs. There are many languages available for simulation programming, and Chapter 7 does not attempt to cover all of these. Instead it illustrates simulation programming, first using SIMSCRIPT, a language specifically designed for simulation programming, and then using a general purpose programming language such as Fortran or PL/I.

GPSS is a widely used simulation language specifically designed to describe the flow of jobs through a system. A model to be simulated using GPSS is described by a block diagram. GPSS is discussed in the books by Fishman and Kobayashi mentioned in the References. The book by Gordon (1975) can serve as a GPSS user's manual. The ease of constructing models using GPSS has led to its wide use. However, the user should be aware that GPSS is considered to have shortcomings with regard to random number generation (e.g., see Section 4.4.9 in the book by Fishman).

As previously discussed, queueing networks can be used to explicitly represent the contention for resources that occurs in computer systems. Chapter 8 describes a set of powerful modeling elements that can be used to define queueing network models that represent many complex system features. The elements have been developed to provide compact representations of system features and to be flexible so that a variety of features can be represented. Furthermore, the elements have pictorial representations so that it is easy to draw a diagram of the network. The class of queueing networks that can be defined by using these elements is far broader than the class of queueing networks that can be mathematically analyzed. While it is possible to simulate these networks using any of the simulation languages mentioned previously, a program package called the RESearch Queueing package (RESQ) has been developed at IBM Research and is specifically designed so that users can easily define these kinds of networks. RESQ builds a simulation program based on the model definition, then carries out the simulation of the model and produces a statistical analysis of the simulation output. The RESQ package also incorporates a program that computes performance measures for those networks that can be exactly analyzed mathematically and hence, do not need to be simulated. Further information about RESQ is contained in Chapter 8 and the references cited therein.

At the end of Section 1.2 we briefly mentioned an important technique for the approximate analysis of performance models, based on decomposing a model into a hierarchy of submodels. This technique is discussed in detail in Chapter 4. Using this technique it may not be possible to mathematically analyze each of the submodels. Instead some of the submodels may have to be simulated. This combined use of analysis and simulation, sometimes called hybrid simulation, may be a cost-effective alternative to the use of pure simulation. The article by Chiu and Chow (1978) describes the hybrid simulation of a performance model of IBM's MVS operating system.

1.4 Validation of Performance Models

The development of a performance model involves characterizing the hardware and software resources that comprise the system, for example, the path lengths of major software components, the scheduling algorithms used, and the speeds of the hardware devices, and also characterizing the workload handled by the system in terms of the demands placed on the various resources. One may decide not to represent certain features of the system structure and the workload in the model and to represent other features in a gross way. This is done in order to simplify the model and in the belief that these features do not have a primary effect on performance. The choice of what to represent and how to represent it is the essence of modeling.

As an example, consider again the simple queueing model, shown in Fig. 1.2 and briefly discussed in Section 1.2, which Lassetre and Scherr (1972) used to predict the performance of OS/360 TSO running a single partition. This model incorporated a number of simplifying assumptions with regard to the system structure and the workload, so that it could be mathematically analyzed (see Chapter 3 for details). For example, in the model the system service (swapping and program execution) is assumed to be provided to a user continuously until completion, whereas time-slicing is employed in the system so that the service for one user is interleaved with the services for other users. In order to assess the usefulness of the model Lassetre and Scherr compared performance predictions obtained from the model with measurements from a running TSO system. The system workload was generated at simulated terminals using TSO benchmark scripts. The measured average system service time was an input to the model and the model was used to predict the average response time. The predicted and measured average response times were compared for 37 different cases (e.g., different numbers of users were considered). In approximately 75% of these cases the predicted average response time differed from the measured average response time by less than 10% and the maximum deviation was 24%. At the time of the study the goodness of the model's predictions was considered surprising due to the simplicity of the model. Today we have a better understanding of why this simple model provided useful predictions. This is due to the robustness of certain models and is discussed in Chapter 3.

One criterion for the validity of a model is that the conclusions that are drawn from experimenting with the model are the same conclusions that would have been drawn from experimenting with the system. However, it is usually not possible to test for this kind of validity in a timely fashion, either because the system has not been built or because it is too expensive to carry out the full set of experiments with the system. These after all are the reasons why the model was developed in the first place. If the system has been built, one should of course compare the performance predictions obtained from the model with the measured performance of the system for at least a few representative workloads and system configurations. Any major discrepancy between the predicted and measured performance would certainly cause one to question the validity of the model. Perhaps some key system feature has not been represented in the model or some aspect of the workload has been ignored. If the model is a simulation model that incorporates randomness, then when comparing model predictions and system measurements one must be careful that any discrepancies are not due to statistical variability in the simulation outputs. One way to test for this is to see whether a measured performance value (e.g., an average response time) lies within a confidence interval for that performance value produced by statistically analyzing the simulation outputs (see Chapter 6 for a thorough discussion of obtaining confidence intervals from simulation outputs). If the measured value lies within the confidence interval then there is no evidence of a discrepancy. Other statistical methods can also be applied to model validation. For example, an application of the statistical design and analysis of experiments to performance model validation is presented by Schatzoff and Tillman (1975).

Often two or more models having different levels of detail are developed to represent a system. For example, there may be a detailed simulation model and a simpler analytic model. If the system has not been built then the validity of the simpler model should be investigated by comparing its predictions with the predictions obtained from a more detailed model. Model validation is not discussed elsewhere in the handbook.

References

Chiu, W. W., and Chow, W.-M. (1978). A performance model of MVS, *IBM Systems J.* **17**, 444–462.

Gordon, G. (1975). "The Application of GPSS V to Discrete System Simulation." Prentice-Hall, Englewood Cliffs, New Jersey.

Lassettre, E. R., and Scherr, A. L. (1972). Modeling the performance of OS/360 Time Sharing Option (TSO), In "Statistical Computer Performance Evaluation" (W. Freiberger, ed.), pp. 57–72. Academic Press, New York.

Sauer, C. H., and MacNair, E. A. (1979). Queueing network software for systems modeling, *Software-Practice and Exp.* **9**, 369–380.

Schatzoff, M., and Tillman, C. C. (1975). Design of experiments in simulator validation, *IBM J. Res. Develop.* **17**, 252–262.

Sherman, S. W., and Browne, J. C. (1975). Trace-driven modeling: Review and overview, *Proc. Symp. Simulat. Comput. Syst.* pp. 200–207. National Bureau of Standards, Gaithersburg, Maryland.

Sherman, S. W. (1976). Trace-driven modeling: An update, *Proc. Symp. Simulat. Comput. Syst.* pp. 87–91. Boulder, Colorado.

The following are recent books that deal with topics covered in this chapter:

Fishman, G. S. (1978). "Principles of Discrete Event Simulation." Wiley, New York. This textbook covers modeling, programming, and statistical aspects of discrete event simulation, with an emphasis on statistical aspects. Most of the examples deal with queueing models, although not specifically applied to computer performance modeling. The statistical portions of the textbook are written at a first year graduate level, but other portions are at an undergraduate level.

Kleinrock, L. (1975 and 1976). "Queueing Systems, Vol. 1: Theory" and "Queueing Systems, Vol. 2: Computer Applications." Wiley, New York. This two volume set presents both the mathematical methods of queueing theory and applications to computer performance. The applications mainly deal with processor scheduling and computer-communication networks. The books are written at the first year graduate level for students in computer science and engineering.

Kobayashi, H. (1978). "Modeling and Analysis: An Introduction to System Performance Evaluation Methodology." Addison-Wesley, Reading, Massachusetts. This textbook on computer performance evaluation covers the following methods – analysis of queueing models, discrete event simulation, and statistical data analysis. It is written at the first year graduate level for students in computer science and engineering.

Sauer, C. H., and Chandy, K. M. (1981). "Computer Systems Performance Modeling." Prentice-Hall, Englewood Cliffs, New Jersey. This textbook on computer performance modeling gives more comprehensive coverage to the analysis and simulation of queueing network models of computer performance than do the books of Kleinrock and Kobayashi. It is written at a senior level for students in computer science and engineering and also oriented towards practicing system designers and developers.

2

Mathematical Prerequisites

Stephen S. Lavenberg

2.1 Probability and Random Variables

The models presented in this handbook involve probabilities and random variables. This is true both for the description of a model and the results given for a model. In this section basic material on probability and random variables is given which will aid a modeler in understanding the assumptions made about a model and the results obtained from the analysis or simulation of the model.

2.1.1 *Random Phenomena and Probability*

A phenomenon is considered to be *random* if its future behavior is not predictable in detail. The most familiar random phenomena are those associated with games of chance.

EXAMPLE 2.1   The tossing of a pair of dice is a random phenomenon since the two numbers which will show are not predictable.   △

EXAMPLE 2.2   The playing of roulette is a random phenomenon since it cannot be predicted which number will occur.   △

Performance phenomena associated with computer and computer/communication systems can be considered to be random because

(i)   The exact demands users will place on the system are not predictable.
(ii)   The interactions among the components of such systems are so complicated that the time it takes the system to service a given set of user demands is very difficult to predict.

EXAMPLE 2.3   Consider a computerized airline reservation system. The times at which requests for seat reservations will arrive at the system are not predictable, nor is the number of requests which will arrive in a fixed length interval of time. Furthermore, the time for the system to respond to a particular request is not predictable since it depends on when other requests arrived and on the very complex scheduling and resource management policies the system uses.   △

Although the future behavior of a random phenomenon is not predictable in detail, the phenomenon may exhibit a certain regularity. This is the case for games of chance.

EXAMPLE 2.4   If a pair of fair dice is tossed many times, the pair of numbers (1,1) will show on approximately $\frac{1}{36}$th of the tosses and the pair (3,4) will show on approximately $\frac{1}{18}$th of the tosses. In fact, the frequency of occurrence of each possible pair of numbers will settle down as the number of tosses increases.   △

EXAMPLE 2.5   In many plays of roulette (using a roulette wheel that has 38 numbers), each number will occur on approximately $\frac{1}{38}$th of the plays.   △

This kind of regularity is a property that is exhibited by many random phenomena.

A procedure that allows a random phenomenon to be observed is called a *random experiment*. The tossing of a pair of dice is a random experiment as is a play of roulette. Tossing dice repeatedly or playing roulette repeatedly are examples of independent trials of a random experiment. *Independent trials* are repetitions of a random experiment that satisfy the following two properties:

(i)   The repetitions are performed under conditions that are identical to the best of our knowledge (e.g., a loaded pair of dice is not used on some performances of the experiment while a fair pair of dice is used on other performances).

(ii)   The outcome of any one performance of the experiment does not affect the outcome of any other performance of the experiment.

If the frequency of occurrence of each possible outcome of a random experiment settles down as the number of independent trials of the experiment increases, the phenomenon is said to exhibit *statistical regularity*. Probability theory provides a quantitative means for studying random phenomena that exhibit statistical regularity. Each possible outcome of a random experiment is assigned a number between zero and one called its *probability*. The probability of an outcome can be interpreted as the frequency of occurrence of the outcome in a large number of independent trials of the experiment.

EXAMPLE 2.6   The probability that the pair of numbers (3,4) will show when a pair of dice is tossed is $\frac{1}{18}$.   △

EXAMPLE 2.7   The probability that the number zero will occur in a play of roulette is $\frac{1}{38}$.   △

While the notions of independent trials and probability are easy to understand in the context of games of chance, they are more difficult to understand in the context of computer systems. This is largely because it is not clear what constitutes independent trials of an experiment.

EXAMPLE 2.8   Consider the random experiment of measuring the number of requests for seat reservations that arrive at an airline reservation system during a five minute interval. The experiment can be repeated for different five minute intervals. In order that the outcome of any one performance of the experiment not affect the outcome of any other performance of the experiment, the intervals should not overlap in time. In order that the experiments are performed under conditions that are "identical to the best of our knowledge" the measurements should be made during periods of similar use of the system. For example, some measurements should not be made during a period of known low use (e.g., early morning) while other measurements are made during a period of known high use (e.g., midmorning). However, it is very difficult to know exactly what constitutes independent trials for this experiment.   △

The notion of independent trials should be considered an idealization which may not be achievable in certain contexts, such as random experiments with computer systems. However, when modeling computer systems we shall make statements like "the probability that exactly k requests arrive at the system in a five minute interval is 0.1." This can be interpreted to mean that if we could make independent trials of the experiment described in Example 2.8, exactly k requests would arrive during approximately 10% of the intervals.

2.1.2   Random Variables

A *random variable* is a function that assigns numerical values to the outcomes of a random experiment. Thus, a random variable takes on a value determined by the outcome of a random experiment. Since the outcome of a random experiment cannot be predicted, the value of a random variable cannot be predicted. Different values of the random variable can occur on repeated trials of the experiment. The values of the random variable that occur on independent trials of the experiment are called independent *observations* or independent *samples* of the random variable.

EXAMPLE 2.9   The sum of the numbers that show when a pair of dice is tossed is a random variable.   △

EXAMPLE 2.10   The number of requests that arrive at an airline reservation system during the first hour of operation is a random variable.   △

EXAMPLE 2.11   The time it takes an airline reservation system to respond to the 100th request is a random variable.   △

In Examples 2.9 and 2.10 the random variable can only assume discrete values. In Example 2.11 the random variable can assume continuous values.

a.   Discrete Random Variables

A random variable that can only assume discrete values is called a *discrete random variable*. The values are commonly integers. The random variable is described by giving the possible values it can assume and by giving the probability of each possible value. If X is a discrete random variable and t is a number we write Prob$\{X = t\}$ to denote the probability that X is equal to t. This probability can be interpreted to be the frequency with which X assumes the value t in a large number of independent trials of the random experiment on which X depends. The collection of these probabilities for all possible values of the discrete random variable is called the *probability distribution* of the random variable. Each probability is nonnegative and the sum of all the probabilities must equal one. Thus, if the possible values of a discrete random variable X are the nonnegative integers, then the probability distribution is given by the probabilities Prob$\{X = k\}$ for $k = 0, 1, \ldots$, where Prob$\{X = k\} \geq 0$ and

$$\sum_{k=0}^{\infty} \text{Prob}\{X = k\} = 1. \tag{2.1}$$

The following are discrete random variables that commonly arise in computer system modeling.

Bernoulli Random Variable.   A Bernoulli random variable has only two possible values. Consider a random experiment, such as tossing a coin, that has two possible outcomes, outcome 1 and outcome 2. Let X equal 1 when outcome 1 occurs and let X equal 2 when outcome 2 occurs. Then X is a Bernoulli random variable. Its probability distribution is given by

$$\text{Prob}\{X = 1\} = p, \qquad \text{Prob}\{X = 2\} = 1 - p, \tag{2.2}$$

where $0 < p < 1$. In a large number of independent trials of the experiment, outcome 1 will occur on approximately $100p$ percent of the trials and outcome 2 will occur on approximately $100(1 - p)$ percent of the trials. If a fair coin is tossed, clearly $p = 0.5$. However, if a biased coin is tossed then $p \neq 0.5$.

Binomial Random Variable. Consider a random experiment that has two possible outcomes. Let p, where $0 < p < 1$, denote the probability that outcome 1 occurs so that $1 - p$ is the probability that outcome 2 occurs. Let X denote the number of times outcome 1 occurs in n independent trials of the experiment. (Independent trials of a random experiment that has two possible outcomes are called *Bernoulli trials.* Repeated tossings of a coin are examples of Bernoulli trials.) Then X is a discrete random variable whose possible values are $0, 1, \ldots, n$. The probability distribution of X is given by

$$\text{Prob}\{X = i\} = \binom{n}{i} p^i (1 - p)^{n-i}, \qquad i = 0, 1, \ldots, n, \tag{2.3}$$

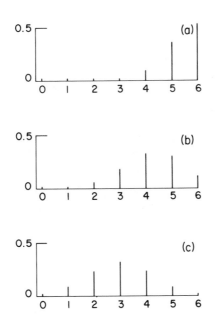

Fig. 2.1 Binomial probability distribution with parameters n and p. (a) $n = 6, p = 0.9$; (b) $n = 6, p = 0.7$; (c) $n = 6, p = 0.5$.

where $\binom{n}{i} = n!/[i!(n-i)!]$, $k! = (k)(k-1) \cdots (2)(1)$ if k is a positive integer and $0! = 1$. This probability distribution is called the *binomial distribution* and it has parameters n and p. The binomial distribution is plotted in Fig. 2.1 for $n = 6$ and several values of p.

EXAMPLE 2.12   Consider a coin for which p is the probability that a head shows. The number of heads that show in n tosses of the coin is a binomial random variable which has parameters n and p. $\triangle$

Geometric Random Variable.   Consider a random experiment that has two possible outcomes. Let p, where $0 < p < 1$, denote the probability that outcome 1 occurs so that $1 - p$ is the probability that outcome 2 occurs. Suppose independent trials of the experiment are performed until outcome 2 occurs for the first time. Let X denote the number of trials up to but not

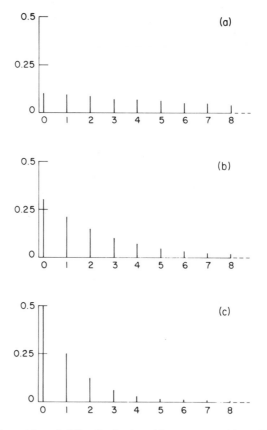

Fig. 2.2   Geometric probability distribution with parameter p. (a) $p = 0.9$; (b) $p = 0.7$; (c) $p = 0.5$.

including the first trial on which outcome 2 occurs. Then X is a discrete random variable whose possible values are $0, 1, \ldots$; that is, X can assume any nonnegative integer value. (The set of possible values for X is not finite.) The probability distribution of X is given by

$$\text{Prob}\{X = i\} = p^i(1 - p), \qquad i = 0, 1, \ldots. \tag{2.4}$$

This probability distribution is called the *geometric distribution* and it has parameter p. The geometric distribution is plotted in Fig. 2.2 for several values of p.

Sometimes the random variable $Y = X + 1$ is of interest. Y is the total number of trials up to and including the first trial on which outcome 2 occurs and it has possible values $1, 2, \ldots$. Y is called a *geometric random variable starting at one* and its probability distribution is given by

$$\text{Prob}\{Y = i\} = p^{i-1}(1 - p), \qquad i = 1, 2, \ldots. \tag{2.5}$$

EXAMPLE 2.13   Consider a coin for which p is the probability that a head shows. Suppose the coin is tossed until the first tail shows. The number of heads before the first tail is a geometric random variable which has parameter p and the total number of tosses is a geometric random variable starting at one which has parameter p.   △

Poisson Random Variable.   Let X denote a discrete random variable whose possible values are $0, 1, \ldots$. X is a Poisson random variable if its probability distribution is given by

$$\text{Prob}\{X = i\} = e^{-\lambda}\lambda^i/i!, \qquad i = 0, 1, \ldots, \tag{2.6}$$

where λ is a positive constant. This probability distribution is called the *Poisson distribution* and it has parameter λ. The Poisson distribution is plotted in Fig. 2.3 for several values of λ.

EXAMPLE 2.14   Let X denote the number of requests that arrive at the central computer of an airline reservation system during a T-second interval. Suppose the interval is divided into n equal subintervals of duration T/n, where n is so large that at most one request can arrive during any subinterval. Then there are two possible outcomes for the random experiment of measuring whether a request arrives during a subinterval: (1) one request arrives; (2) no request arrives. We shall assume that performing this experiment for each subinterval constitutes n independent trials of the experiment. This assumption implies that the presence or absence of a request in any one subinterval does not affect the presence or absence of a request in any other subinterval and that the probability that a request arrives during a subinterval is the same for all subintervals. We shall also assume that the probability that a request arrives during a subinterval is proportional to the length T/n of the subinterval. Then X, the total number of requests which arrive during the n subintervals, is a

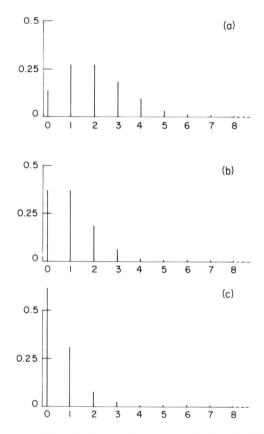

Fig. 2.3 Poisson probability distribution with parameter λ. (a) $\lambda = 2$; (b) $\lambda = 1$; (c) $\lambda = 0.5$.

binomial random variable with parameters n and bT/n, where b is a positive constant of proportionality and $bT/n < 1$. Thus,

$$\text{Prob}\{X = i\} = \binom{n}{i}(bT/n)^i(1 - bT/n)^{n-i}, \qquad (2.7)$$

which is approximately equal to $e^{-bT}(bT)^i/i!$ if n is large. Therefore, under the assumptions we made, the probability distribution for X is approximately a Poisson distribution with parameter bT. △

Expected Value. Let $t_1, t_2, \ldots, t_K$ denote the possible values of a discrete random variable X, where K can be infinite. Let $x_1, x_2, \ldots, x_N$ denote the values of X on N independent trials of the experiment that determines X. The average of the N values is given by

$$S_{N^*} = \frac{1}{N} \sum_{n=1}^{N} x_n = \frac{1}{N} \sum_{k=1}^{K} t_k N_k, \tag{2.8}$$

where N_k is the number of trials on which the value t_k occurs. But N_k/N is the frequency with which the value t_k occurs on the N trials so that N_k/N stabilizes at the value $\text{Prob}\{X = t_k\}$ as N becomes large. Thus, S_N stabilizes at the value

$$E[X] = \sum_{k=1}^{K} t_k \, \text{Prob}\{X = t_k\} \tag{2.9}$$

as N becomes large. This value, denoted by $E[X]$, is called the *expected value* of X.

A function of a random variable is itself a random variable since its value depends on the outcome of a random experiment. If $g(X)$ is a function of a discrete random variable X, then the expected value of $g(X)$ is given by

$$E[g(X)] = \sum_{k=1}^{K} g(t_k) \, \text{Prob}\{X = t_k\}. \tag{2.10}$$

Moments. The expected value of the nth power of X, given by

$$E[X^n] = \sum_{k=1}^{K} t_k^n \, \text{Prob}\{X = t_k\}, \tag{2.11}$$

is called the *nth moment about the origin* of X. The first moment about the origin is simply $E[X]$ and is called the *mean* of X.

The expected value of the nth power of the difference between X and its mean, given by

$$E[(X - E[X])^n] = \sum_{k=1}^{K} (t_k - E[X])^n \, \text{Prob}\{X = t_k\}, \tag{2.12}$$

is called the *nth central moment* of X. The first central moment is equal to zero.

TABLE 2.1

Discrete Random Variables

Random Variable X	Parameters (restrictions)	$E[X]$	$\text{Var}[X]$	$C[X]$
Binomial	n (integer), p $(n \geqslant 1, 0 < p < 1)$	np	$np(1 - p)$	$[(1 - p)/np]^{1/2}$
Geometric	p $(0 < p < 1)$	$p/(1 - p)$	$p/(1 - p)^2$	$1/p^{1/2}$
Geometric starting at one	p $(0 < p < 1)$	$1/(1 - p)$	$p/(1 - p)^2$	$p^{1/2}$
Poisson	λ $(\lambda > 0)$	λ	λ	$1/\lambda^{1/2}$

The second central moment of X is called the *variance* of X and is denoted by $\text{Var}[X]$; i.e.,

$$\text{Var}[X] = E[(X - E[X])^2].\tag{2.13}$$

The variance can also be expressed directly in terms of the mean and the second moment about the origin as follows:

$$\text{Var}[X] = E[X^2] - (E[X])^2.\tag{2.14}$$

The positive square root of the variance is called the *standard deviation*, and the standard deviation divided by the mean is called the *coefficient of variation*. The coefficient of variation of X, denoted by $C[X]$, is thus given by

$$C[X] = (\text{Var}[X])^{1/2}/E[X].\tag{2.15}$$

The coefficient of variation provides information about the variation of a random variable about its mean. This is expressed mathematically by the following inequality, known as *Chebyshev's inequality*:

$$\text{Prob}\{|X - E[X]| \geqslant bE[X]\} \leqslant (C[X]/b)^2,\tag{2.16}$$

where b is any positive number. The probability that X differs from its mean by more than $100b$ percent is less than or equal to the square of the coefficient of variation of X divided by b.

The mean, variance, and coefficient of variation of some discrete random variables are given in Table 2.1.

b. Probability Distribution Function

If X is a random variable and t is a number we write $\text{Prob}\{X \leqslant t\}$ to denote the probability that X is less than or equal to t. The function of t given by $F_X(t) = \text{Prob}\{X \leqslant t\}$ is called the *probability distribution function* of X. A probability distribution function $F_X(t)$ has the following properties:

$$0 \leqslant F_X(t) \leqslant 1,\tag{2.17}$$

$$F_X(-\infty) = 0,\tag{2.18}$$

$$F_X(+\infty) = 1,\tag{2.19}$$

$$t_2 > t_1 \text{ implies that } F_X(t_2) \geqslant F_X(t_1).\tag{2.20}$$

Some probability distribution functions are shown in Fig. 2.4. The probability distribution function $F_X(t)$ of a random variable X completely describes X in the sense that all probabilities involving X can be calculated from $F_X(t)$. The following are examples:

$$\text{Prob}\{t_1 < X \leqslant t_2\} = F_X(t_2) - F_X(t_1), \quad \text{provided} \quad t_1 < t_2, \tag{2.21}$$

$$\text{Prob}\{X = t_3\} = \begin{cases} 0, & \text{if } F_X(t) \text{ is continuous at } t = t_3, \\ p, & \text{if } F_X(t) \text{ has a jump of size } p \text{ at } t = t_3, \end{cases}\tag{2.22}$$

$$\text{Prob}\{X > t_4\} = 1 - F_X(t_4).\tag{2.23}$$

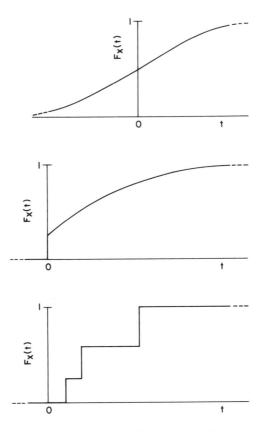

Fig. 2.4   Probability distribution functions.

If X is a discrete random variable then $F_X(t)$ is a staircase function which only changes value by jumps at the possible values of X (see the bottom probability distribution function in Fig. 2.4). The size of the jump at a possible value t is equal to $\text{Prob}\{X = t\}$. Thus, the probability distribution of a discrete random variable completely determines its probability distribution function and vice versa.

c.   Continuous Random Variables

X is called a *continuous random variable* if its probability distribution function is a continuous and differentiable function. (It is, however, allowable that the function not be differentiable at a set of discrete points.) A continuous random variable has a continuum of possible values which is typically an interval $[a,b]$, where $a < b$ and $a = -\infty$ or $b = +\infty$ are allowed. The derivative of the probability distribution function of a continuous random variable is called the *probability density function*. Let $f_X(t)$ denote the probability density function of X. Then $f_X(t)$ and $F_X(t)$ are related as follows:

$$f_X(t) = dF_X(t)/dt, \tag{2.24}$$

$$F_X(t) = \int_{-\infty}^{t} f_X(s)\,ds. \tag{2.25}$$

A probability density function $f_X(t)$ has the following properties:

$$f_X(t) \geqslant 0, \tag{2.26}$$

$$\int_{-\infty}^{\infty} f_X(t)\,dt = 1. \tag{2.27}$$

The probability density function completely describes a continuous random variable. All probabilities involving a continuous random variable can be calculated from its probability density function. Two important examples are

$$\text{Prob}\{t_1 \leqslant X \leqslant t_2\} = \int_{t_1}^{t_2} f_X(t)\,dt, \quad \text{provided} \quad t_1 < t_2, \tag{2.28}$$

$$\text{Prob}\{X > t_3\} = \int_{t_3}^{\infty} f_X(t)\,dt. \tag{2.29}$$

Furthermore, the probability that X is contained in a small interval centered at t is approximately equal to $f_X(t)$ times the length of the interval. As the length of the interval approaches zero this probability approaches zero so that for any real number t, $\text{Prob}\{X = t\} = 0$ if X is a continuous random variable.

The following are continuous random variables that arise in computer system modeling.

Uniform Random Variable. Let X be a continuous random variable that can assume any value in the interval $[a, b]$, where a and b are finite and $a < b$. X is a uniform random variable on the interval $[a, b]$ if

$$f_X(t) = \begin{cases} 0, & t < a \quad \text{or} \quad t > b, \\ 1/(b - a), & a < t < b, \end{cases} \tag{2.30}$$

and, equivalently,

$$F_X(t) = \begin{cases} 0, & t < a, \\ (t - a)/(b - a), & a \leqslant t \leqslant b, \\ 1, & t > b. \end{cases} \tag{2.31}$$

The functions $f_X(t)$ and $F_X(t)$ are plotted in Fig. 2.5. If X is a uniform random

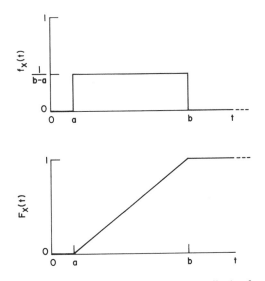

Fig. 2.5 Probability density function and probability distribution function of a uniform random variable on $[a, b]$.

variable on $[a, b]$, then

$$\text{Prob}\{t_1 \leqslant X \leqslant t_2\} = (t_2 - t_1)/(b - a) \qquad (2.32)$$

if $a \leqslant t_1 < t_2 \leqslant b$.

EXAMPLE 2.15 The latency time for a rotating storage device such as a drum can be assumed to be a uniform random variable on the interval $[0, R]$, where R is the time for one complete revolution of the device.   △

Exponential Random Variable. Let X be a continuous random variable that can assume any nonnegative value. X is an exponential random variable if

$$f_X(t) = \begin{cases} 0, & t < 0, \\ \lambda e^{-\lambda t}, & t \geqslant 0, \end{cases} \qquad (2.33)$$

and equivalently,

$$F_X(t) = \begin{cases} 0, & t < 0, \\ 1 - e^{-\lambda t}, & t \geqslant 0. \end{cases} \qquad (2.34)$$

The parameter λ is positive and is called the *rate parameter* of the random variable. The functions $f_X(t)$ and $F_X(t)$ are plotted in Fig. 2.6 for several values of λ.

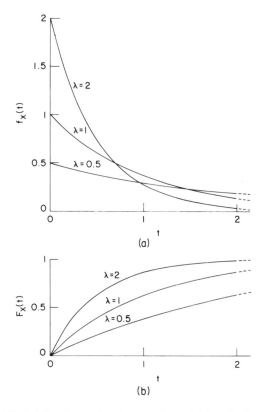

Fig. 2.6 (a) Probability density function and (b) probability distribution function of an exponential random variable with parameter λ.

EXAMPLE 2.16   Consider the arrival of requests at the central computer of an airline reservation system and let X denote the time, starting from zero, until the first request arrives. Divide time into equal subintervals of duration $1/n$, where n is a large positive integer, and make the following assumptions: (1) at most one request can arrive during any subinterval, (2) the presence or absence of a request in any one subinterval does not affect the presence or absence of a request in any other subinterval, and (3) the probability that a request arrives during a subinterval is equal to λ/n for each subinterval, where λ is a positive constant of proportionality and $\lambda/n < 1$. Then X is greater than t if and only if no requests arrive during the first nt subintervals (assuming for convenience that nt is an integer). Thus,

$$\text{Prob}\{X > t\} = \text{Prob}\{\text{no arrivals in first } nt \text{ subintervals}\}$$

$$= (1 - \lambda/n)^{nt} \qquad\qquad (2.35)$$

which is approximately equal to $e^{-\lambda t}$ if n is large. Thus, $\mathrm{Prob}\{X \leqslant t\}$ is approximately equal to $1 - e^{-\lambda t}$, so that the probability distribution function of X is approximately equal to the probability distribution function of an exponential random variable with rate parameter λ. Suppose ns subintervals have elapsed without the first request arriving. It follows from the assumptions we made that the probability that at least nt more subintervals will elapse before the first request arrives does not depend on s and is equal to $(1 - \lambda/n)^{nt}$. This memoryless property also holds for an exponential random variable as seen below. $\triangle$

The exponential random variable plays a fundamental role in the analysis of queueing models of computer systems. This is because it is the only continuous random variable that has the following *memoryless property*:

$$\mathrm{Prob}\{X \leqslant s + t \mid X \geqslant s\} = \mathrm{Prob}\{X \leqslant t\}, \qquad \text{for all } s \geqslant 0, \quad t \geqslant 0. \tag{2.36}$$

The expression to the left of the equal sign denotes the probability that X is less than or equal to $s + t$ given that X is greater than or equal to s (see Section 2.1.3b on conditional probability). The memoryless property states that this probability does not depend on s. Thus, if X is an exponential random variable which has rate parameter λ, then

$$\mathrm{Prob}\{X \leqslant s + t \mid X \geqslant s\} = 1 - e^{-\lambda t}, \qquad \text{for all } s \geqslant 0, \quad t \geqslant 0. \tag{2.37}$$

EXAMPLE 2.17   Assume that the time between successive arrivals of requests at the central computer of an airline reservation system is an exponential random variable X. Consider the following two conditions: (1) a request just arrived; (2) at least s seconds have elapsed since the last request arrived. Due to the memoryless property of the exponential random variable, the probability that the next arrival occurs within t seconds is the same given condition 1 or given condition 2. This is rather surprising and one may ask whether the assumption that the time between successive arrivals is an exponential random variable is a reasonable one. In Section 2.2 on the Poisson process, we shall see that the exponential assumption is often reasonable. $\triangle$

Erlang Random Variable.   Let X be a continuous random variable that can assume any nonnegative value. X is an Erlang random variable if

$$f_X(t) = \begin{cases} 0, & t < 0, \\ e^{-\lambda t} \lambda^k t^{k-1}/(k-1)!, & t \geqslant 0, \end{cases} \tag{2.38}$$

and equivalently,

$$F_X(t) = \begin{cases} 0, & t < 0, \\ 1 - \sum_{j=0}^{k-1} e^{-\lambda t}(\lambda t)^j/j!, & t \geqslant 0, \end{cases} \tag{2.39}$$

where the parameter k is a positive integer and the parameter λ is positive. An Erlang random variable for which $k = 1$ is simply an exponential random variable that has rate parameter λ. If $k > 1$, an Erlang random variable that has parameters k and λ is the sum of k statistically independent (see Section 2.1.3a) exponential random variables, each of which has rate parameter λ. The functions $f_X(t)$ and $F_X(t)$ are plotted in Fig. 2.7 for several values of k and λ.

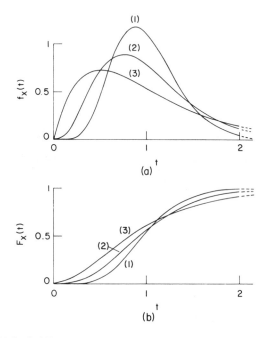

Fig. 2.7   (a) Probability density function and (b) probability distribution function of an Erlang random variable with parameters k and λ (mean = 1). (1) $k = 8$, $\lambda = 8$; (2) $k = 4$, $\lambda = 4$; (3) $k = 2$, $\lambda = 2$.

EXAMPLE 2.18   Assume that the times between successive arrivals of requests at the central computer of an airline reservation system are statistically independent (see Section 2.1.3a) exponential random variables, each of which has rate parameter λ. Then the time between the arrival of the first and $(k + 1)$st request is an Erlang random variable that has parameters k and λ.   △

Gamma Random Variable.   Let X be a continuous random variable that can assume any nonnegative value. X is a gamma random variable if

$$f_X(t) = \begin{cases} 0, & t < 0, \\ e^{-\lambda t}\lambda^{\alpha}\lambda^{\alpha-1}/G(\alpha), & t \geq 0, \end{cases} \qquad (2.40)$$

and equivalently,

$$F_X(t) = \begin{cases} 0, & t < 0, \\ \int_0^t e^{-\lambda s}\lambda^\alpha t^{\alpha-1}/G(\alpha), & t \geqslant 0, \end{cases} \qquad (2.41)$$

where the parameters α and λ are positive and

$$G(\alpha) = \int_0^\infty s^{\alpha-1}e^{-s}\,ds \qquad (2.42)$$

is called the gamma function. [$G(\alpha)$ can be evaluated using the APL scalar function ! with argument $\alpha - 1$.] α is called the shape parameter and λ is called the scale parameter. If α is an integer, then $G(\alpha) = (\alpha - 1)!$ so that a gamma random variable with shape parameter k, where k is an integer, and scale parameter λ is simply an Erlang random variable that has parameters k and λ. The functions $f_X(t)$ and $F_X(t)$ are plotted in Fig. 2.8 for several values of α and λ.

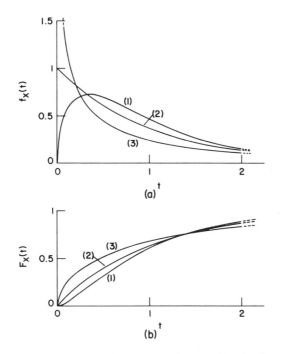

Fig. 2.8 (a) Probability density function and (b) probability distribution function of a gamma random variable with parameters α and λ (mean = 1). (1) $\alpha = 1.5$, $\lambda = 1.5$; (2) $\alpha = 1$, $\lambda = 1$; (3) $\alpha = 0.5$, $\lambda = 0.5$.

Hyperexponential Random Variable. Let X_1 and X_2 be statistically independent (see Section 2.1.3a) exponential random variables which have rate parameters λ_1 and λ_2, respectively, where $\lambda_2 \neq \lambda_1$. Let Y be a Bernoulli random variable that is statistically independent of X_1 and X_2 and has probability distribution

$$\text{Prob}\{Y = 1\} = p, \qquad \text{Prob}\{Y = 2\} = 1 - p. \qquad (2.43)$$

The random variable X, defined by

$$X = \begin{cases} X_1, & \text{if } Y = 1, \\ X_2, & \text{if } Y = 2, \end{cases} \qquad (2.44)$$

is a hyperexponential random variable which has parameters p, λ_1, and λ_2.

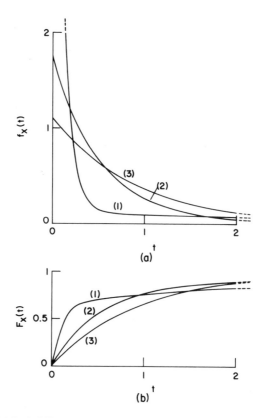

Fig. 2.9 (a) Probability density function and (b) probability distribution function of a hyperexponential random variable with parameters p, λ_1, λ_2 (mean = 1, coefficient of variation = 2). (1) $p = 0.351$, $\lambda_1 = 0.375$, $\lambda_2 = 10$; (2) $p = 0.143$, $\lambda_1 = 0.25$, $\lambda_2 = 2$; (3) $p = 0.00662$, $\lambda_1 = 0.0625$, $\lambda_2 = 1.11$.

X is equal to X_1 with probability p and X is equal to X_2 with probability $1 - p$. The probability density function and probability distribution function of X are given by

$$f_X(t) = \begin{cases} 0, & t < 0, \\ p\lambda_1 e^{-\lambda_1 t} + (1 - p)\lambda_2 e^{-\lambda_2 t}, & t \geqslant 0, \end{cases} \tag{2.45}$$

$$F_X(t) = \begin{cases} 0, & t < 0, \\ 1 - p e^{-\lambda_1 t} - (1 - p)e^{-\lambda_2 t}, & t \geqslant 0. \end{cases} \tag{2.46}$$

The functions $f_X(t)$ and $F_X(t)$ are plotted in Fig. 2.9 for several values of p, λ_1, and λ_2.

Normal Random Variable.   The continuous random variable X is a normal random variable if

$$f_X(t) = (1/2\pi\sigma^2)^{1/2} \exp(-(t - m)^2/2\sigma^2), \qquad \text{for all} \quad t, \tag{2.47}$$

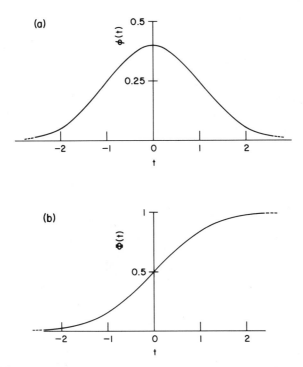

Fig. 2.10   (a) Probability density function and (b) probability distribution function of a unit normal random variable.

and equivalently,

$$F_X(t) = (1/2\pi\sigma^2)^{1/2} \int_{-\infty}^{t} \exp(-(s-m)^2/2\sigma^2)\,ds, \qquad \text{for all} \quad t, \quad (2.48)$$

where m and σ are parameters and σ is positive. (It will be seen later in Table 2.2 that m and σ are the mean and standard deviation of X.) A normal random variable with $m = 0$ and $\sigma = 1$ is called a *unit* normal or *standard* normal random variable. We let $\phi(t)$ and $\Phi(t)$ denote the probability density function and probability distribution function of a unit normal random variable; i.e.,

$$\phi(t) = (1/2\pi)^{1/2} \exp(-t^2/2), \qquad \text{for all} \quad t, \quad (2.49)$$

and

$$\Phi(t) = (1/2\pi)^{1/2} \int_{-\infty}^{t} \exp(-s^2/2)\,ds, \qquad \text{for all} \quad t. \quad (2.50)$$

The functions $\phi(t)$ and $\Phi(t)$ are plotted in Fig. 2.10. If X is a normal random variable with parameters m and σ, then $(X - m)/\sigma$ is a unit normal random variable and

$$f_X(t) = \phi((t-m)/\sigma), \qquad (2.51)$$

$$F_X(t) = \Phi((t-m)/\sigma). \qquad (2.52)$$

A useful property of normal random variables is that if $X_1, X_2, \ldots, X_n$ are statistically independent (see Section 2.1.3a) normal random variables and if $c_1, c_2, \ldots, c_n$ are constants, then $c_1 X_1 + c_2 X_2 + \cdots + c_n X_n$ is a normal random variable. The important role played by the normal random variable in the statistical analysis of simulation outputs is discussed in Chapter 6.

Student's t Random Variable. The continuous random variable X is a Student's t random variable (also called Student's t statistic) if

$$f_X(t) = 1/[n^{1/2} B_n (1 + t^2/n)^{(n+1)/2}], \qquad \text{for all} \quad t, \quad (2.53)$$

and equivalently,

$$F_X(t) = (1/n^{1/2} B_n) \int_{-\infty}^{t} (1 + s^2/n)^{-(n+1)/2}\,ds, \qquad \text{for all} \quad t, \quad (2.54)$$

where n is a positive integer,

$$B_n = G(1/2)G(n/2)/G((n+1)/2), \qquad (2.55)$$

and $G(\alpha)$ is the gamma function defined in Eq. (2.42). The parameter n is called the number of degrees of freedom. The functions $f_X(t)$ and $F_X(t)$ are plotted in Fig. 2.11 for several values of n. As n increases the probability density function and probability distribution function of a Student's t random variable

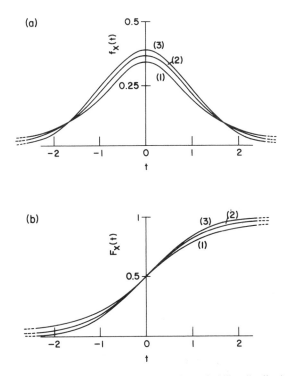

Fig. 2.11 (a) Probability density function and (b) probability distribution function of a Student's t random variable with n degrees of freedom. (1) $n = 2$; (2) $n = 5$; (3) $n = \infty$ (unit normal).

approach those of a unit normal random variable. For $n \geqslant 25$ the probability distribution functions of a Student's t and unit normal random variable differ by less than 0.01.

Student's t random variable arises in the following way. Let $X_1, X_2, \ldots, X_n$ be statistically independent (see Section 2.1.3a) random variables that have the same normal distribution with parameters m and σ. In addition, let

$$\bar{X} = \sum_{i=1}^{n} \frac{X_i}{n} \tag{2.56}$$

and

$$S^2 = \sum_{i=1}^{n} \frac{(X_i - \bar{X})^2}{(n-1)}. \tag{2.57}$$

Then $\sqrt{n}(\bar{X} - m)/S$ is a Student's t random variable which has $n - 1$ degrees of freedom. The important role played by Student's t random variable in the statistical analysis of simulation outputs is due to this result and is discussed in Chapter 6.

Expected Value. The expected value of a continuous random variable X is given by

$$E[X] = \int_{-\infty}^{\infty} t f_X(t)\, dt. \tag{2.58}$$

As is the case with a discrete random variable, the average [given by the first equality in Eq. (2.8)] of the values of X on independent trials of the experiment which determines X stabilizes at the value $E[X]$ as the number of trials becomes large.

If $g(X)$ is a function of a continuous random variable X, then

$$E[g(X)] = \int_{-\infty}^{\infty} g(t) f_X(t)\, dt. \tag{2.59}$$

Moments. The nth moment about the origin of a continuous random variable X is given by

$$E[X^n] = \int_{-\infty}^{\infty} t^n f_X(t)\, dt. \tag{2.60}$$

The nth central moment is given by

$$E[(X - E[X])^n] = \int_{-\infty}^{\infty} (t - E[X])^n f_X(t)\, dt. \tag{2.61}$$

The variance, standard deviation, and coefficient of variation of a continuous random variable are defined in the same way as they are for a discrete random variable [see Eqs. (2.13)–(2.15)] and Chebyshev's inequality [Eq. (2.16)] holds for a continuous random variable. The mean, variance, and coefficient of variation of some continuous random variables are given in Table 2.2.

The coefficient of variation provides information about the variation of a random variable about its mean. The larger the coefficient of variation is, the larger the variation about the mean is. The coefficient of variation of an exponential random variable is equal to one. The coefficient of variation of an Erlang random variable is less than one if the integer parameter k is greater than one. Thus, an Erlang random variable has less variation about its mean than an exponential random variable. A gamma random variable can achieve any specified value of the coefficient of variation by proper choice of the value of the shape parameter α. The coefficient of variation of a hyperexponential random variable is greater than one, and any specified value of the coefficient of variation that is greater than one can be achieved by proper choice of the

TABLE 2.2

Continuous Random Variables

Random variable X	Parameters (restrictions)	$E[X]$	$Var[X]$	$C[X]$
Uniform	a, b $(a < b)$	$(a+b)/2$	$(b-a)^2/12$	$(b-a)/[\sqrt{3}(a+b)]$
Exponential	λ $(\lambda > 0)$	$1/\lambda$	$1/\lambda^2$	1
Erlang	k (integer), λ $(k \geqslant 1, \lambda > 0)$	k/λ	k/λ^2	$1/k^{1/2}$
Gamma	α, λ $(\alpha > 0, \lambda > 0)$	α/λ	α/λ^2	$1/\alpha^{1/2}$
Hyperexponential	p, λ_1, λ_2 $(0 < p < 1, \lambda_1 > 0, \lambda_2 > 0)$	$p/\lambda_1 + (1-p)/\lambda_2$	[a]	[b]
Normal	m, σ $(\sigma > 0)$	m	σ^2	σ/m
Student's t	n (integer) $(n \geqslant 1)$	0 $(n > 1)$	$n/(n-2)$ $(n > 2)$	

[a] $2(p/\lambda_1^2 + (1-p)/\lambda_2^2) - (p/\lambda_1 + (1-p)/\lambda_2)^2$.

[b] $\{[2(p/\lambda_1^2 + (1-p)/\lambda_2^2)/(p/\lambda_1 + (1-p)/\lambda_2)^2] - 1\}^{1/2}$.

values of the parameters p, λ_1, and λ_2. The following choice achieves specified values m and $c > 1$ of the mean and coefficient of variation, respectively, of a hyperexponential random variable:

$$1/\lambda_2 = \text{any positive value less than } m, \qquad (2.62)$$

$$1/\lambda_1 = m\{1 + (c^2 - 1)/[2(1 - 1/\lambda_2 m)]\}, \qquad (2.63)$$

$$p = 2(1 - 1/\lambda_2 m)^2/[c^2 - 1 + 2(1 - 1/\lambda_2 m)^2]. \qquad (2.64)$$

Thus, the choice of values is not unique. For each of the sets of parameter values (chosen according to Eqs. (2.62)–(2.64)) in Fig. 2.9, the mean is equal to one and the coefficient of variation is equal to two. Notice that the probability density functions (and probability distribution functions) are quite different for the different sets of values.

Notice from Table 2.2 that the parameters m and σ of a normal random variable are equal to the mean and standard deviation respectively. The mean of a Student's t random variable exists only if $n > 1$ and the variance exists only if $n > 2$.

d. Percentiles

If X is a random variable and q is a positive number less than one, we let $t_q(X)$ denote the smallest number t for which $F_X(t) \geqslant q$. The number $t_q(X)$ is called the $100q$th *percentile* or *quantile* of X. It has the property that

$$F_X(t) < q, \quad \text{if} \quad t < t_q(X), \qquad F_X(t) \geqslant q, \quad \text{if} \quad t \geqslant t_q(X). \quad (2.65)$$

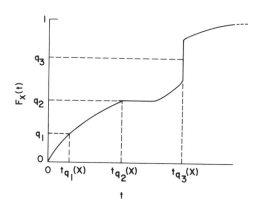

Fig. 2.12   Percentiles of a random variable X.

Percentiles can be determined graphically from $F_X(t)$ as shown in Fig. 2.12. They provide useful information about a random variable. If an infinite number of independent observations of a random variable X were made, then at least $100q$ percent of the observations would be less than or equal to $t_q(X)$. Furthermore, if $t < t_q(X)$, then less than $100q$ percent of the observations would be less than or equal to t. The 50th percentile, i.e., $q = 0.5$, is called the *median*. Often the median and higher percentiles of a random variable are of interest.

EXAMPLE 2.19   Part of the performance specification for the design of an interactive computer system may be expressed in terms of percentiles of the response time, e.g., the 90th percentile of the response time should be less than 2 s.   △

If X is a continuous random variable, then $F_X(t)$ does not have discontinuities such as the one shown in Fig. 2.12. Therefore, if X is a continuous random variable, then $t_q(X)$ is the smallest number t for which $F_X(t) = q$, so that

$$F_X(t_q(X)) = q. \qquad (2.66)$$

EXAMPLE 2.20   If X is an exponential random variable with rate parameter λ, then

$$t_q(X) = - [\ln(1 - q)]/\lambda. \qquad (2.67)$$

Thus, the $100q$th percentile of an exponential random variable is equal to $- \ln(1 - q)$ times the mean. The median and a few higher percentiles of an

TABLE 2.3

Percentiles

q	Exponential random variable with $\lambda=1$	Unit normal random variable
0.5	0.693	0
0.75	1.39	0.674
0.9	2.30	1.28
0.95	3.00	1.64
0.975	3.71	1.96
0.99	4.61	2.33

exponential random variable with rate parameter equal to 1 are given in Table 2.3. Percentiles of an exponential random variable with rate parameter λ can be obtained from the table and Eq. (2.67). $\triangle$

EXAMPLE 2.21   If X is a normal random variable with mean m and variance σ^2, then

$$t_q(X) = \sigma \Phi^{-1}(q) + m, \qquad (2.68)$$

where $\Phi(t)$ is the probability distribution function of a unit normal random variable and is given in Eq. (2.50), and $\Phi^{-1}(q)$ is the inverse of this function. Thus, $\Phi^{-1}(q)$ is the $100q$th percentile of a unit normal random variable. The median and a few higher percentiles of a unit normal random variable are given in Table 2.3. Percentiles of a normal random variable with mean m and variance σ^2 can be obtained from the table and Eq. (2.68). $\triangle$

If X is a discrete random variable which can assume only nonnegative integer values and X has probability distribution

$$\text{Prob}\{X = k\} = p_k, \qquad k = 0, 1, \ldots, \qquad (2.69)$$

then

$$t_q(X) = \begin{cases} 0, & \text{if } q \leqslant p_0, \\ k, & \text{if } \sum_{j=0}^{k-1} p_j < q \leqslant \sum_{j=0}^{k} p_j \text{ and } k \geqslant 1. \end{cases} \qquad (2.70)$$

EXAMPLE 2.22   If X is a geometric random variable with parameter p, then $p_k = p^k(1 - p)$ and $p_0 + p_1 + \cdots + p_k = 1 - p^{k+1}$. It follows that

$$t_q(X) = \lceil \ln(1 - q)/\ln p \rceil - 1, \qquad (2.71)$$

where $\lceil y \rceil$ denotes the smallest integer which is greater than or equal to y. $\triangle$

2.1.3 Multiple Random Variables

Suppose there are several quantities $X_1, X_2, \ldots, X_n$ whose values are determined by the outcome of the same random experiment. Then $X_1, X_2, \ldots, X_n$ are random variables. The values of some of these random variables may affect the values of other of these random variables.

EXAMPLE 2.23   Consider the experiment of tossing a pair of dice, one of which is colored green and the other of which is colored red. The following are random variables determined by this experiment:

$$X_1 = \text{the number that shows on the green die,}$$

$$X_2 = \text{the number that shows on the red die,}$$

$$X_3 = \text{the sum of the numbers which show.}$$

Since $X_3 = X_1 + X_2$, the value of X_1 affects the value of X_3 and vice versa, and the value of X_2 affects the value of X_3 and vice versa. However, the value of X_1 does not affect the value of X_2 and vice versa. △

When considering random variables, $X_1, X_2, \ldots, X_n$, which are determined by the same experiment, one may be interested in probabilities involving more than one of the random variables as well as probabilities involving each of the random variables alone.

EXAMPLE 2.24 X_1 and X_3 are the random variables in Example 2.23. $\text{Prob}\{X_1 = i; X_3 = j\}$ denotes the probability that X_1 assumes the value i and X_3 assumes the value j. If the pair of dice is tossed repeatedly the frequency of tosses on which $X_1 = i$ and $X_3 = j$ stabilizes at the above probability. For example, $\text{Prob}\{X_1 = 2; X_3 = 4\} = \frac{1}{36}$. △

If $X_1, X_2, \ldots, X_n$ are random variables and $t_1, t_2, \ldots, t_n$ are numbers we write $\text{Prob}\{X_1 \leqslant t_1; X_2 \leqslant t_2; \ldots; X_n \leqslant t_n\}$ to denote the probability that $X_1 \leqslant t_1$ and $X_2 \leqslant t_2, \ldots,$ and $X_n \leqslant t_n$.

a. Statistical Independence

If $\text{Prob}\{X_1 \leqslant t_1; X_2 \leqslant t_2; \ldots; X_n \leqslant t_n\} = \text{Prob}\{X_1 \leqslant t_1\} \text{Prob}\{X_2 \leqslant t_2\} \cdots \text{Prob}\{X_n \leqslant t_n\}$ for all $t_1, t_2, \ldots, t_n$, the random variables $X_1, X_2, \ldots, X_n$ are said to be *statistically independent*. Otherwise, they are said to be *statistically dependent*.

EXAMPLE 2.25 $X_1, X_2,$ and X_3 are the random variables in Example 2.23. From Example 2.24, $\text{Prob}\{X_1 = 2; X_3 = 4\} = \frac{1}{36}$. Considering X_1 alone and X_3 alone, $\text{Prob}\{X_1 = 2\} = \frac{1}{6}$ and $\text{Prob}\{X_3 = 4\} = \frac{1}{12}$. Thus, $\text{Prob}\{X_1 = 2; X_3 = 4\} \neq \text{Prob}\{X_1 = 2\} \text{Prob}\{X_3 = 4\}$, so that X_1 and X_3 are statistically dependent. Now consider X_1 and X_2. $\text{Prob}\{X_1 = i; X_2 = j\} = \frac{1}{36}$ for

$i = 1, \ldots, 6$ and $j = 1, \ldots, 6$. Also $\mathrm{Prob}\{X_1 = i\} = \frac{1}{6}$ for $i = 1, \ldots, 6$ and $\mathrm{Prob}\{X_2 = j\} = \frac{1}{6}$ for $j = 1, \ldots, 6$. Thus, $\mathrm{Prob}\{X_1 = i; X_2 = j\} = \mathrm{Prob}\{X_1 = i\}\,\mathrm{Prob}\{X_2 = j\}$ for all i and j, so that X_1 and X_2 are statistically independent. It can also be shown that X_1, X_2, and X_3 are statistically dependent. △

The function of $t_1, t_2, \ldots, t_n$ given by $\mathrm{Prob}\{X_1 \leqslant t_1; X_2 \leqslant t_2; \ldots; X_n \leqslant t_n\}$ is called the *joint probability distribution function* of $X_1, X_2, \ldots, X_n$. If $X_1, X_2, \ldots, X_n$ are statistically independent, then the joint probability distribution function of $X_1, X_2, \ldots, X_n$ is equal to the product of the probability distribution functions of each of the random variables. This is not true if $X_1, X_2, \ldots, X_n$ are statistically dependent. When random variables are statistically independent, the values of any subset of the random variables do not affect the values of the other random variables.

One common way in which statistically independent random variables arise is if each random variable is defined with respect to a different experiment and the outcomes of any subset of the experiments do not affect the outcomes of the other experiments.

EXAMPLE 2.26   The tossing of a pair of colored dice, one of which is green and the other red, can be considered to consist of two experiments, tossing the green die and tossing the red die. Clearly, the outcome of one of these experiments does not affect the outcome of the other. This explains why the random variables X_1 and X_2 in Example 2.23 are statistically independent. △

The notion of statistical independence is an important one. When analyzing queueing models of computer systems, many of the random variables involved are assumed to be statistically independent. Without this assumption it would be impossible to analyze the model mathematically. The statistical analysis of simulation outputs is often complicated by the fact that certain random variables are statistically dependent.

b. Conditional Probability

When dealing with more than one random variable one may be interested in probabilities involving a subset of the random variables given that the other random variables satisfy certain conditions. Such probabilities are called *conditional probabilities*.

EXAMPLE 2.27 X_1, X_2, and X_3 are the random variables in Example 2.23. We write $\mathrm{Prob}\{X_3 = j \,|\, X_1 = i\}$ to denote the probability that X_3 equals j given that X_1 equals i. This conditional probability can be interpreted as follows. Suppose the pair of dice is repeatedly tossed and we consider only those tosses on which $X_1 = i$. The frequency with which $X_3 = j$ on those tosses stabilizes at

$\text{Prob}\{X_3 = j \,|\, X_1 = i\}$. Since the frequency of all tosses on which $X_1 = i$ stabilizes at $\text{Prob}\{X_1 = i\}$ and the frequency of all tosses on which $X_1 = i$ and $X_3 = j$ stabilizes at $\text{Prob}\{X_1 = i;\ X_3 = j\}$, it follows that

$$\text{Prob}\{X_3 = j \,|\, X_1 = i\} = \text{Prob}\{X_1 = i;\ X_3 = j\}/\text{Prob}\{X_1 = i\}. \quad (2.72)$$

For example, $\text{Prob}\{X_1 = 2;\ X_3 = 4\} = \frac{1}{36}$ and $\text{Prob}\{X_1 = 2\} = \frac{1}{6}$ so that $\text{Prob}\{X_3 = 4 \,|\, X_1 = 2\} = \frac{1}{6}$. Since $\text{Prob}\{X_3 = 4\} = \frac{1}{12}$, $\text{Prob}\{X_3 = 4 \,|\, X_1 = 2\}$ is not equal to $\text{Prob}\{X_3 = 4\}$. This is because X_1 and X_3 are statistically dependent. On the other hand X_1 and X_2 are statistically independent so that $\text{Prob}\{X_1 = i;\ X_2 = j\} = \text{Prob}\{X_1 = i\}\,\text{Prob}\{X_2 = j\}$. Therefore, $\text{Prob}\{X_2 = j \,|\, X_1 = i\} = \text{Prob}\{X_1 = i;\ X_2 = j\}/\text{Prob}\{X_1 = i\} = \text{Prob}\{X_2 = j\}$.

$$\triangle$$

If $X_1, X_2, \ldots, X_n$ are random variables and $t_1, t_2, \ldots, t_n$ are real numbers, we write $\text{Prob}\{X_1 \leqslant t_1 \,|\, X_2 \leqslant t_2;\ \ldots;\ X_n \leqslant t_n\}$ to denote the conditional probability that $X_1 \leqslant t_1$ given that $X_2 \leqslant t_2$ and $X_3 \leqslant t_3, \ldots,$ and $X_n \leqslant t_n$. This conditional probability is given by

$$\text{Prob}\{X_1 \leqslant t_1 \,|\, X_2 \leqslant t_2;\ \ldots;\ X_n \leqslant t_n\}$$
$$= \text{Prob}\{X_1 \leqslant t_1;\ X_2 \leqslant t_2;\ \ldots;\ X_n \leqslant t_n\}/\text{Prob}\{X_2 \leqslant t_2;\ \ldots;\ X_n \leqslant t_n\}.$$
$$(2.73)$$

If $X_1, X_2, \ldots, X_n$ are statistically independent, then

$$\text{Prob}\{X_1 \leqslant t_1 \,|\, X_2 \leqslant t_2;\ldots;X_n \leqslant t_n\}$$
$$= \text{Prob}\{X_1 \leqslant t_1\}, \quad \text{for all} \quad t_1, t_2, \ldots, t_n; \quad (2.74)$$

i.e., the conditional probability is equal to the unconditional probability. More generally, if $X_1, X_2, \ldots, X_n$ are statistically independent, then a conditional probability involving any subset of the random variables given conditions on the other random variables is equal to the unconditional probability.

c. Important Relations

If $X_1, X_2, \ldots, X_n$ are random variables (which need not be statistically independent) and $c_1, c_2, \ldots, c_n$ are numbers, then

$$E\left[\sum_{i=1}^{n} c_i X_i\right] = \sum_{i=1}^{n} c_i E[X_i]. \quad (2.75)$$

The mean of a linear combination of random variables is equal to the same linear combination of the means of the random variables.

If $X_1, X_2, \ldots, X_n$ are statistically independent random variables, then

$$E[X_1 X_2 \cdots X_n] = E[X_1]E[X_2] \cdots E[X_n]. \quad (2.76)$$

The mean of a product of statistically independent random variables is equal to the product of the means of the random variables. However, the mean of the product being equal to the product of the means does not imply that the random variables are statistically independent.

The *covariance* of two random variables X and Y, denoted by $\mathrm{Cov}[X, Y]$, is given by

$$\mathrm{Cov}[X, Y] = E[(X - E[X])(Y - E[Y])]. \tag{2.77}$$

Note that $\mathrm{Cov}[X, X] = \mathrm{Var}[X]$. The covariance of X and Y can also be expressed as

$$\mathrm{Cov}[X, Y] = E[XY] - E[X]E[Y]. \tag{2.78}$$

Two random variables X and Y are said to be *uncorrelated* if $\mathrm{Cov}[X, Y] = 0$ and equivalently, $E[XY] = E[X]E[Y]$. Thus, if X and Y are statistically independent they are uncorrelated. However the reverse need not be true. The *correlation coefficient* of X and Y, denoted by $\mathrm{Cor}[X, Y]$, is given by

$$\mathrm{Cor}[X, Y] = \mathrm{Cov}[X, Y]/(\mathrm{Var}[X]\mathrm{Var}[Y])^{1/2}. \tag{2.79}$$

A correlation coefficient can be either positive or negative, but its absolute value cannot exceed one. The absolute value of $\mathrm{Cor}[X, Y]$ is equal to one if and only if $X = b + cY$ for some numbers b and c, that is if X and Y are linearly related.

If $X_1, X_2, \ldots, X_n$ are random variables (which need not be statistically independent) and $c_1, c_2, \ldots, c_n$ are numbers, then

$$\mathrm{Var}\left[\sum_{i=1}^{n} c_i X_i\right] = \sum_{i=1}^{n} c_i^2 \mathrm{Var}[X_i] + 2 \sum_{i=1}^{n-1} \sum_{j=i+1}^{n} c_i c_j \mathrm{Cov}[X_i, X_j]. \tag{2.80}$$

If X_i and X_j are uncorrelated for all $i \neq j$, then

$$\mathrm{Var}\left[\sum_{i=1}^{n} c_i X_i\right] = \sum_{i=1}^{n} c_i^2 \mathrm{Var}[X_i]. \tag{2.81}$$

If $X_1, X_2, \ldots, X_n$ are statistically independent they are uncorrelated, so that Eq. (2.81) holds.

The following are important results for the average of a large number of statistically independent random variables:

Let $X_1, X_2, \ldots, X_n$ be statistically independent random variables each of which has the same probability distribution function with finite mean m and finite positive variance V. Let

$$S_n = \sum_{i=1}^{n} \frac{X_i}{n}. \tag{2.82}$$

As n becomes large, the random variable S_n approaches a constant equal to the mean m. This result is called the *law of large numbers*. Furthermore, as n becomes large the probability distribution function of the random variable $n^{1/2}(S_n - m)/V^{1/2}$ approaches the probability distribution function of a unit normal random variable. This result is called the *central limit theorem*. In Fig. 2.13, the probability density function of $n^{1/2}(S_n - m)/V^{1/2}$ is plotted for various n in the case where $X_1, X_2, \ldots, X_n$ are exponential random variables. The probability density function of a normal random variable that has mean zero and variance one is also plotted.

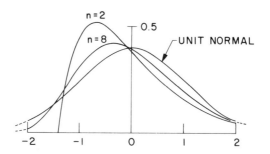

Fig. 2.13 Central limit theorem − probability density function of $\sqrt{n}(S_n - m)/\sqrt{V}$ and of a unit normal random variable.

2.1.4 Transform Methods

a. Probability Generating Function

Let $f_0, f_1, f_2, \ldots$ be a sequence of real numbers and let z be a complex number. Then, the function of z,

$$G(z) = \sum_{k=0}^{\infty} f_k z^k, \qquad (2.83)$$

is called the *z-transform* of the sequence. It may be necessary to restrict the values of z so that the sum exists.

Let X be a discrete random variable that can assume only nonnegative integer values and let

$$p_k = \text{Prob}\{X = k\}, \qquad k = 0, 1, 2, \ldots . \qquad (2.84)$$

The z-transform of the probability distribution $p_0, p_1, p_2, \ldots$, is given by

$$G_X(z) = \sum_{k=0}^{\infty} p_k z^k, \qquad (2.85)$$

and is called the *probability generating function* of X. The sum exists if $|z| \leqslant 1$.

TABLE 2.4

Probability Generating Functions

Random variable X	Parameters (restrictions)	$G_X(z)$
Binomial	n (integer), p ($n \geqslant 1$, $0 < p < 1$)	$[(1 - p) + pz]^n$
Geometric	p ($0 < p < 1$)	$(1 - p)/(1 - pz)$
Geometric starting at one	p ($0 < p < 1$)	$z(1 - p)/(1 - pz)$
Poisson	λ ($\lambda > 0$)	$e^{\lambda(z - 1)}$

The probability generating functions of some discrete random variables are given in Table 2.4.

The probability generating function of a discrete random variable uniquely determines its probability distribution. In Chapter 3, the probability generating function of a discrete random variable is sometimes given, rather than its probability distribution. In such a case, the probabilities can be obtained from the probability generating function by one of two methods.

One method is differentiation, i.e.,

$$p_0 = G_X(0), \tag{2.86}$$

$$p_k = (1/k!)(d^k G_X(z)/dz^k)_{z=0}, \qquad k = 1, 2, \ldots. \tag{2.87}$$

Sometimes, however, the form of $G_X(z)$ is so complicated that it is not practical to obtain more than a few of the probabilities in this manner.

The other method is by a recursive computational procedure. This method can be used if $G_X(z)$ is the ratio of two polynomials in z, i.e., if

$$G_X(z) = (a_0 + a_1 z + \cdots + a_m z^m)/(b_0 + b_1 z + \cdots + b_n z^n). \tag{2.88}$$

The probabilities are computed recursively as follows:

$$p_0 = a_0/b_0, \tag{2.89}$$

$$p_k = \frac{1}{b_0}\left(a_k - \sum_{i=1}^{\min(n,k)} b_i p_{k-i}\right), \qquad k = 1, 2, \ldots, \tag{2.90}$$

where $\min(n, k)$ denotes the minimum of n and k, and $a_k = 0$ if $k > m$. This computation is easy to program on a computer, and as many of the probabilities as are desired can be obtained.

The moments about the origin of a discrete random variable can be obtained from its probability generating function by differentiation. The first two moments about the origin are given by

$$E[X] = (dG_X(z)/dz)_{z=1}, \tag{2.91}$$

$$E[X^2] = (d^2 G_X(z)/dz^2)_{z=1} + E[X]. \tag{2.92}$$

The computation of higher moments is more complicated. The following recursive procedure can be used:

$$E[X^k] = (d^k G_X(z)/dz^k)_{z=1} + \sum_{i=1}^{k-1} a_{ki}E[X^i], \quad k = 3, 4, \ldots, \tag{2.93}$$

$$a_{k1} = (-1)^k(k-1)!, \qquad\qquad k = 3, 4, \ldots, \tag{2.94}$$

$$a_{k,k-1} = k(k-1)/2, \qquad\qquad k = 3, 4, \ldots, \tag{2.95}$$

$$a_{ki} = a_{k-1,i-1} - (k-1)a_{k-1,i}, \qquad j = 2, \ldots, k-2; \quad k = 4, 5, \ldots. \tag{2.96}$$

The following is an important property of the probability generating function:

Let $X_1, X_2, \ldots, X_n$ be statistically independent discrete random variables and let $X = X_1 + X_2 + \cdots + X_n$. Then

$$G_X(z) = G_{X_1}(z)G_{X_2}(z) \cdots G_{X_n}(z). \tag{2.97}$$

b. Laplace Transform of a Probability Density Function

Let $f(t)$, $t \geq 0$, be a real-valued function of t and let s be a complex number. Then, the function of s,

$$L(s) = \int_0^\infty f(t)e^{-st}\,dt, \tag{2.98}$$

is called the *Laplace transform* of the function. It may be necessary to restrict the values of s so that the integral exists.

Let X be a continuous random variable that can assume only nonnegative values and has probability density function $f_X(t)$. The Laplace transform of the probability density function is given by

$$L_X(s) = \int_0^\infty f_X(t)e^{-st}\,dt. \tag{2.99}$$

The integral exists if the real part of s is nonnegative. The Laplace transforms of the probability density functions of some continuous random variables are given in Table 2.5.

The moments about the origin of a nonnegative continuous random variable X can be easily obtained from $L_X(s)$ by differentiation as follows:

$$E[X^k] = (-1)^k(d^k L_X(s)/ds^k)_{s=0}, \qquad k = 1, 2, \ldots. \tag{2.100}$$

The moments about the origin of the random variables in Table 2.5 are given in Table 2.6.

TABLE 2.5

Laplace Transforms of Probability Density Functions

Random variable X	Parameters (restrictions)	$L_X(s)$
Exponential	$\lambda \ (\lambda > 0)$	$\lambda/(\lambda + s)$
Erlang	k (integer), $\lambda \ (k \geqslant 1, \lambda > 0)$	$[\lambda/(\lambda + s)]^k$
Gamma	$\alpha, \lambda \ (\alpha > 0, \lambda > 0)$	$[\lambda/(\lambda + s)]^\alpha$
Hyperexponential	$p, \lambda_1, \lambda_2 \ (0 < p < 1, \lambda_1 > 0, \lambda_2 > 0)$	$p\lambda_1/(\lambda_1 + s) + (1 - p)\lambda_2/(\lambda_2 + s)$

TABLE 2.6

Moments about the Origin

Random variable X	Parameter (restrictions)	$E[X^n]$
Exponential	$\lambda \ (\lambda > 0)$	$n!/\lambda^n$
Erlang	k (integer), $\lambda \ (k \geqslant 1, \lambda > 0)$	$k(k + 1) \cdots (k + n - 1)/\lambda^n$
Gamma	$\alpha, \lambda \ (\alpha > 0, \lambda > 0)$	$\alpha(\alpha + 1) \cdots (\alpha + n - 1)/\lambda^n$
Hyperexponential	$p, \lambda_1, \lambda_2 \ (0 < p < 1, \lambda_1 > 0, \lambda_2 > 0)$	$n![(p/\lambda_1^n) + (1 - p)/\lambda_2^n]$

The Laplace transform of the probability density function of a nonnegative continuous random variable uniquely determines the probability density function and thus uniquely determines the probability distribution function. In Chapter 3, the Laplace transform is sometimes given rather than the probability density function or probability distribution function. In such a case the probability density function can be numerically computed at regularly spaced points over some finite interval by using a computer program that computes the inverse Laplace transform. The Laplace transform of the probability distribution function is given by $L_X(s)/s$, so that the probability distribution function can be numerically computed at regularly spaced points over some finite interval by computing the inverse Laplace transform of $L_X(s)/s$.

The following is an important property of the Laplace transform of a probability density function:

Let $X_1, X_2, \ldots, X_n$ be statistically independent nonnegative continuous random variables and let $X = X_1 + X_2 + \cdots + X_n$. Then

$$L_X(s) = L_{X_1}(s)L_{X_2}(s) \cdots L_{X_n}(s). \tag{2.101}$$

2.2 Poisson Process

Suppose we perform a random experiment and as a result continuously observe the values of some quantity as a function of time. The values at the various times cannot be predicted and, hence, are random variables. A function of time whose values are random variables is called a *stochastic process.*

EXAMPLE 2.28   A gambler plays roulette. Let $M(t)$ be the amount of money he has won after t consecutive hours of playing. The function of time $M(t)$, $t \geq 0$, is a stochastic process.   △

EXAMPLE 2.29   Let $N(t)$ be the number of requests for seat reservations which arrive at the central computer of an airline reservation system during the time interval $[0, t]$. For a particular time t, $N(t)$ is a random variable (e.g., see Example 2.10). Therefore, the function of time $N(t)$, $t \geq 0$, is a stochastic process.   △

2.2.1 Definition

Consider a stochastic process $N(t)$, $t \geq 0$, where $N(t)$ is the number of arrivals at some system during the time interval $[0, t]$. We call such a process an *arrival process.* Let X_1 denote the time from time zero until the first arrival. For $i \geq 2$, let X_i denote the time between the $(i - 1)$st and ith arrivals. The relation between the arrival process $N(t)$, $t \geq 0$, and the *interarrival times* $X_1, X_2, \ldots$ is shown in Fig. 2.14. The interarrival times are random variables. If the interarrival times are statistically independent random variables, each of which has the same probability distribution function, then the arrival process is called a *renewal process.* An important example of a renewal process is a Poisson process. A *Poisson process* is an arrival process whose interarrival times are statistically independent exponential random variables, each of which has rate parameter λ; λ is called the *arrival rate* of the process. The Poisson process just

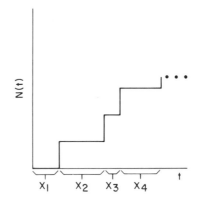

Fig. 2.14   Arrival process $N(t)$, $t \geq 0$ and interarrival times $X_1, X_2, \ldots$.

defined is said to be homogeneous since the arrival rate does not vary with time. The nonhomogeneous Poisson process, which has the property that the arrival rate varies with time, is discussed in Section 5.4.3. Unless stated otherwise, however, we only consider the homogeneous Poisson process.

A common assumption made in order to be able to mathematically analyze a queueing model of a computer system is that the arrival process is a Poisson process. Since the interarrival times are statistically independent exponential random variables, each of which has the same rate parameter, the interarrival times have the memoryless property (see the discussion of the exponential random variable in Section 2.1.2c). This is the reason the Poisson process plays a fundamental role in the analysis of queueing models of computer systems.

2.2.2 Properties

The following are some properties of a Poisson process:

1. The number of arrivals during any interval of time depends only on the length of the interval and not on its starting time.

2. The numbers of arrivals that occur during nonoverlapping time intervals are statistically independent.

3. If t is very small, the probability that exactly one arrival occurs during a time interval of length t is approximately equal to λt, where λ is the arrival rate. The probability that more than one arrival occurs is negligible compared to λt.

The Poisson process is the only arrival process that has these three properties. It is indeed a very special arrival process. Furthermore, if $N(t)$, $t \geq 0$, is a Poisson process that has arrival rate λ, then for each t, $N(t)$ is a Poisson random variable that has parameter λt; that is,

$$\text{Prob}\{N(t) = i\} = e^{-\lambda t}(\lambda t)^i / i!, \qquad i = 0, 1, \dots . \qquad (2.102)$$

Therefore,

$$E[N(t)] = \lambda t, \qquad (2.103)$$

so that λ is equal to the mean number of arrivals per unit of time. This explains why λ is called the arrival rate.

2.2.3 Merging

There may be several sources of arrivals at a system which merge to form the arrival process at the system.

EXAMPLE 2.30   In an airline reservation system, the arrivals generated at each of the terminals that use the system merge to form the arrival process at the central computer.   △

If $N_i(t)$, $t \geqslant 0$, $i = 1, 2, \ldots, n$ are arrival processes, the merged arrival process is given by $N(t) = N_1(t) + N_2(t) + \cdots + N_n(t), t \geqslant 0$. This merging is depicted in Fig. 2.15. If the arrival processes are renewal processes and the interarrival times for the different processes are statistically independent, the arrival processes are said to be statistically independent. The following is an important property of statistically independent Poisson processes: If statistically independent Poisson processes are merged, the merged arrival process is a Poisson process whose arrival rate is the sum of the arrival rates of the individual processes. However, if statistically independent renewal processes are merged, the merged process is not, in general, a renewal process.

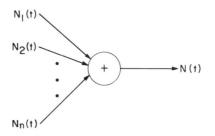

Fig. 2.15   Merging n arrival processes.

Although the Poisson process is a rather special arrival process, arrival processes that are approximately Poisson often arise in practice. The following result indicates why. If an arrival process is obtained by merging a large number of statistically independent renewal processes, then the merged arrival process is approximately a Poisson process, at least over time intervals that are short compared to the interarrival times of the individual arrival processes. This result provides physical conditions under which it may be reasonable to assume Poisson arrivals.

EXAMPLE 2.31   The arrival of calls at a telephone exchange is the merging of the arrivals due to a large number of individual subscribers. Thus, it may be reasonable to assume that the merged arrival process is a Poisson process.   △

EXAMPLE 2.32   The arrival of requests at the central computer of an airline reservation system is the merging of the arrivals generated at a large number of terminals. Thus, it may be reasonable to assume that the merged arrival process is a Poisson process.   △

2.2.4 *Splitting*

Suppose arrivals at a system are routed to n subsystems in the following way. Let $Y_1, Y_2, \ldots$ be statistically independent discrete random variables, each of which has probability distribution

$$\text{Prob}\{Y_i = j\} = p_j, \qquad j = 1, 2, \ldots, n. \tag{2.104}$$

If $Y_i = j$, then the ith arrival is routed to subsystem j. Thus, the ith arrival is routed to subsystem j with probability p_j. If the arrival process at the system is a Poisson process that has arrival rate λ, then the arrival processes at the n subsystems are statistically independent Poisson processes which have arrival rates, $p_1\lambda, p_2\lambda, \ldots, p_n\lambda$. This splitting is depicted in Fig. 2.16.

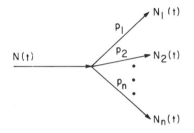

Fig. 2.16 Splitting an arrival process.

2.3   Little's Formula and Its Applications

Consider any system at which customers arrive, spend time in the system, and depart. Let

$N(t)$ = number of arrivals at the system in the time interval $[0, t]$,   (2.105)

$l(t)$ = number of customers in the system at time t,   (2.106)

r_k = time spent in the system by the kth customer to arrive.   (2.107)

r_k is called the system *response time* for the kth customer. These quantities can be considered to be known deterministic quantities or random variables. The only assumptions we make are that the following limits exist and are finite:

$$\lambda = \lim_{t \to \infty} \frac{N(t)}{t}, \tag{2.108}$$

$$L = \lim_{t \to \infty} \frac{1}{t} \int_0^t l(s) \, ds, \tag{2.109}$$

$$R = \lim_{k \to \infty} \frac{1}{k} \sum_{i=1}^{k} r_i. \tag{2.110}$$

[The expression "$\lim_{t \to \infty} N(t)/t$" stands for "the limit as t approaches infinity of $N(t)/t$." The limit is the value at which $N(t)/t$ stabilizes as t becomes large.] The quantity λ is the *arrival rate*, the quantity L is the *average* over all time of the *number of customers in the system*, and the quantity R is the *average* over all arrivals at the system of the *system response time*. These three quantities are related by the formula,

$$L = \lambda R, \tag{2.111}$$

known as *Little's formula*. (The letter W is commonly used instead of R so that Little's formula is commonly written, $L = \lambda W$; R is used here to stand for response time). This formula states that the average number of customers in the system is equal to the product of the arrival rate and the average system response time. This formula can be applied to obtain any one of the quantities L, λ, R given the other two. The following examples indicate some of the applications of Little's formula.

EXAMPLE 2.33   Consider the system consisting of n subsystems depicted in Fig. 2.17. Customers from an external source arrive at the system, spend time

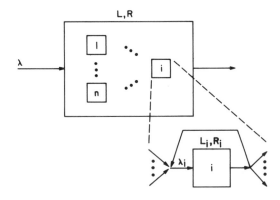

Fig. 2.17   System consisting of n subsystems with external arrivals.

in the system circulating among the subsystems, and eventually depart from the system. λ denotes the arrival rate at the system and is given. L denotes the average over all time of the number of customers in the system and R denotes the average over all arrivals at the system of the system response time. For subsystem i, λ_i denotes the arrival rate at the subsystem, L_i denotes the average number of customers in the subsystem, and R_i denotes the average over all arrivals at the subsystem of the subsystem response time. Note that customers can arrive at subsystem i directly from the source, directly from the other subsystems, and even directly from subsystem i itself. Since a customer in the system is in one of the subsystems,

$$L = L_1 + L_2 + \cdots + L_n. \tag{2.112}$$

Applying Little's formula to the system yields

$$L = \lambda R, \tag{2.113}$$

where λ is given. Usually L is computed from a detailed analysis of the system and R is obtained from Little's formula. Applying Little's formula to each subsystem yields

$$L_i = \lambda_i R_i, \qquad i = 1, 2, \ldots, n. \tag{2.114}$$

Combining Eqs. (2.112)–(2.114) yields

$$R = \sum_{i=1}^{n} \frac{\lambda_i R_i}{\lambda}. \tag{2.115}$$

Thus, the average system response time can be expressed directly in terms of the average subsystem response times and the arrival rates at the system and at each subsystem.

A customer may visit subsystem i more than once while it is in the system. Let R_i^* denote the average over all arrivals at the system of the time a customer spends in subsystem i while it is in the system. The time spent in subsystem i by a customer while it is in the system is not spent continuously. However, Little's formula holds in the following form:

$$L_i = \lambda R_i^*. \tag{2.116}$$

Thus,

$$R_i^*/R = L_i/L, \tag{2.117}$$

so that the fraction of the average system response time that is spent in subsystem i is equal to the fraction of the average number of customers in the system that are in subsystem i. $\triangle$

EXAMPLE 2.34   Consider the same system as in Example 2.33, except that there is no external source of arrivals. Rather there are N customers in the system initially. A customer that departs from the system is immediately fed back as an arrival at the system as shown in Fig. 2.18. Thus, the number of customers in the system is always equal to N so that L, the average number of customers in the system, is equal to N. The system response time is the time spent in the system by a customer between arrival along the feedback path and departure along the feedback path. λ denotes the arrival rate at the system along the feedback path and R denotes the average system response time. Little's formula yields

$$N = \lambda R, \tag{2.118}$$

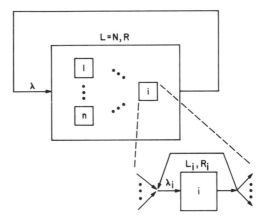

Fig. 2.18   System consisting of n subsystems with N customers in the system.

where N is given. Usually λ is computed from a detailed analysis of the system and R is obtained from this formula. All of the equations in Example 2.33 hold with L replaced by N.   △

In the above examples, no distinction was made among customers. If, however, there are several types of customers, Little's formula holds for each customer type separately as well as for all customers without regard to type.

EXAMPLE 2.35   Suppose in Example 2.33 there are two types of customers, type A and type B, which arrive at the system. Let λ^A and λ^B denote the arrival rates of type A and type B customers at the system, let L^A and L^B denote the average number of type A and type B customers in the system, and let R^A and R^B denote the average system response time for type A and type B customers. Then

$$L^A = \lambda^A R^A, \qquad (2.119)$$

$$L^B = \lambda^B R^B. \qquad (2.120)$$

In fact all the equations in Example 2.33 hold for each type of customer. Of course Little's formula holds without regard to customer type so that

$$L = \lambda R, \qquad (2.121)$$

where $\lambda = \lambda^A + \lambda^B$ and $L = L^A + L^B$. Hence,

$$R = (\lambda^A R^A + \lambda^B R^B)/(\lambda^A + \lambda^B). \qquad (2.122)$$

The average system response time for all types of customers is a linear combination of the average response times for each type of customer. A similar result holds for the average subsystem response times.   △

EXAMPLE 2.36   Suppose in Example 2.34 there are N^A type A customers and N^B type B customers in the system. Then, Little's formula holds for each type of customer, i.e.,

$$N^A = \lambda^A R^A, \tag{2.123}$$

$$N^B = \lambda^B R^B, \tag{2.124}$$

as well as for all types of customers; i.e.,

$$N = \lambda R. \tag{2.125}$$

Since $\lambda = \lambda^A + \lambda^B$ and $N = N^A + N^B$, it follows that

$$R = (\lambda^A R^A + \lambda^B R^B)/(\lambda^A + \lambda^B). \tag{2.126}$$

References

For further reading, the following books deal with topics covered in this chapter.

Çinlar, E. (1975). "Introduction to Stochastic Processes." Prentice-Hall, Englewood Cliffs, New Jersey. This textbook contains a modern mathematical treatment of many important stochastic processes including Poisson processes and renewal processes. It is suitable for a mathematically inclined reader who is familiar with calculus and basic probability theory.

Feller, W. (1968). "An Introduction to Probability Theory and Its Applications." Vol. I, 3rd ed. Wiley, New York. This widely used book treats probability in a rigorous mathematical manner yet contains many examples that help the reader to develop a feel for the subject.

Johnson, N. L., and Kotz, S. (1969). "Discrete Distributions." Houghton Mifflin, Boston, Massachusetts. This book is a useful reference on discrete random variables. It discusses the properties and uses of most discrete random variables of interest to modelers.

Johnson, N. L., and Kotz, S. (1970). "Continuous Univariate Distributions-1" and "Continuous Univariate Distributions-2." Houghton Mifflin, Boston, Massachusetts. These books are useful references on continuous random variables. They discuss the properties and uses of most continuous random variables of interest to modelers.

Trivedi, K. S. (1982). "Probability and Statistics with Reliability, Queueing, and Computer Science Applications." Prentice-Hall, Englewood Cliffs, New Jersey. This textbook provides an introduction to probability, stochastic processes, and statistics suitable for students in computer science and engineering. It also contains computer performance modeling applications.

3

Analytical Results for Queueing Models

Stephen S. Lavenberg and Charles H. Sauer

3.1 Introduction

A *queue* is a waiting line for service. The service is provided by a single *server* or by multiple servers which operate in parallel. A queue and its servers are shown in Fig. 3.1 and are called a *service center*. *Customers* arrive at the service center, wait in line for a server to become free, receive service, and depart.

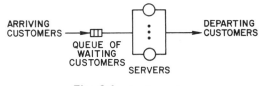

Fig. 3.1 Service center.

EXAMPLE 3.1 Messages generated by a source are to be transmitted one at a time over a communication line. If the line is busy when a message is generated the message temporarily waits in a buffer. Whenever the line becomes free and there are messages in the buffer, one of the messages immediately leaves the buffer and begins to be transmitted. Each message is a customer, the communication line is the server, the transmission of a message is the service, and the messages waiting in the buffer form the queue. △

A queueing model consists of one or more service centers. A customer that departs from a service center may enter another service center, reenter the same service center, or depart from the system. A customer may arrive at the system from an external source, spend time in the system, and depart, or it may be in the system initially and remain there indefinitely.

A queueing model is a mathematical model used to represent a physical system in which there is contention for resources. The purpose is to predict the performance of the system. When using a mathematical model to represent a physical system the modeler must understand which features of the system are represented in the model and which are not, how the features are represented, and the various mathematical assumptions that have been made. The model should be used only if it is a reasonable representation of the system for the performance questions being addressed. The queueing models described in this chapter have been analyzed mathematically. Only the results of an analysis are given, not the analysis itself. The results are either formulas, for such performance measures as utilizations, throughputs, and average response times, or algorithms, which can be used to compute such performance measures. Sources for the results are given in Section 3.9. However, it is not necessary for the reader to refer to the sources in order to understand and apply the results.

In order to fully describe a queueing model it is necessary to describe (i) the arrival of customers at the system, (ii) the service demands of each customer, (iii) the service rate of each server, (iv) the sequence of service centers visited by each customer and (v) the order in which customers in each service center are served. As we shall see, the arrival of customers, the service demands, and the sequence of service centers they visit are described in terms of probabilities and random variables. Also, many performance measures are expressed in terms of probabilities and random variables. Section 2.1 contains material on probability and random variables needed to fully understand the models and results in this chapter.

3.2   Performance Measures

A queueing model is a dynamic probabilistic model; i.e., it uses probabilities to represent the evolution over time of a system. It is very difficult to analyze the transient behavior of such a model, i.e., the behavior as a function of time. The transient behavior is most readily studied via simulation (see Chapter 6). However, it is often possible to analyze the steady-state behavior of such a model.

Let n_s denote the number of customers in the system at time s. Then n_s is a discrete random variable and has a probability distribution that depends on s and on the initial conditions of the system (conditions at time zero). It is very difficult to obtain this probability distribution using analysis. However, for the queueing models we shall consider, as s becomes large n_s behaves exactly like a random variable n whose probability distribution $\text{Prob}\{n = i\}$, $i = 0, 1, \ldots,$ does not depend on the initial conditions or on the time s. The random variable n is called the *steady-state number of customers* and its probability distribution can often be obtained using analysis. The mean and other moments of n can then be computed from the probability distribution; i.e.,

$$E[n^k] = \sum_{i=0}^{\infty} i^k \text{Prob}\{n = i\}. \tag{3.1}$$

For the queueing models we shall consider, the steady-state probabilites $\text{Prob}\{n = i\}$ and the moments $E[n^k]$ are equal to averages over an infinitely long interval of time, called *long-run time averages*. Thus,

$$\text{Prob}\{n = i\} = \lim_{s \to \infty} (\text{fraction of time during the first } s \text{ time units that}$$
$$i \text{ customers are in the system}), \tag{3.2}$$

$$E[n^k] = \lim_{s \to \infty} \frac{1}{s} \int_0^s [n_u]^k \, du. \tag{3.3}$$

Let r_j denote the time spent in the system by the jth customer to arrive. Then r_j, called the jth *response time*, is a random variable (typically a continuous random variable) and has a probability distribution function that depends on j and on the inital conditions. However, for the queueing models we shall consider, as j becomes large r_j behaves exactly like a random variable r whose probability distribution function $\text{Prob}\{r \leqslant t\}$, $t \geqslant 0$, does not depend on j or on the initial conditions. The random variable r is called the *steady-state response time*. If r has probability density function $f_r(t)$, $t \geqslant 0$, then the kth moment of the steady-state response time is given by

$$E[r^k] = \int_0^\infty t^k f_r(t)\, dt. \tag{3.4}$$

For the queueing models we shall consider, $\text{Prob}\{r \leqslant t\}$ and $E[r^k]$ are equal to averages over an infinite number of customers, called *long-run customer averages*. Thus,

$$\text{Prob}\{r \leqslant t\} = \lim_{J \to \infty} \text{ (fraction of the first } J \text{ customers to arrive whose}$$
$$\text{response times are less than or equal to } t), \tag{3.5}$$

$$E[r^k] = \lim_{J \to \infty} \frac{1}{J} \sum_{j=1}^{J} r_j^k. \tag{3.6}$$

The quantities in Eqs. (3.2), (3.3), (3.5), and (3.6) provide information about the performance of the system. The mean number of customers $E[n]$ and the mean response time $E[r]$ are often the simplest of these performance measures to compute. If they are finite we say the system is *stable*. Let Λ denote the long-run rate at which customers depart from the system; i.e.,

$$\Lambda = \lim_{s \to \infty} \frac{1}{s} \text{ (number of customers that depart in the first}$$
$$s \text{ time units).} \tag{3.7}$$

If the system is stable the *throughput* Λ must equal the long-run rate at which customers arrive. Furthermore, Little's formula (see Section 2.3) holds; i.e.,

$$E[n] = \Lambda E[r]. \tag{3.8}$$

If a service center has a single server, the long-run fraction of time that the server is busy is called the *utilization* of the service center. In general a service center has $m \geqslant 1$ servers and the utilization U is defined on a per server basis as follows:

$$U = \frac{1}{m} \lim_{s \to \infty} \frac{1}{s} \text{ (total busy time of all servers during the first}$$
$$s \text{ time units).} \tag{3.9}$$

It is easy to show that U is also equal to the long-run time average of the fraction of servers that are busy, i.e., letting b_s denote the fraction of servers that are busy at time s,

$$U = \lim_{s \to \infty} \frac{1}{s} \int_0^s b_u \, du. \tag{3.10}$$

3.3 Single Service Center Queueing Models

3.3.1 Description and Notation

In this section we present results for queueing models consisting of a single service center (see Fig. 3.1). Customers arrive at the service center, stay in the service center until their service demands are satisfied, and depart. Each server represents a resource, e.g., communication line, processor, or input/output device, and if there are multiple servers they are identical and operate independently and in parallel. A customer can be served by any free server, and unless stated otherwise, a server is never idle if there are customers waiting to be served. In order to fully specify such a queueing model it is necessary to describe the arrival times of customers, their service demands, the number and service rate of the servers, and the order in which customers are served.

Arrival Times. The times between successive arrivals at the service center are called *interarrival times.* The interarrival times are assumed to be statistically independent random variables that have the same probability distribution function. Thus, the arrival process is a renewal process (see Section 2.2). A common additional assumption is that the interarrival times are exponential random variables. In that case the arrival process is a Poisson process (see Section 2.2). In some models different types of customers are distinguished.

EXAMPLE 3.2   Both system control messages and user messages are transmitted over the same communication line. System control messages are short compared to user messages and are given transmission priority over user messages. It may be useful to distinguish between these two types of messages in a model.   △

If there are different types of customers, the type of each arriving customer is assumed to be chosen probabilistically according to fixed probabilites. Let K denote the number of types of customers and let a_k denote the probability that an arriving customer is type k, where $a_1 + \cdots + a_K = 1$. If the overall arrival process is a Poisson process with arrival rate λ, then the arrival processes for the different types of customers are statistically independent Poisson processes with arrival rates $\lambda_1 = a_1\lambda, \ldots, \lambda_K = a_K\lambda$ (see Section 2.2.4). Equivalently, if the arrival processes for the different types of customers are statistically independent Poisson processes with arrival rates $\lambda_1, \ldots, \lambda_K$ then the overall arrival process is a Poisson process with arrival rate $\lambda = \lambda_1 + \cdots + \lambda_K$ and the probability that an arriving customer is type k is given by $a_k = \lambda_k/\lambda$.

Service Demands, Service Rate, and Service Times. The amount of service required by a customer at the service center is called a *service demand*. A service demand is often expressed in units of time, but it can be expressed in other units.

EXAMPLE 3.3   A service demand at a communication line can be expressed in units of bits to be transmitted. With these units the service demand does not depend on the speed on the line.   △

EXAMPLE 3.4   A service demand at a processor can be expressed in units of instructions. With these units the service demand does not depend on the speed of the processor.   △

All service demands are assumed to be statistically independent random variables. Service demands for customers of the same type are assumed to have the same probability distribution function, but service demands for customers of different types can have different probability distribution functions.

The speed of a server in service units per time unit is called the *service rate*. The service units are the same units in which service demands are expressed. All servers at the service center have the same service rate.

EXAMPLE 3.5   The service rate of a communication line can be expressed in bits per second.   △

EXAMPLE 3.6   The service rate of a processor can be expressed in instructions per second.   △

The *service time* of a customer is given by

$$\text{service time} = (\text{service demand})/(\text{service rate}).\qquad(3.11)$$

If the service rate is equal to one then the service time is equal to the service demand.

Queueing Discipline. A queueing discipline is an algorithm that determines the order in which customers in the service center are served. Unless stated otherwise, a server is never idle if there are customers waiting to be served. The queueing disciplines to be considered depend on the order in which customers arrive at the service center and/or priorities assigned to customers and/or the amounts of service already provided to customers. They do not depend on the exact service demands of customers which are unknown.

The queueing discipline in which customers are served in the order of their arrival at the service center is called *first-come-first-served* (FCFS) [also called first-in-first-out (FIFO)].

EXAMPLE 3.7   In some communication networks, messages (customers) are transmitted (served) one at a time over a communication line (server) in the order of their arrival at the transmitting node.   △

EXAMPLE 3.8   Requests (customers) to transfer records from a direct access storage device are often scheduled so that the records are transferred (customers are served) one at a time in the order of arrival of the requests.
△

A queueing discipline in which customers are assigned fixed priorities which determine the order in which they are served is called a *priority* queueing discipline. The next customer to be served is one that has the highest priority among all customers waiting to be served. Customers having the same priority are served in the order of their arrival. If a service, once begun, is not interruptable, the queueing discipline is called *nonpreemptive*. If, on the other hand, an arriving customer interrupts the service of a lower priority customer and begins to be served, the queueing discipline is called *preemptive*. A customer whose service was interrupted resumes service at the point of interruption when there are no higher priority customers to be served. (We do not consider the preemptive queueing discipline in which the interrupted service is repeated from the beginning, rather than resumed, since useful analytical results are not available.)

EXAMPLE 3.9   In some communication networks system control messages are given transmission priority over user messages; that is, the next message to be transmitted over a line is a control message if there are any waiting. Once a message transmission begins it continues to completion without interruption. Control messages are transmitted in the order of their arrival as are user messages. Thus, the queueing discipline is nonpreemptive priority.   △

EXAMPLE 3.10   In some operating systems, system programs are given priority over user programs for execution on the processor. Furthermore, system programs interrupt executing user programs. An interrupted user program later resumes execution at the point of interruption. Thus, the queueing discipline is preemptive priority.   △

In the *round robin* queueing discipline a customer is given continuous service for a maximum interval of time call a *quantum*. If the customer's service demand is not satisfied during the quantum, the customer reenters the queue and waits to receive an additional quantum of service, repeating this process until its service demand is satisfied. Customers in the queue are served in the order in which they last entered the queue. The round robin queueing discipline is depicted in Fig. 3.2. It is designed to provide fast response to customers with small service demands (e.g., service demands that are satisfied within one quantum) at the expense of customers with large service demands.

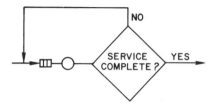

Fig. 3.2   Round robin queueing discipline.

EXAMPLE 3.11   In an interactive computer system it is often desirable to give fast response to short jobs at the expense of long jobs. This is accomplished by time-slicing, i.e., using round robin or a similar algorithm to schedule the processor.   △

The round robin queueing discipline has the effect that if the quantum size is very small all customers appear to receive service simultaneously and share the server equally (here we assume there is a single server). Thus, if there are i customers present each customer appears to receive $(1/i)$th of the server's rate. The queueing discipline in which all customers receive service from a single server simultaneously with equal shares of the service rate is called *processor sharing* (PS). The processor sharing queueing discipline is commonly used to model the effect of the round robin queueing discipline for small quantum size. Analytical results for processor sharing are much simpler than those for round robin and they provide good approximations to round robin results.

Other queueing disciplines will be introduced throughout this chapter.

Notation.   The shorthand notation letter/letter/m is commonly used to partially describe a queueing model consisting of a single service center that has m servers. The first letter refers to the interarrival times and the second letter refers to the service demands. The following letters are used:

M: denotes an exponential random variable; the letter M is used to refer to the memoryless property of an exponential random variable [see Eq. (2.36) and the discussion following it];

D: denotes a deterministic, i.e., constant, quantity;

G: denotes a general nonnegative random variable.

EXAMPLE 3.12   An $M/G/1$ queueing model is one in which all interarrival times are exponential random variables, all service demands are general nonnegative random variables, and there is one server.   △

The following additional notation is used:

T: interarrival time (a random variable),
$\lambda = 1/E[T]$:   arrival rate,
K: number of types of customers,

a_k: probability an arriving customer is type k, where $a_1 + \cdots + a_K = 1$,

$\lambda_k = a_k\lambda$: arrival rate of type k customers,

γ: service rate of each server,

S_k: service demand (service time if $\gamma = 1$) of type k customers (a random variable),

S: service demand (service time if $\gamma = 1$) without regard to customer type (a random variable),

n_k: steady-state number of type k customers in the service center (a random variable),

$n = n_1 + \cdots + n_K$: steady-state number of customers in the service center (a random variable),

r_k: steady-state response time for type k customers (a random variable),

r: steady-state response time without regard to customer type (a random variable),

U_k: utilization due to type k customers,

$U = U_1 + \cdots + U_K$: utilization,

Λ_k: throughput of type k customers,

$\Lambda = \Lambda_1 + \cdots + \Lambda_K$: throughput.

We use the notation of Chapter 2 for a random variable X, i.e.,

$E[X]$: mean,

$\mathrm{Var}[X]$: variance,

$C[X]$: coefficient of variation,

$F_X(t)$: probability distribution function,

$f_X(t)$: probability density function (if X is a continuous random variable),

$L_X(s)$: Laplace transform of $f_X(t)$ (if X is a continuous random variable),

$G_X(z)$: probability generating function (if X is a discrete random variable).

The moments about the origin of S and $S_1, \ldots, S_K$ are related by

$$E[S^j] = \sum_{k=1}^{K} a_k E[S_k^j], \qquad (3.12)$$

and their probability distribution functions are related by

$$F_S(t) = \sum_{k=1}^{K} a_k F_{S_k}(t). \qquad (3.13)$$

Also,

$$E[r^j] = \sum_{k=1}^{K} a_k E[r_k^j] \qquad (3.14)$$

and

$$F_r(t) = \sum_{k=1}^{K} a_k F_{r_k}(t). \tag{3.15}$$

3.3.2 Stability, Utilization, and Throughput

Intuitively, a service center should be stable, i.e., $E[n]$ and $E[r]$ are finite, if customers arrive at a rate that is smaller than the rate at which they can be served. The quantity that governs the stability of a service center is the *traffic intensity* ρ. Unless stated otherwise,

$$\rho = \lambda E[S]/m\gamma \tag{3.16}$$

and a service center is stable if $\rho < 1$ and it is unstable if $\rho > 1$. (The case $\rho = 1$ is omitted since it sometimes presents mathematical difficulties.) Furthermore, unless stated otherwise, if $\rho < 1$ then $U = \rho$ and $\Lambda = \lambda$; i.e., the utilization equals the traffic intensity and the throughput equals the arrival rate. If $\rho \geqslant 1$ then $U = 1$, i.e., on the average all the servers are busy. If there are different types of customers then the traffic intensity given in Eq. (3.16) can also be written as

$$\rho = \sum_{k=1}^{K} \frac{\lambda_k E[S_k]}{m\gamma}. \tag{3.17}$$

If $\rho < 1$ then $U_k = \lambda_k E[S_k]/m\gamma$ and $\Lambda_k = \lambda_k$. Results are only given for stable queueing models.

3.3.3 M/G/1 Queueing Model

The $M/G/1$ queueing model represents the contention for a single server under the assumption that the arrival process is a Poisson process. The single server can be a communication line, a processor, an I/O device, or a serially reusable program. Modeling applications are given in the examples. The mathematical analysis of the $M/G/1$ queueing model has been carried out for a wide variety of queueing disciplines. Consequently, the results presented here provide insight into the effects of queueing disciplines on performance.

Usually we shall give expressions for the mean and variance of the steady-state response time r and the mean and variance of the steady-state number of customers in the system n. While it would be nice to have explicit expressions for the probability distribution function of r and the probability distribution of n, these have only been obtained in special cases. Unless stated otherwise, we assume that the service rate γ is equal to one so that S and S_k are service times. If $\gamma \neq 1$, then S and S_k should be replaced by S/γ and S_k/γ in all expressions.

a. First-Come-First-Served (FCFS) Queueing Discipline

Customers are served in the order of their arrival.

$$E[r] = E[S] + \frac{\lambda E[S^2]}{2(1 - \rho)}, \tag{3.18}$$

$$\text{Var}[r] = \text{Var}[S] + \frac{\lambda E[S^3]}{3(1 - \rho)} + \frac{\lambda^2 (E[S^2])^2}{4(1 - \rho)^2}, \tag{3.19}$$

$$L_r(s) = \frac{L_S(s)s(1 - \rho)}{s - \lambda + \lambda L_S(s)}, \tag{3.20}$$

$$E[n] = \rho + \frac{\lambda^2 E[S^2]}{2(1 - \rho)}, \tag{3.21}$$

$$\text{Var}[n] = E[n] + \lambda^2 \text{Var}[S] + \frac{\lambda^3 E[S^3]}{3(1 - \rho)} + \frac{\lambda^4 (E[S^2])^2}{4(1 - \rho)^2}, \tag{3.22}$$

$$G_n(z) = \frac{L_S(\lambda - \lambda z)(1 - z)(1 - \rho)}{L_S(\lambda - \lambda z) - z}. \tag{3.23}$$

The means and variances in Eqs. (3.18), (3.19), (3.21), and (3.22) increase to infinity as λ approaches $1/E[S]$, i.e., as the traffic intensity ρ defined in Eq. (3.16) approaches one. This behavior is typical of many queueing models as we shall see. Note from Eqs. (3.18) and (3.21) that the mean steady-state response time and the mean steady-state number of customers depend on the service time S only through the mean and second moment about the origin of S. Equation (3.18) can be rewritten as

$$E[r] = E[S] + \frac{\rho E[S](1 + C^2[S])}{2(1 - \rho)}. \tag{3.24}$$

Thus, the mean steady-state response time and mean steady-state number of customers increase as $C[S]$, the coefficient of variation of the service time, increases. (The coefficients of variation of some common random variables are given in Table 2.2.) If $C[S] = 0$, then S is not a random variable but is a deterministic quantity. (In this case all service times have the same constant value.) Thus, the term $\rho E[S]C^2[S]/[2(1 - \rho)]$ is the contribution to the mean response time due to the randomness of the service times. In Fig. 3.3, $E[r]/E[S]$ is plotted as a function of ρ for several values of $C[S]$.

From Eqs. (3.19) and (3.22), the variance of the steady-state response time and the variance of the steady-state number of customers depend on S only through the first three moments about the origin of S. (The moments about the origin of some common random variables are given in Table 2.6.) For $k \geqslant 2$, $E[r^k]$ can be obtained from Eq. (3.20) by differentiation [see Eq.

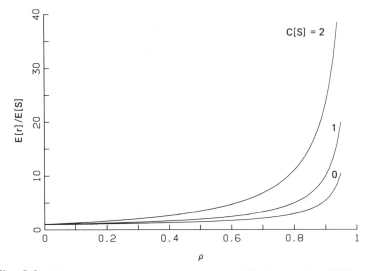

Fig. 3.3 Mean steady-state response time versus traffic intensity for $M/G/1$ queueing model with FCFS queueing discipline.

(2.100)] and $E[n^k]$ can be obtained from Eq. (3.23) by differentiation [see Eqs. (2.93)–(2.96)]. Both $E[r^k]$ and $E[n^k]$ depend on S only through $E[S]$, $E[S^2], \ldots, E[S^{k+1}]$.

$L_r(s)$, the Laplace transform of the probability density function of r, given in Eq. (3.20), and $G_n(z)$, the probability generating function of n, given in Eq. (3.23), are expressed in terms of $L_S(s)$, the Laplace transform of the probability density function of S. (Laplace transforms of probability density functions of some common random variables are given in Table 2.5.) Except in special cases (see $M/M/1$ and $M/D/1$ results below), $L_r(s)$ and $G_n(z)$ cannot be inverted algebraically and explicit expressions for the probability distribution or density function of r or the probability distribution of n have not been obtained. However, these transforms can often be inverted numerically as discussed in Section 2.1.4.

EXAMPLE 3.13   We consider the transfer of records stored on a single disk drive. Requests to transfer a record arrive at the software queue for the disk drive. The requested records are transferred one at a time in the order of arrival of the requests so that the queueing discipline is FCFS. We shall assume that the control unit and channel are always available and only consider the contention for the drive. Thus, the drive is the server. The service time S is the sum of the seek time (time to move the arm from its current position to the cylinder containing the requested record), latency time (time from when the seek is complete until the requested record begins to pass under the head), and data transfer time. (We are neglecting the typically small amount of time required to transfer and execute channel commands.) Denoting the seek, latency, and transfer times by X_S, X_L, and X_T, respectively, then $S = X_S + X_L + X_T$. If we assume that requests arrive according to a Poisson process with rate λ and that successive service times are statistically independent random variables, we can use Eq. (3.24) to compute the mean steady-state response time, where the response time is the time from when a request arrives until the data transfer is complete. [Actually, successive service times are not independent since successive seek times are not independent. This is because the next seek time depends on the current arm position. However, this dependency is ignored in the model. A comparison was made with numerical results (given in Table 1 of Hofri, 1980) for a more complex model which represents this dependence. The comparison showed that the effect of the dependence is small and can be ignored.]

In order to use Eq. (3.24) it is necessary to compute the mean and coefficient of variation of S. Clearly,

$$E[S] = E[X_S] + E[X_L] + E[X_T]. \tag{3.25}$$

It is reasonable to assume that the seek, latency, and transfer times are statistically independent random variables, so that

$$\text{Var}[S] = \text{Var}[X_S] + \text{Var}[X_L] + \text{Var}[X_T]. \tag{3.26}$$

We next compute the mean and variance of X_S, X_L, and X_T.

The seek time X_S depends on the cylinder addresses of successive requested records and on the seek time characteristics of the device, i.e., the time it takes the arm to move a specified number of cylinders. Let C denote the total number of cylinders on the drive. We assume that the cylinder address of a requested record equals the cylinder address of the previous requested record with probability p and it equals a particular one of the other $C - 1$ cylinder addresses with probability $(1 - p)/(C - 1)$. With this assumption the number of cylinders moved, denoted by M, has probability distribution

$$\text{Prob}\{M = i\} = \begin{cases} p, & i = 0, \\ (1 - p)2(C - i)/(C - 1)C, & i = 1, \ldots, C - 1. \end{cases} \tag{3.27}$$

The seek time characteristics of the device are given by the times $t(i)$, $i = 0, \ldots, C - 1$, where $t(i)$ is the time to move i cylinders. The moments of the seek time can then be computed as follows:

$$E[X_S^k] = \sum_{i=1}^{C-1} [t(i)]^k \text{Prob}\{M = i\}. \tag{3.28}$$

The mean and variance of X_S are computed from Eqs. (3.27) and (3.28).

It is reasonable to assume that the latency time X_L is a uniform random variable on the interval $[0, R]$, where R is the time for a full rotation. With this assumption

$$E[X_L] = R/2, \tag{3.29}$$

$$\text{Var}[X_L] = R^2/12. \tag{3.30}$$

If all records are B bytes long, then the transfer time X_T is a constant equal to B/D, where D is the data rate (bytes/second) of the drive. Thus,

$$E[X_T] = B/D, \tag{3.31}$$

$$\text{Var}[X_T] = 0. \tag{3.32}$$

The mean steady-state response time $E[r]$ can now be computed from Eqs. (3.24)–(3.32).

For IBM's 3330-11 disk drive $C = 808$, $R = 0.0167$ s, $D = 806 \times 10^3$ bytes/s and the seek time characteristics can be approximated by

$$t(i) = 0.00859 + 0.00141\sqrt{i}, \qquad i = 1, \ldots, 807. \tag{3.33}$$

For this disk drive $E[X_L] = 0.00835$, $\text{Var}[X_L] = 0.0000232$, and for a fixed record size $B = 2000$ bytes, $E[X_T] = 0.00248$, $\text{Var}[X_T] = 0$. In Table 3.1 we

TABLE 3.1

Values Based on Approximate Seek Time Characteristics
of 3330-11 Disk Drive and Eq. (3.27)

p	$E[X_S]$	$\text{Var}[X_S]$	$E[S]$	$C[S]$	$1/E[S]$
1/808	0.0300	0.0000791	0.0408	0.248	24.5
0.2	0.0240	0.000206	0.0348	0.435	28.7
0.5	0.0150	0.000264	0.0258	0.656	38.7

give the mean and variance of the seek time, the mean and coefficient of variation of the service time, and the maximum throughput $1/E[S]$ (requests/second) for several values of p, the probability that successive requests are for records on the same cylinder. If $p = 1/808$ then it is as probable to reference the same cylinder as it is to reference any other cylinder. As p increases, the performance of the drive improves. Values of p equal to or greater than 0.5 have been observed for real systems. In Fig. 3.4 we plot $E[r]$ versus λ, the arrival rate (requests/second), for $B = 2000$ bytes, and the three values of p in Table 3.1.   △

The expressions given in Eqs. (3.18), (3.19), (3.21), and (3.22) for the mean and variance of r and n simplify considerably if S is an exponential random

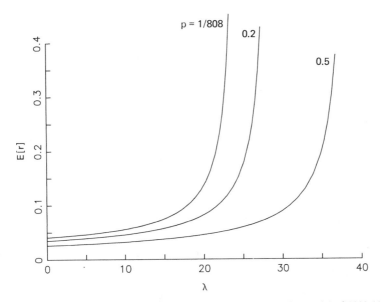

Fig. 3.4 Mean steady-state response time versus arrival rate for model of 3330-11 disk drive (record size = 2000 bytes).

variable or if S is a constant. In these two special cases, expressions have been obtained for the probability distribution function of r and the probability distribution of n.

Exponential Service Times $(M/M/1)$.

$$E[r] = E[S]/(1 - \rho), \tag{3.34}$$

$$\text{Var}[r] = [E[S]/(1 - \rho)]^2, \tag{3.35}$$

$$F_r(t) = \begin{cases} 0, & t \leq 0, \\ 1 - e^{-(1-\rho)t/E[S]}, & t > 0, \end{cases} \tag{3.36}$$

$$E[n] = \rho/(1 - \rho), \tag{3.37}$$

$$\text{Var}[n] = \rho/(1 - \rho)^2, \tag{3.38}$$

$$\text{Prob}\{n = i\} = (1 - \rho)\rho^i, \qquad i = 0, 1, \ldots . \tag{3.39}$$

Notice from Eq. (3.36) that r is an exponential random variable with rate parameter $(1 - \rho)/E[S]$. Thus, the moments about the origin of r can be obtained from Table 2.6 and the percentiles of r can be obtained from Eq. (2.67). It follows from Eq. (3.39) that n is a geometric random variable with parameter ρ. These results only hold in the special case of exponential service times.

Constant Service Times (M/D/1).

$$E[r] = E[S] + \frac{\rho E[S]}{2(1 - \rho)}, \tag{3.40}$$

$$\text{Var}[r] = \frac{\rho(E[S])^2}{3(1 - \rho)} + \frac{\rho^2(E[S])^2}{4(1 - \rho)^2}, \tag{3.41}$$

$$F_r(t) = \begin{cases} 0, & t < E[S], \\ \sum_{k=0}^{i-1} \text{Prob}\{n=k\} + \text{Prob}\{n=i\}(t - iE[S])/E[S], & iE[S] \leqslant t < (i+1)E[S]; \\ & i \geqslant 1, \end{cases} \tag{3.42}$$

$$E[n] = \rho + \frac{\rho^2}{2(1 - \rho)}, \tag{3.43}$$

$$\text{Var}[n] = \rho + \frac{3\rho^2 + 2\rho^3}{6(1 - \rho)} + \frac{\rho^4}{4(1 - \rho)^2}, \tag{3.44}$$

$$\text{Prob}\{n = i\}$$
$$= \begin{cases} 1 - \rho, & i = 0, \\ (1 - \rho)(e^\rho - 1), & i = 1, \\ (1 - \rho)\sum_{j=0}^{i}(-1)^{i-j}(j\rho)^{i-j-1}(j\rho + i - j)e^{j\rho}/(i - j)! & i \geqslant 2. \end{cases} \tag{3.45}$$

Note that the expressions in Eqs. (3.42) and (3.45) are much more complicated than the corresponding expressions [Eqs. (3.36) and (3.39)] for the case of exponential service times. However, it is easy to compute the probabilities in Eq. (3.45) and from these to compute $F_r(t)$, $t \geqslant 0$. Table 3.2 gives the 90th and 95th percentiles of the steady-state response time for $E[S] = 1$ and several values of the traffic intensity ρ for constant service times

TABLE 3.2

Percentiles of the Steady-State Response Time
($E[S] = 1$)

	$M/D/1$		$M/M/1$	
ρ	90th	95th	90th	95th
0.5	2.62	3.08	4.60	6.00
0.75	4.88	6.14	9.20	12.0
0.9	11.8	15.1	23.0	30.0
0.95	23.3	30.2	46.0	60.0

and exponential service times. If $E[S] \neq 1$, the values in the table should be multiplied by $E[S]$.

   *b.   Service Demand Independent Noninterruptable Queueing Disciplines:
   Service In Random Order (SIRO) and Last-Come-First-Served (LCFS)*

The FCFS queueing discipline has the property that the order in which customers begin service does not depend on any aspect of the customers' service demands and a service, once begun, is not interruptable. For any queueing discipline that has this service demand independent noninterruptable property the mean steady-state response time and the probability distribution of the steady-state number of customers in the system are the same as for FCFS. Thus, $E[r]$, $E[n]$, $Var[n]$, and $G_n(z)$ are given in Eqs. (3.18) and

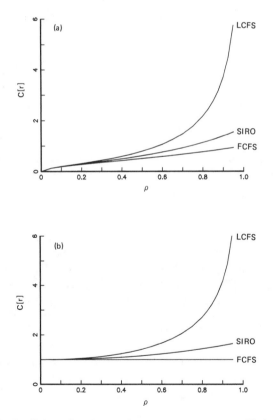

Fig. 3.5 Coefficient of variation of response time versus traffic intensity for $M/G/1$ queueing model (FCFS, SIRO, LCFS queueing disciplines) — (a) constant service times, (b) exponential service times.

(3.21)–(3.23). However, the probability distribution function of the steady-state response time, and in particular its variance, are not the same as for FCFS.

Two such queueing disciplines are SIRO and LCFS. In the SIRO queueing discipline the next customer to be served is chosen probabilistically, with equal probabilities assigned to all waiting customers. Thus, if i customers are waiting when the server becomes free, the probability a particular customer is served next equals $1/i$. In the LCFS queueing discipline customers are served in the reverse order of their arrival. For SIRO

$$\mathrm{Var}[r] = \mathrm{Var}[S] + \frac{2\lambda E[S^3]}{3(1 - \rho)(2 - \rho)} + \frac{\lambda^2(2 + \rho)(E[S^2])^2}{4(1 - \rho)^2(2 - \rho)}, \quad (3.46)$$

which is larger than for FCFS [see Eq. (3.19)], and for LCFS

$$\mathrm{Var}[r] = \mathrm{Var}[S] + \frac{\lambda E[S^3]}{3(1 - \rho)^2} + \frac{\lambda^2(1 + \rho)(E[S^2])^2}{4(1 - \rho)^3}, \quad (3.47)$$

which is larger than for SIRO. (Explicit expressions for the probability distribution function of r have not been obtained for these queueing disciplines, even for exponential service times.) In Fig. 3.5 we plot $C[r]$, the coefficient of variation of r, versus ρ for the FCFS, SIRO, and LCFS queueing disciplines and for both constant and exponential service times.

c. Round Robin and Processor Sharing (PS) Queueing Disciplines

The round robin queueing discipline was described in Section 3.3.1 and depicted in Fig. 3.2. It is intended to give quick response to customers with small service demands at the expense of customers with large service demands. Unfortunately, except in the case of exponential service times, even the calculation of mean response time is complicated (see Sakata et al., 1971). In the case of exponential service times, the mean steady-state response time and the probability distribution of the steady-state number of customers in the system are the same as for the FCFS queueing discipline. Thus, $E[r]$ is given in Eq. (3.34) and $E[n]$, $\mathrm{Var}[n]$, and $\mathrm{Prob}\{n = i\}$ are given in Eqs. (3.37)–(3.39). (Explicit expressions for the variance and probability distribution function of r have not been obtained.) If in reality the server devotes a portion of each quantum to overhead activities associated with implementing this queueing discipline (so that a customer can only be served during the remaining portion of the quantum) the results are not so simple and depend on the quantum size and the amount of overhead (see Sakata et al., 1971). We have assumed the overhead is negligible compared to the quantum size.

The PS queueing discipline (described in Section 3.3.1) approximates the effect of the round robin queueing discipline for small quantum size (neglecting overhead). Each customer simultaneously receives an equal share of the service rate; i.e., if there are i customers present, each customer receives $(1/i)$th of the service rate. Most of the analytical results for PS are very simple and provide a good approximation to results for round robin if the quantum size is small compared to the mean service time. The PS approximation is often used to model a CPU which is scheduled in a round robin manner.

The surprising result about PS is that the mean steady-state response time and the probability distribution of the steady-state number of customers in the system depend on the service demand distribution only through its mean. (This is not true for the probability distribution of the steady-state response time. Useful expressions for this distribution have not been obtained.) We have that

$$E[r] = E[S]/(1 - \rho), \tag{3.48}$$

$$E[n] = \rho/(1 - \rho), \tag{3.49}$$

$$\text{Var}[n] = \rho/(1 - \rho)^2, \tag{3.50}$$

$$\text{Prob}\{n = i\} = (1 - \rho)\rho^i, \qquad i = 0, 1, \ldots. \tag{3.51}$$

These expressions are identical to those for the FCFS queueing discipline if the service times are exponentially distributed [see Eqs. (3.34), (3.37)–(3.39)]. Comparing $E[r]$ for PS in Eq. (3.48) which we denote $E[r]_{\text{PS}}$, with $E[r]$ for FCFS in Eq. (3.24), which we denote $E[r]_{\text{FCFS}}$, it follows that

$$E[r]_{\text{PS}} < E[r]_{\text{FCFS}}, \qquad \text{if} \quad C[S] > 1, \tag{3.52}$$

$$E[r]_{\text{PS}} > E[r]_{\text{FCFS}}, \qquad \text{if} \quad C[S] < 1. \tag{3.53}$$

Also, as $C[S]$ increases, i.e., as the service demands become more variable, the ratio $E[r]_{\text{PS}}/E[r]_{\text{FCFS}}$ decreases. In Fig. 3.6 we plot $E[r]_{\text{PS}}/E[r]_{\text{FCFS}}$ as a function of $C[S]$ for several values of ρ.

Another indication of the effect of PS is obtained by considering the mean steady-state response time for a customer whose service demand is exactly x. Denoting this conditional mean by $E[r \mid S = x]$, we have

$$E[r \mid S = x]_{\text{FCFS}} = x + \frac{\rho E[S](1 + C^2[S])}{2(1 - \rho)}, \tag{3.54}$$

$$E[r \mid S = x]_{\text{PS}} = \frac{x}{1 - \rho}. \tag{3.55}$$

The expression in Eq. (3.55) is smaller than that in Eq. (3.54) if $x < E[S](1 + C^2[S])/2$ and is larger if $x > E[S](1 + C^2[S])/2$. Thus, in comparison with FCFS, PS favors short service demands and discriminates against long service demands.

The effect of overhead in the round robin queueing discipline can be approximately accounted for in the PS queueing discipline as follows. Suppose

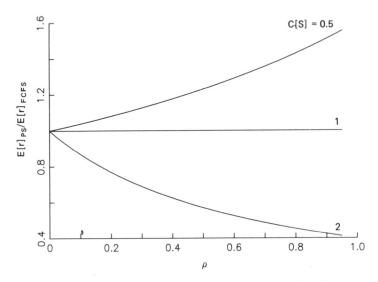

Fig. 3.6 Ratio of mean steady-state response times for PS and FCFS versus traffic intensity for $M/G/1$ queueing model.

a fraction $\Theta, 0 < \Theta < 1$, of each quantum is devoted to overhead activities. Then, in Eqs. (3.48)–(3.51) ρ is replaced by $\rho/(1 - \Theta)$. For stability, it is necessary that $\rho < 1 - \Theta$.

d. Last-Come-First-Served Preemptive Resume (LCFSPR) Queueing Discipline

In the LCFSPR queueing discipline customers are served in the reverse order of their arrival (as in LCFS) and an arriving customer interrupts the current service, if any, and begins to be served. The interrupted service of a customer is resumed when all customers that arrived later than that customer have departed. Although this queueing discipline rarely arises in practice we include it due to the simplicity of the following results. $E[r]$, $E[n]$, $\text{Var}[n]$, and $\text{Prob}\{n = i\}$ are the same as for the PS queueing discipline and are given in Eqs. (3.48)–(3.51). Furthermore,

$$\text{Var}[r] = (\text{Var}[S] + \rho(E[S])^2)/(1 - \rho)^3. \tag{3.56}$$

e. Priority Queueing Disciplines

Priority queueing disciplines were described in Section 3.3.1. They often arise in practice when scheduling service in order to give favored treatment to certain types of customers, e.g., system control messages in a communication system or operating system programs in a computer system.

There are K types of customers. Customers of the same type have the same priority and type 1 customers have the highest priority, type 2 customers have the second highest priority, and so on. We use the notation introduced in Section 3.3.1 to distinguish the different types of customers; e.g., a_k is the probability an arriving customer is type k, $\lambda_k = a_k\lambda$ is the arrival rate of type k customers, and S_k is their service demand. The overall arrival process is a Poisson process with arrival rate $\lambda = \lambda_1 + \cdots + \lambda_K$, and the arrival processes for the different types of customers are statistically independent Poisson processes. Equations (3.12) and (3.13) express the moments about the origin and the probability distribution function of S, the service demand without regard to customer type, in terms of the moments about the origin and the probability distribution functions of $S_1, \ldots, S_K$. We let

$$\rho(k) = \sum_{j=1}^{k} \lambda_j E[S_j] \tag{3.57}$$

denote the traffic intensity due to the first k types of customers. The overall traffic intensity is

$$\rho = \rho(K) = \lambda E[S], \tag{3.58}$$

which, as usual, we assume to be less than one. We next present results for the nonpreemptive and preemptive priority queueing disciplines and then compare these results with results for the FCFS queueing discipline.

Nonpreemptive. For $k = 1, \ldots, K$,

$$E[r_k] = E[S_k] + \frac{\lambda E[S^2]}{2[1 - \rho(k-1)][1 - \rho(k)]}, \tag{3.59}$$

$$\begin{aligned}
\mathrm{Var}[r_k] = \mathrm{Var}[S_k] &+ \frac{\lambda E[S^3]}{3[1 - \rho(k-1)]^2[1 - \rho(k)]} \\
&+ \frac{\lambda E[S^2](2\sum_{j=1}^{k} \lambda_j E[S_j^2] - \lambda E[S^2])}{4[1 - \rho(k-1)]^2[1 - \rho(k)]^2} \\
&+ \frac{\lambda E[S^2]\sum_{j=1}^{k-1} \lambda_j E[S_j^2]}{2[1 - \rho(k-1)]^3[1 - \rho(k)]},
\end{aligned} \tag{3.60}$$

where $\rho(0) = 0$. The mean and variance of r, the overall response time without regard to customer type, are obtained from Eqs. (3.59) and (3.60) as follows.

$$E[r] = \sum_{k=1}^{K} \frac{\lambda_k}{\lambda} E[r_k], \tag{3.61}$$

$$\mathrm{Var}[r] = \sum_{k=1}^{K} \frac{\lambda_k}{\lambda}[\mathrm{Var}[r_k] + (E[r_k])^2] - (E[r])^2. \tag{3.62}$$

From Little's formula (see Section 2.3),

$$E[n_k] = \lambda_k E[r_k], \tag{3.63}$$

$$E[n] = \lambda E[r]. \tag{3.64}$$

Preemptive. For $k = 1, \ldots, K$

$$E[r_k] = \frac{E[S_k]}{1 - \rho(k-1)} + \frac{\sum_{j=1}^k \lambda_j E[S_j^2]}{2[1 - \rho(k-1)][1 - \rho(k)]}, \tag{3.65}$$

$$\text{Var}[r_k] = \frac{\text{Var}[S_k]}{[1 - \rho(k-1)]^2} + \frac{E[S_k]\sum_{j=1}^{k-1} \lambda_j E[S_j^2]}{[1 - \rho(k-1)]^3}$$

$$+ \frac{\sum_{j=1}^k \lambda_j E[S_j^3]}{3[1 - \rho(k-1)]^2[1 - \rho(k)]} + \frac{(\sum_{j=1}^k \lambda_j E[S_j^2])^2}{4[1 - \rho(k-1)]^2[1 - \rho(k)]^2}$$

$$+ \frac{(\sum_{j=1}^k \lambda_j E[S_j^2])(\sum_{j=1}^{k-1} \lambda_j E[S_j^2])}{2[1 - \rho(k-1)]^3[1 - \rho(k)]}. \tag{3.66}$$

Expressions for $E[r]$, $\text{Var}[r]$, $E[n_k]$, and $E[n]$ are obtained from Eqs. (3.65) and (3.66) by using Eqs. (3.61)–(3.64).

Comparison with FCFS. If a priority queueing discipline is not used, but rather customers are served in the order of their arrival then

$$E[r_k] = E[S_k] + \frac{\lambda E[S^2]}{2(1 - \rho)}, \tag{3.67}$$

$$\text{Var}[r_k] = \text{Var}[S_k] + \frac{\lambda E[S^3]}{3(1 - \rho)} + \frac{\lambda^2 (E[S^2])^2}{4(1 - \rho)^2}. \tag{3.68}$$

It follows from Eqs. (3.59), (3.65), and (3.67) that $E[r_1]$ is largest for FCFS, second largest for nonpreemptive priority, and smallest for preemptive priority, while $E[r_K]$ is smallest for FCFS, second smallest for nonpreemptive priority, and largest for preemptive priority. For $k = 2, \ldots, K - 1$, $E[r_k]$ for nonpreemptive priority is smaller than for FCFS if and only if $(1 - \rho) < [1 - \rho(k-1)][1 - \rho(k)]$. For $k = 2, \ldots, K - 1$, the relative values of $E[r_k]$ for preemptive priority and the other two queueing disciplines depend on the first two moments of the service demands as well as on the traffic intensities.

EXAMPLE 3.14 A single processor processes three types of jobs: short interactive jobs, long interactive jobs, and batch jobs. The rates of arrival at the processor of the short interactive, long interactive, and batch jobs are 5 jobs/s, 2 jobs/s, and 0.5 jobs/s, respectively, and their mean processing times are 0.05 s, 0.125 s, and 0.5 s, respectively. We assume that the three types of jobs arrive

TABLE 3.3

Mean (Coefficient of Variation) of Response Time for Example 3.14

	Interactive jobs		Batch jobs	All jobs
	Short	Long		
FCFS	0.725 (1.38)	0.800 (1.25)	1.18 (0.948)	0.775 (1.31)
NP(SI, LI, B)	0.275 (1.35)	0.575 (1.12)	1.85 (1.17)	0.460 (1.78)
PP(SI, LI, B)	0.0667 (1.00)	0.283 (1.04)	2.35 (1.02)	0.277 (3.08)
NP(B, LI, SI)	1.40 (1.70)	0.575 (1.62)	0.725 (0.928)	1.14 (1.80)
PP(B, LI, SI)	1.45 (1.66)	0.583 (1.66)	0.667 (1.00)	1.17 (1.78)

according to independent Poisson processes and that their service times are independent exponentially distributed random variables. In Table 3.3 we compare the response time performance of the processor for the FCFS, nonpreemptive priority (NP), and preemptive priority (PP) queueing disciplines. For each priority queueing discipline we consider two priority orderings: (SI, LI, B) in which type 1 customers are the short interactive jobs and hence have highest priority, type 2 customers are the long interactive jobs and hence have second highest priority, and type 3 customers are the batch jobs and hence have lowest priority; and (B, LI, SI) in which the types and hence the priorities are reversed. The values given in Table 3.3 are the mean response time and in parentheses the coefficient of variation (i.e, the square root of the variance divided by the mean) of the response time for each type of job and for all jobs. These are computed from Eqs. (3.59)–(3.62) and (3.65)–(3.68). Since the service times for each type of customer are exponentially distributed it follows that for type k customers $\text{Var}[S_k] = (E[S_k])^2, E[S_k^2] = 2(E[S_k])^2$, and $E[S_k^3] = 6(E[S_k])^3$ (e.g., see Tables 2.2 and 2.6).

First compare the FCFS results in row 1 of Table 3.3 with the priority results in rows 2 and 3 where highest priority is given to the shortest jobs and lowest priority to the longest jobs. The mean response time for the short interactive jobs is substantially decreased for the NP queueing discipline with a further substantial decrease for the PP discipline. The mean response for long interactive jobs is also decreased, but not as much. These decreases are at the expense of the batch jobs, whose mean response time increases but not drastically. The overall effect is that the mean response time for all jobs is largest for FCFS and smallest for PP. Note that the reverse is true for the coefficient of variation. Next compare these results with the priority results in rows 4 and 5 where highest priority is given to the longest jobs and lowest priority to the shortest jobs. Clearly this is not desirable as the increased mean response time for the shortest jobs causes the mean response time for all jobs to increase.

IBM's MVS operating system allows preemptive priority scheduling of the processor. Typically shorter jobs are given higher priority than longer jobs.

$\triangle$

Composite Priorities. The following priority queueing discipline includes the nonpreemptive and preemptive disciplines as special cases. As before customers of the same type have the same priority and type 1 customers have the highest priority, type 2 customers have the second highest priority, and so on. However, the K types of customers are divided into L levels where types $1, \ldots, K_1$ are in level 1, types $K_1 + 1, \ldots, K_2$ are in level 2, ..., and types $K_{L-1} + 1, \ldots, K$ are in level L. The queueing discipline is nonpreemptive priority among customer types in the same level and it is preemptive priority among customer types in different levels. If $L = 1$ the discipline is strictly nonpreemptive and if $L = K$ the discipline is strictly preemptive.

Let $l(k)$ denote the level that contains type k, i.e., $K_{l(k)-1} + 1 \leqslant k \leqslant K_{l(k)}$. Then for $k = 1, \ldots, K$

$$E[r_k] = \frac{E[S_k]}{1 - \rho(K_{l(k)-1})} + \sum_{j=1}^{K_{l(k)}} \lambda_j E[S_j^2], \tag{3.69}$$

$$\begin{aligned}
\text{Var}[r_k] = {} & \frac{\text{Var}[S_k]}{[1 - \rho(K_{l(k)-1})]^2} + \frac{E[S_k] \sum_{j=1}^{K_{l(k)}-1} \lambda_j E[S_j^2]}{[1 - \rho(K_{l(k)-1})]^3} \\
& + \frac{\sum_{j=1}^{K_{l(k)}-1} \lambda_j E[S_j^3]}{3[1 - \rho(k)][1 - \rho(k-1)]^2} \\
& + \frac{\sum_{j=1}^{K_{l(k)}} \lambda_j E[S_j^2](2 \sum_{j=1}^{k} \lambda_j E[S_j^2] - \sum_{j=1}^{K_{l(k)}} \lambda_j E[S_j^2])}{4[1 - \rho(k-1)]^2[1 - \rho(k)]^2} \\
& + \frac{\sum_{j=1}^{K_{l(k)}} \lambda_j E[S_j^2] \sum_{j=1}^{k-1} \lambda_j E[S_j^2]}{2[1 - \rho(k-1)]^3[1 - \rho(k)]},
\end{aligned} \tag{3.70}$$

where $K_0 = 0, \rho(0) = 0$, and $\rho(k)$ is given by Eq. (3.57).

Expressions for $E[r]$, $\text{Var}[r]$, $E[n_k]$, and $E[n]$ are obtained from Eqs. (3.69) and (3.70) by using Eqs. (3.61)–(3.64).

EXAMPLE 3.15 Consider IBM's 8100 processor which can function as a terminal control unit. The processor has several hardware interrupt levels and the queueing discipline is preemptive priority among requests at different hardware interrupt levels. Within a hardware interrupt level, different types of requests can be assigned different priorities and the queueing discipline is nonpreemptive priority among requests at the same level. In Table 3.4 we give an example with 5 hardware interrupt levels and a total of 10 types of requests. The values of λ_k, $E[S_k]$, and $E[S_k^2]$ are for illustration only; $E[r_k]$ is

TABLE 3.4

A Composite Priorities Example

Hardware interrupt level	Request type k	λ_k	$E[S_k]$	$E[S_k^2]$	$E[r_k]$
(1) Machine check and recovery	1	10^{-7}	2.0	404	2.0
(2) I/O cycle steal	2	0.25	0.08	0.0067	0.0809
(3) Order entry application	3	0.8	0.005	0.00065	0.00835
	4	0.2	0.015	0.00585	0.0186
	5	0.5	0.015	0.00585	0.0187
(4) Inventory update application	6	0.02	0.31	13.9	0.778
	7	0.02	0.25	9.06	0.738
	8	0.005	0.70	71.0	1.21
	9	0.001	1.8	55.1	2.35
(5) Printer	10	0.007	27	1460	35.7

computed from these values using Eqs. (3.57) and (3.69). The overall traffic intensity ρ equals 0.24. △

f. Different Service Time for Customers that Arrive when the System Is Empty

In some applications the service time of a customer that arrives when the system is empty has a different probability distribution function than the service time of a customer that arrives when the system is not empty.

EXAMPLE 3.16   Consider a fixed head per track rotating storage device in which all heads are aligned. Suppose that all records have equal length and that N records completely fill a track. Furthermore, suppose that records on different tracks are aligned so that if there are L tracks, L records begin to pass under the heads simultaneously.

Requests to transfer a record arrive at the control unit, and we assume the device transfers records in the order in which the requests arrived. (In Example 3.17 in Section 3.3.3g we shall consider the case where the device next transfers a requested record having the shortest latency.) We assume that the channel and control unit are always available and only consider contention for the device. Thus, the device is the server. The service time is the sum of the latency time (time from when the device is free until the requested record begins to pass under the heads) and the data transfer time. The data transfer time is a constant which equals R/N, where R is the time for a full rotation of the device and N is the number of records on a track. If a request arrives when other requests are present, the device will become free to service the request at the end of transferring some record. Thus the latency time has possible values iR/N, $i = 0, 1, \ldots, N - 1$, and the service time has possible values $iR/N, i = 1, \ldots, N$.

If on the other hand a request arrives when no requests are present, the heads may be positioned anywhere within a record so that the latency time and hence, the service time need not be an integer multiple of R/N as above. △

Let S^* denote the service time random variable for a customer that arrives when the system is empty and let S denote the service time random variable of a customer that arrives when the system is not empty. The queueing discipline is FCFS. The traffic intensity, $\rho = \lambda E[S]$, is not affected by S^*. If $\rho < 1$, then

$$E[r] = \frac{E[S^*]}{1 - \lambda(E[S] - E[S^*])} + \frac{\lambda(E[S^{*2}] - E[S^2])}{2[1 - \lambda(E[S] - E[S^*])]}$$
$$+ \frac{\lambda E[S^2]}{2(1 - \rho)}, \tag{3.71}$$

$$\text{Var}[r] = \frac{E[S^{*2}]}{1 - \lambda(E[S] - E[S^*])} + \frac{\lambda(E[S^{*3}] - E[S^3])}{2[1 - \lambda(E[S] - E[S^*])]}$$
$$+ \frac{\lambda E[S^3]}{3(1 - \rho)} + \frac{\lambda E[S^2]E[r]}{(1 - \rho)} - (E[r])^2, \tag{3.72}$$

$$L_r(s) = \frac{(1 - \rho)\{\lambda[L_{S^*}(s) - L_S(s)] - sL_{S^*}(s)\}}{[1 - \lambda(E[S] - E[S^*])][\lambda - s - \lambda L_S(s)]}, \tag{3.73}$$

$$E[n] = \lambda E[r], \tag{3.74}$$

$$\text{Var}[n] = \lambda^2 \text{Var}[r] + E[n], \tag{3.75}$$

$$G_n(z) = L_r(\lambda - \lambda z). \tag{3.76}$$

EXAMPLE 3.16 (continued) We assume that requests for the transfer of records arrive according to a Poisson process with rate λ and that requested records are chosen independently with equal probability assigned to each of the N records on a track. We shall use Eq. (3.71) to compute the mean response time, where the response time is the time from when a request arrives until the record transfer is complete.

The service time S for a request that arrives when other requests are present is a discrete random variable that has probability distribution

$$\text{Prob}\{S = iR/N\} = 1/N, \qquad i = 1, \ldots, N. \tag{3.77}$$

Therefore,

$$E[S] = R(N + 1)/2N, \tag{3.78}$$

$$E[S^2] = R^2(N + 1)(N + 1/2)/3N^2. \tag{3.79}$$

The service time S^* for a request that arrives when no requests are present is equal to S plus the time from when the request arrives until the heads are next positioned at the end of a record. This latter time, call it Y, is a continuous random variable that can assume any value between 0 and R/N. It can be shown that the probability density function of Y is given by

$$f_Y(t) = \frac{\lambda e^{\lambda t}}{e^{\lambda R/N} - 1}, \qquad 0 \leqslant t \leqslant \frac{R}{N}, \tag{3.80}$$

and that

$$E[Y] = \frac{R/N}{1 - e^{-R/N}} - \frac{1}{\lambda}, \tag{3.81}$$

$$E[Y^2] = \frac{(R/N)[(R/N) - 2/\lambda]}{1 - e^{-R/N}} + \frac{2}{\lambda^2}. \tag{3.82}$$

Furthermore, Y and S are statistically independent. Since $S^* = S + Y$,

$$E[S^*] = E[S] + E[Y], \tag{3.83}$$

$$E[S^{*2}] = E[S^2] + 2E[S]E[Y] + E[Y^2]. \tag{3.84}$$

Thus, $E[S^*]$ and $E[S^{*2}]$ can be computed using Eqs. (3.78), (3.79), and (3.81)–(3.84). If $\rho = \lambda E[S] = \lambda R(N + 1)/2N < 1$, the mean steady-state response time $E[r]$ can be computed from Eq. (3.71). The final result is that if $\lambda < 2N/[R(N + 1)]$ then

$$E[r] = (R/N) + (R/2) + \frac{\lambda R^2(N + 1)(2N + 1)}{6N[2N - \lambda R(N + 1)]}. \tag{3.85}$$

Thus, the mean response time equals the time to transfer a record plus one-half the rotation time plus a term that increases from zero to infinity as the arrival rate of requests increases from zero to $2N/[R(N + 1)]$, which is the maximum throughput (requests per second). In Example 3.17 in the next section we shall compare the mean response time given by Eq. (3.85) with the mean response time when the device next transfers a requested record having the shortest latency.   △

g. Forced Idle Periods

So far we have assumed that the server is always serving a customer when customers are present. In some modeling applications this may not be true; i.e., there may be periods during which customers are present but no customers can be served. In this section we consider an $M/G/1$ queueing model in which the server operates according to the flow chart in Fig. 3.7. During the forced idle periods no customers are served. Following each forced idle period the queue is inspected in zero time to see if any customers are present. If customers are present, one customer is served. There are two types of forced idle periods:

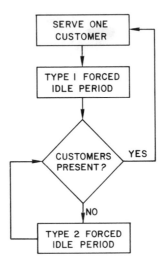

Fig. 3.7   Operation of server with forced idle periods.

type 1 periods which follow the serving of a customer and type 2 periods which follow a forced idle period that ends with no customers present. Customers are served in the order of their arrival.

EXAMPLE 3.17   Consider a fixed head per track rotating storage device with equal size aligned records as described in Example 3.16 in the previous section. However, instead of the device transferring records in first-come-first-served order, we consider the case where the device next transfers a requested record having the shortest latency, i.e., a requested record that next passes under the heads. Records on different tracks that are aligned with each other are said to have the same sector address. Records that have the same sector address and hence pass under the heads simultaneously are transferred in the order in which the requests arrived. (We are assuming that there is no limit on the number of requests that can be stored in the control unit. This is not the case for IBM's 2305 fixed head disk drive, since the 2835 control unit can store at most eight requests for a single device.)

We now show how this shortest latency time first (SLTF) scheduling discipline can be represented using Fig. 3.7. To do this we consider the transfer of records having the same sector address separately from the transfer of records having a different sector address. This can be done for the SLTF scheduling discipline since there is no interference in transferring records that have different sector addresses. Consider how the device behaves with respect to the transfer of records having the same sector address. After transferring such a record in the constant time R/N, the device cannot begin to transfer another record having the same sector address for the remainder of the rotation, i.e., for a period of length $R(N-1)/N$, where N is the number of records per track. This corresponds to a type 1 forced idle period in Fig. 3.7. If at the end of this period there are requests for records having this sector address, one such record will be transferred. (As in Example 3.16, we are assuming that the channel and control unit are always available for transfers.) If there are no such requests, the device becomes unavailable for a full rotation, i.e., for a period of length R. This corresponds to a type 2 forced idle period in Fig. 3.7.   △

Returning to the queueing model, we assume that the durations of type 1 forced idle periods are statistically independent and identically distributed random variables. The same assumption is made for the durations of type 2 forced idle periods. We let I_1 and I_2 denote the duration of a type 1 and type 2 idle period, respectively. I_1, I_2, and S (the service time random variable) can have different distributions. We assume that $S' = S + I_1$ and I_2 are statistically independent. However, S and I_1 can be statistically dependent.

This traffic intensity for this queueing model is

$$\rho' = \lambda E[S']. \tag{3.86}$$

If $\rho' < 1$ (it is not sufficient that $\lambda E[S] < 1$), then

$$E[r] = E[S] + \frac{\lambda E[(S')^2]}{2(1-\rho')} + \frac{E[I_2^2]}{2E[I_2]}, \tag{3.87}$$

$$\text{Var}[r] = \text{Var}[S] + \frac{\lambda E[(S')^2]}{3(1-\rho')} + \frac{\lambda^2 (E[(S')^2])^2}{4(1-\rho')^2}$$

$$+ \frac{E[I_2^3]}{3E[I_2]} - \left(\frac{E[I_2^2]}{2E[I_2]}\right)^2, \tag{3.88}$$

$$L_r(s) = \frac{L_S(s)(1-\lambda\rho')[1-L_{I_2}(s)]}{[s-\lambda+\lambda L_{S'}(s)]E[I_2]}, \tag{3.89}$$

$$E[n] = \lambda E[r], \tag{3.90}$$

$$\text{Var}[n] = \lambda^2 \text{Var}[r] + E[n], \tag{3.91}$$

$$G_n(z) = L_r(\lambda - \lambda z). \tag{3.92}$$

EXAMPLE 3.17 (continued)   As in Example 3.16 we assume that requests for the transfer of records arrive according to a Poisson process with rate λ and that the sector addresses of requested records are chosen independently with equal probability assigned to each of the N sector addresses. We shall use Eq. (3.87) to compute the mean response time.

The arrival process of requests is probabilistically split into N arrival processes, one for each sector address. Due to the probabilistic splitting mechanism these N arrival processes are statistically independent Poisson processes each with rate λ/N (see Section 2.2.4). In the queueing model we consider the arrival process of requests corresponding to one sector address. Hence, the arrival rate is λ/N and not λ. S, I_1, and I_2 are constants and $S = R/N, I_1 = R(N-1)/N, I_2 = R$. Thus, $S' = S + I_1 = R$. From Eq. (3.86) the traffic intensity is $\rho' = (\lambda/N)(R) = \lambda R/N$. Thus, if $\lambda < N/R$ it follows from Eq. (3.87), with λ/N replacing λ, that

$$E[r] = (R/N) + (R/2) + \frac{\lambda R^2}{2(N - \lambda R)}. \tag{3.93}$$

This expression is the same for all sector addresses. Thus, the mean response time for SLTF scheduling equals the time to transfer a record plus one-half the rotation time plus a term that increases from zero to infinity as the arrival rate

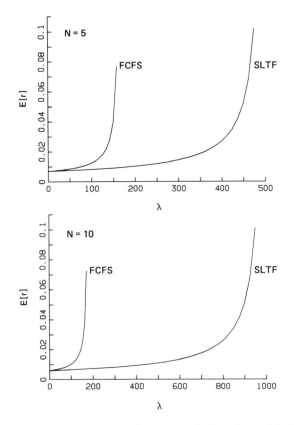

Fig. 3.8 Mean steady-state response time versus arrival rate for model of fixed head disk drive (fixed size aligned records).

of requests increases from zero to N/R, which is the maximum throughput (requests per second). Equation (3.85) gives the mean response time for first-come-first-served (FCFS) scheduling. The mean response time for FCFS is greater than that for SLTF if $\lambda > 0$ and $N > 1$. Further, the maximum throughput (requests per second) for FCFS is $2N/[R(N + 1)]$ while for SLTF it is N/R. In Fig. 3.8 we plot $E[r]$ versus λ for the FCFS and SLTF scheduling disciplines and for $N = 5$ and $N = 10$ records per track. We let $R = 0.01$ s, the rotation time for IBM's 2305-2 fixed head disk drive. $\triangle$

h. Finite Capacity

So far we have assumed that the queue has unlimited capacity so that an arriving customer is never turned away. In this section we consider an $M/G/1$ queueing model with finite capacity N. At most N customers can be in the system at any one time, including the customer receiving service. A customer that arrives when the system is full is lost. Customers that enter the system are served in the order of their arrival.

EXAMPLE 3.18 Messages waiting to be transmitted over a communication line are stored in a buffer. The buffer has finite capacity and a message that arrives when the buffer is full is lost. $\triangle$

The finite capacity queueing model differs from the models we have considered so far in that it is stable even if the traffic intensity, $\rho = \lambda E[S]$, exceeds one, Furthermore, the utilization and throughput do not have the usual values; i.e., it is *not* true that $U = \rho$ and $\Lambda = \lambda$. The following results hold for all finite values of ρ.

$$U = \rho/(\rho + p_N), \tag{3.94}$$

$$\Lambda = \lambda/(\rho + p_N), \tag{3.95}$$

$$E[r] = NE[S] - \sum_{k=1}^{N-1} \frac{kp_k}{\lambda}, \tag{3.96}$$

$$\text{Var}[r] = N\,\text{Var}[S] + \sum_{k=1}^{N-1} \frac{k(k+1)p_k}{\lambda^2} - \left(\sum_{k=1}^{N-1} \frac{kp_k}{\lambda}\right)^2$$

$$- N(N-1)E[S]\frac{p_N}{\lambda}, \tag{3.97}$$

$$L_r(s) = [L_S(s)]^N \sum_{k=1}^{N} p_k\left(\frac{\lambda}{\lambda - s}\right)^k - p_N \frac{s}{\lambda} \sum_{k=1}^{N} \left(\frac{\lambda L_S(s)}{\lambda - s}\right)^k, \tag{3.98}$$

$$E[n] = \left(N\rho - \sum_{k=1}^{N-1} kp_k\right)\Big/(\rho + p_N), \tag{3.99}$$

$$\text{Var}[n] = \left[N\rho + N(N-1)(1-p_N) - 2N \sum_{k=1}^{N-1} kp_k \right.$$

$$\left. + \sum_{k=1}^{N-1} k^2 p_k \right] / (\rho + p_N) - (E[n])^2, \qquad (3.100)$$

$$\text{Prob}\{n = k\} = \begin{cases} p_{N-k}/(\rho + p_N), & k = 0, \ldots, N-1, \\ 1 - 1/(\rho + p_N), & k = N. \end{cases} \qquad (3.101)$$

The quantities $p_1, \ldots, p_N$ in the above equations sum to one and are computed as follows. Let

$$\alpha_k = \int_0^\infty [1 - F_S(t)] \frac{e^{-\lambda t} \lambda^k t^{k-1}}{(k-1)!} dt, \qquad k = 1, 2, \ldots, \qquad (3.102)$$

and let

$$\beta_k = \begin{cases} 1, & k = 0, \\ \alpha_1/(1 - \alpha_1), & k = 1, \\ (\sum_{l=1}^{k-1} \beta_l \alpha_{k+1-l} + \alpha_k)/(1 - \alpha_1), & k = 2, 3, \ldots. \end{cases} \qquad (3.103)$$

Then,

$$p_k = \beta_{N-k} \left/ \sum_{l=0}^{N-1} \beta_l \right., \qquad k = 1, \ldots, N. \qquad (3.104)$$

Once the integral in Eq. (3.102) has been evaluated for $k = 1, \ldots, N-1$ it is easy to compute p_k for $k = 1, \ldots, N$ using Eqs. (3.103) and (3.104). Expressions for α_k are given in Table 3.5 for several service time random variables.

An additional performance measure for a finite capacity queueing model is the probability P_{loss} that an arriving customer is lost. We have that

$$P_{\text{loss}} = 1 - 1/(\rho + p_N). \qquad (3.105)$$

TABLE 3.5

Expressions for α_k

Service time S	Parameters	α_k
Constant	—	$1 - e^{-\rho} \sum_{j=0}^{k-1} \rho^j/j!$
Erlang	i (integer), u	$\sum_{j=0}^{i-1} \binom{j+k-1}{j} \lambda^k u^j \left/ (\lambda + u)^{k+j} \right.$
Exponential	u	$[\rho/(1+\rho)]^k$
Hyperexponential	p, u_1, u_2	$p[\lambda/(\lambda + u_1)]^k + (1-p)[\lambda/(\lambda + u_2)]^k$

In Fig. 3.9 we plot $E[r]/E[S]$ versus ρ for exponential service times and several values of the capacity N. Note that due to the capacity being finite $E[r]$

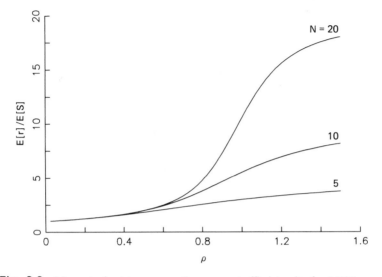

Fig. 3.9   Mean steady-state response time versus traffic intensity for $M/G/1$ queueing model with finite capacity N.

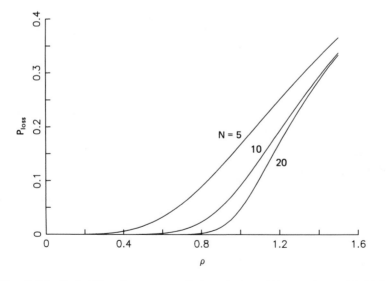

Fig. 3.10   Probability of loss versus traffic intensity for $M/G/1$ queueing model with finite capacity N.

remains finite when ρ exceeds one. In Fig. 3.10 we plot P_{loss} versus ρ for exponential service times and several values of N.

i. Arrival Rate and Service Rate Dependent on the Number of Customers

So far we have only considered models in which the arrival rate and the service rate are constants that do not depend on the number of customers in the service center. In this section we let the arrival rate and/or the service rate change as the number of customers in the service center changes.

Let $\lambda(i)$ denote the arrival rate when there are i customers in the service center; $i = 0, 1, \ldots$. Either all the arrival rates are positive or for some positive integer i_0, $\lambda(i) = 0$ for all $i \geq i_0$. In the latter case the arrival process shuts off whenever there are i_0 customers in the service center.

EXAMPLE 3.19   A source generates messages according to a Poisson process. The messages are to be transmitted one at a time over a communication line and waiting messages are stored in a buffer that has finite capacity. In order to prevent messages from being lost the source shuts off whenever the buffer is full. Thus, the arrival rate is a constant when the buffer is not full and is zero when it is full.   △

Let $\gamma(i)$ denote the service rate of the server when there are i customers in the service center; $i = 1, 2, \ldots$. All the service rates are positive. Sometimes, in order to simplify the analysis of a complex queueing model which consists of many interconnected service centers, a portion of the model is replaced by a single service center whose service rate depends on the number of customers in the service center. Methods for computing the service rates when using this technique are presented in Chapter 4.

We next present analytical results for the FCFS, PS, and last-come-first-served preemptive resume (LCFSPR) queueing disciplines. For the FCFS queueing discipline, the results only hold for exponential service demands $(M/M/1$ queueing model) while for the PS and LCFSPR queueing disciplines the results hold for general service demands $(M/G/1$ queueing model).

FCFS $(M/M/1)$, PS $(M/G/1)$, and LCFSPR $(M/G/1)$.   Equation (3.11) which expresses the service time in terms of the service demand and the service rate does not hold if the service rate depends on the number of customers. Furthermore, the results on stability, utilization, and throughput in Section 3.3.2 do not hold. The stability of the service center is governed by the quantities

$$\rho_i = \lambda(i)E[S]/\gamma(i + 1), \qquad i = 0, 1, 2, \ldots . \tag{3.106}$$

The service center is stable if for some integer I and number $b < 1$, $\rho_i \leq b$, for all $i \geq I$. We first give results for the probability distribution of the number of customers in the service center and then express other performance measures in terms of this distribution. If the service center is stable then

$$\text{Prob}\{n = 0\} = 1 \bigg/ \left[1 + \sum_{j=1}^{\infty} \prod_{i=0}^{j-1} \rho_i \right], \tag{3.107}$$

$$\text{Prob}\{n = k\} = \text{Prob}\{n = 0\} \prod_{i=0}^{k-1} \rho_i, \qquad k = 1, 2, \ldots, \tag{3.108}$$

$$U = 1 - \text{Prob}\{n = 0\}, \tag{3.109}$$

$$\Lambda = \sum_{k=0}^{\infty} \lambda(k) \, \text{Prob}\{n = k\}, \tag{3.110}$$

$$E[n] = \sum_{k=1}^{\infty} k \, \text{Prob}\{n = k\}, \tag{3.111}$$

$$E[r] = E[n]/\Lambda. \tag{3.112}$$

The notation $\prod_{i=0}^{j-1} \rho_i$ stands for the product $\rho_0 \rho_1 \cdots \rho_{j-1}$. Equations (3.107), (3.110), and (3.111) involve summing an infinite number of terms. In the following special case only a finite number of terms need be summed. Suppose for some integer I that $\lambda(i) = \lambda$ and $\gamma(i + 1) = \gamma$ for all $i \geqslant I$ and that $\rho = \lambda E[S]/\gamma < 1$. Then $\rho_i = \rho$ for all $i \geqslant I$ and Eqs. (3.107), (3.110), and (3.111) simplify as follows.

$$\text{Prob}\{n = 0\} = 1 \bigg/ \left[1 + \sum_{j=1}^{I-1} \prod_{i=0}^{j-1} \rho_i + \frac{1}{1 - \rho} \prod_{i=0}^{I-1} \rho_i \right], \tag{3.113}$$

$$\Lambda = \sum_{k=0}^{I-1} \lambda_k \, \text{Prob}\{n = k\} + \frac{\lambda}{1 - \rho} \, \text{Prob}\{n = 0\} \prod_{i=0}^{I-1} \rho_i, \tag{3.114}$$

$$E[n] = \sum_{k=1}^{I-1} k \, \text{Prob}\{n = k\} + \left[\frac{\rho}{(1 - \rho)^2} + \frac{I}{1 - \rho} \right] \text{Prob}\{n = 0\} \prod_{i=0}^{I-1} \rho_i. \tag{3.115}$$

If $\lambda(i) = 0$ for all $i \geqslant i_0$ then Eqs. (3.113)–(3.115) hold with $I = i_0$ and $\rho = 0$.

j. Group Arrivals

We consider an $M/M/1$ queueing model in which a group of customers arrives at each arrival time. The arrival times of groups are determined by a Poisson process with arrival rate λ', and the number of customers in a group is a positive random variable g. The arrival rate of customers is given by $\lambda = \lambda' E[g]$. However, the customer arrival process is not a Poisson process unless g is a constant equal to one. The following results hold for any service demand independent noninterruptable queueing discipline (see Section

3.3.3b). The traffic intensity is given, as usual, by $\rho = \lambda E[S]$. If $\rho < 1$ then

$$E[r] = E[S](1 + E[g^2]/E[g])/2(1 - \rho), \qquad (3.116)$$

$$E[n] = \rho(1 + E[g^2]/E[g])/2(1 - \rho), \qquad (3.117)$$

$$G_n(z) = \frac{(1 - \rho)(1 - z)}{(1 - z) - z(\rho/E[g])(1 - G_g(z))}, \qquad (3.118)$$

where $G_g(z)$ in Eq. (3.118) is the probability generating function of the group size g.

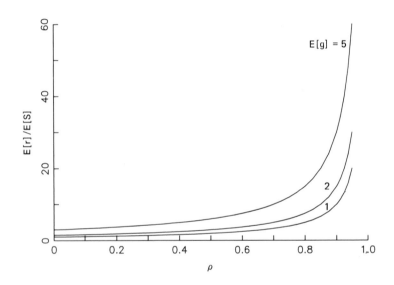

Fig. 3.11   Mean steady-state response time versus traffic intensity for $M/M/1$ queueing model with group arrivals (constant group size).

If the group size is always equal to one then this queueing model is simply the ordinary $M/M/1$ queueing model whose performance measures are given in Eqs. (3.34)–(3.39). However, if the group size is not always equal to one then for the same traffic intensity $E[r]$ and $E[n]$ in Eqs. (3.116) and (3.117) are greater than $E[r]$ and $E[n]$ in Eqs. (3.34) and (3.37). The effect of group arrivals compared to single arrivals is to increase $E[r]$ and $E[n]$ for the same traffic intensity. If the group size is a constant then $E[g^2]/E[g] = E[g]$. In Fig. 3.11 we plot $E[r]/E[S]$ versus ρ for several values of constant group size. If ρ is fixed then the arrival rate of groups is inversely proportional to the group size. Thus, for fixed ρ performance degrades if groups are larger but arrive less frequently.

3.3.4 G/M/1 Queueing Model

The $G/M/1$ queueing model represents the contention for a single server under the assumption that the interarrival times have a general distribution and the service times have an exponential distribution. Compared to the $M/G/1$ queueing model (see Section 3.3.3) few analytical results are available for the $G/M/1$ queueing model. The results given below hold for the FCFS queueing discipline. [Equations (3.120) and (3.123)–(3.125) hold for any service demand independent noninterruptable queueing discipline. See Section 3.3.3b.] As in Section 3.3.3 we assume that $\gamma = 1$.

Let x be the unique positive value less than one that satisfies the equation

$$x = L_T((1 - x)/E[S]). \tag{3.119}$$

[$L_T(s)$ is the Laplace transform of the probability density function of the interarrival time T. Expressions for the Laplace transforms of the probability density functions of some common random variables are given in Table 2.5.] Then

$$E[r] = E[S]/(1 - x), \tag{3.120}$$

$$\text{Var}[r] = [E[S]/(1 - x)]^2, \tag{3.121}$$

$$F_r(t) = \begin{cases} 0, & t \leq 0, \\ 1 - e^{-(1-x)t/E[S]}, & t > 0, \end{cases} \tag{3.122}$$

$$E[n] = \rho/(1 - x), \tag{3.123}$$

$$\text{Var}[n] = \rho(1 + x - \rho)/(1 - x)^2, \tag{3.124}$$

$$\text{Prob}\{n = i\} = \begin{cases} 1 - \rho, & i = 0, \\ \rho x^{i-1}(1 - x), & i = 1, 2, \dots . \end{cases} \tag{3.125}$$

Notice from Eq. (3.122) that r is an exponential random variable with rate parameter $(1 - x)/E[S]$. The above results are similar to those for the $M/M/1$ queueing model given in Eqs. (3.34)–(3.39). The results would be identical if $x = \rho$. In general $x \neq \rho$ and it is necessary to solve Eq. (3.119) numerically in order to obtain x. (For example, Newton's method can be used.)

The following result provides some insight into the effect of the variability of the interarrival times on the mean response time. Let T have a gamma distribution (see Section 2.1.2c). Then by appropriate choice of the parameters of the distribution it is possible to achieve any specified values of the mean and coefficient of variation of T. It can be shown that if $E[T]$ is fixed, then x increases as $C[T]$, the coefficient of variation of T, increases. It then follows from Eq. (3.120) that if $E[T]$ is fixed then $E[r]$ increases as $C[T]$ increases. Thus, the more variable the interarrival times the greater the mean response time (at least if T has a gamma distribution). In Fig. 3.12 we plot

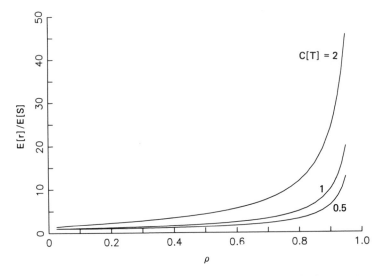

Fig. 3.12 Mean steady-state response time versus traffic intensity for $G/M/1$ queueing model (gamma interarrival times).

$E[r]/E[S]$ versus ρ for several values of $C[T]$ when T has a gamma distribution. The case $C[T] = 1$ corresponds to T having an exponential distribution, i.e., to the $M/M/1$ queueing model.

3.3.5 G/G/1 Queueing Model

So far we have considered queueing models that represent the contention for a single server either under the assumption that the interarrival times have an exponential distribution ($M/G/1$ queueing model) or under the assumption that the service times have an exponential distribution ($G/M/1$ queueing model). Many more analytical results were available for the $M/G/1$ model than for the $G/M/1$ model. When both the interarrival times and the service times have general distributions there are very few results available. In particular explicit expressions have not been obtained for $E[r]$ and $E[n]$. However, the following are simple upper bounds on $E[r]$ and $E[n]$ which hold for any service demand independent noninterruptable queueing discipline (see Section 3.3.3b). As in Section 3.3.3 we assume that $\gamma = 1$.

$$E[r] \leqslant E[S] + \frac{\lambda(\mathrm{Var}[T] + \mathrm{Var}[S])}{2(1 - \rho)}, \tag{3.126}$$

$$E[n] \leqslant \rho + \frac{\lambda^2(\mathrm{Var}[T] + \mathrm{Var}[S])}{2(1 - \rho)}. \tag{3.127}$$

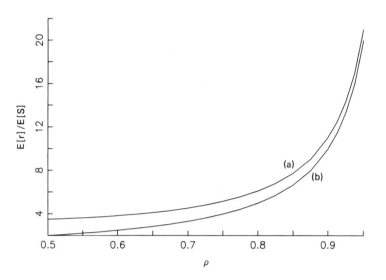

Fig. 3.13 Mean steady-state response time versus traffic intensity for $M/M/1$ queueing model – (a) $G/G/1$ upper bound, (b) exact.

The upper bounds depend on the mean and variance of both T and S. It has been shown that these upper bounds are close approximations to $E[r]$ and $E[n]$ when ρ is close to (but less than) one. For example, for the $M/G/1$ queueing model the upper bound in Eq. (3.126) exceeds the exact value of $E[r]$ given in Eq. (3.18) by an amount $E[S](1 + \rho)/2\rho$ which is small compared to the exact value of $E[r]$ when ρ is close to one. In Fig. 3.13 we plot $E[r]/E[S]$ versus ρ and the upper bound on $E[r]/E[S]$ obtained from Eq. (3.126) versus ρ for the $M/M/1$ queueing model.

3.3.6 M/G/m Queueing Model

The $M/G/m$ queueing model represents the contention for m identical servers that operate independently and in parallel. A customer can be served by any free server and a server is never idle if there are customers waiting to be served. The arrival process is assumed to be a Poisson process. Results for the special case of a single server ($m = 1$) were presented in Section 3.3.3. Far fewer results are available if $m > 1$. For example, if the queueing discipline is FCFS there is no useful expression for $E[r]$ unless the service times are exponentially distributed (see Section 3.3.6a below). Recall (see Section 3.3.2) that if $m > 1$ the traffic intensity ρ is equal to $\lambda E[S]/m\gamma$. As in Section 3.3.3, unless stated otherwise we assume that γ, the service rate of each server, is equal to one so that S is the service time. If $\gamma \neq 1$ then S should be replaced by S/γ in all expressions.

a. *First-Come-First-Served (FCFS) Queueing Discipline*
    (M/M/m Queueing Model)

The following results hold if the queueing discipline is FCFS and if service
times are exponentially distributed. [Equations (3.128) and (3.132)–(3.134)
also hold for any service demand independent noninterruptable queueing
discipline. See Section 3.3.3b.]

$$E[r] = E[S]\left(1 + \frac{\rho(m\rho)^{m-1}}{m!A(1-\rho)^2}\right), \tag{3.128}$$

$$\text{Var}[r] = (E[S])^2\left(1 + \frac{2\rho^2(m\rho)^{m-2}}{m!A(1-\rho)^3} - \left[\frac{\rho(m\rho)^{m-1}}{m!A(1-\rho)^2}\right]^2\right), \tag{3.129}$$

$$F_r(t) = \begin{cases} 0, & t \leq 0, \\ 1 - e^{-t/E[S]} - [(m\rho)^m/m!A(1-\rho)]g(t), & t > 0, \end{cases} \tag{3.130}$$

where

$$g(t) = \begin{cases} (e^{-m(1-\rho)t/E[S]} - e^{-t/E[S]})/[1 - m(1-\rho)], & \rho \neq (m-1)/m, \\ te^{-t/E[S]}/E[S], & \rho = (m-1)/m, \end{cases}$$

$$\tag{3.131}$$

$$E[n] = m\rho + \rho(m\rho)^m/m!A(1-\rho)^2, \tag{3.132}$$

$$\text{Var}[n] = m\rho + \frac{\rho(m\rho)^m}{m!A(1-\rho)}\left[\frac{(1+\rho)}{(1-\rho)^2} + m - \frac{\rho(m\rho)^m}{m!A(1-\rho)^3}\right], \tag{3.133}$$

$$\text{Prob}\{n = i\} = \begin{cases} (m\rho)^i/i!A, & i = 0, 1, \ldots, m, \\ m^m\rho^i/m!A, & i = m+1, m+2, \ldots. \end{cases} \tag{3.134}$$

The quantity A in the above expressions is given by

$$A = \sum_{i=0}^{m-1} \frac{(m\rho)^i}{i!} + \frac{(m\rho)^m}{m!(1-\rho)}. \tag{3.135}$$

It can be verified that if $m = 1$ the above expressions simplify to those for the
$M/M/1$ queueing model given in Eqs. (3.34)–(3.39). (If $m = 1$ then r is an
exponential random variable and thus $C[r]$, the coefficient of variation of r, is
equal to one. If $m > 1$ then r is not an exponential random variable and it can
be shown that $C[r]$ is less than one.) In Fig. 3.14 we plot $E[r]$ versus λ for
$E[S] = 1$ and several values of m and in Fig. 3.15 we plot $C[r]$ versus λ for
$E[S] = 1$ and several values of m. Note that $C[r]$ approaches one as λ
approaches m, i.e., as ρ approaches one. In Section 3.3.9 we shall compare the
mean response times of single server and multiple server queueing models, and
we shall use Eq. (3.128) to obtain numerical results.

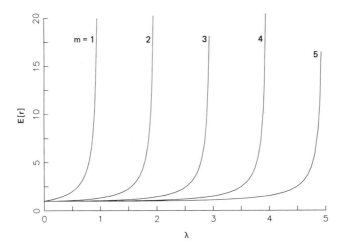

Fig. 3.14 Mean steady-state response time versus arrival rate for $M/M/m$ queueing model ($E[S] = 1$).

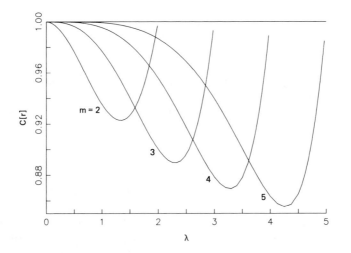

Fig. 3.15 Coefficient of variation of steady-state response time versus arrival rate for $M/M/m$ queueing model ($E[S] = 1$).

b. *Processor Sharing (PS) Queueing Discipline*

The PS queueing discipline was described in Sections 3.3.1 and 3.3.3c in the case of a single server. In the case of $m > 1$ servers the PS queueing discipline operates as follows. If there are i customers in the service center and $i \leqslant m$, each customer simultaneously receives the full service rate of one of the servers;

i.e., each customer simultaneously receives service at rate γ. If there are i customers in the service center and $i > m$, then the total service rate $m\gamma$ of the m servers is equally divided among the i customers; i.e., each customer simultaneously receives service at rate $m\gamma/i$. As in the case of a single server, the surprising result is that the mean steady-state response time and the probability distribution of the steady-state number of customers in the system depend on the service time distribution only through its mean. (This is not true for the probability distribution function of the steady-state response time. Useful expressions for this distribution function have not been obtained.) Assuming that $\gamma = 1$ we have that

$$E[r] = E[S](1 + \rho(m\rho)^{m-1}/m!A(1-\rho)^2), \tag{3.136}$$

$$E[n] = m\rho + \rho(m\rho)^m/m!A(1-\rho)^2, \tag{3.137}$$

$$\text{Var}[n] = m\rho + \frac{\rho(m\rho)^m}{m!A(1-\rho)}\left[\frac{(1+\rho)}{(1-\rho)^2} + m - \frac{\rho(m\rho)^m}{m!A(1-\rho)^3}\right], \tag{3.138}$$

$$\text{Prob}\{n = i\} = \begin{cases} (m\rho)^i/i!A, & i = 0, 1, \ldots, m, \\ m^m\rho^i/m!A, & i = m+1, m+2, \ldots. \end{cases} \tag{3.139}$$

The quantity A in the above expressions is given by

$$A = \sum_{i=0}^{m-1} \frac{(m\rho)^i}{i!} + \frac{(m\rho)^m}{m!(1-\rho)}. \tag{3.140}$$

These expressions are identical to those for the FCFS queueing discipline if the service times are exponentially distributed [see Eqs. (3.128) and (3.132)–(3.135)]. (If $m > 1$ and service times are general we cannot compare $E[r]$ for PS with $E[r]$ for FCFS, as we did in Section 3.3.3c when $m = 1$, since we do not have an expression for $E[r]$ for FCFS.)

c. No Waiting (M/G/∞ Queueing Model and M/G/m Loss Model)

First consider a service center in which the number of servers is so large that an arriving customer never has to wait for a server to become free. Under the assumption of Poisson arrivals it is possible for an arbitrarily large number of customers to arrive in any particular time period so that an arbitrarily large, i.e., an infinite, number of servers is required to guarantee that an arriving customer will never wait. If an arriving customer never waits the response time is equal to the service time and the number of customers in the service center is equal to the number of busy servers. Furthermore the service center is always stable. We have for the steady-state number of customers in the service center that

$$E[n] = \lambda E[S], \tag{3.141}$$

$$\text{Var}[n] = \lambda E[S], \tag{3.142}$$

$$\text{Prob}\{n = i\} = e^{-\lambda E[S]}(\lambda E[S])^i/i!, \qquad i = 0, 1, \ldots. \tag{3.143}$$

The above expressions depend on the service time distribution only through its mean. Furthermore, n is a Poisson random variable with parameter $\lambda E[S]$ (see Section 2.1.2b).

EXAMPLE 3.20   Consider an idealized communication system with an infinite number of identical parallel lines. If messages arrive according to a Poisson process then the probability distribution of the number of busy lines is given by Eq. (3.143).   △

Of course in a real system the number of servers is finite. An interesting model with no waiting which arose in telephony is the $M/G/m$ loss model. There are m identical parallel servers and a customer that arrives when all m servers are busy is lost; i.e., there is no buffer to hold waiting customers. The response time of a customer that is not lost is equal to its service time, and the number of customers in the service center is equal to the number of busy servers. Furthermore, the service center is stable for all values of $\rho = \lambda E[S]/m$. We have for the steady-state number of customers in the system that

$$E[n] = m\rho(1 - (m\rho)^m/m!A), \tag{3.144}$$

$$\mathrm{Var}[n] = m\rho\left[1 - \frac{(m\rho)^m}{m!A}\left(m - 1 + m\rho + \frac{(m\rho)^{m+1}}{m!A}\right)\right], \tag{3.145}$$

$$\mathrm{Prob}\{n = i\} = (m\rho)^i/i!A, \qquad i = 0, 1, \dots. \tag{3.146}$$

The quantity A in Eqs. (3.144)–(3.146) is given by

$$A = \sum_{i=0}^{m} \frac{(m\rho)^i}{i!}. \tag{3.147}$$

An additional performance measure is the probability that an arriving customer is lost, denoted P_{loss}, which is given by

$$P_{\mathrm{loss}} = \mathrm{Prob}\{n = m\} = (m\rho)^m/m!A. \tag{3.148}$$

The utilization per server U and the throughput Λ are related to the probability of loss by

$$U = \rho(1 - P_{\mathrm{loss}}), \tag{3.149}$$

$$\Lambda = \lambda(1 - P_{\mathrm{loss}}). \tag{3.150}$$

The above expressions depend on the service time distribution only through its mean.

EXAMPLE 3.21   Consider a communication system with m identical parallel lines and no buffering. If messages arrive according to Poisson process then the probability that an arriving message is lost is given by Eq. (3.148). In Fig. 3.16 we plot P_{loss} versus λ for $E[S] = 1$ and several values of m.   △

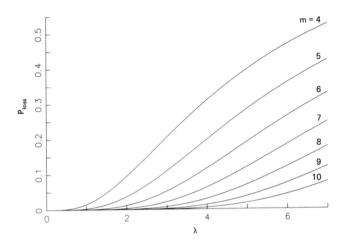

Fig. 3.16   Probability of loss versus arrival rate for $M/G/m$ loss model ($E[S] = 1$).

d.   Arrival Rate and Service Rate Dependent on the Number of Customers

In this section, as in Section 3.3.3i, we let the arrival rate and/or the service rate of each server change as the number of customers in the service center changes. As in Section 3.3.3i we let $\lambda(i), i = 0, 1, \ldots,$ denote the arrival rate and $\gamma(i), i = 1, 2, \ldots,$ denote the service rate of each server when there are i customers in the service center. Either all the arrival rates are positive or for some positive integer i_0, $\lambda(i) = 0$ for all $i \geqslant i_0$. All the service rates are positive. See Section 3.3.3i for an example of the arrival rate depending on the number of customers and for further discussion. Here we give an example of the service rate depending on the number of customers.

EXAMPLE 3.22   In a multiprocessor computer system, when more than one processor is executing instructions the effective service rate (instructions per second) of each executing processor is typically less than the service rate of a processor executing alone. This is due to memory interference and lock contention. Consider a dual processor system where each processor has a 1 MIP service rate when it executes alone and a 0.8 MIP service rate when both processors are executing. The two processors are represented as a service center with two servers. Customers in the service center represent programs that are executing or waiting to be executed. The service rates of each server in instructions per second are $\gamma(1) = 10^6$, $\gamma(i) = 0.8 \times 10^6$, $i = 2, 3, \ldots$. Thus, if two or more customers are present so that both servers are busy the service rate of each server is 0.8×10^6. $\triangle$

We next present analytical results for the FCFS and PS queueing disciplines and for the $M/G/\infty$ queueing model. For the FCFS queueing discipline the results only hold for exponential service demands ($M/M/m$ queueing model), while for the PS queueing discipline they hold for general service demands ($M/G/m$ queueing model).

FCFS ($M/M/m$), PS ($M/G/m$), and $M/G/\infty$. Equation (3.11), which expresses the service time in terms of the service demand and the service rate, does not hold if the service rate depends on the number of customers. Furthermore, the results on stability, utilization, and throughput in Section 3.3.2 do not hold.

We first consider the FCFS ($M/M/m$) and PS ($M/G/m$) cases. The stability of the service center is governed by the quantities

$$\rho_i = \begin{cases} \lambda(i)E[S]/[(i+1)\gamma(i+1)], & i = 0, 1, \ldots, m-1, \\ \lambda(i)E[S]/(m\gamma(i+1)), & i = m, m+1, \ldots. \end{cases} \tag{3.151}$$

The service center is stable if for some integer I and number $b < 1$, $\rho_i \leqslant b$ for all $i \geqslant I$. If the service center is stable then $\text{Prob}\{n = i\}$, $i = 0, 1, \ldots, \Lambda, E[n]$, and $E[r]$ are given in Eqs. (3.107), (3.108), and (3.110)–(3.112) in Section 3.3.3i, where ρ_i is given in Eq. (3.151) instead of Eq. (3.106). The utilization per server is given by

$$U = 1 - \frac{1}{m} \sum_{k=0}^{m-1} (m - k)\, \text{Prob}\{n = k\}. \tag{3.152}$$

Suppose for some integer $I \geqslant m$ that $\lambda(i) = \lambda$ and $\gamma(i+1) = \gamma$ for all $i \geqslant I$ and that $\rho = \lambda E[S]/m\gamma < 1$. Then $\rho_i = \rho$ for all $i \geqslant I$ and the expressions for $\text{Prob}\{n = 0\}$, Λ, and $E[n]$ simplify and are given by Eqs. (3.113)–(3.115) in Section 3.3.3i.

The stability of the $M/G/\infty$ service center is governed by the quantities

$$\rho_i = \lambda(i)E[S]/[(i+1)\gamma(i+1)], \qquad i = 0, 1, \ldots. \tag{3.153}$$

The service center is stable if for some integer I and number $b < 1$, $\rho_i \leqslant b$ for all $i \geqslant I$. If the service center is stable then Eqs. (3.107), (3.108), and (3.110)–(3.112) hold with ρ_i given in Eq. (3.153).

3.3.7 G/M/m Queueing Model

The $G/M/m$ queueing model represents the contention for m identical servers that operate independently and in parallel under the assumption that the interarrival times have a general distribution and the service times have an exponential distribution. Results for the special case of a single server ($m = 1$) were presented in Section 3.3.4. If $m = 1$, the computation of performance measures is simple once Eq. (3.119) is solved numerically. If $m > 1$, Eq. (3.154) given below, which is similar to Eq. (3.119), must be solved numerically, but additional very complicated calculations are required to compute performance measures. Therefore, we only give bounds on certain performance measures in this section. The bounds in Eqs. (3.155)–(3.158) hold for any service demand independent noninterruptable queueing discipline (see Section 3.3.3b). The bound in Eq. (3.159) only holds if the queueing discipline is FCFS. We assume that $\gamma = 1$.

Let x be the unique positive value less than one which satisfies the equation

$$x = L_T(m(1 - x)/E[S]). \qquad (3.154)$$

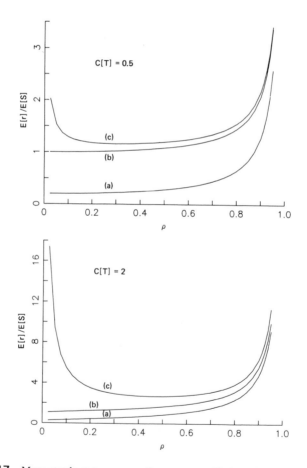

Fig. 3.17   Mean steady-state response time versus traffic intensity for $G/M/m$ queueing model ($m = 5$, gamma interarrival times) – (a) lower bound [Eq. (3.155)], (b) upper bound [Eq. (3.155)], (c) upper bound [Eq. (3.157)].

Then,

$$\frac{E[S]}{m(1-x)} \leqslant E[r] \leqslant \frac{E[S]}{m(1-x)} + \frac{(m-1)E[S]}{m} \qquad (3.155)$$

$$\frac{\rho}{1-x} \leqslant E[n] \leqslant \frac{\rho}{1-x} + (m-1)\rho. \qquad (3.156)$$

The differences between the lower and upper bounds in Eqs. (3.155) and (3.156) are small compared to $E[r]$ and $E[n]$ when ρ is close to one. Note that when $m = 1$ the lower and upper bounds are equal to the exact values for the $G/M/1$ queueing model given in Eqs. (3.120) and (3.123). The following equations give upper bounds on $E[r]$ and $E[n]$ which are easier to compute but are larger than the above upper bounds.

$$E[r] \leqslant E[S] + \frac{\lambda[\mathrm{Var}[T] + (E[S]/m)^2]}{2(1-\rho)}, \qquad (3.157)$$

$$E[n] \leqslant m\rho + \frac{\lambda^2 \mathrm{Var}[T] + \rho^2}{2(1-\rho)}. \qquad (3.158)$$

The upper bounds in Eqs. (3.157) and (3.158) are close approximations to $E[r]$ and $E[n]$ when ρ is close to one. In Fig. 3.17 we plot the lower and upper bounds on $E[r]/E[S]$ in Eq. (3.155) and the upper bound in Eq. (3.157) versus ρ for $m = 5$ and two values of $C[T]$ when T has a gamma distribution.

The following is a lower bound on the probability distribution function of r which holds if the queueing discipline is FCFS.

$$F_r(t) \geqslant 1 - e^{-t/E[S]} + \frac{x(e^{-t/E[S]} - e^{-m(1-x)t/E[S]})}{1 - m(1-x)}, \qquad t \geqslant 0. \qquad (3.159)$$

3.3.8   G/G/m Queueing Model

So far we have considered queueing models that represent the contention for multiple servers under the assumption that the interarrival times have an exponential distribution ($M/G/m$ queueing model) or under the assumption that the service times have an exponential distribution ($G/M/m$ queueing model). When both the interarrival times and the service times have general distributions there are very few results available. The following are simple upper bounds on $E[r]$ and $E[n]$ which hold for any service demand independent noninterruptable queueing discipline (see Section 3.3.3b). We assume that $\gamma = 1$.

$$E[r] \leqslant E[S] + \frac{\lambda[\mathrm{Var}[T] + (\mathrm{Var}[S]/m)]}{2(1-\rho)}, \qquad (3.160)$$

$$E[n] \leqslant m\rho + \frac{\lambda^2[\mathrm{Var}[T] + (\mathrm{Var}[S]/m)]}{2(1-\rho)}. \qquad (3.161)$$

The upper bounds depend only on m and on the mean and variance of T and S. Note that if $m = 1$ the upper bounds are identical to those for the $G/G/1$ queueing model given in Eqs. (3.126) and (3.127). However, if $m > 1$ the upper bounds are not necessarily close approximations to the true values of $E[r]$ and $E[n]$ when ρ is close to one. For example, upper bounds on $E[r]$ and $E[n]$ for the $G/M/m$ queueing model were given in Eqs. (3.157) and (3.158). For the $G/M/m$ queueing model the upper bound in Eq. (3.160) exceeds the upper bound in Eq. (3.157) by an amount $[(m - 1)/m]\rho E[S]/[2(1 - \rho)]$ which is very large when ρ is close to one.

3.3.9 Comparison of Single Server and Multiple Server Queueing Models

It is interesting to compare the mean response times of

(i) a service center having a single server,

(ii) a service center having m servers each of which is m times slower than the server in (i), and

(iii) a service center having a single server which is m times slower than the server in (i) and where the service center handles $(1/m)$th of the customers; either every mth arriving customer enters the service center or an arriving customer enters the service center with probability $1/m$.

Let $r(m, \lambda, \gamma)$ denote the steady-state response time of a $G/G/m$ queueing model for which the arrival rate is λ and each server has service rate γ. For case (i) above the steady-state response time is $r(1, \lambda, \gamma)$, for case (ii) it is $r(m, \lambda, \gamma/m)$, and for case (iii) it is $r(1, \lambda/m, \gamma/m)$. The service demand S is the same in each case so that the traffic intensity for each case is given by $\rho = \lambda E[S]/\gamma$. For any service demand independent noninterruptable queueing discipline (see Section 3.3.3b),

$$E[r(1, \lambda, \gamma)] < E[r(m, \lambda, \gamma/m)] < E[r(1, \lambda/m, \gamma/m)], \qquad (3.162)$$

where the first inequality always holds if the coefficient of variation of S does not exceed one, but may not hold if it exceeds one. The second inequality always holds.

EXAMPLE 3.23 Suppose we have the choice of providing one high speed line for the transmission of messages or m identical parallel slow speed lines, each having $(1/m)$th the speed of the high speed line. It follows from the first inequality in Eq. (3.162) that it is better to provide the high speed line. (Of course we have not taken factors like cost and reliability into account.)

In order to obtain illustrative numerical results we assume Poisson arrivals and exponentially distributed message lengths, i.e., an $M/M/m$ queueing model. Using the expressions for $E[r]$ given in Eqs. (3.34) and (3.128), with $E[S]$ divided by the service rate, we plot $E[r(m, \lambda, \gamma/m)]/E[r(1, \lambda, \gamma)]$ versus ρ

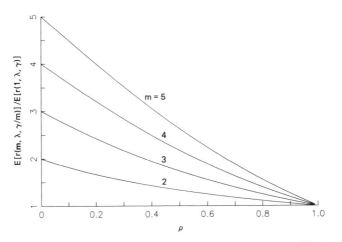

Fig. 3.18 Ratio of mean steady-state response times versus traffic intensity for Example 3.23.

for several values of m in Fig. 3.18. Note that this ratio approaches m as ρ approaches zero and it approaches one as ρ approaches one.   △

EXAMPLE 3.24   Suppose we have m identical parallel lines for the transmission of messages along a single path and we have the choice of providing a single buffer that is shared by the m lines or a separate buffer for each line. In the former case a message waiting in the buffer can be transmitted when any line becomes free. In the latter case a message waiting in a buffer can only be transmitted when the line it is waiting for becomes free. We assume in the latter case that either arriving messages are assigned to the buffers cyclically, i.e., every mth arrival enters the same buffer, or they are assigned to the buffers randomly and the probability of entering a particular buffer is $1/m$. It follows from the second inequality in Eq. (3.162) that it is better to provide a single shared buffer.

In order to obtain illustrative numerical results we assume Poisson arrivals and exponentially distributed message lengths. We first assume in the case of separate buffers that the assignment of arriving customers to the separate buffers is random. With random assignment the arrival processes to each of the m buffers are Poisson processes with arrival rates equal to $(1/m)$th of the overall arrival rate. Thus, each buffer and its line behave like an $M/M/1$ queueing model. Next we assume in the case of separate buffers that the assignment of arriving customers to the separate buffers is cyclic. With cyclic assignment the interarrival time for a particular buffer is the sum of m independent exponential random variables and hence has an Erlang distribution (see Section 2.1.2c). Thus, each buffer and its line behave like a $G/M/1$ queueing model with Erlang interarrival times having parameters m and λ, where λ is the overall arrival rate. The arrival rate to each buffer is λ/m. An Erlang random variable has coefficient of variation less than one so that $E[r]$ is less than it would be for Poisson arrivals (see the discussion at the end of Section 3.3.4). Thus, $E[r]$ is less for cyclic assignment than for random assignment, but from the second inequality in Eq. (3.162) it is still greater than for the case of a single shared buffer. Using the expressions for $E[r]$ given in Eqs. (3.34), (3.120), and (3.128), with $E[S]$ divided by the service rate, we plot in Fig. 3.19 $E[r(1, \lambda/m, \gamma/m)]/E[r(m, \lambda, \gamma/m)]$ versus ρ for random assignment and cyclic assignment and for several values of m. Note that these ratios approach one as ρ approaches zero and they approach m as ρ approaches one. $\triangle$

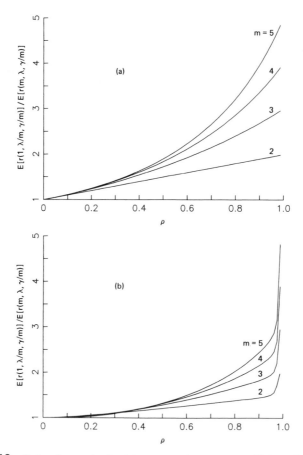

Fig. 3.19   Ratio of mean steady-state response times versus traffic intensity for Example 3.24 – (a) random assignment, (b) cyclic assignment.

3.4 Introduction to Queueing Networks

So far we have only considered queueing models that consist of a single service center. In the remainder of this chapter we shall consider queueing models that consist of two or more interconnected service centers. Such models, called queueing networks, are widely used to represent contention for the multiple resources that comprise a system. Queueing networks such as the one shown in Fig. 3.20 in which customers arrive from an external source, spend time in the network, and depart are said to be *open*. In an open queueing network a customer that completes service at a service center immediately enters another service center, reenters the same service center, or departs from the network. Queueing networks such as the one shown in Fig. 3.21 in which there is no external source of customers are said to be *closed*. In a closed queueing network a fixed number of customers circulate indefinitely among the service centers. A customer that completes service at a service center immediately enters another service center or reenters the same service center. Closed queueing networks are used to represent systems in which a fixed number of users contend for resources.

When describing a queueing network it is necessary to specify the number of servers, the service demands, the service rate, and the queueing discipline for

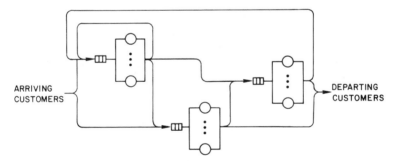

Fig. 3.20   Open queueing network.

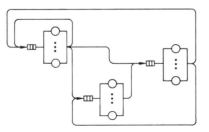

Fig. 3.21   Closed queueing network.

each service center. This will be done using terminology and notation consistent with that used in Section 3.3. As in Section 3.3, if there is more than one server at a service center the servers are identical and operate independently and in parallel. All service demands at all service centers are assumed to be statistically independent random variables. Unless stated otherwise, service demands at a particular service center for customers of the same type are assumed to have the same probability distribution function. The service rate for each server can depend in general on the number of customers in the service center. If the service rate does not depend on the number of customers in the service center and is equal to one, then the service time is equal to the service demand. Analytical results for queueing networks have not been obtained for all queueing disciplines considered in Section 3.3. For the most part results have only been obtained for networks in which each service center has either the first-come-first-served (FCFS), processor sharing (PS), or last-come-first-served preemptive resume (LCFSPR) queueing discipline or there is a large enough number of servers at the service center so that queueing never occurs. If the queueing discipline at a service center is FCFS the results we shall present hold only if, at the service center, the service demands for different types of customers have the same exponential distribution. However, if the queueing discipline is PS or LCFSPR or if queueing never occurs, the results hold if different types of customers have different general service demand distributions at the service center.

In Sections 3.4.1 and 3.4.2, we shall introduce the use of queueing networks in performance modeling by presenting analytical results and applications for two examples of closed queueing networks, the machine repair model and the central server model. Results and applications for more general queueing networks will be presented in subsequent sections. For the closed queueing networks we consider in Section 3.4.1 and 3.4.2, all customers are of the same type. In addition, all service rates are equal to one so that service times are equal to service demands. The following notation will be used:

N: number of customers in the network;

J: number of service centers;

$S_{(j)}$:   service demand ($=$ service time) at service center j (a random variable);

$n_{(j)}$:   steady-state number of customers in service center j (a random variable);

$r_{(j)}$:   steady-state response time of service center j (a random variable); the response time of a service center is the time from when a customer enters the service center until it departs;

$U_{(j)}$:   utilization of service center j;

$\Lambda_{(j)}$:   throughput of service center j.

3.4.1 Machine Repair Model

Consider the closed queueing network consisting of two service centers shown in Fig. 3.22. There are N identical customers in the network. Service center 1 has N servers. Since there are as many servers at service center 1 as there are customers in the network, a customer arriving at service center 1 always finds a free server and never queues for service. Thus, no queue is shown in front of the servers and no queueing discipline is required. Service demands at service center 1 can have a general distribution. Service center 2 has a single server and the queueing discipline is FCFS. Service demands at service center 2 are assumed to be exponentially distributed. A customer that completes service at service center 1 immediately enters service center 2, and a customer that completes service at service center 2 immediately enters service center 1.

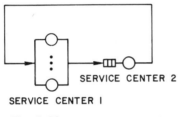

SERVICE CENTER I

Fig. 3.22   Machine repair model.

This network was originally used to model a situation in which several identical machines that operate independently and in parallel are subject to breakdown and there is a single person to repair the machines. Hence, it is commonly called the machine repair model. Each customer in the network represents a machine, and each machine is either (i) running, i.e., in service center 1, (ii) broken down and waiting for repair, i.e., waiting in the queue in service center 2, or (iii) being repaired, i.e., receiving service at service center 2. A machine that is repaired immediately begins to run again and keeps running until it next breaks down and requires repair. Performance measures include the mean number of machines that are running and the utilization of the repair person. Of more interest to us is the use of the machine repair model in computer performance modeling.

EXAMPLE 3.25   The machine repair model was used in the late 1960s during the development of OS/360 TSO to predict the performance of TSO running a single partition in main memory (Lassettre and Scherr, 1972). In a time-sharing system such as TSO an interactive user at a terminal alternately thinks, enters input, waits for the computer to execute a program in response to the input (during which time the keyboard is locked), and receives output. The time it takes to receive output, think, and enter input is lumped together and called the "think" time. Upon completion of a think time the user's input enters a queue of work for the system. In OS/360 TSO the service provided by the system consists of handling terminal I/O, swapping a user's program in and out of main memory, and executing the program. The time it takes to provide this service is called the system service time. If there is only a single time-sharing partition in main memory, the system can provide service to only one user at a time. Hence, the system acts as a single server. However, system service for different users is interleaved in time by using time-slicing.

In the model there is one customer for each interactive user. Thus, the number of interactive users is assumed to be constant. Service center 1 represents the terminals (there is one terminal for each user) and a service time at service center 1 represents a think time. Service center 2 represents the system and its queue of requests. A service time at service center 2 represents a system service time. Since the queueing discipline at service center 2 is FCFS, the interleaving of system service for different users via time-slicing is not represented in the model. It would have been more appropriate to model time-slicing by assuming the queueing discipline to be processor sharing. However, when this model was used in the late 1960s results for processor sharing had not yet been obtained. We shall discuss this further after we present analytical results for the model.

The model was primarily used to predict the number of interactive users the system could support for a given mean think time, mean system service time, and required mean system response time. (The system response time is represented in the model by the response time of service center 2.) △

The following results hold for the machine repair model. We let

$$b = E[S_{(1)}]/E[S_{(2)}], \qquad (3.163)$$

$$A_N = \sum_{i=0}^{N} \frac{b^i}{i!}. \qquad (3.164)$$

Then

$$U_{(2)} = A_{N-1}/A_N, \qquad (3.165)$$

$$\Lambda_{(2)} = U_{(2)}/E[S_{(2)}], \qquad (3.166)$$

$$E[r_{(2)}] = (NE[S_{(2)}]/U_{(2)}) - E[S_{(1)}], \qquad (3.167)$$

$$F_{r_{(2)}}(t) = \begin{cases} 0, & t \leqslant 0, \\ 1 - [e^{-t/E[S_{(2)}]} \sum_{i=0}^{N-1} ((b + t/E[S_{(2)}])^i/i!)]/A_{N-1}, & t > 0, \end{cases}$$

$$(3.168)$$

$$E[n_{(2)}] = N - U_{(2)}b, \tag{3.169}$$

$$\text{Prob}\{n_{(2)} = i\} = b^{N-i}/(N-i)!A_N, \qquad i = 0, 1, \ldots, N. \tag{3.170}$$

A_N is a normalizing constant whose value, given in Eq. (3.164), is determined by the requirement that the probabilities in Eq. (3.170) sum to one.

EXAMPLE 3.25 (continued)   We now describe one way in which the model was used in conjunction with measurements during the development of OS/360 TSO. For a more complete discussion see Lassettre and Scherr (1972). The mean system service time $E[S_{(2)}]$ was estimated from measurements on an actual TSO system with a second computer system used to simulate the interactive users. TSO benchmark scripts provided the inputs to be entered by the simulated users. Think times were simulated by independently sampling from an exponential distribution whose mean $E[S_{(1)}]$ was specified. The number of users, the mean system service time, and the mean think time were used in Eqs. (3.163)–(3.165) and (3.167) to compute $E[r_{(2)}]$. This predicted value was compared with the measured average response time. A substantial difference between the predicted and measured values was usually an indication of bugs in the control program. The correction of these bugs eliminated any serious discrepancy between the predicted and measured values. Once the bugs were corrected, if the average response time exceeded the specification for the TSO benchmark, the interactive programs and/or the system configuration were modified in an attempt to improve system performance. The above procedure was then repeated.

The predicted and measured average response times were compared in 37 different cases (e.g., different numbers of users were considered). In approximately 75% of these cases the predicted and measured values differed by less than 10%. The maximum deviation was 24%. The quality of the model's predictions was surprising due to the assumptions made; i.e., time-slicing was not represented and system service times were assumed to be exponentially distributed. It would have been more appropriate to model time-slicing by assuming the queueing discipline at service center 2 to be PS (processor sharing) instead of FCFS. It is now known that the results given in Eqs. (3.163)–(3.167), (3.169), and (3.170) hold if the queueing discipline is PS. Furthermore, if the queueing discipline is PS these results hold if the service times have a general distribution. [The expression for the response time distribution given in Eq. (3.168) only holds if the queueing discipline is FCFS and the service times are exponentially distributed.] Thus, the quality of the model's predictions of the average response time is no longer surprising.

It can be shown from Eqs. (3.163)–(3.165) that as N increases to infinity the utilization $U_{(2)}$ increases to one. It follows from Eqs. (3.166) and (3.167) that if N is so large that $U_{(2)} \approx 1$ then

$$\Lambda_{(2)} \approx 1/E[S_{(2)}] \tag{3.171}$$

and

$$E[r_{(2)}] \approx NE[S_{(2)}] - E[S_{(1)}]. \qquad (3.172)$$

Thus, if the utilization is close to one, increasing the number of customers has little effect on the throughput $\Lambda_{(2)}$, but each additional customer increases the mean response time $E[r_{(2)}]$ for all customers by an amount approximately equal to the mean service time $E[S_{(2)}]$. We illustrate this behavior in Fig. 3.23 by plotting $\Lambda_{(2)}$ versus N and $E[r_{(2)}]$ versus N for $E[S_{(1)}] = 35$ and $E[S_{(2)}] = 1$. (As we shall see in Section 3.5 the throughput and mean response time behave in a similar way for much more complex models of interactive systems, where the system itself is represented by a network of service centers

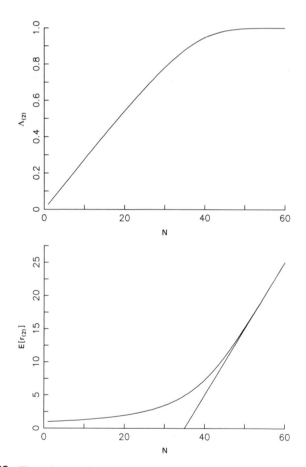

Fig. 3.23 Throughput and mean response time versus number of users for machine repair model of time sharing system ($E[S_{(1)}] = 35, E[S_{(2)}] = 1$).

rather than by a single service center.) An approximation to the value of N at which the throughput begins to flatten out and the mean response time begins to rise almost linearly is obtained by setting the right-hand side of Eq. (3.172), which is the asymptote of $E[r_{(2)}]$ for large N and is plotted as the straight line in Fig. 3.23, equal to $E[S_{(2)}]$, which is the value of $E[r_{(2)}]$ for $N = 1$. The resulting value of N is given by

$$N^* = 1 + (E[S_{(1)}]/E[S_{(2)}]). \tag{3.173}$$

The values of $E[S_{(1)}]$ and $E[S_{(2)}]$ for Fig. 3.23 are 35 and 1, respectively, so that $N^* = 36$.   △

We now discuss the generality of the results given in Eqs. (3.163)–(3.170). The relations between $U_{(2)}$, $\Lambda_{(2)}$, $E[r_{(2)}]$, and $E[n_{(2)}]$ given in Eqs. (3.165)–(3.167) and (3.169) hold under much more general assumptions than we have made about the queueing discipline at service center 2 and about the service times. For example, the relations hold for any service demand independent noninterruptable queueing discipline (see Section 3.3.3b) and they hold if $S_{(2)}$ has a general distribution. This is because these equations follow directly from suitable applications of Little's formula (see Section 2.3). Equation (3.166) is Little's formula applied to the server at service center 2. Equation (3.167) follows from the application of Little's formula to the entire closed system as discussed in Example 2.34. (Replace λ by $\Lambda_{(2)}$ and replace R by $E[S_{(1)}] + E[r_{(2)}]$ in Eq. (2.118). Then solve for $E[r_{(2)}]$.) Finally, Eq. (3.169) follows from Eqs. (3.166) and (3.167) and Little's formula applied to service center 2; i.e., $E[n_{(2)}] = \Lambda_{(2)}E[r_{(2)}]$.

The results given in Eqs. (3.163)–(3.170) are very simple and depend on $S_{(1)}$ and $S_{(2)}$ only through their means. This is true even though $S_{(1)}$ can have a general distribution. Furthermore, as discussed above in Example 3.25, if the queueing discipline at service center 2 is PS then, with the exception of Eq. (3.168), these results hold when $S_{(2)}$ has a general distribution. However, if the queueing discipline at service center 2 is FCFS then Eqs. (3.165), (3.168), and (3.170) hold only if $S_{(2)}$ has an exponential distribution.

Results have been obtained for the machine repair model if the queueing discipline at service center 2 is FCFS and $S_{(2)}$ has a general distribution, but only if $S_{(1)}$ has an exponential distribution. In this case

$$U_{(2)} = 1 - 1 \left/ \left[1 + \frac{N}{b} + \frac{N}{b} \sum_{k=1}^{N-1} \binom{N-1}{k} g(k) \right] \right., \tag{3.174}$$

where

$$g(k) = \prod_{i=1}^{k} \frac{1 - L_{S_{(2)}}(i/E[S_{(1)}])}{L_{S_{(2)}}(i/E[S_{(1)}])}, \qquad k = 1, 2, \dots . \tag{3.175}$$

$L_{S_{(2)}}(s)$ is the Laplace transform of the probability density function of $S_{(2)}$.

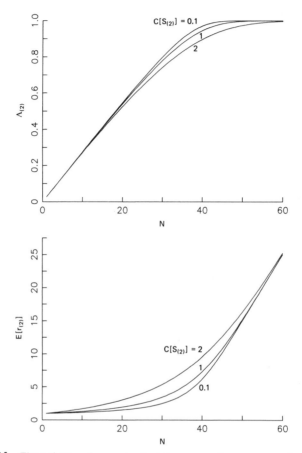

Fig. 3.24 Throughput and mean steady-state response time versus number of customers for machine repair model with FCFS queueing discipline ($S_{(1)}$ has exponential distribution, $S_{(2)}$ has gamma distribution).

Note that this expression for $U_{(2)}$ depends on the distribution of $S_{(2)}$ in a complicated way. Once $U_{(2)}$ has been computed, $\Lambda_{(2)}$, $E[r_{(2)}]$, and $E[n_{(2)}]$ can again be easily obtained from Eqs. (3.166), (3.167), and (3.169). In Fig. 3.24 we plot $\Lambda_{(2)}$ versus N and $E[r_{(2)}]$ versus N when $S_{(2)}$ has a gamma distribution (see Section 2.1.2c). The plots are for $E[S_{(1)}] = 35$, $E[S_{(2)}] = 1$, and different values of $C[S_{(2)}]$.

3.4.2 Central Server Model

Consider the closed queueing network consisting of J service centers shown in Fig. 3.25. There are N identical customers in the network. Each service

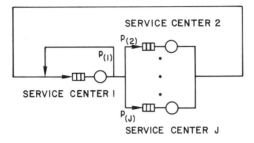

Fig. 3.25 Central server model.

center has a single server. The queueing discipline at service center 1 is either FCFS, in which case the service demands at service center 1 are assumed to have an exponential distribution, or PS, in which case the service demands can have a general distribution. The queueing discipline at service center j, $j \neq 1$, is FCFS and the service demands are assumed to have an exponential distribution. A customer that completes service at service center 1 immediately enters service center j with probability $p_{(j)} \geqslant 0$, where $p_{(1)} + \cdots + p_{(J)} = 1$. Thus, the next service center visited by a customer that completes service at service center 1 is selected randomly according to the probability distribution $p_{(j)}$, $j = 1, \ldots, J$. If $p_{(1)} > 0$ then a customer can immediately re-enter service center 1. A customer that completes service at service center j, $j \neq 1$, immediately enters service center 1. The server at service center 1 is called the central server.

The central server model was originally introduced to model the contention among programs for the processor and I/O devices in a multiprogrammed computer system.

EXAMPLE 3.26 Consider a multiprogrammed computer system with virtual memory having a fixed number N of initiators and operating under heavy demand; i.e., there is always a program waiting to be allocated a memory region. Suppose there is sufficient main memory available so that N programs are always allocated memory regions. Such a system operates with a fixed level of multiprogramming equal to N. Suppose the system has a single processor and several I/O devices, where each I/O device is used either for paging I/O or file I/O. For example, there may be several drums used for paging I/O and several disks used for file I/O. Until a program terminates, it alternately executes on the processor and receives I/O service. Since there are several programs in the system, queueing delays can occur at the processor and at any of the I/O devices. Time-slicing is used to schedule the processor and the scheduling discipline at each I/O device is first-come-first-served. When a program page faults or issues a file transfer request, and other programs are waiting to be executed, a task switch occurs and one of the waiting programs begins execution. When a program terminates its execution a new program is initiated.

In applying the central server model to represent the contention for the processor and I/O devices we let customers in the model represent programs that have been allocated a memory region. The time a program waits to be allocated a memory region is not represented in the model. The model only represents the time spent by a program after it has been allocated a memory region. Service center 1 represents the processor and its queue of programs and service center j, $j \neq 1$, represents an I/O device and its queue of programs. Since time-slicing is used at the processor the queueing discipline at service center 1 is assumed to be PS rather than FCFS. The queueing discipline at the other service centers is FCFS. The termination of a program and initiation of a new program is represented by a customer re-entering service center 1 upon completing a service at service center 1. (We are assuming that the last service received by program is a processor service. By letting $p_{(1)} = 0$ the central server model can also represent the case where the last service received by a program is an I/O service.) It is assumed that each I/O device can access and transfer data for only one program at a time and that different I/O devices do not interfere with each other, e.g., by contending for the same channel. Since a channel is essentially only busy when an I/O device is busy, channels need not be represented in the model if there are a sufficient number of channels so that I/O data accesses and transfers are not substantially delayed by having to wait for a channel to become free. Other features of real systems not represented in this model include overlap of processing and I/O activities for a program, scheduling program execution on the processor based on priorities, I/O device scheduling algorithms other than first-come-first-served, different behavior for different programs (e.g., batch programs and interactive programs), and variations in the level of multiprogramming. In addition, probabilistic assumptions are made for this model, e.g., exponentially distributed I/O service times and random routing of an I/O request to the I/O devices, which may not be realistic. Some of these shortcomings will be addressed in the remaining sections of this chapter. However, it is not possible to redress all the grievances we might have about the realism of this model and still have the model remain analytically tractable. Nonetheless, this model and the more realistic models we shall consider later in this chapter are useful in addressing computer performance evaluation problems. We shall continue this example after presenting analytical results for the central server model. $\triangle$

We next present a simple procedure for computing the utilization, throughput, mean steady-state number of customers, and mean steady-state response time for each service center in the central server model. (In later sections we shall present procedures to compute the probability distribution of the number of customers in a service center for more general queueing networks). The procedure is recursive with respect to the number of customers in the network. Therefore, when describing the procedure, we shall use the notation $U_{(j)}(i)$, $\Lambda_{(j)}(i)$, $n_{(j)}(i)$, and $r_{(j)}(i)$ to denote the utilization, throughput, steady-state number of customers, and steady-state response time for service center j in a central server model with i customers. For simplicity of notation we let $L_{(j)}(i) = E[n_{(j)}(i)]$ and $R_{(j)}(i) = E[r_{(j)}(i)]$. $U_{(j)}(i)$, $\Lambda_{(j)}(i)$, $L_{(j)}(i)$, and $R_{(j)}(i)$ can be computed for $j = 1, \ldots, J$ and $i = 1, \ldots, N$ as follows:

$$L_j(0) = 0, \qquad j = 1, \ldots, J. \tag{3.176}$$

For $i = 1, \ldots, N$,

$$R_{(j)}(i) = E[S_{(j)}][1 + L_{(j)}(i - 1)], \qquad j = 1, \ldots, J, \tag{3.177}$$

$$\Lambda_{(1)}(i) = i \bigg/ \left[R_{(1)}(i) + \sum_{j=2}^{J} p_{(j)} R_{(j)}(i) \right], \tag{3.178}$$

$$\Lambda_{(j)}(i) = p_{(j)} \Lambda_{(1)}(i), \qquad j = 2, \ldots, J, \tag{3.179}$$

$$L_{(j)}(i) = \Lambda_{(j)}(i) R_{(j)}(i), \qquad j = 1, \ldots, J, \tag{3.180}$$

$$U_{(j)}(i) = \Lambda_{(j)}(i) E[S_{(j)}], \qquad j = 1, \ldots, J. \tag{3.181}$$

Equations (3.178), (3.180), and (3.181) follow directly from suitable applications of Little's formula (see Section 2.3). Equation (3.178) is Little's formula applied to the entire closed network as discussed in Example 2.34. To make this application clearer the central server model has been redrawn in Fig. 3.26 to correspond to Fig. 2.18. Thus, in Eq. (2.118) N is replaced by i, λ is replaced by $\Lambda_{(1)}(i)$, and R is replaced by $R_{(1)}(i) + p_{(2)}R_{(2)}(i) + \cdots + p_{(J)}R_{(J)}(i)$. Equation (3.180) is Little's formula applied to service center j and Eq. (3.181) is Little's formula applied to the server at service center j. Equation (3.179) follows from the fact that $p_{(j)}$ is the long-run fraction of the customers leaving

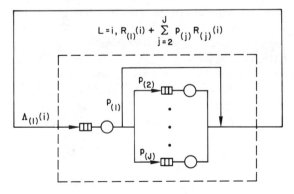

Fig. 3.26   Application of Little's formula to central server model.

service center 1 that enter service center j. Equation (3.177) relates the mean response time at service center j for the network with i customers to the mean number of customers in service center j for the network with $i - 1$ customers. [For an interpretation of this equation see Reiser and Lavenberg (1980).] It is the key to the recursive procedure. Values computed for $i < N$ need not be stored once the values for $i + 1$ have been computed unless performance measures for i customers in the network are of interest. If the utilizations are not of interest Eq. (3.181) can be dropped, and if the throughputs for $j \neq 1$ are not of interest then Eqs. (3.179) and (3.180) can be combined to yield

$$L_{(j)}(i) = p_{(j)} \Lambda_{(1)}(i) R_{(j)}(i), \qquad j = 1, \ldots, J. \tag{3.182}$$

EXAMPLE 3.26 (continued)   The throughput of the processor and I/O subsystem is the rate at which programs terminate and is given by $p_{(1)} \Lambda_{(1)}$ in the model. The response time of the subsystem is the time from when a program is initiated until it terminates. (Note again that the time a program waits for memory is not included in this response time.) The mean steady-state response time is given by

$$R = \frac{N}{p_{(1)} \Lambda_{(1)}} = \left(R_{(1)} + \sum_{j=2}^{J} p_{(j)} R_{(j)} \right) \Big/ p_{(1)}. \tag{3.183}$$

It can be shown that $\Lambda_{(1)}$ and R in the model are both increasing functions of N. Thus, increasing the level of multiprogramming should increase the throughput. However, we know this need not be the case in a real system if memory is not managed properly.

In a real system, as the level of multiprogramming is increased, the amount of memory allocated to each program decreases (assuming the total amount of main memory is fixed). Thus, the average number of instructions executed by a program between page faults decreases as the level of multiprogramming increases. More programs are running, but the average time between page faults for an executing program is less. The overall effect on throughput is not clear. We now use the model to predict this effect.

For simplicity we consider a system with no file I/O. We now relate some parameters that characterize a program to parameters in the model. Let l denote the average path length of a program (average number of instructions executed between initiation and termination), and let ω denote the average number of references per instruction. Neglecting processor overhead associated with a page fault l does not depend on the level of multiprogramming N. However, the miss ratio for a program (average number of page faults per reference) does depend on N, and we denote this dependence by $\delta(N)$. The average number of page faults for a program is $l\omega\delta(N)$. In the model the number of page faults for a program is a geometric random variable with parameter $1 - p_{(1)}$ (see Section 2.1.2a). Therefore, the mean number of page faults is $(1 - p_{(1)})/p_{(1)}$. Setting the mean number of page faults in the model equal to $l\omega\delta(N)$, it follows that

$$p_{(1)}(N) = 1/[1 + l\omega\delta(N)], \qquad (3.184)$$

where we have denoted the dependence of $p_{(1)}$ on N. Let γ denote the speed of the processor in instructions per second so that l/γ is the average execution time for a program between initiation and termination. In the model the mean number of execution intervals for a program between initiation and terminal is $1/p_{(1)}(N)$ (one plus the mean number of page faults), and the mean time for an execution interval is $E[S_{(1)}]$. Therefore, the mean execution time for a program between initiation and termination is $E[S_{(1)}]/p_{(1)}(N)$. Setting $E[S_{(1)}]/p_{(1)}(N)$ equal to l/γ, it follows that

$$E[S_{(1)}(N)] = p_{(1)}(N)l/\gamma, \qquad (3.185)$$

where we have denoted the dependence of $E[S_{(1)}]$ on N. Let f_j denote the fraction of page faults for a program that are to paging device j, $j = 1, \ldots, J - 1$. It is reasonable to assume that f_j does not depend on N. In the model, for $j = 2, \ldots, J, p_{(j)}/(1 - p_{(1)}(N))$ is the probability that a page fault is to device $j - 1$, so that

$$p_{(j)}(N) = f_{j-1}(1 - p_{(1)}(N)), \qquad j = 2, \ldots, J, \qquad (3.186)$$

where we have denoted the dependence of $p_{(j)}$ on N. (Note that $p_{(j)}(N)$ should

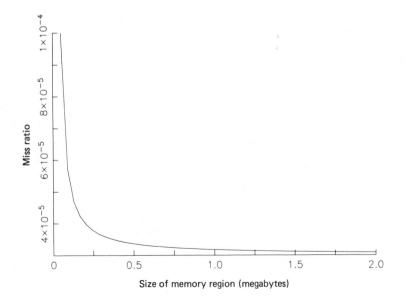

Fig. 3.27 Miss ratio curve for a program.

be substituted for $p_{(j)}$ and $E[S_{(1)}(N)]$ should be substituted for $E[S_{(1)}]$ in the recursive procedure given in Eqs. (3.177)–(3.181). However, now the intermediate values $U_{(j)}(i)$, $\Lambda_{(j)}(i)$, $L_{(j)}(i)$, and $R_{(j)}(i)$ for $i < N$ computed by the procedure are not the actual values for i customers in the network since in general $p_{(j)}(i) \neq p_{(j)}(N)$ and $E[S_{(1)}(i)] \neq E[S_{(1)}(N)]$ if $i < N$. However, the final values for $i = N$ are correct.)

Let A denote the total amount of main memory available for user programs. We assume that if the level of multiprogramming is N, each user is allocated a region of size A/N. In Fig. 3.27 we show a hypothetical plot of the miss ratio for a program versus the size of its main memory region in megabytes. (The miss ratio curve of course depends on the page size and the memory management algorithm.) We assume that each program has the same miss ratio curve. (This would be the case for a multiprogramming benchmark workload of N identical programs.) We consider the basic parameters of the workload and system to be

l:	the average path length,
ω:	the average number of references per instruction,
γ:	the speed of the processor,
N:	the level of multiprogramming,
$\delta(N)$:	the miss ratio,
$J - 1$:	the number of paging devices,
$E[S_{(j)}]$:	the mean service time of paging device $j - 1$, $j = 2, \ldots, J$,
f_j:	the fraction of page faults that are to I/O device j, $j = 1, \ldots, J - 1$.

$\delta(N)$ is obtained by evaluating the miss ratio curve at A/N. The model parameters $p_{(j)}(N)$, $j = 1, \ldots, J$ and $E[S_{(1)}(N)]$ are obtained from the workload and system parameters and Eqs. (3.184)–(3.186). In Fig. 3.28 we plot the throughput, $p_1(N)\Lambda_1(N)$, versus N for $A = 2$ megabytes, the miss ratio curve in Fig. 3.27 and $l = 0.25 \times 10^6$, $\omega = 1.2$, $\gamma = 2 \times 10^6$, $J = 3$, $E[S_{(2)}] = E[S_{(3)}] = 0.02$, $f_1 = f_2 = 0.5$. Note that the throughput first increases as N increases, achieves its maximum value for $N = 10$, and then decreases if N is increased further. This illustrates what can happen if memory is not managed properly. Fortunately, memory management algorithms are often designed so that a program is allocated memory only if it can be allocated a sufficiently large portion (e.g., a portion large enough to contain its working set) so that it page faults infrequently. This kind of memory management attempts to limit the maximum level of multiprogramming to acceptable values.

We have not discussed the representation in the model of processor overhead due to such operating system activities as page fault and I/O handling, processor scheduling, and program initiation. A common way to do this in the central server model is to assume that the total processor overhead is equally divided among all programs and among all execution intervals. Thus,

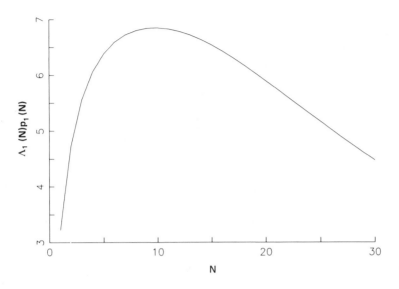

Fig. 3.28 Throughput versus level of multiprogramming for central server model in Example 3.26 and miss ratio curve in Fig. 3.27.

the total execution time for a program should include the associated processor overhead time. △

3.5 Closed Product Form Queueing Networks[†]

A closed network is one with a fixed number of customers. In this section we consider general closed networks that have a "product form" solution in the sense that

$$P(\mathscr{S}_{(1)}, \ldots, \mathscr{S}_{(J)}) = P_{(1)}(\mathscr{S}_{(1)}) \cdots P_{(J)}(\mathscr{S}_{(J)})/G(N), \qquad (3.187)$$

where $P(\mathscr{S}_{(1)}, \ldots, \mathscr{S}_{(J)})$ is the steady-state probability of a network state in a network with J service centers, $P_{(j)}(\mathscr{S}_{(j)}), j = 1, \ldots, J$, is a factor corresponding to the steady-state probability of the state of service center j in isolation, N is the number of customers in the network, and $G(N)$ is a normalizing constant. The normalizing constant $G(N)$ is equal to the sum of $P_{(1)}(\mathscr{S}_{(1)}) \cdots P_{(J)}(\mathscr{S}_{(J)})$ over all feasible network states. Thus the sum of $P(\mathscr{S}_{(1)}, \ldots, \mathscr{S}_{(J)})$ over all feasible network states is equal to one. The state of a service center might be

[†] Material in Sections 3.5–3.7 based in part on K. M. Chandy and C. H. Sauer, Computational algorithms for product form queueing networks, *Comm. ACM* **23**, 573–583. Copyright 1980, Association for Computing Machinery, Inc., reprinted by permission.

defined by the number of customers in the center or the number of customers of each type in the center. (More detailed definitions are also used, but we shall not consider them.)

The two networks we have examined so far, the machine repair model and the central server model, have this product form solution. For the machine repair model we can rewrite Eq. (3.170) as

$$\text{Prob}\{n_{(1)} = i, n_{(2)} = N - i\} = \frac{\{(E[S_{(1)}])^i/i!\}(E[S_{(2)}])^{N-i}}{G(N)}, \quad (3.188)$$

where

$$G(N) = \sum_{i=0}^{N} \frac{(E[S_{(1)}])^i}{i!}(E[S_{(2)}])^{N-i}. \quad (3.189)$$

For the central server model

$$\text{Prob}\{n_{(1)} = i_1, \dots, n_{(J)} = i_J\} = \frac{(E[S_{(1)}])^{i_1}(p_{(2)}E[S_{(2)}])^{i_2} \cdots (p_{(J)}E[S_{(J)}])^{i_J}}{G(N)},$$

$$(3.190)$$

where $i_1 + \cdots + i_J = N$ and

$$G(N) = \sum_{i_1 + \cdots + i_J = N} (E[S_{(1)}])^{i_1}(p_{(2)}E[S_{(2)}])^{i_2} \cdots (p_{(J)}E[S_{(J)}])^{i_J}. \quad (3.191)$$

[We shall shortly discuss efficient methods for obtaining $G(N)$ which should be used instead of direct evaluation of Eq. (3.191).] Both of these networks are special cases of the product form networks we shall define.

If a queueing network does not have a product form solution, then we usually must use fairly general numerical techniques (e.g., solution of Markov balance equations, see Sauer and Chandy, 1981) for its solution. In this case we shall find the exact solution of the network intractable unless it is fairly small, i.e., it has few service centers and/or customers.

For a network to have a product form solution, only certain queueing disciplines can be allowed. If a service center has an "infinite" number of servers (at least N servers) so that queueing never occurs, we shall say that it has an infinite server (IS) queueing discipline. We shall assume in Sections 3.5–3.7 that only FCFS, PS, and IS disciplines are allowed. See Section 3.8 for further discussion of queueing disciplines allowed in product form networks.

3.5.1 Single Chain Networks

First we consider closed networks in which all customers are homogeneous; i.e., there is a single customer type. However, service centers may consist of several "classes" which allow customers to have different sets of routing probabilities for different visits to a service center. (Both the machine repair and central server models we have discussed have exactly one class per center.) If a service center has a PS or IS discipline, then there may be different service demand distributions for the different classes at a service center. In these cases, the service demand distributions affect the performance measures we shall consider only through the mean service demand. If a service center has a FCFS discipline, then all classes at that center must have the same exponential service demand distribution. There are C classes in the network numbered from 1 to C. The set of classes belonging to service center j is $\mathscr{C}_j$, $j = 1, \ldots, J$. Figure 3.29 shows a network with two service centers and four classes. Class 1 belongs to center 1 and the remaining classes belong to center 2.

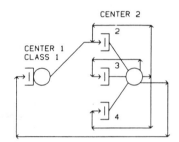

Fig. 3.29 Network with two service centers and four classes.

In product form networks with homogeneous customers, classes are primarily useful in representing routing behavior such as that depicted by Fig. 3.29, where a customer's future routing depends on its past routing. See Section 3.8 for further discussion of routing generalizations in product form networks.

EXAMPLE 3.27 Figure 3.30 shows a queueing network that can be considered a combination of the machine repair model and the central server model. The diagram assumes a small interactive computer system with one floppy disk and one hard disk. Since this is a small system these devices are likely used for file I/O as well as paging (or swapping if there is not paging).

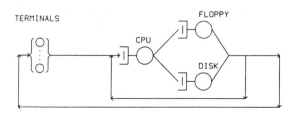

Fig. 3.30 Computer system model of Example 3.27.

Note that this model does not consider memory contention. If we attempt to add memory contention to this model then we will not be able to obtain a product form network. (The model with memory contention will be discussed in Chapters 4 and 8. Most published applications of models based on this one include memory contention. See Brown *et al.*, 1977, for example.) As with the machine repair and central server model, this network has one class per service center.   △

EXAMPLE 3.28   The network of Fig. 3.31 is a refinement of the network of Fig. 3.30. Both networks may be considered models of the same computer

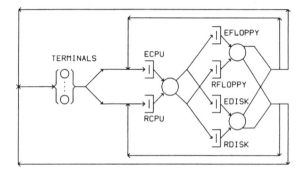

Fig. 3.31   Computer system model of Example 3.28.

system and both assume that all customers (interactive users) are homogeneous. The second network distinguishes between types of commands: sometimes a user issues a command to an editor (presumably such commands are likely to have low CPU service demands) while other times a user issues a command to run a program other than an editor (presumably these commands have higher CPU service times). Each of the service centers other than the one for the terminals has two classes: one for editing commands and one for "running" commands. Assuming that scheduling at the CPU is represented by the PS discipline, then we can have distinct service demand distributions at the two CPU classes. Assuming that device scheduling is FCFS, then the two floppy disk classes must have the same exponential distribution and the two hard disk classes must have the same exponential distribution, but the floppy disk classes need not have the same mean service demand as the hard disk classes.   △

If a customer at class c can reach class d, possibly after passing through intermediate classes, we shall say that d is *reachable* from c. A set of classes is called a *closed routing chain* if (1) for any pair of classes c and d in the set, d is reachable from c and c is reachable from d and if (2) there is no class e that is not in the set such that e is reachable from some class in the set or some class in the set is reachable from e. For the networks of this section all classes belong to a single closed routing chain.

The mean service demand for a customer at class c is $E[S_c]$, $c = 1, \ldots, C$. Service center j has associated with it a capacity function $\mu_{(j)}(n)$ which is the total service rate when there are n customers in the service center. If, as in Section 3.3.6d, we let $\gamma_{(j)}(n)$ denote the service rate of each server at center j, then $\mu_{(j)}(n) = \min(m_{(j)}, n)\gamma_{(j)}(n)$ where $m_{(j)}$ is the number of servers at center j.

The probability that a customer completing service in class c joins class d is p_{cd}, $c = 1, \ldots, C$, $d = 1, \ldots, C$. Let the relative throughput of class c be y_c in the sense that if Λ_c is the throughput of class c, y_d is the relative throughput of class d and Λ_d is the throughput of class d, $c = 1, \ldots, C$, $d = 1, \ldots, C$, then $\Lambda_c = \Lambda_d y_c / y_d$. The set of relative throughputs $\{y_c\}$ is any set of positive values satisfying the following set of C linear equations:

$$y_c = \sum_{d=1}^{C} y_d p_{dc}, \qquad c = 1, \ldots, C. \tag{3.192}$$

Note that these equations are linearly dependent and thus the relative throughputs are not determined uniquely by Eq. (3.192). By replacing any one equation, say the ith equation, with an equation equating the relative throughput to a constant, i.e., $y_i = a$, a set of linearly independent equations is obtained. That set can be solved by usual numerical procedures such as Gaussian elimination or Crout reduction. Given any set of relative throughputs, we can obtain another valid set of relative throughputs by multiplying the given set by a positive constant. With some computational algorithms we must be careful about our choice of relative throughputs, as we shall discuss in Section 3.5.2b.

We shall find it most convenient to first obtain metrics by service center and then obtain class specific metrics from the service center metrics. Let $y_{(j)}$ be the relative throughput at service center j, i.e.,

$$y_{(j)} = \sum_{c \text{ in } \mathscr{C}_j} y_c, \qquad j = 1, \ldots, J. \tag{3.193}$$

The mean service demand at service center j is $E[S_{(j)}]$, where

$$E[S_{(j)}] = \frac{\sum_{c \text{ in } \mathscr{C}_j} y_c E[S_c]}{y_{(j)}}. \tag{3.194}$$

Let the relative service demand of class c be

$$b_c = y_c E[S_c]. \tag{3.195}$$

If class c belongs to a queue with unit capacity, i.e., $\mu_{(j)}(n) = 1$, $n = 1, \ldots, N$, then b_c is also the relative utilization of class c in the sense that if both classes c and d belong to queues (either the same queue or different queues) with unit capacity, U_c is the utilization of class c, b_d is the relative service demand of class d, and U_d is the utilization of class d, $c = 1, \ldots, C$, $d = 1, \ldots, C$, then $U_c = U_d b_c / b_d$. Analogously, let the relative service demand at service center j be

$$b_{(j)} = \sum_{c \text{ in } \mathscr{C}_j} b_c, \qquad j = 1, \ldots, J. \tag{3.196}$$

The product form solution for the distribution of the number of customers at the service centers is

$$P(n_{(1)}, \ldots, n_{(J)}) = X_{(1)}(n_{(1)}) \cdots X_{(J)}(n_{(J)})/G(N) \tag{3.197}$$

where $n_{(j)}$ is the number of customers at service center j, the numbers of customers at the centers sum to N, and

$$X_{(j)}(n) = \frac{b_{(j)}^n}{\prod_{i=1}^n \mu_{(j)}(i)}, \qquad n = 0, \ldots, N, \tag{3.198}$$

where we assume the product in the denominator to be defined to be one when $n = 0$. The product form solution for the distribution of the number of customers at the classes is

$$P(n_1, \ldots, n_C) = X_{(1)}(n_c \; \forall c \text{ in } \mathscr{C}_1) \cdots X_{(J)}(n_c \; \forall c \text{ in } \mathscr{C}_J)/G(N), \tag{3.199}$$

where n_c is the number of customers at class c, the numbers of customers at the classes sum to N, and

$$X_{(j)}(n_c \; \forall c \text{ in } \mathscr{C}_j) = \frac{n_{(j)}! \prod_{c \text{ in } \mathscr{C}_j} (b_c^{n_c}/n_c!)}{\prod_{i=1}^{n_{(j)}} \mu_{(j)}(i)}, \tag{3.200}$$

where the number of customers at center j is $n_{(j)}$ and as before we assume the product in the denominator to be defined to be one when $n_{(j)} = 0$.

Note that the only parameters in these solutions are numbers of customers, relative service demands, and service capacities. In particular, the routing probabilities do not explicitly appear.

3.5.2 Computational Algorithms for Single Chain Networks

We describe three algorithms for closed product form networks: the Convolution algorithm, the Mean Value Analysis (MVA) algorithm and the Local Balance Algorithm for Normalizing Constants (LBANC). (All three algorithms extend to the full class of networks known to have a product form solution.) We discuss several algorithms because no one algorithm is best for all problems and for implementation on all machines. Historically, the order of development was first the Convolution algorithm, followed by the original version of MVA, the original version of LBANC, a modified version of MVA, and a modified version of LBANC. The historical order is of interest because the algorithms other than Convolution were developed, at least in part, to alleviate problems of that algorithm.

Convolution remains the dominant algorithm at this writing and a reasonable choice for general purpose use. MVA and LBANC are the dominant algorithms for the special case where all networks to be solved have only single server fixed capacity service centers and IS service centers. If in this case the machine's memory is not severely constrained, then MVA is the algorithm of choice. If in this case the machine's memory is severely constrained, (e.g., the solution is to be implemented on a programmable calculator) and the number of centers is not too large, then LBANC or MVA will be the algorithm of choice.

In general, i.e., when we consider networks without the above restrictions, the basic problem in making a choice between Convolution, MVA, and LBANC is making a tradeoff between potential numerical instability and potentially prohibitive computational expense. The original and modified versions of MVA (and LBANC) differ in their treatment of service centers with general capacity functions ($\mu_{(j)}$). The modified version of MVA has the best numerical stability of the known algorithms, but also has prohibitive computational expense for networks with more than a very few centers with general capacity functions. The original version of MVA has potentially disastrous numerical problems for certain networks with general capacity functions but has essentially the same computational expense as Convolution and the original version of LBANC. The Convolution algorithm is much less expensive than the modified version of MVA but has two numerical problems: (1) The normalizing constant $G(N)$ may exceed the floating point range of some machines for problems with reasonable parameter values. MVA avoids normalizing constants and their associated numerical problems. (2) For normalizing constants near the lower limit (in magnitude) of the floating point range, truncation errors will cause gross inaccuracy in the determination of $G(N)$. LBANC uses equations closely related to those of MVA but also uses the same normalizing constants as Convolution. Thus LBANC has the same problem of normalizing constants not being representable within the floating point range of a given machine. However, LBANC does not have the second numerical problem of Convolution. The modified version of LBANC has the same problem of computational expense as the modified MVA and the original version of LBANC has the same potential for numerical disaster as the original MVA.

In developing a state-of-the-art solution package, there seem to be three reasonable options: (1) use Convolution exclusively, (2) use the modified MVA exclusively, or (3) use a hybrid LBANC-Convolution approach where LBANC is used for fixed capacity and IS centers, the centers which are handled most easily by LBANC, and Convolution is used for general capacity service centers. The first option will likely require the least implementation effort. The second option will likely require the most implementation effort. The third option will likely require intermediate implementation effort, the lowest computational expense, and the best numerical properties obtainable without the modified version of MVA or the modified version of LBANC.

The following sections are written to be as self-contained as possible. The sections on Convolution, 3.5.2a, and MVA, 3.5.2c, are independent of each other except that Section 3.5.2c refers to equations in Section 3.5.2a that are used to obtain individual class measures from service center measures. The section on LBANC, 3.5.2d, is to a small degree dependent on the Convolution section. The hybrid LBANC–Convolution section, 3.5.2e, is dependent on both the LBANC and Convolution sections, of course. The section on programmable calculator implementations, 3.5.2f, is dependent on the previous sections. Convolution and LBANC require the scaling techniques of Section 3.5.2b to minimize the problem of normalizing constants outside of a machine's floating point range.

To summarize the notation we use in the computational algorithms, the following are the input parameters for service center j:

$y_{(j)}$:   relative throughput,
$E[S_{(j)}]$:   mean service demand,
$b_{(j)}$:   relative service demand,
$\mu_{(j)}(n)$: service capacity given n customers at center,
$m_{(j)}$:   number of servers.

The following input parameters are used to determine class specific performance measures for class c:

y_c: relative throughput,
$E[S_c]$:   mean service demand,
b_c: relative service demand.

The following variables are the performance measures for service center j given N customers in the network:

$\Lambda_{(j)}(N)$: throughput,
$U_{(j)}(N)$: utilization of each server,
$L_{(j)}(N)$: mean queue length (number of customers at center),
$R_{(j)}(N)$: mean response time.

The following variables are the performance measures for class c given N customers in the network:

$\Lambda_c(N)$: throughput,
$U_c(N)$: utilization of each server,
$L_c(N)$: mean queue length (number of customers at center),
$R_c(N)$: mean response time.

Where appropriate, the number of customers N will be left implicit.

a. Convolution

The Convolution algorithm derives its name from the manner in which the normalizing constant $G(N)$ is obtained from the factors $X_{(j)}(n_{(j)}), j = 1, \ldots, J,$ similarly to the convolution of discrete probability distributions. The algorithm is simply a computationally efficient and numerically appropriate method for summing the feasible numerators of Eq. (3.197).

The method requires iteration over the centers of the network and over the possible numbers of customers in each center. Either iteration may be nested inside the other. Usually implementations will nest the iteration over numbers of customers inside the iteration over the centers in order to facilitate trading computational efficiency in favor of storage efficiency. We shall assume this nesting.

Let G_j contain the summations over the first j centers, $j = 1, \ldots, J,$ for each possible number of customers $n, n = 0, \ldots, N,$ in those centers. $G_1 = X_1$ where X_1 is a vector of length $N + 1$ with elements defined by Eq. (3.198) with $j = 1$. For $j = 2, \ldots, J,$

$$G_j(n) = \sum_{i=0}^{n} G_{j-1}(i)X_j(n - i), \qquad n = 0, \ldots, N, \qquad (3.201)$$

where X_j is a vector of length $N + 1$ with elements defined by Eq. (3.198). Let $G = G_J,$ so that $G(N) = G_J(N)$.

Simplifications are possible for some types of centers. It will simplify the discussion if we assume that service centers are numbered so that centers 1 to J' are IS centers; i.e., $\mu_{(j)}(n) = n\mu_{(j)}(1), j = 1, \ldots, J', n = 1, \ldots, N,$ and centers $J' + 1$ to J'' are single server fixed capacity centers, i.e., $\mu_{(j)}(n) = \mu_{(j)}(1),$ $j = J' + 1, \ldots, J'', n = 1, \ldots, N.$ For IS service centers Eq. (3.198) simplifies to

$$X_{(j)}(n) = b_{(j)}^n / (\mu_{(j)}(1))^n n!, \qquad n = 0, \ldots, N, \qquad (3.202)$$

and if $J' > 0$ we can use

$$G_{J'}(n) = \frac{(\sum_{j=1}^{J'} b_{(j)} / \mu_{(j)}(1))^n}{n!}, \qquad n = 0, \ldots, N, \qquad (3.203)$$

rather than Eq. (3.201). For single server fixed capacity service centers, Eq. (3.198) simplifies to

$$X_{(j)}(n) = (b_{(j)} / \mu_{(j)}(1))^n, \qquad n = 0, \ldots, N, \qquad (3.204)$$

and Eq. (3.201) simplifies to

$$G_j(n) = G_{j-1}(n) + \frac{b_{(j)}}{\mu_{(j)}(1)} G_j(n - 1), \qquad (3.205)$$

$j = \max(2, J' + 1), \ldots, J'', n = 1, \ldots, N. \ [G_j(0) = 1, j = 1, \ldots, J.]$

Performance measures are obtained from the above quantities and $\mathbf{G}_{J-(j)}$, the normalizing constant vector with service center j excluded from the summation. ($\mathbf{G}_{J-(j)}$ may be thought of as the normalizing constant vector for the network with service center j removed.)

The throughput of service center j is

$$\Lambda_{(j)} = y_{(j)}G(N - 1)/G(N). \tag{3.206}$$

For service centers with general capacity functions ($\mu_{(j)}$), the queue length distribution must be obtained in order to obtain utilizations, mean queue lengths, and mean response times. (We use "queue length" synonymously with "number of customers at a center.") The queue length distribution for service center j is given by

$$\text{Prob}\{n_{(j)} = i\} = X_{(j)}(i)G_{J-(j)}(N - i)/G(N), \qquad i = 0, \ldots, N. \tag{3.207}$$

Let there be $m_{(j)}$ servers at service center j. The utilization of each server at service center j is

$$U_{(j)} = \frac{\sum_{i=1}^{N} \min(i, m_{(j)}) \, \text{Prob}\{n_{(j)} = i\}}{m_{(j)}}. \tag{3.208}$$

Similarly,

$$E[n_{(j)}] = \sum_{i=1}^{N} i \, \text{Prob}\{n_{(j)} = i\}. \tag{3.209}$$

From Little's formula

$$E[r_{(j)}] = E[n_{(j)}]/\Lambda_{(j)}. \tag{3.210}$$

If service center j has an IS queueing discipline, then the mean queue length at service center j is

$$E[n_{(j)}] = \Lambda_{(j)}E[S_{(j)}]/\mu_{(j)}(1). \tag{3.211}$$

If service center j is a single server center with fixed capacity then the following simplifications are possible. We can obtain the queue length distribution without the expense of obtaining (saving) $\mathbf{G}_{J-(j)}$. If we define $G(i) = 0$ for $i < 0$, then

$$\text{Prob}\{n_{(j)} = i\} = \frac{(b_{(j)}/\mu_{(j)}(1))^i (G(N - i) - (b_{(j)}/\mu_{(j)}(1))G(N - i - 1))}{G(N)}, \tag{3.212}$$

$i = 0, \ldots, N$. The utilization of the server at service center j is

$$U_{(j)} = \Lambda_{(j)}E[S_{(j)}]/\mu_{(j)}(1). \tag{3.213}$$

The mean queue length is

$$E[n_{(j)}] = \sum_{i=1}^{N} \frac{(b_{(j)}/\mu_{(j)}(1))^i G(N - i)}{G(N)}. \tag{3.214}$$

If service center j has $m_{(j)}$ fixed rate servers, i.e., $\mu_{(j)}(n) = \min(n, m_{(j)})\mu_{(j)}(1)$, $n = 1, \ldots, N$, then the utilization of each server at service center j is

$$U_{(j)} = \Lambda_{(j)} E[S_{(j)}]/\mu_{(j)}(1)m_{(j)}. \tag{3.215}$$

The performance measures for individual classes can be obtained from the service center measures as follows. Assume that class c is part of service center j. The throughput of class c is

$$\Lambda_c = (y_c/y_{(j)})\Lambda_{(j)}. \tag{3.216}$$

The queue length distribution for class c is given by

$$\text{Prob}\{n_c = i\} = \sum_{n=i}^{N} \frac{n!}{i!(n-i)!} \frac{b_c^i (b_{(j)} - b_c)^{n-i}}{b_{(j)}^n} \text{Prob}\{n_{(j)} = n\}, \tag{3.217}$$

$i = 0, \ldots, N$. The utilization of each server at service center j by customers in class c is

$$U_c = (b_c/b_{(j)})U_{(j)}. \tag{3.218}$$

Similarly,

$$E[n_c] = (b_c/b_{(j)})E[n_{(j)}]. \tag{3.219}$$

From Little's formula

$$E[r_c] = E[n_c]/\Lambda_c. \tag{3.220}$$

We now give a more programlike definition of the algorithm. We assume that queue length distributions are only obtained when necessary for other performance measures. We will not obtain measures for individual classes. We assume that the relative service demands have already been determined. T is used to hold $\mathbf{G}_{j-1}$. The variable t is used to collect IS service centers for computation of $\mathbf{G}_{j'}$. We use $L_{(j)}$ to represent $E[n_{(j)}]$ and use $R_{(j)}$ to represent $E[r_{(j)}]$. Where a tradeoff must be made between memory usage and computation, we make the tradeoff in favor of greater memory usage and lesser computation. (Methods of shifting of the tradeoff toward lesser memory usage and greater computation should be obvious, but the shift toward the tradeoffs we make is less obvious.)

{CONVOLUTION ALGORITHM}
    {Compute normalizing constants}
        {IS service centers}
            If $J' = 0$
                $\mathbf{G} = (1, 0, \ldots, 0)$
            $t = 0$
            For $j = 1$ to J'
                $t = t + b_{(j)}/\mu_{(j)}(1)$

$G(0) = 1$
For $n = 1$ to N
 $G(n) = G(n - 1) \times t/n$
{Fixed capacity service centers}
 For $j = J' + 1$ to J''
 $\mathbf{T} = \mathbf{G}$
 For $n = 1$ to N
  $G(n) = T(n) + (b_{(j)}/\mu_{(j)}(1)) \times G(n - 1)$
{Other service centers}
 For $j = J'' + 1$ to J
 $\mathbf{T} = \mathbf{G}$
 $\mathbf{G}_{J-(j)} = \mathbf{G}$
 $X_{(j)}(0) = 1$
 For $n = 1$ to N
  $G(n) = 0$
  $X_{(j)}(n) = X_{(j)}(n - 1) \times b_{(j)}/\mu_{(j)}(n)$
  For $i = 1$ to n {Convolution}
   $G(n) = G(n) + X_{(j)}(i) \times T(n - i)$
 For $j = J'' + 1$ to $J - 1$
 For $j' = j + 1$ to J
  $\mathbf{T} = \mathbf{G}_{J-(j')}$
  For $n = 1$ to N
   $\mathbf{G}_{J-(j')}(n) = 0$
   For $i = 1$ to n {Convolution}
    $\mathbf{G}_{J-(j')}(n) = T(n) + X_{j'}(i) \times T(n - i)$
{Finished computing normalizing constants}
{Throughputs}
 For $j = 1$ to J
 $\Lambda_{(j)} = y_{(j)} \times G(N - 1)/G(N)$
{Other measures depend on center type}
 For $j = 1$ to J' {IS service centers}
 {Utilizations}
 $U_{(j)} = 0$
 {Mean queue lengths}
 $L_{(j)} = \Lambda_{(j)} \times E[S_{(j)}]/\mu_{(j)}(1)$
 {Mean response times}
 $R_{(j)} = E[S_{(j)}]/\mu_{(j)}(1)$
 For $j = J'$ to J'' {Fixed capacity service centers}
 {Utilizations}
 $U_{(j)} = \Lambda_{(j)} \times E[S_{(j)}]/\mu_{(j)}(1)$
 {Mean queue lengths}
 $L_{(j)} = 0$
 For $n = 1$ to N

$$L_{(j)} = L_{(j)} + (b_{(j)}/\mu_{(j)}(1))^n \times G(N - n)$$
$$L_{(j)} = L_{(j)}/G(N)$$
{Mean response times}
$$R_{(j)} = L_{(j)}/\Lambda_{(j)}$$
For $j = J'' + 1$ to J {Other service centers}
{Utilizations}
$$U_{(j)} = 0$$
For $n = 1$ to N
$$U_{(j)} = U_{(j)} + \min(n, m_{(j)}) \times X_{(j)}(n) \times G_{J-(j)}(N - n)$$
$$U_{(j)} = U_{(j)}/(G(N) \times m_{(j)})$$
{Mean queue lengths}
$$L_{(j)} = 0$$
For $n = 1$ to N
$$L_{(j)} = L_{(j)} + n \times X_{(j)}(n) \times G_{J-(j)}(N - n)$$
$$L_{(j)} = L_{(j)}/G(N)$$
{Means response times}
$$R_{(j)} = L_{(j)}/\Lambda_{(j)}$$
{END CONVOLUTION ALGORITHM}

EXAMPLE 3.27 (continued)   Let us assume that in the network of Fig. 3.30 the mean think time is 10 sec, the mean CPU time is 50 ms, the mean floppy disk time is 220 ms, and the mean hard disk time is 19 ms. The CPU scheduling is PS, and the device scheduling is FCFS. The probability a customer goes to the floppy disk after leaving the CPU is 0.1 (the probability a customer goes to the hard disk after leaving the CPU is 0.9), and the probability a customer returns to the CPU after leaving a device is 0.875 (the number of CPU–I/O cycles has a geometric distribution starting at one with mean 8 cycles). Figure 3.32 plots Λ,

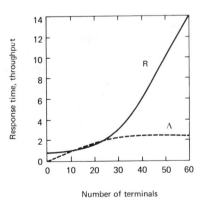

Fig. 3.32   Mean steady-state response time and throughput versus number of terminals for network of Example 3.27.

the throughput through the terminals, and R, the mean response time, i.e., the mean time between issuing a command and receiving a response, as a function of the number of terminals N as N ranges from 1 to 60. (The mean response time can be obtained by applying Little's formula, i.e., by summing the mean CPU and disk queue lengths and dividing by $\varLambda$.) Note the similarity between the throughput and response time trends in this figure and those in Fig. 3.23.

$\triangle$

b. Scaling

There is a major problem with the Convolution algorithm that we ignored in Section 3.5.2a. If care is not used in the choice of the relative service demands, then it is likely that elements of **G** will be outside of the floating point range of many computers. Floating point range problems are especially likely in networks with large numbers of customers and/or service centers with highly variable capacity functions, e.g., IS service centers. LBANC encounters similar problems.

Though we cannot eliminate this problem in general, we can greatly alleviate it by proper choice of the relative throughputs. Given a set of relative throughputs and service demands satisfying Eqs. (3.192)–(3.196), we can scale these sets so that no element of **G** will be too large for a given floating point range.

Let ε be a constant chosen so that $1/\varepsilon$ is slightly less than the upper limit of the given floating point range. For example, $\varepsilon = 10^{-75}$ could be used for the IBM 360/370 series of computers. δ is an arbitrary constant slightly less than 1, e.g., 0.99. The following algorithm will scale a set of relative throughputs such that $NG(n) < \varepsilon^{-1}$, $n = 0, \ldots, N$. (Thus overflow will not occur in computing mean queue lengths, either.) It assumes the numbering scheme just used with the Convolution algorithm; i.e., service centers $1, \ldots, J'$ are IS service centers, service centers $J' + 1, \ldots, J''$ are single server fixed capacity service centers, and service centers $J'' + 1, \ldots, J$ have general capacity functions. Let $g_{(j)}$ be an integer such that $1 \leqslant g_{(j)} \leqslant N$ and $\mu_{(j)}(n) = \mu_{(j)}(g_{(j)})$ for $n \geqslant g_{(j)}$. (For single server fixed capacity service centers $g_{(j)} = 1$ and for IS service centers $g_{(j)} = N$.)

{SCALING ALGORITHM}
$\quad D = 1/\max(b_{(1)}/\mu_{(1)}(N), \ldots, b_{(J)}/\mu_{(J)}(N))$.
$\quad$ Repeat
$\quad\quad D = \delta \times D$
$\quad\quad P = 1$
$\quad\quad$ If $J' \neq 0$
$\quad\quad\quad P = \exp(- D \times (b_{(1)} + \cdots + b_{(J')}))$
$\quad\quad$ If $J' \neq J''$
$\quad\quad\quad P = P \times (1 - D \times b_{(J'+1)}/\mu_{(J'+1)}(1)) \times \cdots \times (1 - D \times b_{(J'')}/\mu_{(J'')}(1))$

For $j = J'' + 1$ to J

$$P = P \times \frac{1 - [(D \times b_{(j)})/\mu_{(j)}(g_{(j)})]}{1 + \sum_{i=1}^{g_{(j)}-1} \left(\frac{1}{\prod_{h=1}^{i} \mu_{(j)}(h)} - \frac{1}{\mu_{(j)}(g_{(j)}) \times \prod_{h=1}^{i-1} \mu_{(j)}(h)} \right) \times (D \times b_{(j)})^i}$$

Until $P > N\varepsilon$
For $c = 1$ to C
$\quad y_c = D \times y_c$
Redetermine $\{y_{(j)}\}$, $\{b_c\}$, and $\{b_{(j)}\}$
{END SCALING ALGORITHM}

It will still be possible for some elements of $\mathbf{G}$ *to be too small for the given floating point range.* It is also possible that underflow will occur in executing the Convolution algorithm even when the elements of $\mathbf{G}$ are within the given floating point range. When $G(n)$ for some n is nearly too small for a given floating point range, then the Convolution algorithm is likely to be numerically unstable and produce highly erroneous results. LBANC does not have this problem with numerical instability and can be used to obtain $G(n)$ in such cases.

In Lam (1982) a scaling approach is proposed which varies the scaling factor during the execution of the primary algorithm, e.g., the Convolution algorithm. Though this approach effectively eliminates floating point range problems with the Convolution algorithm, it is not clear at this writing whether the approach is useful in practice.

c. Mean Value Analysis

The Mean Value Analysis algorithm avoids the numerical problems of the Convolution algorithm by avoiding computation of the normalizing constant of Eq. (3.197). It is the algorithm of choice for networks with only IS and single server fixed capacity centers (unless the number of centers is small enough and memory is so constrained that LBANC becomes attractive.) However, the computational complexity of (the modified version of) MVA grows combinatorially with the number of service centers with general capacity functions, i.e., centers other than single server fixed capacity and IS centers. The real complexity problem is that MVA must obtain queue length distributions for service centers with general capacity functions; the computational complexity of MVA grows with the number of service centers where queue length distributions are obtained. [We have not discussed computational complexity in quantitative terms because it is not really an issue unless several service centers have general capacity functions. In that case Convolution will be much less expensive than the modified MVA or the modified LBANC. For quantitative discussion of computational complexity of Convolution and MVA, see Reiser (1977, 1981) and Reiser and Lavenberg (1980). The computational complexity of LBANC is essentially the same as that of MVA.] We have already seen a restricted version of MVA in Eqs. (3.176)–(3.180).

The key to MVA is being able to give a recursive expression for the mean response time of a service center in terms of measures for the network with one less customer. For IS service centers

$$R_{(j)}(N) = E[S_{(j)}]/\mu_{(j)}(1), \qquad N > 0. \tag{3.221}$$

For single server fixed capacity service centers

$$R_{(j)}(N) = \frac{E[S_{(j)}]}{\mu_{(j)}(1)}(1 + L_{(j)}(N - 1)), \qquad N > 0. \tag{3.222}$$

We temporarily defer the general capacity function case. As we shall see when we give a programlike definition of MVA, we would not actually use recursion but rather iteration over number of customers starting at one and stopping at N. The following equations would allow the iteration to proceed. First we would obtain the throughputs by applying Little's formula to the mean cycle time, i.e., the mean time between a customer's arrivals at a queue.

$$\Lambda_{(j)}(N) = \frac{N}{\sum_{i=1}^{J} (y_{(i)}/y_{(j)})R_{(i)}(N)}, \qquad j = 1, \ldots, J. \tag{3.223}$$

[This equation is analogous to Eq. (3.178) for the central server model.] We would then obtain mean queue lengths for fixed capacity centers by using Little's formula again:

$$L_{(j)}(N) = \Lambda_{(j)}(N)R_{(j)}(N), \qquad j = 1, \ldots, J. \tag{3.224}$$

Now we can use Eqs. (3.221) and (3.222) at the next higher number of customers to continue the iteration. The name of the algorithm comes from the fact that the above equations deal with mean performance values. There is no use of normalizing constants or even marginal distributions.

When general capacity service centers are allowed, marginal queue length distributions appear in the equations for those centers. Let us use $P_{(j)}(i|N)$ for Prob$\{n_{(j)} = i\}$ in a network with N customers. For service centers with general capacity functions

$$R_{(j)}(N) = E[S_{(j)}] \sum_{i=1}^{N} \frac{i}{\mu_{(j)}(i)} P_{(j)}(i - 1 \,|\, N - 1), \qquad N > 0. \tag{3.225}$$

Equation (3.223) still holds with general capacity centers. To obtain the queue length distribution, we can use

$$P_{(j)}(i|N) = \frac{E[S_{(j)}]\Lambda_{(j)}(N)}{\mu_{(j)}(i)} P_{(j)}(i - 1 \,|\, N - 1), \qquad i = 1, \ldots, N. \tag{3.226}$$

However, we now arrive at the critical problem which leads to the computational complexity we have been emphasizing. The problem is the computation of $P_{(j)}(0 \mid N)$. The original approach,

$$P_{(j)}(0 \mid N) = 1 - \sum_{i=1}^{N} P_{(j)}(i \mid N), \tag{3.227}$$

fails numerically as $P_{(j)}(0 \mid N)$ tends to zero. Problems may arise with very small values of N, say 10, for some networks. The numerically stable, but potentially expensive, modified approach is to use

$$P_{(j)}(0 \mid N) = \frac{\Lambda_{(i)}(N)}{\Lambda_{(i)}^{J-(j)}(N)} P_{(j)}(0 \mid N - 1), \tag{3.228}$$

where i is any service center other than j and $\Lambda_{(i)}^{J-(j)}(N)$ is the throughput for center i in the network with center j removed. (We do not need to consider the routing probabilities in solving that network; it is sufficient to simply omit center j from the sets of relative throughputs, service demands, etc.) Determining $\Lambda_{(i)}^{J-(j)}(N)$ is nearly as expensive as determining $\Lambda_{(i)}(N)$, so for a given number of service centers it is nearly twice as expensive to solve a network with one service center with a general capacity function as it is to solve a network with only single server fixed capacity and IS centers. If a network has two centers with general capacity functions, say centers $J - 1$ and J, then it will be necessary to obtain $\Lambda_{(i)}^{J-(J-1,J)}(N)$, $\Lambda_{(i)}^{J-(J-1)}(N)$, and $\Lambda_{(i)}^{J-(J)}(N)$, so the solution will be nearly four times as expensive as if the network had only single server fixed capacity and IS service centers. This combinatorial increase in complexity may be prohibitive if there are more than a few centers with general capacity functions. In general, assuming $J > J''$, the number of additional networks to be considered is $2^{J-J''} - 1$.

We now give a more programlike definition of the algorithm. As before we assume service centers $1, \ldots, J'$ are IS service centers, service centers $J' + 1, \ldots, J''$ are single server fixed capacity service centers, and service centers $J'' + 1, \ldots, J$ have general capacity functions. We assume that the relative throughputs have already been determined. We assume that if there are general capacity centers, i.e., if $J > J''$, that $J'' > 0$ and that $\Lambda_{(1)}^{J-(j)}(n)$, $n = 1, \ldots, N$, has already been determined for $j = J'' + 1, \ldots, J$. T is used to gather the weighted sum of response times. We assume that we are only interested in measures for number of customers N and will reuse variables as convenient. Thus we shall omit the indices that indicate numbers of customers where the same variable can be used for all numbers of customers.

{MEAN VALUE ANALYSIS}
   {Initialization}
      For $j = J' + 1$ to J''
         $L_{(j)} = 0$

For $j = J'' + 1$ to J
$P_{(j)}(0) = 1$
{Number of customers loop}
For $n = 1$ to N
  {Mean response times}
  $T = 0$
  For $j = 1$ to J' {IS service centers}
  $R_{(j)} = E[S_{(j)}]/\mu_{(j)}(1)$
  $T = T + y_{(j)} \times R_{(j)}$
  For $j = J' + 1$ to J'' {Fixed capacity service centers}
  $R_{(j)} = (E[S_{(j)}]/\mu_{(j)}(1)) \times (1 + L_{(j)})$
  $T = T + y_{(j)} \times R_{(j)}$
  For $j = J'' + 1$ to J {General capacity service centers}
  $R_{(j)} = 0$
  For $i = 1$ to n {Iterate over queue lengths}
    $R_{(j)} = R_{(j)} + i \times P_{(j)}(i - 1)/\mu_{(j)}(i)$
  $R_{(j)} = E[S_{(j)}] \times R_{(j)}$
  $T = T + y_{(j)} \times R_{(j)}$
{End mean response times}
{Throughputs}
  $T = n/T$
  For $j = 1$ to J
  $\Lambda_{(j)} = y_{(j)} \times T$
{Mean queue lengths–fixed capacity service centers}
  For $j = J' + 1$ to J''
  $L_{(j)} = \Lambda_{(j)} \times R_{(j)}$
{Queue length distributions–general capacity service centers}
  For $j = J'' + 1$ to J
  For $i = n$ down to 1 {Iterate over queue lengths}
    $P_{(j)}(i) = E[S_{(j)}] \times \Lambda_{(j)} \times P_{(j)}(i - 1)/\mu_{(j)}(i)$
  $P_{(j)}(0) = P_{(j)}(0) \times \Lambda_{(1)}/\Lambda_{(1)}^{J - (j)}(n)$
{End number of customers loop}
{Mean queue lengths not already determined}
  For $j = 1$ to J', J'' to J
  $L_{(j)} = \Lambda_{(j)} \times R_{(j)}$
{Utilizations}
  For $j = 1$ to J' {IS service centers}
  $U_{(j)} = 0$
  For $j = J' + 1$ to J'' {Fixed capacity service centers}
  $U_{(j)} = \Lambda_{(j)} \times E[S_{(j)}]/\mu_{(j)}(1)$
  For $j = J'' + 1$ to J {Other service centers}
  $U_{(j)} = 0$
  For $n = 1$ to N

$$U_{(j)} = U_{(j)} + \min(n, m_{(j)}) \times P_{(j)}(n)$$
$$U_{(j)} = U_{(j)}/m_{(j)}$$
{END MEAN VALUE ANALYSIS}

d. Local Balance Algorithm for Normalizing Constants

LBANC was inspired by MVA, but unlike MVA, LBANC explicitly requires computation of normalizing constants. The equations largely parallel those of MVA, but because of the explicit use of normalizing constants the equations are generally simpler. LBANC has the same problem as Convolution with regard to normalizing constants having values outside of a given floating point range, but LBANC does not have the instability of Convolution near the lower limit of the floating point range. Let $\tilde{L}_{(j)}(n)$ be the unnormalized mean queue length of service center j given n customers in the network; i.e.,

$$\tilde{L}_{(j)}(n) = L_{(j)}(n)G(n), \qquad n = 0, \dots, N. \tag{3.229}$$

LBANC yields unnormalized mean queue lengths as intermediate results. From the unnormalized mean queue lengths we can use

$$G(n) = \frac{\sum_{j=1}^{J} \tilde{L}_{(j)}(n)}{n}, \qquad n = 1, \dots, N. \tag{3.230}$$

Normalized mean queue lengths are available once $G(N)$ is determined. Throughputs can be obtained from Eqs. (3.206) and (3.216) and mean response times from Little's formula. As with MVA the queue length distribution must be obtained by LBANC for general capacity service centers. LBANC has a computational complexity problem with such service centers corresponding to that of Mean Value Analysis. Utilizations can be obtained from Eqs. (3.208), (3.212), (3.215), and (3.218) as appropriate.

For IS service centers

$$\tilde{L}_{(j)}(n) = \frac{b_{(j)}}{\mu_{(j)}(1)} G(n-1), \qquad n = 1, \dots, N. \tag{3.231}$$

For single server fixed capacity service centers,

$$\tilde{L}_{(j)}(n) = \frac{b_{(j)}}{\mu_{(j)}(1)} (G(n-1) + \tilde{L}_{(j)}(n-1)), \qquad n = 1, \dots, N. \tag{3.232}$$

For service centers other than fixed capacity single server and IS, we can obtain

$$\tilde{P}_{(j)}(i \mid n) = \frac{b_{(j)}}{\mu_{(j)}(i)} \tilde{P}_{(j)}(i-1 \mid n-1), \qquad i = 1, \dots, n, \quad n = 1, \dots, N, \tag{3.233}$$

where $\tilde{P}_{(j)}(i \mid n)$ is the unnormalized probability of queue length i at service center j given n customers in the network, i.e.,

$$\tilde{P}_{(j)}(i\,|\,n) = P_{(j)}(i\,|\,n)G(n). \tag{3.234}$$

After using Eq. (3.233) we use

$$\tilde{L}_{(j)}(n) = \sum_{i=1}^{n} i\tilde{P}_{(j)}(i\,|\,n), \qquad n = 1,\ldots,N. \tag{3.235}$$

$G(n)$ is then obtained from Eq. (3.230). To keep the iteration going we must obtain $\tilde{P}_{(j)}(0\,|\,n)$. Doing so we face the same problems as discussed with Mean Value Analysis and Eqs. (3.227) and (3.228). The equation corresponding to Eq. (3.227) is

$$\tilde{P}_{(j)}(0\,|\,n) = G(n) - \sum_{i=1}^{n} \tilde{P}_{(j)}(i\,|\,n), \qquad n = 1,\ldots,N, \tag{3.236}$$

and the equation corresponding to Eq. (3.228) is simply

$$\tilde{P}_{(j)}(0\,|\,n) = G_{J-(j)}(n), \qquad n = 1,\ldots,N. \tag{3.237}$$

Though Eq. (3.237) is simpler than Eq. (3.228), the computational effort of obtaining $G_{J-(j)}(n)$ is essentially the same as that of obtaining $A_{(i)}^{J-(j)}(n)$.

We now give a programlike definition of LBANC. As before we assume service centers $1,\ldots,J'$ are IS service centers, service centers $J'+1,\ldots,J''$ are single server fixed capacity service centers, and service centers $J''+1,\ldots,J$ have general capacity functions. We assume that the relative service demands have already been determined. We assume that we are primarily interested in measures for number of customers N and shall reuse variables along the way; i.e., we will drop the n subscripts from all of the above variables, except G. We will continue to use the "tilde" for clarity, but note that the final, normalized values can use the same storage as the unnormalized values. We assume that $G_{J-(j)}(n)$, $n = 1,\ldots,N$, has already been determined for $j = J''+1,\ldots,J$.

{Local Balance Algorithm for Normalizing Constants}
  {Initialization}
    $G(0) = 1$
    For $j = J'+1$ to J''
      $\tilde{L}_{(j)} = 0$
    For $j = J''+1$ to J
      $\tilde{P}_{(j)}(0) = 1$
  {Number of customers loop}
    For $n = 1$ to N
      $G(n) = 0$
      {Unnormalized mean queue lengths}
        For $j = 1$ to J' {IS service centers}

$$\tilde{L}_{(j)} = (b_{(j)}/\mu_{(j)}(1)) \times G(n-1)$$
$$G(n) = G(n) + \tilde{L}_{(j)}$$

For $j = J' + 1$ to J'' {Fixed capacity service centers}
$$\tilde{L}_{(j)} = (b_{(j)}/\mu_{(j)}(1)) \times (G(n-1) + \tilde{L}_{(j)})$$
$$G(n) = G(n) + \tilde{L}_{(j)}$$

For $j = J'' + 1$ to J {General capacity service centers}
$$\tilde{L}_{(j)} = 0$$

For $i = n$ down to 1 {Iterate over queue lengths}
$$\tilde{P}_{(j)}(i) = b_{(j)} \times \tilde{P}_{(j)}(i-1)/\mu_{(j)}(i)$$
$$\tilde{L}_{(j)} = \tilde{L}_{(j)} + i \times \tilde{P}_{(j)}(i)$$
$$G(n) = G(n) + \tilde{L}_{(j)}$$

{Normalizing constant}
$$G(n) = G(n)/n$$

{Unnormalized probability center is empty}
$$\tilde{P}_{(j)}(0) = G_{J-(j)}(n)$$

{End number of customers loop}

For $j = 1$ to J {Normalized mean queue lengths}
$$L_{(j)} = \tilde{L}_{(j)}/G(N)$$

For $j = 1$ to J {Throughputs and mean response times}
$$\Lambda_{(j)} = y_{(j)}G(N-1)/G(N)$$
$$R_{(j)} = L_{(j)}/\Lambda_{(j)}$$

For $j = 1$ to J' {IS service center utilizations}
$$U_{(j)} = 0$$

For $j = J' + 1$ to J'' {Fixed capacity service center utilizations}
$$U_{(j)} = \Lambda_{(j)} \times E[S_{(j)}]/\mu_{(j)}(1)$$

For $j = J'' + 1$ to J {Other service center utilizations}
$$U_{(j)} = 0$$

For $n = 1$ to N
$$U_{(j)} = U_{(j)} + \min(n, m_{(j)}) \times \tilde{P}_{(j)}(n)$$
$$U_{(j)} = U_{(j)}/(G(N) \times m_{(j)})$$

{End LOCAL BALANCE ALGORITHM FOR NORMALIZING CONSTANTS}

Note that we do not have to save $G(0), \ldots, G(N-2)$. However, if we do save these values, then we can readily recompute measures for individual service centers for numbers of customers less than N, *without recomputing measures for other service centers*. This is especially significant when using machines with very limited memory, e.g., programmable calculators and home computers. This is an advantage of LBANC over Mean Value Analysis in such memory limited situations. Note that LBANC and Mean Value Analysis can be used with pocket calculators with large single chain numbers of customers because the storage required is independent of the number of customers [assuming we do not save $G(0), \ldots, G(N-2)$ with LBANC].

With LBANC it is also possible to use Eq. (3.212) to obtain the queue length distribution for fixed capacity service centers. This expression has the advantage that it can be used to obtain a desired probability without obtaining other probabilities first as would be the case if Eq. (3.233) were used. This is also important when memory is limited.

e. Hybrid Use of LBANC with Convolution

The equations given for LBANC and Convolution in the previous sections can be used together without the addition of any new equations. The basic idea is to use LBANC for fixed capacity and IS service centers to avoid the numerical instability of Convolution for $G(N)$ near the lower limit of floating point magnitude and to use Convolution for other centers to avoid the computational expense of LBANC. The following gives a programlike definition of the hybrid algorithm.

{HYBRID LBANC–CONVOLUTION ALGORITHM}
  {Initialization}
    $G(0) = 1$
    For $j = J' + 1$ to J''
    $\tilde{L}_{(j)} = 0$
  {Number of customers loop (LBANC)}
    For $n = 1$ to N
    $G(n) = 0$
      {Unnormalized mean queue lengths}
      For $j = 1$ to J' {IS service centers}
      $\tilde{L}_{(j)} = (b_{(j)}/\mu_{(j)}(1)) \times G(n - 1)$
      $G(n) = G(n) + \tilde{L}_{(j)}$
      For $j = J' + 1$ to J'' {Fixed capacity service centers}
      $\tilde{L}_{(j)} = (b_{(j)}/\mu_{(j)}(1)) \times (G(n - 1) + \tilde{L}_{(j)})$
      $G(n) = G(n) + \tilde{L}_{(j)}$
    {Normalizing constant}
      $G(n) = G(n)/n$
  {End number of customers loop (LBANC)}
  {Convolution for other service centers}
    For $j = J'' + 1$ to J
    $\mathbf{T} = \mathbf{G}$
    $\mathbf{G}_{J-(j)} = \mathbf{G}$
    $X_{(j)}(0) = 1$
    For $n = 1$ to N
    $G(n) = 0$
    $X_{(j)}(n) = X_{(j)}(n - 1) \times b_{(j)}/\mu_{(j)}(n)$
    For $i = 1$ to n {Convolution}
      $G(n) = G(n) + X_{(j)}(i) \times T(n - i)$

For $j = J'' + 1$ to $J - 1$
  For $j' = j + 1$ to J
  $\mathbf{T} = \mathbf{G}_{J-(j')}$
  For $n = 1$ to N
    $\mathbf{G}_{J-(j')}(n) = 0$
    For $i = 1$ to n {Convolution}
      $G_{J-(j')}(n) = T(n) + X_{j'}(i) \times T(n - i)$
{Finished computing normalizing constants}
{(Re)determine unnormalized measures}
  For $j = 1$ to J' {IS service centers}
  $\tilde{L}_{(j)} = (b_{(j)}/\mu_{(j)}(1)) \times G(N - 1)$
  For $j = J' + 1$ to J'' {Fixed capacity service centers}
  $\tilde{L}_{(j)} = 0$
  For $n = 1$ to N
    $\tilde{L}_{(j)} = (b_{(j)}/\mu_{(j)}(1)) \times (G(n - 1) + \tilde{L}_{(j)})$
  For $j = J'' + 1$ to J {General capacity service centers}
  $\tilde{L}_{(j)} = 0$
  For $i = 1$ to N {Iterate over queue lengths}
    $\tilde{P}_{(j)}(i) = X_{(j)}(i) \times G_{J-(j)}(N - i)$
    $\tilde{L}_{(j)} = \tilde{L}_{(j)} + i \times \tilde{P}_{(j)}(i)$
{Determine normalized measures}
  For $j = 1$ to J
  $L_{(j)} = \tilde{L}_{(j)}/G(N)$
  For $j = 1$ to J
  $\Lambda_{(j)} = y_{(j)}G(N - 1)/G(N)$
  $R_{(j)} = L_{(j)}/\Lambda_{(j)}$
  For $j = 1$ to J' {IS service centers}
  $U_{(j)} = 0$
  For $j = J' + 1$ to J'' {Fixed capacity service centers}
  $U_{(j)} = \Lambda_{(j)} \times E[S_{(j)}]/\mu_{(j)}(1)$
  For $j = J'' + 1$ to J {Other service centers}
  $U_{(j)} = 0$
  For $n = 1$ to N
    $U_{(j)} = U_{(j)} + \min(n, m_{(j)}) \times \tilde{P}_{(j)}(n)$
  $U_{(j)} = U_{(j)}/(G(N) \times m_{(j)})$
{END HYBRID LBANC–CONVOLUTION ALGORITHM}

f. Programmable Calculator Implementations

Significant queueing network problems can be solved using the above three algorithms on programmable calculators. The principal problem is that a programmable calculator usually has a very small memory, often less than 50 registers (words), so memory usage becomes the dominant factor in comparing the algorithms. Consideration of service centers other than IS and single server fixed capacity dramatically increases memory usage, so we assume that only these types of centers are to be handled in a calculator implementation. It simplifies both our discussion and actual implementation if we assume, without loss of generality, that $\mu_{(j)}(1) = 1$, $j = 1, \ldots, J$.

In order to conserve memory as far as possible, an implementation may require that the user enter some parameters twice, at different stages of the computation, so that the parameter values need not be saved in registers. Consider the Convolution implementation in Section 3.5.2a with the above restrictions on service centers. First the program may request $b_{(j)}, j = 1, \ldots, J'$, one at a time, to determine t. Then it can determine $\mathbf{G}_{J'}$ while only retaining N, n, t, and the elements of $\mathbf{G}_{J'}$. After that, it requests the values $b_{(j)}$, $j = J' + 1, \ldots, J'' = J$, and determines $\mathbf{G}_j$ while only retaining $N, n, \mathbf{T}, b_{(j)}$, and the newly computed elements of $\mathbf{G}_j$. Thus the normalizing constant vector is obtained with the maximum number of registers used at a given time roughly equal to twice the number of customers (N). Performance measures can then be obtained on a *center by center* basis, with the user re-entering the input parameters for that center. (The storage for this phase is less than that for the previous phase.)

Chandy and Sauer (1980) proposed an algorithm (CCNC) for programmable calculators with the claim that it required less storage than the algorithms we have considered. However, that algorithm has the same storage requirements as the Convolution implementation we have described. It is more expensive computationally than Convolution.

Where N is sufficiently large that it is not practical to store both the vectors required in the above Convolution approach, LBANC and MVA may still be feasible if the number of centers J is not too large. Because of the iteration over number of customers in MVA and LBANC, it is impractical to ask the user to re-enter the individual queue parameters at each step of that iteration. However, it is not necessary to retain the values dependent on the number of customers except for the values determined at the last iteration step in order to proceed to the next step. In our LBANC implementation it is only necessary to retain N, n, $G(n - 1)$, $G(n)$, $b_{(j)}, j = 1, \ldots, J$, and $\tilde{L}_{(j)}, j = 1, \ldots, J$. So the number of registers needed is roughly twice the number of centers. In our MVA implementation it is necessary to retain N, n, T, $y_{(j)}, j = 1, \ldots, J, E[S_{(j)}]$, $j = 1, \ldots, J, R_{(j)}, j = 1, \ldots, J$, and $L_{(j)}, j = 1, \ldots, J$. So the number of registers needed is roughly four times the number of centers. However, it is possible to devise an alternate MVA implementation which retains $b_{(j)}, j = 1, \ldots, J$, and $\hat{R}_{(j)}, j = 1, \ldots, J$, where $\hat{R}_{(j)} = y_{(j)}R_{(j)}$. Such an implementation may or may not be less convenient for the user, depending on the desired performance measures. As with LBANC, the number of registers needed is roughly twice the number of centers.

3.5.3 Multiple Chain Networks

Now we consider closed product form networks with K routing chains. Typically, there are different types of customers in different routing chains. There are C classes and J service centers, as before, but now the classes are partitioned among the chains as well as the centers. Let $\mathcal{K}_k$ be the set of classes in chain $k, k = 1, \ldots, K$. Each chain k is such that for any pair of classes c and d in $\mathcal{K}_k$, d is reachable from c and c is reachable from d; furthermore, there is no class e which is not in $\mathcal{K}_k$, such that e is reachable from some class in $\mathcal{K}_k$ or that some class in $\mathcal{K}_k$ is reachable from e. It is not necessary that a given chain have classes at all service centers.

EXAMPLE 3.29   The network of Fig. 3.33 is similar to that of Fig. 3.31 but has two closed chains. The network of Fig. 3.31 assumes that homogeneous

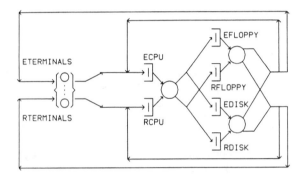

Fig. 3.33   Computer system model of Example 3.29.

users switch (frequently) between editing and "running" modes. In the network of Fig. 3.33 there are two heterogeneous sets of users, one set which stays in editing mode and one which stays in running mode.   △

EXAMPLE 3.30   In a communication network with end-to-end flow control, there is a limit to the number of messages (or packets) that may be in transit between a given source and a given destination. Such a communication network may be represented by a closed queueing network with a different routing chain for each (source, destination) pair. The number of customers in each routing chain is set equal to the limit to the number of messages which may be in transit between the given source and destination. Note that each routing chain typically visits only a small subset of the service centers.   △

The probability that a customer completing service in class c joins class d is p_{cd}, as before. The relative throughput of class c is y_c, as before. Though Eq.

(3.192) still holds, for computational purposes we should consider K such sets of linear equations of the form

$$y_c = \sum_{d \text{ in } \mathscr{K}_k} y_d p_{dc}, \quad c \text{ in } \mathscr{K}_k, \quad k = 1, \dots, K. \tag{3.238}$$

In each set one equation should be replaced by an equation of the form $y_c = a_k$, where a_k is a positive constant, to obtain a set of linearly independent equations. Let $y_{(k,j)}$ be the relative throughput of chain k customers at service center j; i.e.,

$$y_{(k,j)} = \sum_{c \text{ in } \mathscr{K}_k, c \text{ in } \mathscr{C}_j} y_c, \quad k = 1, \dots, K, \quad j = 1, \dots, J. \tag{3.239}$$

The mean service demand at class c remains $E[S_c]$. The mean service demand at service center j for a chain k customer is $E[S_{(k,j)}]$ where

$$E[S_{(k,j)}] = \frac{\sum_{c \text{ in } \mathscr{K}_k, c \text{ in } \mathscr{C}_j} y_c E[S_c]}{y_{(k,j)}}, \quad k = 1, \dots, K, \quad j = 1, \dots, J. \tag{3.240}$$

The relative service demand of class c is b_c, as before. Let the chain k relative service demand at service center j be

$$b_{(k,j)} = \sum_{c \text{ in } \mathscr{K}_k, c \text{ in } \mathscr{C}_j} b_c, \quad k = 1, \dots, K, \quad j = 1, \dots, J. \tag{3.241}$$

Let N_k, $k = 1, \dots, K$, be the number of customers of chain k, and let $\mathbf{N} = (N_1, \dots, N_K)$. Let $\mathbf{e}_k$, $k = 1, \dots, K$, be a vector with K dimensions with the kth element equal to one and all other elements equal to zero.

We will assume the same capacity functions as before, i.e., service capacity as a function of queue length independent of class or chain distinctions. See Section 3.8 for discussion of other capacity functions.

The product form solution for the distribution of the number of customers of each chain at the service centers is

$$P(\mathbf{n}_{(1)}, \dots, \mathbf{n}_{(J)}) = X_{(1)}(\mathbf{n}_{(1)}) \cdots X_{(J)}(\mathbf{n}_{(J)})/G(\mathbf{N}), \tag{3.242}$$

where $\mathbf{n}_{(j)}$ is a vector whose components are the number of customers of each chain at center j, the vectors of numbers of customers at the centers sum to $\mathbf{N}$, and

$$X_{(j)}(\mathbf{n}) = \frac{(n!/n_1! \cdots n_K!) b_{(1,j)}^{n_1} \cdots b_{(K,j)}^{n_K}}{\prod_{i=1}^{n} \mu_{(j)}(i)}, \quad \mathbf{n} = \mathbf{0}, \dots, \mathbf{N}, \tag{3.243}$$

where $\mathbf{n} = (n_1, \dots, n_K)$, n is the sum of the elements of $\mathbf{n}$, $\mathbf{0}$ is a vector with K dimensions with all elements equal to zero, and we assume the product in the denominator to be defined to be one when $n = 0$. The product form solution for the distribution of the number of customers at the classes is

$$P(n_1, \dots, n_C) = \frac{X_{(1)}(n_c \, \forall c \text{ in } \mathscr{C}_1) \cdots X_{(J)}(n_c \, \forall c \text{ in } \mathscr{C}_J)}{G(\mathbf{N})}, \tag{3.244}$$

where n_c is the number of customers at class c, the numbers of customers at the classes of chain k sum to N_k, $k = 1, \ldots, K$, and the factors $X_{(j)}(n_c \, \forall c$ in $\mathscr{C}_j)$ are defined by Eq. (3.200).

Note that, as before, the only parameters in these solutions are numbers of customers, relative service demands, and service capacities.

3.5.4   Computational Algorithms for Multiple Chain Networks

All of the algorithms of Section 3.5.2 extend to multiple chain closed networks. The discussion of programmable calculator implementations also extends, but we shall not further discuss such implementations explicitly. To summarize the notation we use in the computational algorithms, the following are the input parameters for service center j:

$y_{(k,j)}$:	chain k relative throughput,
$E[S_{(k,j)}]$:	chain k mean service demand,
$b_{(k,j)}$:	chain k relative service demand,
$\mu_{(j)}(n)$:	service capacity given n customers at center,
$m_{(j)}$:	number of servers.

For the cases where there are no classes belonging to both chain k and center j, our equations will still hold if we assume that the relative throughput, mean service demand, and relative service demand are all zero for that (k,j) pair. The same variables are used for class input parameters as in the single chain case. The following variables are the performance measures for chain k for service center j given the vector $\mathbf{N}$ of the number of customers of each chain in the network:

$\Lambda_{(k,j)}(\mathbf{N})$:	throughput,
$U_{(k,j)}(\mathbf{N})$:	utilization of each server,
$L_{(k,j)}(\mathbf{N})$:	mean queue length,
$R_{(k,j)}(\mathbf{N})$:	mean response time.

Where appropriate, the network vector of numbers of customers $\mathbf{N}$ will be left implicit. The same variables are used for class performance measures as in the single chain case, with $\mathbf{N}$ replacing N where $\mathbf{N}$ is made explicit.

a.   Convolution

Corresponding to the single chain case, $\mathbf{G}_j$ is a matrix with K dimensions which contains the summation over the first j service centers for each possible vector of numbers of customers $\mathbf{n}$, $\mathbf{n} = \mathbf{0}, \ldots, \mathbf{N}$, in those centers. $\mathbf{G}_1 = \mathbf{X}_1$ where $\mathbf{X}_1$ is a vector with K dimensions with elements defined by Eq. (3.243) with $j = 1$. For $j = 2, \ldots, J$,

$$G_j(\mathbf{n}) = \sum_{i_1 = 0}^{n_1} \cdots \sum_{i_K = 0}^{n_K} G_{j-1}(\mathbf{i}) X_j(\mathbf{n} - \mathbf{i}), \qquad \mathbf{n} = \mathbf{0}, \ldots, \mathbf{N}, \qquad (3.245)$$

where $\mathbf{X}_j$ is defined by Eq. (3.243). Let $\mathbf{G} = \mathbf{G}_J$, so that $G(\mathbf{N}) = G_J(\mathbf{N})$.

As before, simplifications are possible for some types of centers. We continue the previous assumptions about numbering of centers; i.e., service centers $1, \ldots, J'$ are IS service centers, service centers $J' + 1, \ldots, J''$ are single server fixed capacity service centers, and service centers $J'' + 1, \ldots, J$ have general capacity functions. For IS centers Eq. (3.243) simplifies to

$$X_{(j)}(\mathbf{n}) = \frac{(1/n_1! \cdots n_K!) b_{(1,j)}^{n_1} \cdots b_{(K,j)}^{n_K}}{(\mu_{(j)}(1))^n}, \qquad \mathbf{n} = \mathbf{0}, \ldots, \mathbf{N}, \qquad (3.246)$$

and if $J' > 0$ we can use

$$G_{J'}(\mathbf{n}) = \frac{1}{n_1! \cdots n_K!} \left(\sum_{j=1}^{J'} \frac{b_{(1,j)}}{\mu_{(j)}(1)} \right)^{n_1} \cdots \left(\sum_{j=1}^{J'} \frac{b_{(K,j)}}{\mu_{(j)}(1)} \right)^{n_K}, \qquad \mathbf{n} = \mathbf{0}, \ldots, \mathbf{N}, \tag{3.247}$$

rather than using Eq. (3.245). For single server fixed capacity centers Eq. (3.243) simplifies to

$$X_{(j)}(\mathbf{n}) = \frac{(n!/n_1! \cdots n_K!) b_{(1,j)}^{n_1} \cdots b_{(K,j)}^{n_K}}{(\mu_{(j)}(1))^n}, \qquad \mathbf{n} = \mathbf{0}, \ldots, \mathbf{N}, \qquad (3.248)$$

and Eq. (3.245) simplifies to

$$G_j(\mathbf{n}) = G_{j-1}(\mathbf{n}) + \sum_k \frac{b_{(k,j)}}{\mu_{(j)}(1)} G_j(\mathbf{n} - \mathbf{e}_k), \qquad (3.249)$$

$j = \max(2, J' + 1), \ldots, J'', \mathbf{n} = \mathbf{0}, \ldots, \mathbf{N}$, where the summation is taken over k such that $\mathbf{n} \geqslant \mathbf{e}_k$ (the relationship "$\geqslant$" between vectors is applied element by element). Analogous to our definition for products over empty ranges (defined to be one) we define sums over empty ranges, e.g., the above sum for $\mathbf{n} = \mathbf{0}$, to be zero.

As before, performance measures are obtained from the above quantities and $\mathbf{G}_{J-(j)}$. The chain k throughput of service center j is

$$\Lambda_{(k,j)} = y_{(k,j)} \frac{G(\mathbf{N} - \mathbf{e}_k)}{G(\mathbf{N})}, \qquad \mathbf{N} \geqslant \mathbf{e}_k, \quad k = 1, \ldots, K, \qquad (3.250)$$

and the center throughput $\Lambda_{(j)}$ is the sum of the chain throughputs. The joint queue length distribution for service center j is given by

$$\text{Prob}\{\mathbf{n}_{(j)} = \mathbf{i}\} = \frac{X_{(j)}(\mathbf{i}) G_{J-(j)}(\mathbf{N} - \mathbf{i})}{G(\mathbf{N})}, \qquad \mathbf{i} = \mathbf{0}, \ldots, \mathbf{N}, \qquad (3.251)$$

and the marginal queue length distributions are obtained by appropriate summations, e.g.,

$$\text{Prob}\{n_{(j)} = i\} = \sum_{|\mathbf{n}| = i} \text{Prob}\{\mathbf{n}_{(j)} = \mathbf{n}\}, \qquad i = 0, \ldots, N, \qquad (3.252)$$

and

$$\text{Prob}\{n_{(k,j)} = i_k\} = \sum_{n_k = i_k} \text{Prob}\{\mathbf{n}_{(j)} = \mathbf{n}\}, \qquad i_k = 0, \ldots, N_k. \qquad (3.253)$$

Equations (3.208) and (3.209) still hold (where N is taken to be the summation of the components of $\mathbf{N}$) and Eq. (3.210) still holds. The mean number of chain k customers at center j is

$$E[n_{(k,j)}] = \sum_{i=1}^{N_k} i\,\text{Prob}\{n_{(k,j)} = i\}. \qquad (3.254)$$

From Little's formula the mean response time for chain k customers at center j is

$$E[r_{(k,j)}] = E[n_{(k,j)}]/\Lambda_{(k,j)}. \qquad (3.255)$$

If service center j has an IS discipline, the mean number of chain k customers is also given by

$$E[n_{(k,j)}] = \Lambda_{(k,j)}E[S_{(k,j)}]/\mu_{(j)}(1). \qquad (3.256)$$

If service center j has a single fixed rate server, then the following simplifications are possible. If we define $G(\mathbf{i}) = 0$ if any element of $\mathbf{i}$ is less than zero, then

$$\text{Prob}\{n_{(k,j)} = i\}$$
$$= \frac{[b_{(k,j)}/\mu_{(j)}(1)]^i\{G(\mathbf{N} - i\mathbf{e}_k) - [b_{(k,j)}/\mu_{(j)}(1)]G(\mathbf{N} - (i+1)\mathbf{e}_k)\}}{G(\mathbf{N})},$$
$$(3.257)$$

$i = 0, \ldots, N_k$, $k = 1, \ldots, K$. The mean chain k queue length is

$$E[n_{(k,j)}] = \sum_{i=1}^{N_k} \frac{[b_{(k,j)}/\mu_{(j)}(1)]^i G(\mathbf{N} - i\mathbf{e}_k)}{G(\mathbf{N})}. \qquad (3.258)$$

If service center j has $m_{(j)}$ fixed rate servers then Eq. (3.215) still holds.

Performance measures for individual classes can be obtained from the above measures as follows. Assume that class c is part of service center j and chain k. The throughput of class c is

$$\Lambda_c = (y_c/y_{(k,j)})\Lambda_{(k,j)}. \qquad (3.259)$$

The queue length distribution for class c is given by

$$\text{Prob}\{n_c = i\} = \sum_{n_k = i}^{N_k} \frac{n_k!}{i!(n_k - i)!} \frac{b_c^i(b_{(j)} - b_c)^{n_k - i}}{b_{(j)}^{n_k}} \text{Prob}\{n_{(k, j)} = n_k\}, \qquad (3.260)$$

$i = 0, \ldots, N$. The mean queue length of class c customers is

$$E[n_c] = (b_c/b_{(k, j)})E[n_{(k, j)}]. \qquad (3.261)$$

Of course, Eq. (3.220), Little's formula, holds.

The program implementation for the multiple chain case closely parallels that of the single chain case. The primary difference is that the iteration over number of customers becomes iteration over vectors of numbers of customers. We shall not present a programlike definition for the multiple chain case.

b. Scaling

The scaling algorithm of Section 3.5.2b extends immediately to multiple closed chains with the following changes:

1. *For the purpose of scaling only*, $b_{(j)} = \sum_{k=1}^{K} b_{(k, j)}, j = 1, \ldots, J$.
2. N is interpreted as the sum of the components of $\mathbf{N}$.
3. The last statement of the algorithm becomes: Redetermine $\{y_{(k, j)}\}$, $\{b_c\}$, and $\{b_{(k, j)}\}$.

c. Mean Value Analysis

The equations for the single chain case are easily rewritten for the multiple chain case. For IS service centers Eq. (3.221) becomes

$$R_{(k, j)}(\mathbf{N}) = E[S_{(k, j)}]/\mu_{(j)}(1), \qquad k = 1, \ldots, K, \quad \mathbf{N} \neq \mathbf{0}. \qquad (3.262)$$

For single server fixed capacity service centers Eq. (3.222) becomes

$$R_{(k, j)}(\mathbf{N}) = \frac{E[S_{(k, j)}]}{\mu_{(j)}(1)}(1 + L_{(j)}(\mathbf{N} - \mathbf{e}_k)), \qquad k = 1, \ldots, K, \quad \mathbf{N} \geq \mathbf{e}_k. \qquad (3.263)$$

Equation (3.223) becomes

$$\Lambda_{(k, j)}(\mathbf{N}) = y_{(k, j)} \frac{N_k}{\sum_{i=1}^{J} y_{(k, i)} R_{(k, i)}(\mathbf{N})}, \qquad k = 1, \ldots, K, \quad j = 1, \ldots, J. \qquad (3.264)$$

Equation (3.224) becomes

$$L_{(k, j)}(\mathbf{N}) = \Lambda_{(k, j)}(\mathbf{N}) R_{(k, j)}(\mathbf{N}), \qquad k = 1, \ldots, K, \quad j = 1, \ldots, J. \qquad (3.265)$$

As in the single chain case, only mean values are required to obtain performance measures for IS and fixed capacity centers.

Let us use $P_{(j)}(i \,|\, \mathbf{N})$ for $\text{Prob}\{n_{(j)} = i\}$ in a network with vector of number of customers $\mathbf{N}$. For service centers with general capacity functions, Eq. (3.225) becomes

$$R_{(k,j)}(\mathbf{N}) = E[S_{(k,j)}] \sum_{i=1}^{N} \frac{i}{\mu_{(j)}(i)} P_{(j)}(i-1 \mid \mathbf{N} - \mathbf{e}_k), \qquad (3.266)$$

$k = 1, \ldots, K$, $\mathbf{N} \geqslant \mathbf{e}_k$. Equation (3.226) becomes

$$P_{(j)}(i \mid \mathbf{N}) = \frac{1}{\mu_{(j)}(i)} \sum_{k} E[S_{(k,j)}] \Lambda_{(k,j)}(\mathbf{N}) P_{(j)}(i-1 \mid \mathbf{N} - \mathbf{e}_k), \qquad (3.267)$$

$i = 1, \ldots, N$, where the summation is taken over k such that $\mathbf{N} \geqslant \mathbf{e}_k$. Equation (3.227) becomes

$$P_{(j)}(0 \mid \mathbf{N}) = 1 - \sum_{i=1}^{N} P_{(j)}(i \mid \mathbf{N}) \qquad (3.268)$$

[and fails numerically as $P_{(j)}(0 \mid \mathbf{N})$ tends to zero]. Equation (3.228) becomes

$$P_{(j)}(0 \mid \mathbf{N}) = \frac{\Lambda_{(k,i)}(\mathbf{N})}{\Lambda_{(k,i)}^{J-(j)}(\mathbf{N})} P_{(j)}(0 \mid \mathbf{N} - \mathbf{e}_k), \qquad (3.269)$$

where i is any service center other than j and any k such that $N_k > 0$ may be used.

The program implementation for the multiple chain case closely parallels that of the single chain case. The primary difference is that the iteration over number of customers becomes iteration over vectors of numbers of customers. In implementing MVA for multiple chains, storage may be prohibitive if iteration over numbers of customers is done in the obvious manner using nested loops, e.g.,

For $n_1 = 0$ to N_1

   For $n_2 = 0$ to N_2

      $\cdots$

      For $n_K = 0$ to N_K

      If $\mathbf{n} \neq \mathbf{0}$

         {Mean response times}

      $\cdots$

Rather, iteration over numbers of customers should be organized so that the sum of chain numbers of customers is nondecreasing, e.g.,

For $n = 1$ to N

   For $n_1 = \max(0, n - (N_2 + \cdots + N_K))$ to $\min(n, N_1)$

      For $n_2 = \max(0, n - (n_1 + N_3 + \cdots + N_K))$ to $\min(n - n_1, N_2)$

      $\cdots$

For $n_{K-1} = \max(0, n - (n_1 + n_2 + \cdots + n_{K-2} + N_K))$
$$\text{to } \min(n - (n_1 + \cdots + n_{K-2}), N_{K-1})$$
$n_K = n - (n_1' + \cdots + n_{K-1})$
{Mean response times}

$\cdots$

Using such an organization, only variables for total numbers of customers n and $n-1$ are needed; storage for variables with smaller total numbers of customers can be reused. We shall not present the rest of a programlike definition for the multiple chain case.

d. Local Balance Algorithm for Normalizing Constants

The equations for the single chain case are easily rewritten for the multiple chain case. Equation (3.230) becomes

$$G(\mathbf{n}) = \frac{\sum_{j=1}^{J} \sum_{k=1}^{K} \tilde{L}_{(k,j)}(\mathbf{n})}{n}, \qquad \mathbf{n} \neq \mathbf{0}. \tag{3.270}$$

For IS service centers Eq. (3.231) becomes

$$\tilde{L}_{(k,j)}(\mathbf{n}) = \frac{b_{(k,j)}}{\mu_{(j)}(1)} G(\mathbf{n} - \mathbf{e}_k), \qquad k = 1, \ldots, K, \quad \mathbf{n} \geqslant \mathbf{e}_k. \tag{3.271}$$

For single server fixed capacity service centers Eq. (3.232) becomes

$$\tilde{L}_{(k,j)}(\mathbf{n}) = \frac{b_{(k,j)}}{\mu_{(j)}(1)} (G(\mathbf{n} - \mathbf{e}_k) + \tilde{L}_{(j)}(\mathbf{n} - \mathbf{e}_k)), \qquad k = 1, \ldots, K, \quad \mathbf{n} \geqslant \mathbf{e}_k. \tag{3.272}$$

For service centers other than fixed capacity single server and IS, Eq. (3.233) becomes

$$\tilde{P}_{(j)}(i \mid \mathbf{n}) = \frac{1}{\mu_{(j)}(i)} \sum_{k} b_{(k,j)} \tilde{P}_{(j)}(i - 1 \mid \mathbf{n} - \mathbf{e}_k), \tag{3.273}$$

$i = 1, \ldots, n$, where the summation is taken over k such that $n_k > 0$. Equation (3.235) becomes

$$\tilde{L}_{(j)}(\mathbf{n}) = \sum_{i=1}^{n} i \tilde{P}_{(j)}(i \mid \mathbf{n}), \qquad \mathbf{n} \neq \mathbf{0}. \tag{3.274}$$

Equation (3.236) becomes

$$\tilde{P}_{(j)}(0 \mid \mathbf{n}) = G(\mathbf{n}) - \sum_{i=1}^{n} \tilde{P}_{(j)}(i \mid \mathbf{n}), \qquad \mathbf{n} \neq \mathbf{0}. \tag{3.275}$$

and the equation corresponding to Eq. (3.237) is

$$\tilde{P}_{(j)}(0 \mid \mathbf{n}) = G_{J-(j)}(\mathbf{n}), \qquad \mathbf{n} \neq \mathbf{0}. \tag{3.276}$$

The discussion of iteration over numbers of customers for MVA applies to LBANC as well. We shall not present the rest of a programlike definition for the multiple chain case.

As in the single chain case, it is straightforward to provide a hybrid LBANC–Convolution implementation where LBANC is used for the IS and fixed capacity centers and Convolution is used for the others.

3.6 Open Product Form Queueing Networks

An open network has a potentially unlimited number of customers. In this section we consider general open networks that have a product form solution in the sense that

$$P(\mathcal{S}_{(1)}, \ldots, \mathcal{S}_{(J)}) = \frac{P_{(1)}(\mathcal{S}_{(1)}) \cdots P_{(J)}(\mathcal{S}_{(J)})}{G}, \tag{3.277}$$

where $P(\mathcal{S}_{(1)}, \ldots, \mathcal{S}_{(J)})$ is the steady-state probability of a network state in a network with J service centers, $P_{(j)}(\mathcal{S}_{(j)}), j = 1, \ldots, J$, is a factor corresponding to the steady-state probability of the state of service center j in isolation, and G is a normalizing constant. The normalizing constant G is equal to the sum of $P_{(1)}(\mathcal{S}_{(1)}) \cdots P_{(J)}(\mathcal{S}_{(J)})$ over all feasible network states. Thus the sum of $P(\mathcal{S}_{(1)}, \ldots, \mathcal{S}_{(J)})$ over all feasible network states is equal to one. The state of a service center might be defined by the number of customers in the center or the number of customers of each type in the center. (More detailed definitions are also used, but we shall not consider them.)

EXAMPLE 3.31   Figure 3.34 is similar to the example of Fig. 3.30, but has no terminals. Rather, it has a source of arriving customers and a sink for departing customers. (Our figures use the same pentagonal symbol for both sources and sinks; the two are distinguished by the direction of associated arrows, out or in, respectively.) A computer system handling batch jobs may be more appropriately represented by an open network such as this than by a closed network. If a transaction oriented interactive system, e.g., a data base system, has hundreds of terminals, then an open network model such as this may be more

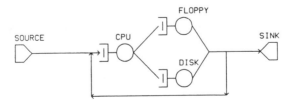

Fig. 3.34   Computer system model of Example 3.31.

practical than a closed network model. As before, a major deficiency of this model is that it does not consider memory contention.   △

EXAMPLE 3.32   Figure 3.35 depicts an open network model of a communication network organized in a ring. An arriving message (customer) goes through one or more communication links (service centers) to get to its

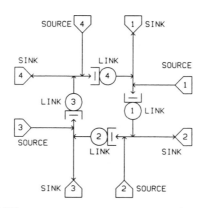

Fig. 3.35 Communication system model of Example 3.32.

destination. The origin of a message may be represented by a source in the queueing network and the destination may be represented by a sink. A message from origin 1 goes through link 1 to get to destination 2, through links 1 and 2 to get to destination 3, and through links 1, 2, and 3 to get to destination 4. A message from origin 2 goes through link 2 to get to destination 3, through links 2 and 3 to get to destination 4, and through links 2, 3, and 4 to get to destination 1. Messages from origins 3 and 4 behave similarly. In order to obtain a product form solution, the arrival processes are assumed to be Poisson. Further it is assumed, à la Kleinrock (1976), that transmission times for a given message at different links are independent. This is not an accurate assumption, since transmission times are usually determined primarily by message lengths, but simulation studies indicate that this assumption does not seem to affect model results for this network and many others. It is assumed that scheduling is FCFS and service demands are exponential.   △

As with closed product form networks, we allow service centers to have FCFS, PS, and IS queueing disciplines. With FCFS disciplines all classes at a service center must have the same exponential service demand distribution. At other centers there may be different service demand distributions for different classes at a center. All external arrival processes are assumed to be Poisson.

A quite remarkable result for open networks with product form solution is "Jackson's theorem," which we discuss in the next section. For networks with constant arrival rates, Jackson's theorem allows us, for most purposes, to examine service centers individually, largely ignoring the other service centers of the network. Thus computational effort is negligible and we shall not develop computational algorithms for the constant arrival rate case.

We next consider open product form networks with a single chain and constant arrival rates. As we shall discuss, multiple chains can be represented by a single chain in open networks with constant arrival rates. This is in contrast to multiple chains in closed networks. In Section 3.6.2 we consider single chain open networks with arrival rates dependent on the number of customers in the network. In both of these sections, the notation used is essentially the same as in Section 3.5.2, but a few additional variables are required.

3.6.1 Constant Arrival Rates

An open network consists of J service centers and C classes, as in a closed network. In addition, there are sources of arriving customers and sinks for departing customers. If a network has a single source and a single sink and if all classes are reachable from the source and the sink is reachable from all classes, then the network has a single open routing chain. It is not necessary, however, that all classes be reachable from each other.

Customer arrivals from the source form a Poisson process with rate λ. The probability an arriving customer goes to class c is p_{0c}. Note that we must have

$$\sum_{c=1}^{C} p_{0c} = 1. \qquad (3.278)$$

The probability a customer at class c goes to the sink is p_{c0}. The probability a customer at class c goes to class d is p_{cd}, as before. The equations for relative throughputs are

$$y_c = p_{0c} + \sum_{d=1}^{C} y_d p_{dc}, \qquad c = 1, \ldots, C. \qquad (3.279)$$

Note that the relative throughputs are uniquely determined by these equations because of the addition of p_{0c}. The definitions of Eqs. (3.193), (3.194), (3.195), and (3.196) are valid for open networks with the definition of y_c in Eq. (3.279). We assume that unless service center j has an IS discipline, in which case $\mu_{(j)}(n) = n\mu_{(j)}(1)$ for positive n, service center $j, j = 1, \ldots, J$, has a finite value $g_{(j)}$ associated with its capacity function such that $\mu_{(j)}(n) = \mu_{(j)}(g_{(j)})$ for $n \geq g_{(j)}$. These centers are referred to as "limited queue-dependent" centers because the capacity depends on the queue length, i.e., the number of customers at the center, only for queue lengths up to $g_{(j)}$. For single server fixed capacity centers $g_{(j)} = 1$. For limited queue-dependent centers we define

$$\rho_{(j)} = \lambda b_{(j)}/\mu_{(j)}(g_{(j)}). \tag{3.280}$$

An open network is stable if and only if $\rho_{(j)} < 1$ for all limited queue-dependent centers. We assume network stability in all that follows. Throughputs are given by

$$\Lambda_c = \lambda y_c, \qquad c = 1, \dots, C, \tag{3.281}$$

and

$$\Lambda_{(j)} = \lambda y_{(j)}, \qquad j = 1, \dots, J. \tag{3.282}$$

We shall find it notationally convenient to define

$$\tilde{\rho}_c = \lambda b_c, \qquad c = 1, \dots, C, \tag{3.283}$$

and

$$\tilde{\rho}_{(j)} = \lambda b_{(j)}, \qquad j = 1, \dots, J. \tag{3.284}$$

We shall find it convenient to define sums over empty ranges, e.g., from 1 to 0, to be zero and to define products over empty ranges to be one. The marginal queue length distribution for center j is given by

$$\text{Prob}\{n_{(j)} = q\} = \frac{\tilde{\rho}_{(j)}^q}{\prod_{i=1}^{q} \mu_{(j)}(i)} \text{Prob}\{n_{(j)} = 0\}. \tag{3.285}$$

For IS centers

$$\text{Prob}\{n_{(j)} = 0\} = \exp(-\tilde{\rho}_{(j)}/\mu_{(j)}(1)). \tag{3.286}$$

For single server fixed capacity centers

$$\text{Prob}\{n_{(j)} = 0\} = 1 - \rho_{(j)}. \tag{3.287}$$

For other limited queue-dependent capacity centers, i.e., $g_{(j)} > 1$,

$$\text{Prob}\{n_{(j)} = 0\} = \left[\frac{\mu_{(j)}(g_{(j)})}{\mu_{(j)}(g_{(j)} - 1)} \frac{1}{1 - \rho_{(j)}} \right. $$
$$\left. + \sum_{i=0}^{g_{(j)}-2} \tilde{\rho}_{(j)}^i \left(\frac{1}{\prod_{h=1}^{i} \mu_{(j)}(h)} - \frac{1}{\mu_{(j)}(g_{(j)} - 1)(\mu_{(j)}(g_{(j)}))^{i-1}} \right) \right]^{-1}. \tag{3.288}$$

Jackson's theorem states that we can use the last four equations for the factors in Eq. (3.277), with the normalizing constant chosen to be one. Alternately, we could use

$$\text{Prob}\{n_{(j)} = q\}/\text{Prob}\{n_{(j)} = 0\} \tag{3.289}$$

as the factors and let

$$G = \frac{1}{\text{Prob}\{n_{(1)} = 0\} \cdots \text{Prob}\{n_{(J)} = 0\}}. \tag{3.290}$$

This second choice of factors is more consistent with our treatment of closed networks and is more appropriate to the discussion of mixed networks (Section 3.7). We assume here, as in Section 3.5, that our primary interest is in performance measures for the service centers, not for the overall network. Thus we shall not further discuss Jackson's theorem per se.

For all centers

$$\text{Prob}\{n_c = q_c, c \text{ in } \mathscr{C}_j\} = \frac{q!}{\prod_{c \text{ in } \mathscr{C}_j} q_c!} \frac{\prod_{c \text{ in } \mathscr{C}_j} \tilde{\rho}_c^{q_c}}{\prod_{i=1}^{q} \mu_{(j)}(i)} \text{Prob}\{n_{(j)} = 0\}, \tag{3.291}$$

where $q = \sum_c q_c$. At IS service centers the utilization of each server is zero. For single server fixed capacity centers

$$U_{(j)} = \rho_{(j)}. \tag{3.292}$$

In general, at limited queue-dependent centers the utilization of each server is

$$U_{(j)} = \frac{\sum_{i=1}^{\infty} \min(i, m_{(j)})\text{Prob}\{n_{(j)} = i\}}{m_{(j)}}. \tag{3.293}$$

For IS service centers the mean queue length is

$$E[n_{(j)}] = \Lambda_{(j)} E[S_{(j)}]/\mu_{(j)}(1). \tag{3.294}$$

For single server fixed capacity centers

$$E[n_{(j)}] = \rho_{(j)}/(1 - \rho_{(j)}). \tag{3.295}$$

For other limited queue-dependent centers

$$E[n_{(j)}] = \tilde{\rho}_{(j)}\text{Prob}\{n_{(j)} = 0\}\left[\frac{\mu_{(j)}(g_{(j)})}{\mu_{(j)}(g_{(j)} - 1)} \frac{1}{(1 - \rho_{(j)})^2} \right.$$
$$\left. + \sum_{i=0}^{g_{(j)} - 2} i\tilde{\rho}_{(j)}^i \left(\frac{1}{\prod_{h=2}^{i+1} \mu_{(j)}(h)} - \frac{1}{\mu_{(j)}(g_{(j)} - 1)(\mu_{(j)}(g_{(j)}))^{i-1}} \right) \right]. \tag{3.296}$$

For class c belonging to service center j

$$E[n_c] = (\tilde{\rho}_c/\tilde{\rho}_{(j)})E[n_{(j)}]. \tag{3.297}$$

Of course, we can apply Little's formula to obtain

$$E[r_c] = (E[n_c]/\Lambda_c), \qquad c = 1, \ldots, C, \tag{3.298}$$

and

$$E[r_{(j)}] = E[n_{(j)}]/\Lambda_{(j)}, \qquad j = 1, \ldots, J. \tag{3.299}$$

We have assumed that there was a single routing chain in the open network. If there are K sources and the classes are partitioned into K disjoint subsets such that for $k = 1, \ldots, K$, all classes in subset k are reachable from source k and are not reachable from any other sources or any classes in any other subsets, then there are K open routing chains. The sink must be reachable from all classes.

In formulating a queueing network model it is often convenient to assume that there are multiple routing chains, as we did implicitly in the discussion of Example 3.32. However, for computational purposes it is desirable to represent multiple chains by a single aggregate chain. If we have K chains, each with a source with Poisson arrivals with constant rate λ_k, $k = 1, \ldots, K$, we can treat the K open chains as a single aggregate chain if we give that aggregate chain an arrival rate

$$\lambda = \sum_{k=1}^{K} \lambda_k \tag{3.300}$$

and where class c belonged to chain k in the original network, make the replacement

$$p_{0c} = (\lambda_k/\lambda)p_{0c}, \qquad c = 1, \ldots, C. \tag{3.301}$$

As we shall illustrate in the following, aggregation of open chains in this manner may also simplify description of the network.

EXAMPLE 3.32 (continued)   If we assume that there are four sources, and thus four chains, then we need six classes per center to describe the routing. For example, for service center 2 we need classes for (origin, destination) pairs $(2, 3)$, $(2, 4)$, $(2, 1)$, $(1, 3)$, $(1, 4)$, and $(4, 3)$. On the other hand, if we assume a single (aggregate) chain then we only need three classes per center, one for each possible destination. For example, for center 2 we need classes for destinations 3, 4, and 1. Let us assume that the mean time between message arrivals from each origin is 0.4 s. Then we could have four sources each with rate 2.5 customers per second or a single source with rate 10 customers per second. Let us assume each possible destination for a message is equally likely. The mean message length is 360 bits. Each link has a capacity of 2400 baud. Thus the mean service demand is 0.15 s. If we assume a single chain we can describe each class as a (center, destination) pair. Let class 1 be for (center, destination) pair $(1, 2)$, class 2 be for pair $(1, 3)$, class 3 be for pair $(1, 4)$, class 4 be for pair $(2, 3)$, etc. With the assumptions we have made, each class is equally likely to be entered on arrival, i.e., $p_{0c} = \frac{1}{12}$ for $c = 1, \ldots, 12$. For classes 1, 4, 7, and 10 $p_{c0} = 1$. $p_{cd} = 1$ for class pairs $(c, d) = (2, 4)$, $(3, 5)$, $(5, 7)$, $(6, 8)$, $(8, 10)$,

(9, 11), (11, 1), and (12, 2). All other routing probabilities are zero. From Eq. (3.279) the relative throughput for classes 1, 4, 7, and 10 is $\frac{1}{4}$, for classes 2, 5, 8, and 11 is $\frac{1}{6}$ and for classes 3, 6, 9, and 12 is $\frac{1}{12}$. The relative throughput for each center is then $\frac{1}{2}$ and the utilization at each center is $10 \times 0.5 \times 0.15 = 0.75$. Thus from Eq. (3.295) the mean queue length at each center is 3 and from Eq. (3.299) the mean response time at each center is 0.6 s. The mean response time for each message is a weighted sum of one, two, and three center mean response times, with each weight being $\frac{1}{3}$. Thus the mean response time for a message is 1.2 s.   △

3.6.2 *Arrival Rates Dependent on the Number of Customers in the Network*

The assumption that arrival rates are constant, independent of system state, may not be reasonable for some systems. One way to relax the constant rate assumption is to allow the arrival rate to depend on the current number of customers in the network. We restrict attention here to single chain networks. See Section 3.8 for references on multiple chain networks with arrival rates dependent on the numbers of customers in the network.

EXAMPLE 3.33 In a communication network, such as the one of Fig. 3.35, the arrival rates of messages may depend upon the congestion in the network. A user of the network may be less likely to send a message if he or she expects that there will be a long response time. Thus the arrival rate of messages decreases as the number of messages currently in the network increases. △

Let the arrival rate given the number of customers in the network n be $\lambda(n)$, $n = 0, \ldots, \infty$. We retain the same definitions of relative throughput, relative service demand, and mean service demand as in the previous section. Though it is not mathematically necessary, for practical application we must assume that there is a nonnegative finite integer a such that $\lambda(n) = \lambda(a)$ for $n \geq a$. $\lambda(a)$ may be zero. For computational purposes it is desirable to distinguish between the cases where $\lambda(a)$ is zero and where $\lambda(a)$ is positive.

In the first case, $\lambda(a) = 0$, we can define an equivalent closed network which has the same solution as the given open network. This is done by deleting the source and sink and adding a new service center, center 0, with $y_{(0)} = 1$, $E[S_{(0)}] = 1$, and $\mu_{(0)}(n) = \lambda(a - n)$, $n = 1, \ldots, a$, and letting the resulting closed network have population $N = a$. All of the performance measures involving centers 1 to J will be the same in the two networks.

For the remainder of this section we assume the second case, i.e., $\lambda(a) > 0$. The network will be stable if and only if

$$\lambda(a) b_{(j)} / \mu_{(j)}(g_{(j)}) < 1 \qquad (3.302)$$

for all limited queue-dependent centers. In all that follows we assume network stability. For convenience let us define

$$A(n) = \prod_{i=0}^{n-1} \lambda(i), \qquad n = 0, \ldots, \infty. \tag{3.303}$$

Let $G(n)$ be as defined in Section 3.5.2, e.g., by Eq. (3.201) and associated discussion, using our current definition of relative service demand $(b_{(j)})$ obtained from Eqs. (3.279), (3.193), (3.194), (3.195), and (3.196). Then for the network as a whole

$$\text{Prob}\{n = i\} = A(i)G(i)/G, \tag{3.304}$$

where

$$G = \sum_{n=0}^{\infty} A(n)G(n). \tag{3.305}$$

We can rewrite Eq. (3.305) as

$$\begin{aligned}
G &= \sum_{n=0}^{a-1} A(n)G(n) + \sum_{n=a}^{\infty} A(a)(\lambda(a))^{n-a}G(n) \\
&= \sum_{n=0}^{a-1} A(n)G(n) + \frac{A(a)}{(\lambda(a))^a}\left(\frac{1}{P(\phi \mid \lambda = \lambda(a))} - \sum_{n=0}^{a-1}(\lambda(a))^n G(n)\right),
\end{aligned} \tag{3.306}$$

where $P(\phi \mid \lambda = \lambda(a))$ is the probability the network would be empty if it had constant arrival rate $\lambda(a)$, as given by the product over $j = 1$ to J of probabilities the individual centers are empty [Eqs. (3.286), (3.287), and (3.288)]. Note that even though we may have used scaling to keep $G(n)$ from being too large for all n, $A(n)G(n)$ or G may be too large for floating point representation. It is possible to deal with this problem by rescaling the necessary values after $G(n)$ has been obtained for the necessary values of n. We can determine a value d such that $A(n)d^nG(n)$ is within range for the necessary values of n and then replace $G(n)$ by $d^nG(n)$. (We would also multiply relative throughputs and utilizations by d. If LBANC has been used, then we can replace the unnormalized mean queue lengths by $d^n\tilde{L}_{(j)}(n)$ for the necessary values of n.) Mean queue length is given by

$$L_{(j)} = \frac{\sum_{n=1}^{\infty} A(n)G(n)L_{(j)}(n)}{G} = \frac{\sum_{n=1}^{\infty} A(n)\tilde{L}_{(j)}(n)}{G}, \tag{3.307}$$

where, as in the discussion of LBANC, $\tilde{L}_{(j)}(n) = G(n)L_{(j)}(n)$. This suggests that LBANC may be most appropriate for use with number of customer dependent arrivals, especially when service centers are either single server fixed rate or IS. Equation (3.307) may be rewritten as

$$L_{(j)} = \frac{\displaystyle\sum_{n=1}^{a-1} A(n)\tilde{L}_{(j)}(n) + \frac{A(a)}{(\lambda(a))^a}\left(\frac{L_{(j)}(\lambda = \lambda(a))}{P(\phi \mid \lambda = \lambda(a))} - \sum_{n=1}^{a-1}(\lambda(a))^n \tilde{L}_{(j)}(n)\right)}{G} \tag{3.308}$$

where $L_{(j)}(\lambda = \lambda(a))$ is the mean queue length if the network had constant arrival rate $\lambda(a)$, obtained from Eq. (3.294), (3.295), or (3.296), as appropriate. Similarly, throughput is given by

$$\Lambda_{(j)} = \frac{\sum_{n=1}^{\infty} A(n)G(n)\Lambda_{(j)}(n)}{G} = \frac{\sum_{n=1}^{\infty} A(n)y_{(j)}G(n-1)}{G}. \tag{3.309}$$

Equation (3.309) may be rewritten as

$$\Lambda_{(j)} = \frac{\sum_{n=1}^{a-1} A(n)y_{(j)}G(n-1) + \frac{A(a)}{(\lambda(a))^a}\left(\frac{\Lambda_{(j)}(\lambda = \lambda(a))}{P(\phi|\lambda = \lambda(a))} - \sum_{n=1}^{a-1}(\lambda(a))^n y_{(j)}G(n-1)\right)}{G}. \tag{3.310}$$

Mean response times can then be obtained by Little's formula,

$$R_{(j)} = L_{(j)}/\Lambda_{(j)}. \tag{3.311}$$

For centers with fixed rate servers Eq. (3.213) can be used for utilizations. For general capacity function centers

$$U_{(j)} = \frac{\sum_{n=1}^{\infty} A(n)G(n)U_{(j)}(n)}{G} = \frac{\sum_{n=1}^{\infty} A(n)\tilde{U}_{(j)}(n)}{G}, \tag{3.312}$$

where $\tilde{U}_{(j)}(n) = G(n)U_{(j)}(n)$. Equation (3.312) can be rewritten

$$U_{(j)} = \frac{\sum_{n=1}^{a-1} A(n)\tilde{U}_{(j)}(n) + \frac{A(a)}{(\lambda(a))^a}\left(\frac{U_{(j)}(\lambda = \lambda(a))}{P(\phi|\lambda = \lambda(a))} - \sum_{n=1}^{a-1}(\lambda(a))^n \tilde{U}_{(j)}(n)\right)}{G}.$$

$$\tag{3.313}$$

3.7   Mixed Product Form Queueing Networks

A mixed network is one with both open and closed chains. The open chains are defined as in open networks and the closed chains are defined as in closed networks. (Closed and open networks are degenerate cases of mixed networks that have no open or closed chains, respectively). We shall restrict attention here to mixed networks with a single open chain with constant arrival rates. Let the open chain be numbered zero and let the closed chains be numbered from 1 to K. We assume the respective previous definitions of relative throughputs and relative service demands, obtained from Eqs. (3.192) and (3.279) as appropriate to the chain type, and from Eqs. (3.193), (3.194), (3.195), and (3.196), with the open chain definitions modified to allow zero as a chain index. We assume the open chain has arrival rate λ. Mixed network stability is defined by the same condition as for open networks, i.e., a mixed network is stable if and only if $\rho_{(j)} < 1$ for all centers other than IS centers. Note that closed chains do not affect the stability of mixed networks.

EXAMPLE 3.34 Suppose that our previously described interactive computer system must also support batch jobs as well as terminal users. These batch jobs may be submitted by terminal commands and/or by spooled devices

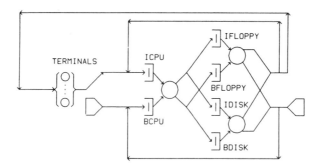

Fig. 3.36 Computer system model of Example 3.34.

such as a card reader. (Note that our queueing network models so far have ignored spooled devices such as card readers and line printers. Spooled devices will be considered in Section 8.3.) This batch load may be represented by adding an open chain to our network as in Fig. 3.36. △

The product form solution for the distribution of the number of customers of each chain at the service centers is

$$P(\mathbf{n}_{(1)}, \ldots, \mathbf{n}_{(J)}) = \frac{X_{(1)}(\mathbf{n}_{(1)}) \cdots X_{(J)}(\mathbf{n}_{(J)})}{G(N_1, \ldots, N_K)}. \tag{3.314}$$

Note the notation for the normalizing constant does not consider the number of open chain (chain 0) customers, just as in Section 3.6. In Eq. (3.314) $\mathbf{n}_{(j)}$ is a vector with $K + 1$ dimensions whose elements are the number of customers of each chain at center j, the numbers of chain k customers at the centers sum to $N_k, k = 1, \ldots, K$, and

$$X_{(j)}(\mathbf{n}) = \frac{(n!/n_0! \cdots n_K!)\tilde{\rho}_{(j)}^{n_0} b_{(1,j)}^{n_1} \cdots b_{(K,j)}^{n_K}}{\prod_{i=1}^{n} \mu_{(j)}(i)}, \tag{3.315}$$

where $\mathbf{n} = (n_0, \ldots, n_K)$, is any vector with nonnegative integer elements such that $n_k \leqslant N_k, k = 1, \ldots, K, n$ is the sum of the elements of $\mathbf{n}$ and we assume the product in the denominator to be defined to be one when $n = 0$. The product form solution for the distribution of the number of customers at the classes is

$$P(n_1, \ldots, n_C) = \frac{X_{(1)}(n_c \, \forall c \text{ in } \mathscr{C}_1) \cdots X_{(J)}(n_c \, \forall c \text{ in } \mathscr{C}_J)}{G(N_1, \ldots, N_K)}, \qquad (3.316)$$

where n_c is the number of customers at class c, the numbers of customers at the classes of chain k sum to $N_k, k = 1, \ldots, K$, and the factors $X_{(j)}(n_c \, \forall c \text{ in } \mathscr{C}_j)$ are defined by

$$X_{(j)}(n_c \, \forall c \text{ in } \mathscr{C}_j) = \frac{n_{(j)}! \prod_{c \text{ in } \mathscr{C}_j} (u_c^{n_c}/n_c!)}{\prod_{i=1}^{n_{(J)}} \mu_{(j)}(i)}, \qquad (3.317)$$

where $u_c = \tilde{\rho}_c$ if class c is in the open chain and $u_c = b_c$ if class c is in a closed chain, the number of customers at center j is $n_{(j)}$, and as before we assume the product in the denominator to be defined to be one when $n_{(j)} = 0$.

The open and closed chains of a mixed network have limited impact on each other. For the performance measures we consider we can continue to consider centers individually, except for normalizing constants and similar values, e.g., $\mathbf{G}_{J-(j)}$. All three computational algorithms can be applied to mixed networks. The basic approach is the same for all three, so we shall focus on the Convolution algorithm and indicate where MVA and LBANC require different steps.

The basic approach is to transform the mixed network to obtain a closed network which has the same closed chain performance measures as the mixed network. This closed network will have

$$X_{(j)}(\mathbf{n}) = \frac{(n!/n_1!, \ldots, n_K!) b_{(1,j)}^{n_1} \cdots b_{(K,j)}^{n_K}}{\prod_{i=1}^{n} \mu_{(j)}(i)} \alpha_{(j)}(n), \qquad \mathbf{n} = \mathbf{0}, \ldots, \mathbf{N}, \qquad (3.318)$$

where the vectors considered now have K dimensions instead of $K + 1$ dimensions, i.e., the open chain is not explicitly considered in the vectors of numbers of customers. For IS centers

$$\alpha_{(j)}(n) = \exp(\tilde{\rho}_{(j)}). \qquad (3.319)$$

For limited queue-dependent centers

$$\alpha_{(j)}(n) = \frac{\mu_{(j)}(g_{(j)})}{\mu_{(j)}(g_{(j)} - 1)} \frac{1}{(1 - \rho_{(j)})^{n+1}}$$

$$+ \sum_{i=0}^{g_{(j)}-2} \frac{(n+i)!}{i! n!} \tilde{\rho}_{(j)}^i \left(\frac{1}{\prod_{h=n+1}^{n+i} \mu_{(j)}(h)} - \frac{1}{\mu_{(j)}(g_{(j)} - 1)(\mu_{(j)}(g_{(j)}))^{i-1}} \right) \qquad (3.320)$$

for $n < g_{(j)} - 1$, and

$$\alpha_{(j)}(n) = 1/(1 - \rho_{(j)})^{n+1} \qquad (3.321)$$

for $n \geqslant g_{(j)} - 1$. Note that although Eq. (3.320) is not simple it is not significantly less complex without the closed chains ($n = 0$); i.e., it is of comparable complexity to the equations for the queue-dependent rate center in isolation. Convolution applies directly with these definitions. The normalizing constant G will be the same as the one in Eqs. (3.314) and (3.316). MVA and LBANC can be applied using the rate function

$$\mu'_{(j)}(n) = \mu_{(j)}(n)\alpha_{(j)}(n - 1)/\alpha_{(j)}(n). \tag{3.322}$$

For LBANC to give the same value of G as Eq. (3.214), one must start with

$$G(0) = \alpha_1(0) \cdots \alpha_M(0). \tag{3.323}$$

The open chain marginal queue length distribution is given by

$$\text{Prob}\{n_{(0,j)} = p\} = \tilde{\rho}^p_{(j)} \sum_{i=0}^{N} \frac{(p + i)!}{p!i!\alpha_{(j)}(i) \prod_{h=i+1}^{i+p} \mu_{(j)}(h)} P_{(j)}(i \,|\, \mathbf{N}),$$

$$p = 0, \ldots, \infty, \tag{3.324}$$

where i is the sum of the components of $\mathbf{i}$ and $P_{(j)}(i \,|\, \mathbf{N})$ is the closed network marginal distribution obtained by Eq. (3.252) for Convolution, by Eq. (3.267) for MVA and Eq. (3.273) and normalization for LBANC. The open chain mean queue length is given by

$$E[n_{(0,j)}] = \tilde{\rho}_{(j)} \sum_{i=0}^{N} \frac{(i + 1)\alpha_{(j)}(i + 1)}{\mu_{(j)}(i + 1)\alpha_{(j)}(i)} P_{(j)}(i \,|\, \mathbf{N}) \tag{3.325}$$

for limited queue-dependent centers, which simplifies to

$$E[n_{(0,j)}] = \frac{\rho_{(j)}}{1 - \rho_{(j)}} (1 + L_{(j)}(\mathbf{N})) \tag{3.326}$$

for constant rate centers. Of course, for IS centers

$$E[n_{(0,j)}] = \tilde{\rho}_{(j)}/\mu_{(j)}(1). \tag{3.327}$$

The following modifications should be made to the scaling algorithm of Section 3.5.4b. First, for the purpose of scaling only, $b_{(j)}$ is defined as in Section 3.5.4b; i.e., the open chain is not included. Second, in the expressions for P in Section 3.5.2b, replace $D \times b_{(j)}$ by $\tilde{\rho}_{(j)} + D \times b_{(j)}$, for all j.

EXAMPLE 3.34 (continued)   Let us suppose that the closed chain of Fig. 3.36 has the same parameters as in the network of Example 3.27. The mean service demands at the disk devices for the open chain must be the same as those of the closed chain since FCFS scheduling is assumed. Let us assume that 20% of the batch job disk accesses are to the floppy disk with the remainder going to the hard disk. The mean service demand at the CPU need not be the same for the open and closed chains since PS scheduling was assumed. Let the

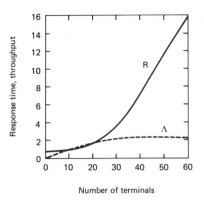

Fig. 3.37 Mean steady-state response time and throughput versus number of terminals for network of Example 3.34.

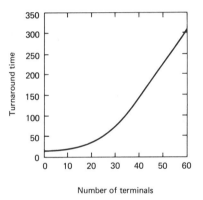

Fig. 3.38 Mean steady-state batch turnaround time versus number of terminals for network of Example 3.34.

mean batch job CPU service time per visit be 75 ms. and let the mean number of batch job CPU-I/O cycles be 100, so that the probability an open chain customer returns to the CPU after leaving an I/O device is 0.99. Figures 3.37 and 3.38 show mean interactive response time and throughput and mean batch job turnaround time, respectively, as functions of the number of terminals given batch job arrivals at the rate of 0.01 jobs per second. The CPU queue saturates (i.e., $\tilde{\rho}_{(j)} = 1$ for the CPU queue) at a batch arrival rate of 0.1333 jobs per second, regardless of the number of terminals. The batch job turnaround time is defined as the time from arrival to departure; the mean turnaround time can be obtained by summing the open chain mean queue lengths to get the mean number of batch jobs in the system and dividing by the arrival rate

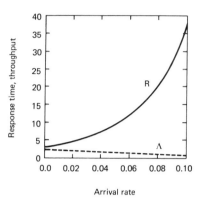

Fig. 3.39   Mean steady-state response time and throughput versus arrival rate for network of Example 3.34.

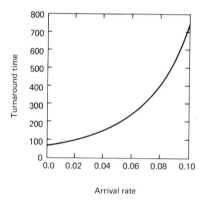

Fig. 3.40   Mean steady-state batch turnaround time versus arrival rate for network of Example 3.34.

(Little's formula). Figures 3.39 and 3.40 show mean interactive response time and throughput and mean batch job turnaround time, respectively, as functions of the batch arrival rate given 30 terminals in use.   △

3.8   Further Results for Product Form Queueing Networks

The product form results we have given apply to many other queueing disciplines, including two (LCFSPR and SIRO) that we have considered in previous sections, and a general class of disciplines known as "station balancing" disciplines. LCFSPR is allowed in product form networks exactly as PS is and yields the same values of PS for the performance measures we have considered. IS, PS, and LCFSPR are all examples of the station balancing disciplines defined by Chandy *et al.* (1977). SIRO is allowed in product form networks exactly as FCFS is and yields the same values as FCFS for the performance measures we have considered (Spirn, 1979).

In addition to the forms of state-dependence we have considered, i.e., service capacity dependent on total queue length and arrival rate dependent on number of customers in the network, generalizations of these forms and another form of state-dependence are allowed in product form networks.

Service capacity functions where the capacity available to each chain (class) depends on the number of customers of that chain (class) at the center are allowed in product form networks (Baskett *et al.*, 1975). Service capacity functions, where the capacity available to each chain (class) depends on the number of customers of each chain (class) at the center, are sometimes allowed in product form networks (Chandy *et al.*, 1975; Sauer, 1981). It is possible to construct capacity functions such that the service capacity at a service center depends on the number of customers in a subnetwork which contains that center, and to have that network be product form (Baskett *et al.*, 1975).

Arrival rate functions where the arrival rate for each chain depends on the number of customers of that chain in the network are allowed in product form networks (Baskett *et al.*, 1975). It is also possible to describe arrival rate functions with constraints on the number of customers in the network. The basic characteristic added by such functions is to allow chains that are in effect neither open nor closed. Rather, these chains are constrained to a range of feasible numbers of customers. Such chains can be considered to be open chains. Only slight revision of Section 3.6.2 is required to allow single chain networks with such functions. The full generality of such functions in multiple chain networks is addressed by Lam (1977).

There are two forms of state-dependent routing allowed in product form networks. One provided by Kobayashi and Reiser (1975) can be obtained by appropriate use of classes; Fig. 3.29 illustrates such use of classes. The other, provided by Towsley (1980), allows certain routing decisions dependent on the numbers of customers at service centers and in subnetworks containing those centers. It is very closely related to the generalization of capacity functions discussed above.

Extensions of all three computational algorithms (Convolution, MVA and LBANC) for all of these forms of state-dependence are given by Sauer (1981).

Certain minor efficiency improvements are possible for handling of limited queue-dependent service centers by considering queue lengths greater than $g_{(j)}$ collectively rather than individually. For discussion in regard to Convolution see Reiser (1977) and for discussion in regard to MVA and LBANC see Reiser and Lavenberg (1980) and Neuse and Chandy (1981). A queueing network analogue of Norton's theorem for electrical circuits (Chandy *et al.*, 1975) can be used to reduce computational effort in parametric studies of queueing networks. This theorem is much more important in approximate solution of nonproduct form networks. We discuss the theorem from that point of view in Chapter 4.

In product form networks with many closed chains and /or large numbers of customers in closed chains, the algorithms we have given may have prohibitive memory and computational requirements. For some such networks with "nice" properties, e.g., the customers of each chain visit only a small subset of the service centers, the "tree" version of the Convolution algorithm has dramatically lower memory and computational requirements (Lam and Lien, 1981). For other such networks, the approximate algorithms we discuss in Chapter 4 may be appropriate.

We have completely ignored the so called "operational analysis" approach to queueing models. This approach is based on assumptions about the deterministic behavior, over a finite time interval, of the system being modeled. No probabilistic assumptions are made. Using the operational approach, one can obtain the same product form solution for closed networks as discussed in Section 3.5, but with nonprobabilistic assumptions about the networks. Instead of obtaining the steady-state probability of a network state, one obtains the fraction of the time interval that the network is in a state. Except for these closed network results, the operational approach has not provided a significant alternative to the probabilistic approach we discuss. For further discussion of the operational approach, see Denning and Buzen (1978) and Sevcik and Klawe (1979).

3.9   Sources for Equations

In this section references are given for the equations contained in this chapter. Typically the equations are presented in this chapter in a different form and/or using a different notation from that in the references.

Section 3.3. General.   Many references for single service center queueing models give equations for the waiting time which does not include the service time rather than for the response time which includes the service time. If w denotes the waiting time than unless stated otherwise

$$E[r] = E[S] + E[w], \tag{3.328}$$

$$\text{Var}[r] = \text{Var}[S] + \text{Var}[w], \tag{3.329}$$

and

$$L_r(s) = L_S(s)L_w(s). \tag{3.330}$$

The mean and variance of r and n can always be obtained from $L_r(s)$ and $G_n(z)$, respectively, by differentiation [see Eqs. (2.100), (2.91), and (2.92)]. Thus, whenever $L_r(s)$ and $G_n(z)$ are given we do not give references for the mean and variance of r and n. The mean and variance of r and n can also be obtained directly from the probability distributions of r and n so that whenever these distributions are given we do not give references for the mean and variance. Furthermore, $E[r]$ and $E[n]$ are always related by Little's formula (see Section 2.3).

Section 3.3.3a. Equations (3.20) and (3.23) follow from Eqs. (5.100) and (5.86) in Kleinrock (1975). Equations (3.36) and (3.39) follow from Eqs. (5.119) and (3.23) in Kleinrock (1975). Equation (3.45) follows from Eq. (3.330) in Kobayashi (1978). Equation (3.42) is easy to derive but has not to our knowledge appeared elsewhere.

Section 3.3.3b. Equations (3.46) and (3.47) follow from Eqs. (3.37) on page 431 and (3.12) on page 421 in Cohen (1969). The equations in Cohen are for the waiting time rather than the response time.

Section 3.3.3c. Equation (3.51) is a special case of results for open networks presented in Section 3.6.1. Equations (3.54) and (3.55) follow from Eqs. (4.13) and (4.17) in Kleinrock (1976).

Section 3.3.3d. Equation (3.56) follows from the fact that the response time distribution for the LCFSPR queueing discipline is equal to the busy period distribution [see page 171 in Kleinrock (1976)] and from Eq. (1.91) in Kleinrock (1976) which gives the variance of the busy period.

Section 3.3.3e. Equations (3.59) and (3.60) follow from Eqs. (68) and (69) for the waiting time in Takacs (1964). Equations (3.65) and (3.66) follow from Eqs. (3.19), (3.20), (3.27), and (3.28) in Miller (1960). Equations (3.69) and (3.70) follow from Eqs. (1), (2), (5), (6), (10), and (11) in Gay and Seaman (1975).

Section 3.3.3f. Equations (3.73) and (3.76) follow from Eq. (3) and the expression for $\Psi(s)$ given in Theorem 4 in Welch (1964). Equation (3.75) can be obtained from Eq. (3.76) by differentiation.

Section 3.3.3g. Equations (3.89) and (3.92) follow from Eqs. (5)–(7) in Skinner (1967). Equation (3.91) can be obtained from Eq. (3.92) by differentiation.

Section 3.3.3h. Equation (3.98) follows from Eq. (8) for the waiting time in Lavenberg (1975). Equation (3.101) follows from results in Section 3.11.3 in Kobayashi (1978). Equations (3.94), (3.95), and (3.105) can be obtained using Eq. (3.101).

Section 3.3.3i. For exponential service times Eqs. (3.107) and (3.108) follow from Eqs. (3.11) and (3.12) for birth-death processes in Kleinrock

(1975). Equations (3.107) and (3.108) are also known to hold for general service times if the queueing discipline is PS or LCFSPR.

Section 3.3.3j.   Equation (3.118) follows from Eq. (4.49) in Kleinrock (1975).

Section 3.3.4.   Equations (3.119) and (3.122) follow from Eqs. (6.28) and (6.30) for the waiting time in Kleinrock (1975). Equation (3.125) follows from the discussion given after Eq. (6.28) in Keinrock (1975).

Section 3.3.5.   Equation (3.126) follows from Eq. (2.22) for the waiting time in Kleinrock (1976).

Section 3.3.6a.   Equation (3.130) follows from Eqs. (3.136) and (3.142) for the waiting time in Kobayashi (1978). Equation (3.134) follows from Eq. (3.37) in Kleinrock (1975).

Section 3.3.6b.   Equation (3.139) is a special case of results for open networks presented in Section 3.6.1.

Section 3.3.6c.   Equation (3.143) follows from Eq. (1.98) in Kleinrock (1976). Equation (3.146) follows from Eq. (1.74) in Kleinrock (1976). This equation is given in Kleinrock for the $M/M/m$ loss model but it also holds for the $M/G/m$ loss model.

Section 3.3.6d.   For exponential service times the results can be obtained from Eqs. (3.11) and (3.12) in Kleinrock (1975). The results are also known to hold for general service times if the queueing discipline is PS or if there is an infinite number of servers.

Section 3.3.7.   Equations (3.155) and (3.157) follow from Eqs. (2.73) and (2.72) for the waiting time in Kleinrock (1976). Equation (3.159) follows from the discussion on bounding the waiting time distribution given on the top of page 50 in Kleinrock (1976).

Section 3.3.8.   Equation (3.160) follows from Eq. (11) for the waiting time in Wolff (1977).

Section 3.3.9.   The first inequality in Eq. (3.162) follows from results on page 289 in Kleinrock (1976). The second inequality in Eq. (3.162) follows from Eq. (11) for the waiting time in Wolff (1977).

Section 3.4.1.   Equations (3.163)–(3.170) follow from Eqs. (3.152), (3.170)–(3.175), (3.178), and (3.187) in Kobayashi (1978). Equation (3.174) follows from our Eq. (3.169) and from Eqs. (4.4) and (4.7) in Chapter II of Jaiswal (1968).

Section 3.4.2.   Equations (3.177)–(3.180) follow from Eqs. (3.1), (3.3), and (3.4) in Reiser and Lavenberg (1980).

Sections 3.5, 3.6, and 3.7. General.   The organization of these sections does not correspond to the chronological appearance of the results in the literature, because of the close relationships between the material in these sections. The product form solution was first obtained for single chain open networks by Jackson (1963). Jackson's results could be interpreted in terms of closed networks by proper choice of arrival rate functions. Jackson did not consider a number of characteristics subsequently shown to result in the same product form solution. The most important generalization of Jackson's work is that of Baskett *et al.* (1975), which allowed multiple chains, queueing disciplines other than FCFS, nonexponential service demands, and most forms of state-dependent behavior currently known to result in the product form solution. The class notation we have used is due to Reiser (1977); it is much less cumbersome than the notation used by Baskett, Chandy, Muntz, and Palacios-Gomez. Further, relatively minor generalizations were provided by Chandy *et al.* (1977) and by Towsley (1980).

Computational algorithms have generally not been considered in the papers that presented and extended the product form solution. The Convolution algorithm is due to Buzen (1973). Generalizations of the Convolution algorithm are found in Chandy *et al.* (1975), Reiser and Kobayashi (1975), Towsley (1980), and Sauer (1981). A formal numerical analysis of the Convolution algorithm is given by Reiser (1977). Mean Value Analysis is due to Reiser and Lavenberg (1980). The modified MVA is found in Reiser (1981); extensions to MVA are given by Sauer (1981). LBANC is due to Chandy and Sauer (1980), with extensions by Sauer (1981).

Many of the equations we have presented follow immediately from the product form solution and/or appear in many of the above references. The most comprehensive sources for these sections are Sauer and Chandy (1981) and Sauer (1981). In the following we shall mainly pay attention to results that are especially important and/or appear in only a few other sources.

Section 3.5.2a.   All of these equations are fairly easily derived from the product form solution. Except for Eq. (3.203) and the class specific results, all of these equations are found in Buzen (1973) or follow directly from equations there. Equation (3.203) and the class specific results follow immediately from results in Reiser (1977).

Section 3.5.2b.   This scaling approach is due to Reiser (1977). It is based on constructing an open network corresponding to the given closed (or mixed) network. The algorithm forces NG to be less than the upper limit of floating point range, where G is the normalizing constant of Eq. (3.290). $G(N)$ must be less than G for any N. For further discussion see Sauer and Chandy (1981).

Section 3.5.2c.   Equation (3.226) follows from substituting Eq. (3.206) in Eq. (3.207). Equation (3.225) then follows from the definition of expected queue length and the application of Little's formula. Equation (3.222) is a simplified form of Eq. (3.225). Equation (3.228) also follows from Eqs. (3.206) and (3.207).

Section 3.5.2d. Equations (3.233) and (3.237) follow from Eq. (3.207). Equations (3.231) and (3.232) follow from Eq. (3.205).

Section 3.5.4a. Again, these equations largely follow directly from the product form solution. See Reiser (1977) and Sauer and Chandy (1981) for further discussion.

Section 3.5.4c. Unlike the single chain case, the primary equations (3.266) and (3.267) are derived independently. See Reiser and Lavenberg (1980) for their derivation. Otherwise the derivations follow the single chain case.

Section 3.5.4d. See Sauer and Chandy (1981) for derivations.

Section 3.6.1. These results all follow from the product form solution. Most of them are found in most of the above general references. In the derivation of Eq. (3.296) [and Eq. (3.288)], the following is useful:

$$\sum_{i=0}^{\infty} \frac{(n+i)!}{n!i!} p^i = \frac{1}{(1-p)^{n+1}}, \qquad |p| < 1, \quad n = 0, 1, 2, \dots . \quad (3.331)$$

This relationship follows from induction on n from the well-known special case for $n = 0$. It is also important for the mixed network derivations.

Section 3.6.2. The equations here follow directly from the product form solution, though some of the derivations are quite tedious.

Section 3.7. These equations also follow directly from the product form solution. The transformation from the mixed network to the corresponding closed network is obtained by summation over all possible numbers of customers in the open chain. Equation (3.331) is used in the transformation and in the open chain equation derivations. See Sauer and Chandy (1981) for further discussion.

References

Baskett, F., Chandy, K. M., Muntz, R. R., and Palacios-Gomez, F. (1975). Open, closed, and mixed networks of queues with different classes of customers, *J. Assoc. Comput. Mach.* **22**, 248–260.

Brown, R. M., Browne, J. C., and Chandy, K. M. (1977). Memory management and response time, *Comm. ACM* **20**, 153–165.

Buzen, J. P. (1973). Computational algorithms for closed queueing networks with exponential servers, *Comm. ACM* **16**, 527–531.

Chandy, K. M., and Sauer, C. H. (1980). Computational algorithms for product form queueing networks, *Comm. ACM* **23**, 573–583.

Chandy, K. M., Herzog, U., and Woo, L. S. (1975). Parametric analysis of queueing networks, *IBM J. Res. Develop.* **19**, 43–49.

Chandy, K. M., Howard, J. H., and Towsley, D. F. (1977). Product form and local balance in queueing networks, *J. Assoc. Comput. Mach.* **24**, 250–263.

Cohen, J. W. (1969). "The Single Server Queue." North-Holland Publ., Amsterdam.

Denning, P. J., and Buzen, J. P. (1978). The operational analysis of queueing network models, *Comput. Surveys* **10**, 225–261.

Gay, T. W., and Seaman, P. H. (1975). Composite priority queue, *IBM J. Res. Develop.* **19**, 78–81.

Hofri, M. (1980). Disk scheduling: FCFS vs SSTF revisited, *Comm. ACM* **23**, 645–653.

Jackson, J. R. (1963). Jobshop-like queueing systems, *Management Sci.* **10**, 131–142.

Jaiswal, N. K. (1968). "Priority Queues." Academic Press, New York.

Kleinrock, L. (1975). "Queueing Systems, Vol. 1, Theory." Wiley, New York.

Kleinrock, L. (1976). "Queueing Systems, Vol. 2, Computer Applications." Wiley, New York.

Kobayashi, H. (1978). "Modeling and Analysis: An Introduction to System Performance Evaluation Methodology." Addison-Wesley, Reading, Massachusetts.

Kobayashi, H., and Reiser, M. (1975). On Generalization of Job Routing Behavior in a Queueing Network Model. IBM Research Rep. RC-5252, Yorktown Heights, New York.

Lam, S. S. (1977). Queueing networks with population size constraints, *IBM J. Res. Develop.* **21**, 370–378.

Lam, S. S. (1982). Dynamic Scaling and Growth Behavior of Queueing Network Normalization Constants. *J. Assoc. Comput. Mach.* **29**, 492–513.

Lam, S. S., and Lien Y. L. (1981). A Tree Convolution Algorithm for the Solution of Queueing Networks, Technical Rep. TR-165. Dept. of Computer Sciences, Univ. of Texas, Austin, Texas; to appear in *Comm. ACM*.

Lassettre, E. R., and Scherr, A. L. (1972). Modelling the performance of OS/360 time sharing option (TSO), *In* "Statistical Performance Evaluation" (W. Freiberger, Ed.). Academic Press. New York.

Lavenberg, S. S. (1975). The steady-state queueing time distribution for the $M/G/1$ finite capacity queue, *Management Sci.* **21**, 501–506.

Miller, R. G. (1960). Priority queues, *Ann. of Math. Statist.* **37**, 86–103.

Neuse, D., and Chandy, K. M. (1981). SCAT: a heuristic algorithm for queueing network models of computing systems, *Performance Eval. Rev.* **10**, 59–79.

Reiser, M., and Kobayashi, H. (1975). Queueing networks with multiple closed chains: Theory and computational algorithms, *IBM J. Res. Develop.* **19**, 283–294.

Reiser, M. (1977). Numerical methods in separable queueing networks, *Stud. Management Sci.* **7**, 113–142.

Reiser, M. (1981). Mean-value analysis and convolution method for queue-dependent servers in closed queueing networks, *Performance Eval.* **1**, 7–18.

Reiser, M., and Lavenberg, S. S. (1980). Mean-value analysis of closed multichain queueing networks, *J. Assoc. Comput. Mach.* **27**, 313–322.

Reiser, M., and Sauer, C. H. (1978). Queueing network models: Methods of solution and their program implementation, "Current Trends in Programming Methodology, Vol. III, Software Modeling and Its Impact on Performance," pp. 115–167. (K. M. Chandy and R. T. Yeh, ed.), Prentice-Hall, Englewood Cliffs, New Jersey.

Sakata, M., Noguchi, S., and Oizumi, J. (1971). An analysis of the $M/G/1$ queue under round-robin scheduling, *Oper. Res.* **19**, 371–385.

Sauer, C. H. (1981). Computational Algorithms for State-Dependent Queueing Networks, IBM Research Rep. RC-8698, Yorktown Heights, New York; to appear in *ACM Trans. Computer Systems*.

Sauer, C. H., and Chandy, K. M. (1981). "Computer Systems Performance Modeling". Prentice-Hall, Englewood Cliffs, New Jersey.

Sevcik, K. C., and Klawe, M. M. (1979). Operational analysis versus stochastic modelling of computer systems, *Proc. Comput. Sci. Statist. Ann. Symp. Interface, 12th.* Univ. of Waterloo, Ontario.

Skinner, C. E. (1967). A priority queueing system with server-walking time, *Oper. Res.* **15**, 278–285.

Spirn, J. R. (1979). Queueing networks with random selection for service, *IEEE T-SE* **5**, 287–289.

Takacs, L. (1964). Priority queues, *Oper. Res.* **12**, 63–74.

Towsley, D. F. (1980). Queueing network models with state-dependent routing, *J. Assoc. Comput. Mach.* **27**, 323–337.

Welch, P. D. (1964). On a generalized $M/G/1$ queueing process in which the first customer of each busy period receives exceptional service, *Oper. Res.* **12**, 736–752.

Wolff, R. W. (1977). An upper bound for multichannel queues, *J. Appl. Probab.* **14**, 884–888.

4

Approximate Analysis of Queueing Networks

Stephen S. Lavenberg and Charles H. Sauer

4.1 Introduction

In Sections 3.5–3.8 exact analytical results were presented for queueing networks that have a product form solution. (A familiarity with Chapter 3, particularly Sections 3.5–3.8, will be useful in understanding this chapter.) In addition, computational algorithms were given which make it possible to efficiently compute performance measures for these networks. These networks have been widely applied in performance modeling due to their computational tractability. In this chapter we consider the approximate analysis of queueing networks for which either exact analytical results are not available or if they are available the computation of performance measures is prohibitively expensive. This is typically the case for queueing networks that do not have a product form solution. There are many features of systems whose representation in queueing networks results in networks that do not have a product form solution. These include simultaneous possession of more than one resource by a customer (e.g., simultaneous possession of memory and a processor or of a disk and a channel), priority scheduling disciplines, and finite buffers which cause blocking or losses. Furthermore, networks that have chain dependent exponential service demand distributions at FCFS service centers or general service demand distributions at FCFS service centers do not have a product form solution. In addition, the computation of performance measures for queueing networks that have a product form solution can become prohibitively expensive if there are many closed chains and large numbers of customers in the chains. This is because the storage and number of computations required grows at least as fast as the product of the number of customers in each chain.

The approximate analysis of queueing networks is an area of continuing research activity. However, several approaches have evolved which appear to be practically useful and we shall cover some of these in this chapter. One difficulty with approximate analysis techniques is that it is not yet possible to put useful bounds on the errors in the computed performance measures introduced by the approximate analysis. However, for the methods we cover, numerical comparisons have been made between the approximate performance measures and either exact analysis results in special cases or simulation estimates in more general cases. For some methods it is clear that further assessment is required, but all the methods presented appear promising. It should be emphasized that the errors to which we refer are analysis errors, i.e., differences between the exact and approximate performance measures for the model. They are not modeling errors, i.e., differences between the exact performance measures for the model and the system. Analysis errors of a few percent in utilizations and throughputs and of up to 20% in mean response times are quite tolerable for purposes such as discarding very bad system designs and capacity planning. Furthermore, such analysis errors are also tolerable considering the errors introduced by the modeling process itself; i.e., the model is an abstraction of the system and the values of input parameters for the model may be rough estimates.

In Sections 4.2 and 4.3 we shall present two main approaches that have been developed for the approximate analysis of queueing networks. The approach in Section 4.2 involves the heuristic development of equations similar to those of the Mean Value Analysis algorithm for product form queueing networks (see Sections 3.5.2c and 3.5.4c). The approach in Section 4.3 involves decomposing a model into submodels, analyzing the submodels (either exactly or approximately), and then using the submodel solutions to construct an overall model solution. In Section 4.4 we shall present a method that has been developed to approximately analyze open queueing network models of disk systems. Finally, in Section 4.5 we shall briefly discuss other methods for open networks.

4.2   Mean Value Analysis Methods

4.2.1   Closed Product Form Networks

In Sections 3.5.2 and 3.5.4 we presented computational algorithms that make it possible to efficiently compute performance measures for closed product form queueing networks. The number of multiplications and the number of additions required by these algorithms are each at least as large as

$$JK \prod_{k=1}^{K} (1 + N_k) \qquad (4.1)$$

and the number of storage locations required is at least as large as

$$\prod_{k=1}^{K} (1 + N_k) \qquad (4.2)$$

where we have used the notation

J: number of service centers,
K: number of routing chains,
N_k: number of customers in chain k.

(We use the same notation for closed multiple chain queueing networks as was used in Section 3.5. A familiarity with Sections 3.5.1, 3.5.2c, 3.5.3, and 3.5.4c is essential to understanding Section 4.2.) For some applications the number of chains and the number of customers in each chain are so large that the time and storage requirements make the use of these algorithms prohibitively expensive.

EXAMPLE 4.1   Consider a closed product form queueing network model of an interactive computer system such as the network shown in Fig. 3.33 in which different types of interactive users are represented by customers in different routing chains. (In general there will be more than two I/O devices represented in the model.) When the system being modeled has several types of users and a large number of users of each type the time or space requirements of the computational algorithms may be excessive. For example, the Mean Value Analysis algorithm described in Section 3.5.4c was implemented in APL and run under VS APL on an IBM 370/168. The execution time to compute performance measures for a network with $J = 4$ service centers, $K = 2$ routing chains, $N_1 = 200$ customers, and $N_2 = 100$ customers was approximately 200 s. If the number of customers in each chain were doubled the execution time would increase by a factor of approximately 4. It is unlikely that one would be willing to spend over 10 min. of CPU time computing performance measures for so simple a model. Typically, one wishes to compute performances in at most a few seconds. △

EXAMPLE 4.2 A packet switching store and forward communication network using a virtual channel window flow control mechanism can be modeled as a closed multiple chain queueing network with one chain for each virtual channel. A virtual channel consists of a sequence of physical channels that connect a packet source to a packet sink. A physical channel is modeled by a FCFS single server fixed capacity service center if the channel is half duplex and by two such service centers if it is full duplex. A source or a sink is also modeled by such a service center. The acknowledgment delay for a packet (time for an acknowledgment to travel from the sink to the source) is modeled by an IS service center. The number of customers in a routing chain is equal to the window size of the virtual channel, i.e., the maximum number of packets allowed on the virtual channel. Customers in a routing chain repeatedly visit in sequence service centers representing the source, the sequence of physical channels that comprise the virtual channel, the sink, and the acknowledgment delay. A portion of such a queueing network model is shown in Fig. 4.1. Two of the routing chains are shown. When more than one chain visit a service center separate waiting lines, representing the separate classes, are shown in the

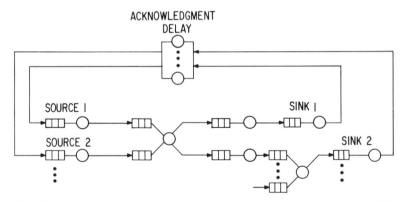

Fig. 4.1 Portion of a queueing network model of a window flow controlled communication network.

figure. (Classes are discussed in Section 3.5.) Note that while the source nodes and sink nodes are represented in the queueing network, the intermediate processor nodes are not represented (intermediate processing delays are assumed to be negligible) nor is the effect of finite buffers in the intermediate nodes represented. A more detailed discussion of this model and its limitations is given in Reiser (1979).

In order for such a queueing network to have a product form solution it is necessary to assume that (1) the packet lengths of a given packet at each physical channel are independent random variables [for a further discussion of this independence assumption see Kleinrock (1976)], (2) all packet lengths are exponentially distributed, and (3) the mean packet lengths for all virtual channels that use the same physical channel are identical. These assumptions are required since service demands at different service centers must be independent random variables and if a service center has a FCFS queueing discipline all service demands at the service center must have the same exponential distribution. [We discuss the approximate analysis of networks in which assumption (3) is relaxed in Section 4.2.2.] For communication networks with dozens of virtual channels the computation of performance measures using the algorithms of Chapter 3 is prohibitively expensive even for small window sizes. △

In the above examples it is desirable to quickly compute reasonably accurate approximations for performance measures instead of computing exact performance measures. We shall next present Mean Value Analysis methods for doing this when, as is the case in the above examples, the network has only single server fixed capacity service centers and IS service centers. Methods for handling networks which include service centers with general capacity functions are not yet fully developed.

Equations (3.262)–(3.265) are the Mean Value Analysis equations for a network that has only single server fixed capacity and IS service centers. We assume that service centers are numbered so that centers $1, \ldots, J'$ are IS and centers $J' + 1, \ldots, J$ are single server fixed capacity. We allow $J' = 0$ but do not allow $J' = J$ since if $J' = J$; i.e., all service centers are IS, Eqs. (3.262), (3.264), and (3.265) can be used to trivially obtain $R_{(k,j)}(\mathbf{N})$, $\Lambda_{(k,j)}(\mathbf{N})$, and $L_{(k,j)}(\mathbf{N})$. For convenience we let $\mu_{(j)}(1) = 1$, so that the service demand $S_{(k,j)}$ equals the service time. It follows from Eqs. (3.262)–(3.265) that for $k = 1, \ldots, K$

$$R_{(k,j)}(\mathbf{N}) = E[S_{(k,j)}], \qquad\qquad j = 1, \ldots, J', \quad \mathbf{N} \geqslant \mathbf{e}_k, \qquad (4.3)$$

$$R_{(k,j)}(\mathbf{N}) = E[S_{(k,j)}](1 + L_{(j)}(\mathbf{N} - \mathbf{e}_k)), \quad j = J' + 1, \ldots, J, \quad \mathbf{N} \geqslant \mathbf{e}_k, \qquad (4.4)$$

$$L_{(k,j)}(\mathbf{N}) = N_k \frac{y_{(k,j)} R_{(k,j)}(\mathbf{N})}{\sum_{i=1}^{J} y_{(k,i)} R_{(k,i)}(\mathbf{N})}, \qquad j = 1, \ldots, J, \qquad (4.5)$$

where we have combined Eqs. (3.264) and (3.265) to obtain Eq. (4.5). [If $N_k = 0$ then we let $R_{(k,j)}(\mathbf{N}) = 0$. If chain k does not visit service center j then we let $E[S_{(k,j)}] = 0$ and $y_{(k,j)} = 0$. If service center j, $J' + 1 \leqslant j \leqslant J$, has a FCFS queueing discipline then Eq. (4.4) only holds if $E[S_{(k,j)}]$ does not depend on k for all chains that visit service center j.]

Note that Eq. (4.4) involves the mean queue length with one less customer in chain k. Thus, in order to compute performance measures for a given $\mathbf{N}$ using these equations it is necessary to recursively compute performance measures for all $\mathbf{n} \leqslant \mathbf{N}$. Several authors have suggested ways to approximate

$$L_{(j)}(\mathbf{N} - \mathbf{e}_k) = \sum_{l=1}^{K} L_{(l,j)}(\mathbf{N} - \mathbf{e}_k) \qquad (4.6)$$

and thus avoid this recursive computation. We next present one of these approximations, which we have chosen because of its simplicity and reasonable accuracy and also because it has been used as part of a more complex and more accurate approximation method which we shall also present.

a. Simple Method

The following approximation was given in Schweitzer (1979). For $j = J' + 1, \ldots, J$

$$L_{(l,j)}(\mathbf{N} - \mathbf{e}_k) = L_{(l,j)}(\mathbf{N}), \qquad l \neq k, \qquad (4.7)$$

and

$$L_{(k,j)}(\mathbf{N} - \mathbf{e}_k) = \frac{(N_k - 1)}{N_k} L_{(k,j)}(\mathbf{N}). \qquad (4.8)$$

It has the following interpretation. Divide both sides of Eq. (4.7) by N_l and divide both sides of Eq. (4.8) by $N_k - 1$ so that both sides of these equations give the mean fraction of a chain's customers in service center j. The approximation states that these fractions do not change if there is one less chain k customer in the network. Substituting Eqs. (4.7) and (4.8) into Eq. (4.6) yields an approximation for $L_{(j)}(\mathbf{N} - \mathbf{e}_k)$ which when substituted into Eq. (4.4) yields the approximation

$$R_{(k,j)}(\mathbf{N}) = E[S_{(k,j)}]\left(1 + L_{(j)}(\mathbf{N}) - \frac{L_{(k,j)}(\mathbf{N})}{N_k}\right), \qquad j = J' + 1, \ldots, J. \quad (4.9)$$

Equations (4.9) and (4.5) are simultaneous nonlinear equations in the unknowns $R_{(k,j)}(\mathbf{N}), k = 1, \ldots, K, j = J' + 1, \ldots, J$, and $L_{(k,j)}(\mathbf{N}), k = 1, \ldots, K$, $j = 1, \ldots, J$. [$R_{(k,j)}(\mathbf{N})$ is known and equals $E[S_{(k,j)}]$ for $j = 1, \ldots, J'$.] These $K(2J - J')$ equations in as many unknowns can be reduced in a fairly straightforward way to K equations in K unknowns. We next present the resulting equations. Let $j(k)$ be a designated service center visited by chain k and for $k = 1, \ldots, K$ let

$$a_{kj} = E[S_{(k,j)}]y_{(k,j)}/y_{(k,j(k))}, \qquad j = 1, \ldots, J, \tag{4.10}$$

$$b_k = \sum_{j=1}^{J'} a_{kj}, \tag{4.11}$$

$$x_k = \Lambda_{(k,j(k))}(\mathbf{N}). \tag{4.12}$$

The K unknowns are x_k, $k = 1, \ldots, K$, where x_k is the approximate chain k throughput at the designated service center $j(k)$, and they satisfy the following simultaneous nonlinear equations:

$$N_k = x_k \left[b_k + \sum_{j=J'+1}^{J} \frac{a_{kj}}{\left(1 + \dfrac{a_{kj}x_k}{N_k}\right)\left[1 - \sum_{l=1}^{K} \dfrac{a_{lj}x_l}{1 + (a_{lj}x_l/N_l)}\right]} \right],$$

$$k = 1, \ldots, K. \tag{4.13}$$

The quantity $a_{lj}x_l$ is the approximate chain l utilization of service center j. The vector $\mathbf{x} = (x_1, \ldots, x_K)$ is said to be a feasible solution of Eq. (4.13) if $x_k > 0$, $k = 1, \ldots, K$, and if

$$\sum_{l=1}^{K} a_{lj}x_l \leqslant 1, \qquad j = J' + 1, \ldots, J. \tag{4.14}$$

Equation (4.14) restricts the approximate utilization of each single server fixed capacity service center to be no greater than one. It can be shown that Eq. (4.13) has at least one feasible solution. There are many algorithms to numerically solve simultaneous nonlinear equations (e.g., see Ortega and Reinboldt, 1970). Rather than writing a program to implement one of these algorithms it is recommended that Eq. (4.13) be solved using an existing well-tested program. An example is the FORTRAN program Minpack-1 described in Moré *et al.* (1980) and available from Argonne National Laboratory or IMSL. Once the solution $\mathbf{x}$ has been obtained approximate values of the other performance measures can be obtained as follows:

$$\Lambda_{(k,j)}(\mathbf{N}) = x_k y_{(k,j)}/y_{(k,j(k))}, \qquad\qquad j = 1, \ldots, J, \tag{4.15}$$

$$L_{(k,j)}(\mathbf{N}) = \Lambda_{(k,j)}(\mathbf{N})E[S_{(k,j)}], \qquad\qquad j = 1, \ldots, J', \tag{4.16}$$

$$L_{(k,j)}(\mathbf{N}) = \frac{a_{kj}x_k}{\left(1 + \dfrac{a_{kj}x_k}{N_k}\right)\left[1 - \sum_{l=1}^{K}\dfrac{a_{lj}x_l}{1 + (a_{lj}x_l/N_l)}\right]}, \qquad j = J'+1, \ldots, J,$$

$$\tag{4.17}$$

$$R_{(k,j)}(\mathbf{N}) = L_{(k,j)}(\mathbf{N})/\Lambda_{(k,j)}(\mathbf{N}), \qquad\qquad j = J' + 1, \ldots, J. \tag{4.18}$$

Reports on the extensive use of this approximation method can be found in Bard (1980) and Chandy and Neuse (1981). Rather than reducing the $K(2J - J')$ equations in (4.9) and (4.5) to the K equations in (4.13) and then numerically solving Eq. (4.13), Eqs. (4.9) and (4.5) are numerically solved in these papers. In both papers the equations are solved using the method of successive approximation, e.g., substitute estimates for the $L_{(k,j)}(\mathbf{N})$ into Eq. (4.9) and then compute the next estimates for the $L_{(k,j)}(\mathbf{N})$ using Eq. (4.5). Continue to iterate in this manner until the successive estimates are sufficiently close. Equation (4.5) guarantees that at each iteration the sum over j of the estimates for the $L_{(k,j)}(\mathbf{N})$ is equal to N_k. Although the papers did not report any convergence problems using successive approximation, the method is not guaranteed to converge and convergence can in general be quite slow.

Bard (1980) has applied the approximation method to hundreds of networks and reported that "results are generally within 5 percent of the exact solution." Chandy and Neuse (1982) have applied the method to both randomly selected networks and networks chosen to stress the approximation.

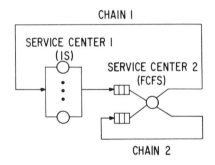

Fig. 4.2 Network for which the simple approximation gives large errors.

Of the more than 70 networks they considered the largest error occurred for the network with two routing chains shown in Fig. 4.2. Chain 1 customers cyclically visit service centers 1 and 2 and chain 2 customers only visit service center 2. There are $N_1 = 8$ chain 1 customers, $N_2 = 1$ chain 2 customers, and $E[S_{(1,1)}] = 8, E[S_{(1,2)}] = E[S_{(2,2)}] = 1$. Large errors occurred in approximating $R_{(2,2)}$, the mean chain 2 response time at service center 2, and $A_{(2,2)}$, the chain 2 throughput at service center 2. The relative errors [relative error in percent = $100 \cdot$ (approximate value $-$ exact value)/exact value] were 35% for $R_{(2,2)}$ and -26% for $A_{(2,2)}$. These large errors occur because decreasing the number of chain 2 customers by one, i.e., from one to zero, has a substantial effect on the mean number of chain 1 customers at service center 2, in contradiction to the assumption in Eq. (4.7). Thus, large errors can occur using the method. However, the method worked well on most networks tested.

b. More Complex Method

The above simple approximation method is based on the assumption that the mean fractions of each chain's customers in each of the single server fixed capacity service centers do not change if there is one less customer in the network. Let $\delta_{ljk}(\mathbf{N})$ denote the actual change in these fractions, i.e., for $j = J' + 1, \ldots, J$

$$\delta_{ljk}(\mathbf{N}) = \begin{cases} (L_{(l,j)}(\mathbf{N} - \mathbf{e}_k)/N_l) - L_{(l,j)}(\mathbf{N})/N_l, & l \neq k, \\ (L_{(k,j)}(\mathbf{N} - \mathbf{e}_k)/(N_k - 1)) - L_{(k,j)}(\mathbf{N})/N_k, & l = k. \end{cases} \quad (4.19)$$

We assume for the time being that the $\delta_{ljk}(\mathbf{N})$ are known. It follows from Eq. (4.19) that for $j = J' + 1, \ldots, J$

$$L_{(l,j)}(\mathbf{N} - \mathbf{e}_k) = L_{(l,j)}(\mathbf{N}) + N_l \delta_{ljk}(\mathbf{N}), \quad l \neq k, \quad (4.20)$$

and

$$L_{(k,j)}(\mathbf{N} - \mathbf{e}_k) = \frac{N_k - 1}{N_k} L_{(k,j)}(\mathbf{N}) + (N_k - 1)\delta_{kjk}(\mathbf{N}). \quad (4.21)$$

Substituting Eqs. (4.20) and (4.21) into Eq. (4.6) yields an expression for $L_{(j)}(\mathbf{N} - \mathbf{e}_k)$ which when substituted into Eq. (4.4) yields

$$R_{(k,j)}(\mathbf{N}) = E[S_{(k,j)}]\left(1 + L_{(j)}(\mathbf{N}) - \frac{L_{(k,j)}(\mathbf{N})}{N_k}\right.$$

$$\left. + \sum_{l=1}^{K} N_l \delta_{ljk}(\mathbf{N}) - \delta_{kjk}(\mathbf{N}) \right), \quad j = J' + 1, \ldots, J. \quad (4.22)$$

Equations (4.22) and (4.5) are simultaneous nonlinear equations in the unknowns $R_{(k,j)}(\mathbf{N}), k = 1, \ldots, K, j = J' + 1, \ldots, J$, and $L_{(k,j)}(\mathbf{N}), k = 1, \ldots, K$, $j = 1, \ldots, J$. These equations can be reduced to K equations in the K unknowns, $x_k, k = 1, \ldots, K$, which were defined in Eq. (4.12). For $k = 1, \ldots, K$ and $j = J' + 1, \ldots, J$ let

$$\varepsilon_{kj} = \sum_{l=1}^{K} N_l \delta_{ljk}(\mathbf{N}) - \delta_{kjk}(\mathbf{N}). \quad (4.23)$$

Then $x_k, k = 1, \ldots, K$, satisfy the following simultaneous nonlinear equations:

$$N_k = x_k \left[b_k + \sum_{j=J'+1}^{J} \frac{a_{kj}\left[1 + \varepsilon_{kj} + \sum_{l=1}^{K} \dfrac{a_{lj}x_l(\varepsilon_{lj} - \varepsilon_{kj})}{1 + (a_{lj}x_l/N_l)}\right]}{\left(1 + \dfrac{a_{kj}x_k}{N_k}\right)\left[1 - \sum_{l=1}^{K} \dfrac{a_{lj}x_l}{1 + (a_{lj}x_l/N_l)}\right]} \right],$$

$$k = 1, \ldots, K. \quad (4.24)$$

Since the $\delta_{ljk}(\mathbf{N})$ are not known, approximate values for them are needed in order to solve Eq. (4.24). In Section 4.2.1a the approximation $\delta_{ljk}(\mathbf{N}) = 0$ was used. Equation (4.24) is more complicated than Eq. (4.13), but reduces to Eq. (4.13) if $\varepsilon_{kj} = 0$ for all k and j. It can be shown that if $\varepsilon_{lj} > -1$ for all l and j then Eq. (4.24) has at least one solution $\mathbf{x} = (x_1, \ldots, x_K)$ for which $x_k > 0$, $k = 1, \ldots, K$, and

$$\sum_{l=1}^{K} \frac{a_{lj}x_l}{1 + (a_{lj}x_l/N_l)} < 1, \qquad j = J' + 1, \ldots, J. \tag{4.25}$$

However, unlike Eq. (4.13) it has not been shown that a solution satisfies Eq. (4.14) that restricts the approximate utilization of each single server fixed capacity service center to be no greater than one. [Before solving Eq. (4.24) the condition $\varepsilon_{lj} > -1$ for all l and j should be checked since if this condition does not hold there is no guarantee that Eq. (4.24) has a solution.] Once a solution $\mathbf{x}$ has been obtained, e.g., by using a well-tested program for solving simultaneous nonlinear equations, then provided $\mathbf{x}$ satisfies Eq. (4.14), approximate values for $\Lambda_{(k,j)}(\mathbf{N})$, $j = 1, \ldots, J$, $L_{(k,j)}(\mathbf{N})$, $j = 1, \ldots, J'$, and $R_{(k,j)}(\mathbf{N})$, $j = J' + 1, \ldots, J$, can be obtained from Eqs. (4.15), (4.16), and (4.18) and approximate values for $L_{(k,j)}(\mathbf{N}), j = J' + 1, \ldots, J$, can be obtained as follows:

$$L_{(k,j)}(\mathbf{N}) = \frac{a_{kj}x_k\left[1 + \varepsilon_{kj} + \sum_{l=1}^{K} \frac{a_{lj}x_l(\varepsilon_{lj} - \varepsilon_{kj})}{1 + (a_{lj}x_l/N_l)}\right]}{\left(1 + \dfrac{a_{kj}x_k}{N_k}\right)\left[1 - \sum_{l=1}^{K} \frac{a_{lj}x_l}{1 + (a_{lj}x_l/N_l)}\right]}, \qquad j = J' + 1, \ldots, J. \tag{4.26}$$

We next give a programlike definition of a method for approximating performance measures in which approximate values for the $\delta_{ljk}(\mathbf{N})$ are computed. The method is based on Chandy and Neuse (1982).

{ALGORITHM FOR APPROXIMATING PERFORMANCE MEASURES}
    {Initialize}
        For $l = 1$ to K, $j = J' + 1$ to J, $k = 1$ to K
        $\delta_{ljk}^{(0)}(\mathbf{N}) = 0$
    For $I = 1$ to I'
        {Step 1 — Obtain approximate values for mean queue lengths}
        For $k = 1$ to K, $j = J' + 1$ to J
            Obtain ε_{kj} from Eq. (4.23) with $\delta_{ljk}(\mathbf{N})$ replaced by $\delta_{ljk}^{(I-1)}(\mathbf{N})$ for $l = 1$ to K
        Solve Eq. (4.24)
        For $k = 1$ to K, $j = J' + 1$ to J
            Obtain $L_{(k,j)}^{(I)}(\mathbf{N})$ by substituting the solution to Eq. (4.24) into Eq. (4.26)

If $I < I'$
{Step 2 – Obtain approximate values for changes in mean queue length fractions with one less customer}
   For $i = 1$ to K
      For $l = 1$ to K, $j = J' + 1$ to J, $k = 1$ to K
         $\delta_{ljk}^{(I-1)}(\mathbf{N} - \mathbf{e}_i) = \delta_{ljk}^{(I-1)}(\mathbf{N})$
         Obtain $L_{(k,j)}^{(I)}(\mathbf{N} - \mathbf{e}_i)$ for $k = 1$ to K, $j = J' + 1$ to J by performing the computations in Step 1 with $\mathbf{N}$ replaced by $\mathbf{N} - \mathbf{e}_i$ in all equations
      For $l = 1$ to K, $j = J' + 1$ to J, $k = 1$ to K
         Obtain $\delta_{ljk}^{(I)}(\mathbf{N})$ from Eq. (4.19) with all mean queue lengths replaced by their most recent approximate values
{END OF ALGORITHM}

If $I' = 1$ Step 1 is performed once, Step 2 is not performed and the method is identical to the one in Section 4.2.1a since $\delta_{ljk}^{(0)}(\mathbf{N}) = 0$. If $I' > 1$ the method attempts to obtain better approximations for the $\delta_{ljk}(\mathbf{N})$ in Step 2 and hence better approximations for the mean queue lengths. Upon termination the algorithm yields approximate values for $L_{(k,j)}(\mathbf{N})$, $k = 1, \ldots, K$, $j = J' + 1$, $\ldots, J$. Approximate values for the other performance measures are obtained from Eqs. (4.15), (4.16), and (4.18) where the most recent solution to Eq. (4.24) is used in Eq. (4.15).

A report on the use of the method for $I' = 3$ was given in Chandy and Neuse (1982). Rather than reducing Eqs. (4.22) and (4.5) to Eq. (4.24) and numerically solving Eq. (4.24), they numerically solved Eqs. (4.22) and (4.5) using successive approximation. They applied the method to the same randomly selected and stress networks that they used to test the simple approximation method. They found that the method always resulted in smaller errors than the simple method and a reduction of the errors by a factor of at least ten was common. For the network shown in Fig. 4.2 the relative errors in approximating $R_{(2,2)}$ and $\Lambda_{(2,2)}$ were reduced from 35% and -26% to -0.4% and 0.4%, respectively. However, the method requires that $I' + K(I' - 1)$ sets of simultaneous nonlinear equations be solved (one set each time Step 1 is performed and K sets each time Step 2 is performed) rather than a single set of equations as in the simple method. Thus, there is a tradeoff between cost and accuracy in chosing between this method and the simple method. More detailed information on this tradeoff can be found in Chandy and Neuse (1982).

4.2.2   *Closed Networks without Product Form*

For a network to have a product form solution it is necessary to assume that the service demands at a FCFS service center are exponentially distributed and have the same mean for all chains which visit the service center. In this section we present an approximation method for the case of chain dependent means. This method is useful when modeling communication networks.

EXAMPLE 4.2 (continued)   In Example 4.2 it was assumed that the mean lengths of packets sent over different virtual channels are identical. The assumption of identical means may be reasonable in a packet switching network which uses the same packet size on all virtual channels. However, in a message switching network the mean message lengths will in general be different for different virtual channels.   △

We shall restrict our consideration to networks that have only single server fixed capacity FCFS service centers and IS service centers, and we shall use the same notation as in Section 4.2.1. In particular, service centers $1, \ldots, J'$ are IS and service centers $J' + 1, \ldots, J$ are single server fixed capacity FCFS. We allow the mean service demands at the FCFS service centers to be chain dependent. However, the service demands at these centers are still assumed to be exponentially distributed. Equations (4.3) and (4.5) still hold in this case, but Eq. (4.4) only holds if $E[S_{(k,j)}]$ does not depend on k for all chains that visit service center j. Reiser (1979) proposed that Eq. (4.4) be replaced by the following approximation for all chains that visit service center j:

$$R_{(k,j)}(\mathbf{N}) = E[S_{(k,j)}] + \sum_{l=1}^{K} E[S_{(l,j)}]L_{(l,j)}(\mathbf{N} - \mathbf{e}_k),$$

$$j = J' + 1, \ldots, J, \quad \mathbf{N} \geq \mathbf{e}_k. \tag{4.27}$$

[If chain k does not visit service center j then $R_{(k,j)}(\mathbf{N}) = 0$.] Note that if $E[S_{(l,j)}] = E[S_{(k,j)}]$ for all chains that visit service center j then Eq. (4.27) simplifies to Eq. (4.4).

Equation (4.27) has the following heuristic interpretation. For a closed product form queueing network it has been shown that $L_{(l,j)}(\mathbf{N} - \mathbf{e}_k)$ is the mean number of chain l customers in service center j upon arrival of a chain k customer at service center j (Lavenberg and Reiser, 1980). Unfortunately, this result does not hold for networks without product form. Suppose, however, that it did hold. Then the summation on the right-hand side of Eq. (4.27) would be the mean time until the departure of all customers that were in service center j upon arrival of the chain k customer, i.e., the mean time the arriving customer waits in the queue. We have used here the memoryless property of the exponential distribution (see Section 2.1.2c). Since the mean response time equals the mean waiting time plus the mean service time, Eq. (4.27) is an approximation for the mean response time.

In order to avoid the recursive computation implied by Eqs. (4.3), (4.27), and (4.5) we use the approximation that was given in Eqs. (4.7) and (4.8). Substituting these equations into Eq. (4.27) yields the following approximation for all chains that visit service center j:

$$R_{(k,j)}(\mathbf{N}) = E[S_{(k,j)}] + \sum_{l=1}^{K} E[S_{(l,j)}]L_{(l,j)}(\mathbf{N})$$

$$- \frac{E[S_{(k,j)}]L_{(k,j)}(\mathbf{N})}{N_k}, \qquad j = J' + 1, \ldots, J. \qquad (4.28)$$

Equations (4.28) and (4.5) are simultaneous nonlinear equations in the unknowns $R_{(k,j)}(\mathbf{N}), k = 1, \ldots, K, j = J' + 1, \ldots, J$, and $L_{(k,j)}(\mathbf{N}), k = 1, \ldots, K,$ $j = 1, \ldots, J$. ($R_{(k,j)}(\mathbf{N})$ is known and equals $E[S_{(k,j)}]$ for $j = 1, \ldots, J'$.) The solution of these equations was investigated by Schweitzer (1979) and we now summarize his results. The equations have been shown to have at least one nonnegative solution. The equations can be reduced to $K + J$ equations in the following $K + J$ unknowns:

$$Z_j = \sum_{k=1}^{K} E[S_{(k,j)}]L_{(k,j)}(\mathbf{N}), \qquad j = 1, \ldots, J, \qquad (4.29)$$

$$Y_k = \sum_{j=1}^{J} y_{(k,j)}R_{(k,j)}(\mathbf{N}), \qquad k = 1, \ldots, K. \qquad (4.30)$$

The $K + J$ equations are

$$Z_j = \sum_{k=1}^{K} N_k y_{(k,j)} \frac{(E[S_{(k,j)}])^2}{Y_k}, \qquad j = 1, \ldots, J', \qquad (4.31)$$

$$Z_j = \sum_{k=1}^{K} N_k y_{(k,j)} E[S_{(k,j)}] \frac{E[S_{(k,j)}] + Z_j}{Y_k + y_{(k,j)}E[S_{(k,j)}]}, \qquad j = J' + 1, \ldots, J, \qquad (4.32)$$

$$1 = \left(\sum_{j=1}^{J'} y_{(k,j)} \frac{E[S_{(k,j)}]}{Y_k} \right) + \sum_{j=J'+1}^{J} y_{(k,j)} \frac{E[S_{(k,j)}] + Z_j}{Y_k + y_{(k,j)}E[S_{(k,j)}]}, \qquad k = 1, \ldots, K. \qquad (4.33)$$

[These equations differ somewhat from those in Schweitzer (1979) in that he did not include IS service centers. If $J' = 0$ then these equations are identical to Schweitzer's.] Note that for fixed $\mathbf{Z} = (Z_1, \ldots, Z_J)$ Eq. (4.33) is for each k a single nonlinear equation in the single unknown Y_k. Each of these equations has a unique solution and can be easily solved using the Newton–Raphson method. Note also that Eq. (4.31) expresses Z_j explicitly in terms of $\mathbf{Y} = (Y_1, \ldots, Y_K)$ for $j = 1, \ldots, J'$. Let

$$F_j(\mathbf{Y}) = \sum_{k=1}^{K} \frac{N_k y_{(k,j)} E[S_{(k,j)}]}{Y_k + y_{(k,j)}E[S_{(k,j)}]}, \qquad j = J' + 1, \ldots, J. \qquad (4.34)$$

If $F_j(\mathbf{Y}) < 1$ then it follows from Eq. (4.32) that Z_j can be expressed explicitly in terms of **Y** as follows:

$$Z_j = \frac{\sum_{k=1}^{K} N_k y_{(k,j)} (E[S_{(k,j)}])^2 / (Y_k + y_{(k,j)} E[S_{(k,j)}])}{1 - F_j(\mathbf{Y})}, \qquad j = J' + 1, \ldots, J.$$

(4.35)

A nonnegative solution to Eqs. (4.31)–(4.33) can therefore be obtained as follows: Given an estimate of **Z** obtain an estimate of **Y** by solving Eq. (4.33) for each k using the Newton–Raphson method. Next obtain a new estimate of **Z** by obtaining a new estimate of Z_j from Eq. (4.31) if $j = 1, \ldots, J'$ and from Eq. (4.35) if $j = J' + 1, \ldots, J$ and if $F_j(\mathbf{Y}) < 1$. If for any $j = J' + 1, \ldots, J$, $F_j(\mathbf{Y}) \geqslant 1$ then let the new estimate of Z_j be equal to the right-hand side of Eq. (4.32) where the current estimate for Z_j is used in the right-hand side. Continue to iterate in this manner until successive estimates of **Z** and **Y** are sufficiently close. Once **Z** and **Y** have been obtained, approximate values for the performance measures can be obtained as follows:

$$R_{(k,j)}(\mathbf{N}) = (E[S_{(k,j)}] + Z_j)/(1 + y_{(k,j)} E[S_{(k,j)}]/Y_k), \quad j = J' + 1, \ldots, J, \quad (4.36)$$

$$\Lambda_{(k,j)}(\mathbf{N}) = N_k y_{(k,j)}/Y_k, \qquad\qquad\qquad j = 1, \ldots, J, \qquad (4.37)$$

$$L_{(k,j)}(\mathbf{N}) = \Lambda_{(k,j)}(\mathbf{N}) E[S_{(k,j)}], \qquad\qquad j = 1, \ldots, J', \qquad (4.38)$$

$$L_{(k,j)}(\mathbf{N}) = \Lambda_{(k,j)}(\mathbf{N}) R_{(k,j)}(\mathbf{N}), \qquad\qquad j = J' + 1, \ldots, J. \quad (4.39)$$

Schweitzer (1979) found that this iterative scheme converged rapidly and was typically two orders of magnitude faster than solving Eqs. (4.28) and (4.5) using successive approximation.

Unfortunately, there has not yet been a comprehensive accuracy assessment of this approximation method. Schweitzer (1979) reported that limited comparisons with simulation results revealed relative errors which were typically less than 5% but occasionally greater than 10%.

Reiser (1979) has investigated an approximation method in which the quantities $L_{(l,j)}(\mathbf{N} - \mathbf{e}_k)$ in Eq. (4.27) are approximated by solving single chain networks rather than using the simple approximation given in Eqs. (4.7) and (4.8). This method is therefore more expensive computationally than Schweitzer's method. Reiser presented a limited comparison of the results obtained using his method with simulation results. The relative errors are in the same range as reported by Schweitzer for his method. Reiser also extended his method to handle nonexponential service demands at FCFS service centers. See Reiser (1979) for details.

Bard (1979) proposed methods similar to Schweitzer's for closed queueing networks with simultaneous resource possession and with other features that do not allow a product form solution. However, we prefer the decomposition methods of Sections 4.3.3c and 4.3.4d for networks with simultaneous resource possession. [See Sauer (1981a) for a comparison of these methods.]

4.3 Decomposition Methods for Networks without Product Form[†]

In Sections 3.5–3.7 we considered queueing networks that have a product form solution and computational algorithms for exact numerical solution of those networks. In Section 4.2 we focused attention on computational methods for approximate numerical solution of product form queueing networks. (We also considered extension of those methods to networks with FCFS service centers with chain-dependent service demands.) These approximate methods are intended for applications where exact numerical solution is either prohibitively expensive or unnecessary. In this section we focus attention on queueing networks that do not have a product form solution and on methods for approximate solution of these networks.

There are many approaches to approximate solution of queueing networks. Some of these will be surveyed in Section 4.5. In this section we consider "decomposition" methods. These methods decompose a network into subnetworks, solve the subnetworks independently, and aggregate the results of those independent solutions to obtain an approximate solution of the original network. (These methods are also referred to as "flow-equivalence" or "Norton's theorem" methods.) In Section 4.3.1 we consider the need for approximate numerical solution. In Section 4.3.2 we consider the theoretical basis for decomposition methods. In Section 4.3.3 we consider decomposition methods for closed networks with a single routing chain. In Section 4.3.4 we consider decomposition methods for closed networks with multiple routing chains. In Section 4.3.5 we discuss the application of decomposition methods to open and mixed networks.

4.3.1 Need for Approximate Numerical Solution

There are system characteristics (which we have already cited) such as simultaneous resource possession or nonexponential service demands at FCFS service centers, which if included in a queueing network model will preclude a product form solution for that model. If these characteristics *can* be significant in performance of the system, then they should be considered in performance models of that system.

Unfortunately, if a queueing network does not have a product form solution, then exact numerical solution of that network will usually be infeasible. If a queueing network does not have a product form solution but has a small number of customers and a small number of service centers, then exact numerical solution may be feasible. The most generally applicable approach to

---

[†] Material in Section 4.3 based in part on C. H. Sauer and K. M. Chandy, Approximate solution of queueing models, *Computer* **13**, 25–32. Copyright 1980, Institute of Electrical and Electronics Engineers.

exact numerical solution of a queueing network without a product form solution is to (1) determine a Markov process representation of the network, (2) obtain a set of linear equations equating flow in and out of the states of the Markov process, (3) solve the linear equations using an iterative numerical technique such as Gauss–Seidel iteration, to obtain steady-state probabilities of the states of the Markov process, and (4) determine performance measures from the state probabilities. [If we are to obtain a Markov process representation, it is usually required that the service demand distributions have an exponential stages representation. Distributions with an exponential stages representation include the exponential, Erlang, hyperexponential, and branching Erlang distributions (Section 8.4).]

The key computational issue in this approach is the solution of the set of linear equations. (We shall say more about specific numerical techniques in Section 4.3.2.) There will be the same number of equations as states of the Markov process. If the number of states is fairly small, say on the order of 100, then this approach will be sufficiently inexpensive for most applications. If the number of states is moderate, say on the order of 1000, then this approach will be feasible but too expensive for some applications. If the number of states is larger than 10,000, this approach will be prohibitively expensive for most applications, and if the number of states is much larger than 10,000 then this approach will be infeasible. We cannot be very specific about memory and computational costs in general, because these are very dependent on the specific Markov process, i.e., the specific queueing network, being considered. However, solution of a network involving a few thousand states can easily require several minutes of CPU time on a processor capable of several million instructions per second. The memory requirement is also very problem dependent. It is not attractive to attempt to store a 1000 by 1000 element matrix (representing the set of linear equations) directly as an array. Usually specialized data structures will be used that only store the nonzero matrix elements. So the memory requirement depends directly on the sparseness of the matrix.

The above discussion is in terms of numbers of states of a Markov process, or equivalently, in terms of numbers of equations in sets of linear equations. An open queueing network or a mixed queueing network will usually have an infinite set of states if represented as a Markov process, so the above approach applies primarily to closed networks. (With an infinite set of states, it may be possible to truncate the state space and consider a finite set of states. However, we are unaware of any such truncation methods which are successful in general application.) A simple closed network may easily have tens of thousands of states if represented as a Markov process. For example, consider the network of Fig. 4.3. This network is essentially the same as that of Fig. 3.30 except that we have included a service center to represent memory as well as the centers representing the processor and disks. Let us assume that all service demand

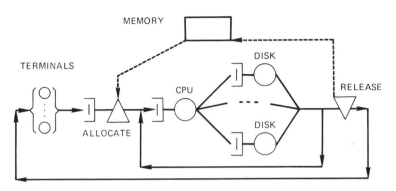

Fig. 4.3 Computer system model with memory.

distributions are exponential, that PS scheduling is used at the CPU, and FCFS scheduling is used at the disks. Let us also assume that the memory is organized in partitions and that processing of a terminal command requires exactly one partition. Memory scheduling is FCFS. Table 4.1 gives the numbers of states of a Markov process representing this network for four disks and various combinations of numbers of terminals and memory partitions. Note that for more than a few terminals and memory partitions, exact numerical solution is expensive or infeasible with the above approach. Yet this is a very simple model. Exact numerical solution is far out of reach for many, only slightly more complex, models. However, if we can decompose a network into subnetworks and solve these subnetworks separately, then the cost of solution

TABLE 4.1

Numbers of Markov States for Network of Fig. 4.3 with Four Disks

| | Partitions | | | | | |
Terminals	2	4	6	8	10	12
5	66	196	252	252	252	252
10	141	546	1302	2277	3003	3003
15	216	896	2352	4752	8008	11648
20	291	1246	3402	7227	13013	20748
25	366	1596	4452	9702	18018	29848
30	441	1946	5502	12177	23023	38948
35	516	2296	6552	14652	28028	48048
40	591	2646	7602	17127	33033	57148
45	666	2996	8652	19602	38038	66248
50	741	3346	9702	22077	43043	75348

may be small even though the subnetworks do not satisfy product form. As we shall see in Section 4.3.3c, the computational expense of approximately solving this particular model is negligible if a decomposition approximation is used.

4.3.2 Theoretical Basis for Decomposition

Our application of decomposition will be approximate and heuristic. However, these decomposition methods can be applied exactly in product form networks and in limiting cases of some other networks. Understanding of these cases where decomposition is exact is useful in understanding the application to approximate solution.

a. The Chandy–Herzog–Woo Theorem (Norton's Theorem)

In electrical circuits, Norton's theorem allows replacement of all but one component of a network of components by a current source. The objective is to study the one component without directly considering the others. The amount of current provided by the source can be determined by considering the network with the component of interest shorted and measuring the current flow through the short in the modified network.

Chandy *et al.* (1975) developed a theorem for product form queueing networks which is analogous to Norton's theorem. Their theorem applies to the entire class of product form queueing networks. In this section we shall restrict attention to the theorem for single chain closed networks. In Sections 4.3.4 and 4.3.5 we shall briefly discuss the theorem for other product form networks.

In the queueing network theorem, a service center is designated with the intent that the remainder of the network be replaced by a single center that is "flow-equivalent" to the subnetwork it replaces. Thus we are decomposing the given network into two subnetworks, the designated center and the remaining centers. We then aggregate the remaining centers to obtain the flow-equivalent center and a new network that is equivalent to the original network as far as the designated center is concerned. See Figs. 4.4, 4.5, and 4.6.

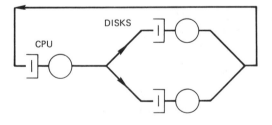

Fig. 4.4 Central server network.

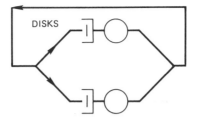

Fig. 4.5 Figure 4.4 network with central server "shorted."

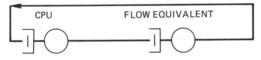

Fig. 4.6 Figure 4.4 network with I/O centers replaced by flow-equivalent center.

The proof of the theorem is very closely related to the discussion of the Convolution algorithm in Section 3.5.2a. We assume the reader is familiar with that section. We assume for simplicity's sake that there is exactly one class per service center; extension to the general single chain case is straightforward. We use the same notation as in Sections 3.5.1 and 3.5.2. To repeat that notation, there are N customers in a network of J service centers. The following are input parameters for service center j:

$y_{(j)}$:   relative throughput,
$E[S_{(j)}]$:   mean service demand,
$b_{(j)}$:   relative service demand,
$\mu_{(j)}(n)$:   service capacity given n customers at center.

The following variables are performance measures for service center j given n customers in the network:

$\Lambda_{(j)}(n)$:   throughput,
$U_{(j)}(n)$:   utilization of each server,
$L_{(j)}(n)$:   mean queue length (number of customers at center),
$R_{(j)}(n)$:   mean response time.

As in our discussion of Eq. (3.228), we shall use superscripts on the variables representing performance measures when we are considering a subset of the service centers. When we consider subsets of the service centers, we assume that the sets of relative throughputs, service demands, etc., are unchanged except that only the values for the centers of the subset are included.

Let us assume that service center J is the designated center of the above discussion. (We do *not* use the numbering convention of the computational algorithms sections, i.e., service center J may be an IS or single server fixed capacity center.) Consider the network obtained by "shorting" center J, e.g., the network of Fig. 4.5. The throughput through the "short," given n customers in this network, can be obtained from Eq. (3.206) as

$$\Lambda_S^{J-(J)}(n) = y_{(J)}G_{J-1}(n-1)/G_{J-1}(n), \qquad n = 1, \ldots, N. \tag{4.40}$$

We have used the subscript S to refer to the "short." The normalizing constant values (G) are obtained from Eq. (3.201).

Once we have the throughputs from Eq. (4.40) we can construct a new network consisting of only the designated center (J) and a new center, the flow-equivalent, which represents the centers other than the designated center from the original network. The flow-equivalent center, which we designate by subscript F, is constructed so that is produces the same flow of customers to the designated center when there are n customers, $n = 1, \ldots, N$, in the flow-equivalent center as the remaining subnetwork produces to the designated center when there are n customers in that subnetwork in the original network. This can be accomplished by letting $y_F = y_{(J)}$, $E[S_F] = 1$, and

$$\mu_F(n) = \Lambda_S^{J-(J)}(n), \qquad n = 1, \ldots, N. \tag{4.41}$$

(We may choose any queueing discipline satisfying product form and these requirements; the specific discipline does not otherwise matter.) Using these definitions and Eq. (3.198), we can verify that

$$X_F(n) = G_{J-1}(n), \qquad n = 0, \ldots, N, \tag{4.42}$$

so the network consisting of only the designated center and the flow-equivalent center will have the same values of the performance measures relating to the designated center as the original network, for the measures we consider. Thus the decomposition and aggregation we have described is exact for closed single chain product form networks.

Though we have assumed we are interested only in the case where all but one service center is represented by a single flow-equivalent center, this assumption is not necessary. It is a small step to consider partitioning the network into several subnetworks and represent these by separate flow-equivalent centers. Collections of these flow-equivalent centers may, in turn, be represented by flow-equivalent centers, thus producing a hierarchy of flow-equivalents.

These results say nothing directly about approximations based on the flow-equivalent representations. However, it is a small leap of faith to say that if a network is close to meeting the requirements of the product form solution, then a decomposition based on these flow-equivalents should lead to small errors. It is difficult to define "close to product form," but judgements can be made based on such criteria as (1) How many centers violate product form requirements? For example, how many FCFS centers do not have exponential service demand distributions? (2) How severely do these centers violate product form requirements? For example, does a FCFS center have a service distribution similar to the exponential distribution or a much more variable distribution? Does a FCFS center with nonexponential service demand distribution have enough servers that it may be considered similar to an IS center? (3) What is the relative load (considering both service demand and service rate) at the centers that violate product form requirements? If a center is lightly loaded, then there is likely to be little queueing and the center may be considered similar to an IS center.

Of course, a given network may have characteristics that make it seem qualitatively unlike a product form network. For example, the memory representation of Fig. 4.3 makes that network seem quite different from any of the product form networks we have considered. Whether or not a network seems similar to a product form network, the evaluation of the accuracy of a decomposition approximation usually must be made empirically. However, even if the network does not seem similar to a product form network, it may be possible to justify (and assume accurate) a decomposition approximation based on the weak-coupling results we now discuss.

b. Weakly Coupled Subnetworks

In many queueing networks it is possible to identify one or more subnetworks such that the average rate of interaction between such a subnetwork and the remainder of the network is much lower than the average rate of interaction between the centers of the subnetwork. Such a subnetwork is said to be "weakly coupled" to the remainder of the network because, from the "point of view" of a center in the subnetwork, that center is much more closely tied to the other centers of the subnetwork than to service centers outside the subnetwork. If we can identify weakly coupled subnetworks in a given network, then we can decompose the network along the boundaries of these subnetworks. We can then obtain separate solutions for the subnetworks and aggregate the results of these separate solutions to find a solution for the original network, much the same as in the case of the theorem for product form networks discussed in the previous section. It is intuitive that as a weakly coupled subnetwork becomes less coupled to the remainder of the network, that subnetwork, in the limit, becomes strictly independent of the remainder of the network and the network is strictly decomposable, i.e., no error is introduced by decomposition.

Substantial formal arguments have been developed that support and clarify the above statements. We shall only discuss an example network and present a few points that have been made in formal arguments. Our discussion is loosely based on the material in Courtois (1975). It is not necessary that this form of decomposition be viewed in terms of subnetworks or similar physical interpretations. Much of the formal work has dealt with the underlying stochastic processes; the physical interpretation we choose is one special case of the general theory. A comprehensive treatment is given by Courtois (1977).

Figure 4.7 depicts a computer system model similar to one we considered in Chapter 3. (See Fig. 3.30 and accompanying discussion.) As the mean number of CPU–I/O cycles increases, i.e., as the probability that a customer completing service at a disk returns to the CPU tends to one, the CPU–I/O subnetwork tends to become independent of the terminals. Thus even if the network of Fig. 4.7 does not satisfy requirements of the product form solution, e.g., if the disk service demand distributions are nonexponential, we can justify a simplified representation of the CPU–I/O subnetwork if the mean number of CPU–I/O cycles is large.

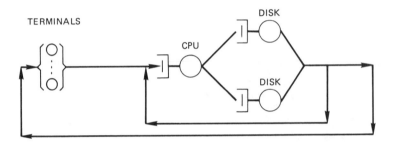

Fig. 4.7 Computer system model.

To obtain the representation of a weakly coupled subnetwork, we can follow these abstract steps: First, we consider the subnetwork in isolation and determine the states of that subnetwork that are important in the subnetwork's effect on the remainder of the network. These states generally capture the long term dynamics of the subnetwork, but ignore the short term dynamics. We then examine (solve) the subnetwork in each of these states to determine the rates at which the subnetwork will leave these states, i.e., interact with the remainder of the network. Third, we solve the network with this simplified representation of the weakly coupled subnetwork.

In practice, these steps may be accomplished by the same procedure that we followed in describing the Chandy–Herzog–Woo theorem, i.e., we consider the subnetwork with the remainder of the network "shorted," determine the throughput through the short for each possible number of customers of the subnetwork, specify a flow-equivalent center with effective service rates equal to these throughputs, and solve the network with the subnetwork replaced by the flow-equivalent center. For example, we can take the network of Fig. 4.7 and "short" the terminals center to obtain the network of Fig. 4.8. After obtaining the throughput through the short for n customers in the subnetwork, $n = 1, \ldots, N$, we can specify the flow-equivalent center exactly as before.

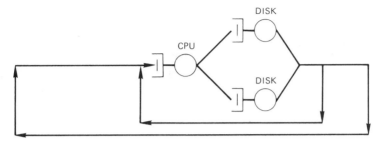

Fig. 4.8   Subnetwork of network of Fig. 4.7.

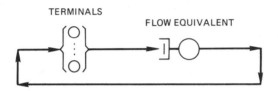

Fig. 4.9   Network of Fig. 4.7 with subnetwork flow-equivalent.

We can solve the network with the flow-equivalent center (Fig. 4.9) and interpret these results in terms of the original network, as discussed in the next section.

These concepts and this procedure depend only on the coupling between subnetworks and not on the presence or absence of characteristics associated with the product form solution. Thus it is clear that since both product form and weak-coupling are sufficient conditions to justify decomposition, and neither requires the other, that neither can be a necessary condition for decomposition to be accurate. If neither condition is present, decomposition may still be an effective approach to approximate solution. In such a situation, the effectiveness of decomposition will have to be evaluated empirically.

The concept of weakly coupled subnetworks applies to systems not representable by Markov processes with finite sets of states. However, if the system can be represented as a finite state Markov process, it is interesting to consider the implications in terms of that process. With appropriate labeling of the Markov states, it is possible to observe a special block structure in the matrix representing the balance equations equating flow in and out of the Markov states. This block structure can be seen in more frequent state transitions involving the weakly coupled subnetwork(s) remaining in the same aggregate state, as far as the remainder of the network is concerned, and relatively infrequent transitions to other aggregate states. Further, where the network can be represented by a Markov process with a finite set of states, it is possible, in principle, to estimate the error introduced by the decomposition.

This requires a complete description of the Markov process, i.e., enumeration of the Markov states and determination of the matrix of balance equations. Obtaining this description is quite a formidable task with the large numbers of states involved in most interesting queueing networks. Thus error estimates from these results are usually not obtained in practice. For further discussion, see Courtois (1977).

c. Performance Measures for Centers of a Subnetwork

Once a solution has been obtained for the network resulting from decomposition of the original network and aggregation of the centers of the subnetwork(s) into a corresponding flow-equivalent center(s), e.g., the networks of Figs. 4.6 and 4.9, there remains the problem of computing performance measures for the centers of the original network that have been represented by a flow-equivalent(s). We assume for sake of simplicity that we are given the solution for a network consisting of service center J of the original network and a flow-equivalent center representing the remainder of the original network, i.e., centers $1, \ldots, J - 1$. Extension to cases with several flow-equivalent centers and with all centers of the original network represented by flow-equivalents is straightforward. Performance measures for center j, $j = 1, \ldots, J - 1$, may be obtained as follows.

Throughput. Given the throughput for center J and the relative throughput for both centers j and J, then

$$\Lambda_{(j)} = (y_{(j)}/y_{(J)})\Lambda_{(J)}. \tag{4.43}$$

Queue Length Distribution. Let $P_{(j)}^{J-(J)}(n|i)$ be the steady-state probability of n customers, $n = 0, \ldots, i$, at center j in the network with center J "shorted," given i customers in that network. For the network consisting of center J and the flow-equivalent, let $P_{(J)}(N - i|N)$ be the steady-state probability of $N - i$ customers, $i = 0, \ldots, N$, at center J, i.e., i customers at the flow-equivalent center, given N customers in that network. Let $P_{(j)}(n|N)$ be the steady-state probability of n customers at center j in the original network, given N customers in that network. Then

$$P_{(j)}(n|N) = \sum_{i=n}^{N} P_{(J)}(N - i|N)P_{(j)}^{J-(J)}(n|i), \qquad n = 0, \ldots, N. \tag{4.44}$$

This follows immediately from the concepts of weakly coupled networks, where those concepts apply. For a proof for product form networks, see Sauer and Chandy (1981, p. 183).

Utilization. Utilization may be obtained from Eq. (3.208), (3.213), or (3.215), depending on the characteristics of center j.

Mean Queue Length. If service center j is an IS center, then Eq. (3.211) should be used. Otherwise, let $L_{(j)}^{J - (J)}(n)$ be the mean queue length at service center j in the network with center J shorted with n customers in that network. Let $L_{(j)}(N)$ be the mean queue length at service center j in the original network with N customers in that network. Then

$$L_{(j)}(N) = \sum_{n=1}^{N} P_{(J)}(N - n \mid N) L_{(j)}^{J - (J)}(n). \qquad (4.45)$$

Again, this follows immediately from the concepts of weakly coupled subnetworks, where those concepts apply. For a proof for product form networks, see Sauer and Chandy (1981, p. 184).

Mean Response Time. Little's formula [Eq. (2.111)] may be used to obtain mean response time.

4.3.3 Decomposition Approximations for Single Chain Closed Networks

There are two characteristics in single chain closed networks that have received significant attention with regard to approximate solutions: (1) presence of FCFS centers with nonexponential service demand distributions, and (2) simultaneous resource possession, i.e., a customer simultaneously holds more than one resource, as in Fig. 4.3. Neither of these characteristics is allowed in product form networks. Some other characteristics, e.g., priority queueing disciplines, have been primarily considered in the multiple chain context, while others of potential interest, e.g., state-dependent routing other than that allowed in product form networks, have received little attention. We first consider the case where a single center violates product form conditions, i.e., is a FCFS center with a nonexponential service demand distribution, while the remaining centers of the network satisfy product form conditions (Section 4.3.3a). We then consider networks where several centers violate product form conditions (Section 4.3.3b). Then we consider simultaneous resource possession (Section 4.3.3c).

a. Networks with a Single Center Violating Product Form

In networks with a single center violating product form, the obvious (and commonly used) heuristic is to follow the steps of Section 4.3.2a, with the designated center being the one violating product form, until we must solve the network consisting of the designated center and the flow-equivalent. Since that network does not satisfy product form, we must use a solution method other than those we have considered. Assuming such a solution is available, we can then complete the solution of the original network as discussed in Section 4.3.2c.

The principal issue here is then the solution of the network consisting of only the designated center and the flow-equivalent. It is convenient, though not absolutely necessary, to assume that the service demand distribution of the designated center is represented by exponential stages, e.g., by the Erlang, hyperexponential, or branching Erlang (see Section 8.4). (The branching Erlang is especially important in this regard since it includes the Erlang and hyperexponential distributions as special cases.) Making this assumption, we can then determine a Markov process representation of the network, with the number of states much smaller than for the original network. [See Tables 6.1 and 6.2 in Sauer and Chandy (1981) for comparisons of the number of Markov states in various central server networks and in the corresponding networks obtained by decomposition.]

There are many numerical techniques that can be applied to the solution of Markov processes such as this. Of the practical techniques, the most general are iterative methods such as the classical Gauss–Seidel method. See Sauer and Chandy (Section 3.3, 1981) for an introduction to such methods and Stewart (1978) for a comprehensive treatment. Though general, these iterative methods are potentially expensive. The recursive method proposed by Herzog *et al.* (1975) is popular because it is inexpensive. See Sauer and Chandy (1981) Section 3.5 for an introduction to this method. There are two limitations to the method of Herzog, Woo, and Chandy. First, the method is much more specialized, so a separate program is usually written for different models, e.g., one program might be used only for the case where the designated center has a single server, another might be used only for two servers, etc. (With more general iterative methods, a single program would normally handle both of these and other cases.) Second, the method is subject to numerical problems similar to the numerical problems we discussed with Mean Value Analysis and Eq. (3.227). These problems are usually not troublesome in practice. Marie (1980) has proposed methods that are similar to the method of Herzog *et al.*, but that avoid the numerical problems. Marie's method is probably the method of choice in this particular application, but it has not been extended to multiple chain problems as has the method of Herzog *et al.*

Many studies have empirically demonstrated the accuracy of this approach. For examples, see Sauer and Chandy (1975), Balbo (1979), and Tripathi (1979).

b. *Networks with Multiple Centers Violating Product Form*

When more than one center violates product form conditions, there is an additional problem beyond those just discussed: we must obtain the solution for the subnetwork obtained by "shorting" a designated center in the original network, and this network does not satisfy product form. A number of methods have been proposed for dealing with this problem. The most successful seems to be that of Marie (1979), which we now describe.

The discussion of the method is much simpler if we assume that wherever a product form network must be solved, the Convolution algorithm (Section 3.5.2a) is used. This is especially true when we consider extension to multiple chains. However, MVA and LBANC can also be used with this method. The discussion in Marie (1979) is less specific to the Convolution algorithm.

Marie's method iterates to refine the solution from a previous iteration step and terminates the iteration when certain criteria are satisfied [see inequalities (4.47) and (4.48) below]. There is no guarantee that the iteration terminates, or that if it does terminate, it obtains a solution that is close to the correct one. However, limited experience indicates that the iteration does terminate within a few steps and that the results are close to those obtained by simulation (Marie, 1979; Balbo, 1979).

Each iteration step involves up to J substeps, where each queue violating product form conditions is treated as the designated queue in a "Norton's theorem" decomposition. For the first iteration step, in determining a flow-equivalent center each center in the corresponding subnetwork that violates product form is replaced by one that satisfies product form and otherwise is as close to the center it replaces as possible. In our context of assuming that the only way centers violate product form is in having FCFS scheduling and a nonexponential service demand distribution, this replacement of centers is simply that if center j, not the designated center, has random variable $S_{(j)}$ with mean $E[S_{(j)}]$ for its service demand, then we use an exponential random variable with mean $E[S_{(j)}]$ in determining the flow-equivalent. The network consisting of the designated and flow-equivalent centers is then solved as discussed in Section 4.3.3a.

Let j be the designated center of a particular substep. In solving the network with only the designated and flow-equivalent centers, in addition to the usual performance measures, we determine $\tilde{X}_{(j)}(n)$, $n = 0, \ldots, N$, where

$$\tilde{X}_{(j)}(n) = \frac{P_{(j)}(n)}{P_{(j)}(0)} \frac{G_{J-(j)}(N)}{G_{J-(j)}(N-n)}, \tag{4.46}$$

$P_{(j)}(n)$ is the steady-state probability of queue length n at the designated center in the network with the flow-equivalent center, and $\mathbf{G}_{J-(j)}$ is the normalizing constant vector for the network without center j (i.e., with center j "shorted"), as in Section 3.5.2. [Obtaining $\tilde{X}_j(n)$ requires negligible additional effort with any of the numerical methods described in Section 4.3.3a.]

For the second and subsequent iteration steps, in determining a flow-equivalent center, for each FCFS center i in the corresponding subnetwork with nonexponential service demand distribution, $\tilde{X}_{(i)}(n)$ is used for $X_{(i)}(n)$, $n = 0, \ldots, N$. For the case of product form networks, it can be shown from Eq. (3.207) that $X_{(i)}(n) = \tilde{X}_{(i)}(n)$, $n = 0, \ldots, N$. For a network with two centers, where one satisfies product form and the other is FCFS with nonexponential service demand distribution, a similar replacement is exact; this is the basis of the numerical method of Marie (1980). For other networks, the replacement is approximate. The effect of this replacement is to give center i a new service rate function that is intended to capture the effect of the nonexponential service demand distribution at that center. The intent of the iteration is to refine these new service rate functions until an accurate solution is obtained. In Marie (1979) the iteration is terminated (if and) when

$$\left| \frac{N - \sum_{j=1}^{J} L_{(j)}}{N} \right| < \varepsilon \tag{4.47}$$

and

$$\left| \frac{(\Lambda_{(j)}/y_{(j)}) - \sum_{i=1}^{J} (\Lambda_{(i)}/Jy_{(i)})}{\sum_{i=1}^{J} (\Lambda_{(i)}/Jy_{(i)})} \right| < \varepsilon, \qquad j = 1, \ldots, J, \tag{4.48}$$

where ε is a small constant, e.g., 10^{-3}. Note that many other criteria could be used for terminating the iteration.

Note that for each service center we have a number of ways to determine the performance measures for that center. For the centers with FCFS scheduling and nonexponential service demand distribution, we may use the values for that center determined when that center was a designated center, or we may use values determined when some other center was a designated center, by the methods of Section 4.3.2c. For the centers satisfying product form conditions, we may choose between values obtained by the methods of Section 4.3.2c for different designated centers, or we could designate these centers as well and use the values obtained in that manner. If the results from the various substeps were consistent, then it should not matter which choices we made, but in fact the results from different substeps are likely to be inconsistent. In Marie (1979) each center is designated, even if some centers satisfy product form conditions; i.e., there are J substeps, and the results used for each center are those obtained when that center was a designated center.

Following is a sketch of a program implementation of Marie's method. $\tilde{X}^s_{(j)}$ is the value of the vector for center j at the end of the sth iteration step.

```
{ITERATIVE APPROXIMATE SOLUTION ALGORITHM}
   {Initialize}
      For j = 1 to J
      X̃⁰₍ⱼ₎(0) = 1
      For n = 1 to N
      X̃⁰₍ⱼ₎(n) = y₍ⱼ₎E[S₍ⱼ₎]X̃⁰₍ⱼ₎(n − 1)/μ₍ⱼ₎(n)
      s = 0
   {Iteration}
      Repeat
         For j = 1 to J {Substep: designate center j}
```

Solve product form subnetwork to determine flow-equivalent
using $\tilde{X}^s_{(i)}$ for $X_{(i)}$, $i \neq j$, and Eq. (4.41)
Solve network of center j and flow-equivalent
Determine $\tilde{X}^{s+1}_{(j)}$ using Eq. (4.46)
$s = s + 1$
Until inequalities (4.47) and (4.48) are satisfied
{END ITERATIVE APPROXIMATE SOLUTION ALGORITHM}

c. Simultaneous Resource Possession

We now consider single chain networks where the number of customers in
some subnetwork of centers is constrained, as in the network of Fig. 4.3,
because customers hold one resource, e.g., memory in Fig. 4.3, while waiting
for and holding other resources, e.g., the CPU and disks in Fig. 4.3. Most
applications of the techniques of this section have been to models of memory
contention such as in Fig. 4.3, (often with more complex memory organization
and scheduling) but other applications are possible (Keller, 1977; Chandy and
Sauer, 1978). We shall restrict attention to applications similar to the model of
Fig. 4.3. We shall also assume that the networks involved satisfy product form
except for the memory contention. In many cases it is straightforward to
combine the methods of this section with those of Sections 4.3.3a and 4.3.3b to
consider FCFS centers with nonexponential service demand distributions, as
well.

For the network of Fig. 4.3 we can follow a decomposition similar to that
we followed for Fig. 4.7. In both cases we can consider the subnetwork
consisting of the CPU and disks and represent this subnetwork by a flow-
equivalent center. In the case of Fig. 4.3, however, the network containing the
flow-equivalent center also contains the memory representation of the original
network. See Fig. 4.10. Once the network with the flow-equivalent has been

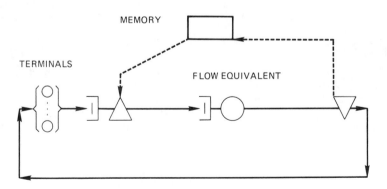

Fig. 4.10   Network of Fig. 4.3 with subnetwork flow-equivalent.

obtained, the remaining steps depend heavily on the specific memory representation. In general we may have to obtain a numerical solution for the network of Fig. 4.10, but in some interesting special cases we can transform the network of Fig. 4.10 into one without the memory representation, e.g., Fig. 4.9. If that is possible, the resulting network will usually satisfy product form and its solution will be much simpler.

Let us make the assumptions that we made when first considering this model, i.e., that memory is organized into partitions, that a customer requires exactly one partition to be able to use the CPU or a disk, and that memory scheduling is FCFS. Let there be T memory partitions. Let the terminals center be center J, and let the flow-equivalent center of Fig. 4.10 have the service capacity function μ_F of Eq. (4.41), relative throughput $y_F = y_{(J)}$, and mean service demand $E[S_F] = 1$.

With these assumptions, there are two cases to consider in the transformation from the network of Fig. 4.10 to the network of Fig. 4.9. In one case, $T \geqslant N$, there is no memory contention and we may use the same flow-equivalent center in both networks. In the other case, $T < N$, there is memory contention that must be reflected in the flow-equivalent center of the network of Fig. 4.10. Let this flow-equivalent have the same characteristics as that of Fig. 4.9, except that it has service capacity function $\mu_{F'}$. With no more than T customers at the new flow-equivalent, it should have the same characteristics as the flow-equivalent that does not represent memory. When there are more than T customers at the new flow-equivalent, then it should serve customers at the same rate as if there were T customers there. Thus, for both cases, we use

$$\mu_{F'}(n) = \mu_F(\min(n, T)), \qquad n = 1, \ldots, N. \qquad (4.49)$$

The most extensive empirical studies for models such as this are found in Keller (1976).

EXAMPLE 4.3 Let us consider a computer system model as in Example 3.27, but with memory contention considered as in Fig. 4.3 and the above discussion, i.e., partitioned memory and FCFS scheduling. All parameters of Example 3.27 are used in this new model. Figure 4.11 shows steady-state mean response time and throughput for N from 1 to 60 for T, the number of partitions, fixed at 4. This figure is similar to Fig. 3.32, but for example, for $N = 60$, the mean response time is higher and the throughput is lower in Fig. 4.11 than in Fig. 3.32. In Section 8.3 we shall give simulation results for $N = 30$ and $T = 4$. (The simulation results agree with these results.) Figure 4.12 shows steady-state mean response time and throughput for T from 1 to 10 for N fixed at 30. △

We should point out that, for some combinations of parameter values that do not satisfy weak-coupling assumptions, this decomposition may lead to significant error. For example, if in the network we have been considering we

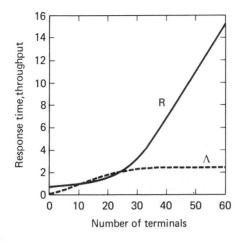

Fig. 4.11   Mean steady-state response time and throughput versus number of terminals for network of Example 4.3.

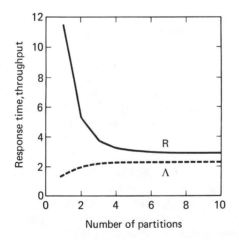

Fig. 4.12   Mean steady-state response time and throughput versus number of partitions for network of Example 4.3.

let T be 1 and let the probability of cycling back to the CPU after a disk service be 0, then the network reduces to a machine repair model (see Section 3.4), since the total number of jobs in the CPU and disk centers will never be more than one and there will be no queueing at those centers. However, this equivalent machine repair model has a nonexponential repair time distribution, and our decomposition would effectively assume an exponential repair time distribution. For some choices of parameters for the CPU and disks, e.g., with small relative service demand at all of these centers but one disk, the differences due to this implicit distributional assumption may be quite noticeable. This is an extreme case, but cases similar to this have arisen in applications of these techniques.

The transformation we just described can be accomplished for other memory representations. The transformation applies for some paged memory systems. For example, some paged memory systems attempt to allow a process into memory only if its entire "working set" will fit into memory. If the size of the working set is approximately constant, then we may use essentially the same discussion as above with T being the number of working sets that will fit into memory. In systems where the number of units (e.g., partitions, pages, words) of memory required by a customer is different for different requests for memory and can be represented by a probability distribution, then the transformation is possible for certain scheduling algorithms similar to those used in practice. See Brown *et al.* (1977) and Sauer and Chandy (1981, Section 9.4). In other cases it may be necessary to obtain a solution for the network of Fig. 4.10.

Methods similar to these can also be used to approximate response time distributions in networks such as that of Fig. 4.3 (Salza and Lavenberg, 1981). These methods use a different representation of the flow-equivalent center.

4.3.4   Decomposition for Multiple Chain Closed Networks

As we shall discuss in the following subsections, much of Section 4.3.3 extends simply to multiple closed chains. However, there are several issues to be considered in addition to those of that section: (1) The characterization of the flow-equivalent center must be different from characterizations we have seen before to both be exact for product form networks and be useful in approximate solutions. (2) The number of chains and the number of customers per chain may be small, in comparison to values that are computationally tractable in product form networks, and still present major computational problems. (3) The transformation from the network of Fig. 4.10 to that of Fig. 4.9 is difficult in some relatively simple cases. In addition to these issues there is the problem of a lack of empirical evaluation of accuracy, in comparison with the single chain cases.

a.   The Chandy–Herzog–Woo Theorem

The Chandy–Herzog–Woo theorem holds for multiple chain product form networks. The proof is simple using the point of view of the Convolution algorithm. The most interesting aspect of the theorem is the physical interpretation provided, i.e., the analogy to Norton's theorem for electrical circuits and the application to approximate solution. In the single chain case, the flow-equivalent center has the characteristics of centers we previously considered in product form networks and necessarily satisfies product form conditions. In the multiple chain case, the flow-equivalent center must have a service capacity function for each chain and each function depends on the numbers of customers of each chain at the flow-equivalent center. Such capacity functions do not in general satisfy product form conditions, but they do for the capacity functions obtained using the theorem.

Considering the network with designated center J "shorted" we can obtain [corresponding to Eq. (4.40)]

$$\Lambda_{(k,S)}^{J-(J)}(\mathbf{n}) = y_{(k,J)}G_{J-1}(\mathbf{n} - \mathbf{e}_k)/G_{J-1}(\mathbf{n}), \qquad \mathbf{n} \geqslant \mathbf{e}_k, \quad k = 1,\ldots,K, \qquad (4.50)$$

where the subscript S refers to the "short." This follows from Eq. (3.250). The flow-equivalent center may be specified to have $y_{(k,F)} = y_{(k,j)}$, $E[S_{(k,F)}] = 1$, and

$$\mu_{(k,F)}(\mathbf{n}) = \Lambda_{(k,S)}^{J-(J)}(\mathbf{n}), \qquad \mathbf{n} \geqslant \mathbf{e}_k, \quad k = 1,\ldots,K, \qquad (4.51)$$

where $\mu_{(k,F)}(\mathbf{n})$ is the service capacity available to chain k customers at the flow-equivalent center when there are $\mathbf{n}$ customers at that center. There are two important points to be made about this service capacity function. First, there are different characterizations of the flow-equivalent center in terms of queueing discipline and number of servers that achieve these capacity functions. Perhaps the simplest characterization is that there are K servers, each one dedicated to customers of a specific chain and providing service capacity dependent on the number of customers of each chain present at the *center*. Second, as we mentioned before, service capacity functions that are different for different chains and depend on the number of customers in each chain do not necessarily satisfy product form (see Sauer, 1981b, Section 6.1). Functions of this type will satisfy product form when obtained via Eqs. (4.50) and (4.51) from product form networks but will not necessarily satisfy product form when obtained from nonproduct form networks.

Though the weak-coupling arguments of Section 4.3.2b extend to multiple chains, there has been little published work in this area.

Performance measures for centers represented by the flow-equivalent center are obtained in essentially the same manner as the single-chain case. For example, the following equation may be used for mean queue length:

$$L_{(k,j)}(\mathbf{N}) = \sum_{\mathbf{n} \neq \mathbf{0}}^{\mathbf{N}} P_{(J)}(\mathbf{N} - \mathbf{n} \mid \mathbf{N})L_{(k,j)}^{J-(J)}(\mathbf{n}). \qquad (4.52)$$

b. *Networks with a Single Center Violating Product Form*

Besides FCFS scheduling with nonexponential service demand distributions, two characteristics of service centers that violate product form and have been considered in decomposition approximations are FCFS scheduling with chain-dependent service demand distributions and priority scheduling.

Conceptually, the decomposition approximations used when a single center violates product form because of these characteristics are straightforward extensions of the single chain case. The center violating product form is designated, a flow-equivalent representing the remainder of the network is obtained using Eqs. (4.50) and (4.51), and a network consisting of the designated center and the flow-equivalent center is constructed. This network may be solved by iterative methods or the method of Herzog *et al.* (1975).

With FCFS scheduling and multiple chains, a Markov process representation of a queueing network must consider the ordering of the customers of different chains at the FCFS centers. Thus the number of Markov states grows combinatorially as the number of chains and the number of customers per chain increase. In practice, if the designated center has FCFS scheduling, then exact numerical solution may be intractable with more than two chains. Several works have used SIRO scheduling as an approximation for FCFS, but there has been no evaluation of the effect of this approximation. With priority scheduling, little or no ordering information is required in a Markov process representation, depending on preemption strategies. Still, with more than a few (say three) chains and significant numbers of customers per chain (say ten), exact numerical solution may be intractable.

With problems that are still intractable after aggregation of service centers, because of the number of chains and the numbers of customers in the chains, aggregation of chains has been proposed, i.e., one chain is designated and the remaining chains are represented by one or two aggregate chains. An aggregate chain may have mean service demand at center j which is a weighted sum of the mean service demands at center j for the chains being represented by the aggregate chain. Similarly, routing probabilities for the aggregate chain may be obtained as weighted sum. The weights considered are usually based on estimates of throughput, though they may be based on numbers of customers (Chandy and Sauer, 1978). In Sauer and Chandy (1975) the estimates of throughput are based on a product form network similar to the network to be solved. In Chow and Yu (1980), for a network with priority scheduling, the estimates of throughput are based on a network that ignores some of the chains. Chow and Yu use iteration to refine their initial estimates. Iteration could also be used to refine the estimates used by Sauer and Chandy. Empirical assessments of accuracy are given in both Sauer and Chandy (1975) and Chow and Yu (1980).

c. Networks with Multiple Centers Violating Product Form

Marie's method extends very naturally to multiple chains (Neuse and Chandy, 1982). Equation (4.46) becomes

$$\tilde{X}_{(j)}(\mathbf{n}) = \frac{P_{(j)}(\mathbf{n})}{P_{(j)}(0)} \frac{G_{J-(j)}(\mathbf{N})}{G_{J-(j)}(\mathbf{N}-\mathbf{n})}. \qquad (4.53)$$

Otherwise, the description, in Section 4.3.3b applies. However, (1) the computational problems just discussed in Section 4.3.4b are magnified by the number of networks solved in the iterative process and (2) there has been relatively little empirical evaluation of accuracy in the multiple chain context.

d. Simultaneous Resource Possession

The extension to multiple chains is straightforward in the case where the "passive" resource (the resource held while contending for other resources), memory in our examples, has different units dedicated to different chains. The steps are essentially the same as before, including the transformation of the network with the passive resource (e.g., Fig. 4.10) to the network without the passive resource (e.g., Fig. 4.9). Equation (4.49) becomes

$$\mu_{(k,F')}(\mathbf{n}) = \mu_{(k,F)}(\min(\mathbf{n}, \mathbf{T})), \qquad \mathbf{n} \geqslant \mathbf{e}_k, \tag{4.54}$$

where $\mathbf{T}$ is the vector of units of memory (e.g., partitions) dedicated to each chain and **min** is the element by element minimum of its arguments. For empirical studies, see Sauer (1981a).

Where the units of memory are not dedicated, but are shared among customers of different chains, the transformation from the network of Fig. 4.10 to that of Fig. 4.9 has not been successful for interesting cases. However, solution of the network of Fig. 4.10 may be tractable, though more expensive than the solution of the network of Fig. 4.9. For further discussion and empirical studies, see Sauer (1981a).

4.3.5 Open and Mixed Networks

Decomposition may be applied in a similar manner to open and mixed networks, but there has been little published work for such networks. For open product form networks, the Chandy–Herzog–Woo results are closely related to Jackson's theorem (see Section 3.6), i.e., in considering a designated center, we may replace the remainder of the network by a Poisson source with arrival rate equal to the throughput of the designated center (assuming no center is saturated). Avi-Itzhak and Heyman (1973) considered approximations for simultaneous resource possession in open networks which are essentially the same as those we have considered for closed single chain networks. For mixed product form networks, the network may be transformed to a closed network as discussed in Section 3.7, and then the decomposition approaches for closed networks can be used.

**4.4   Extended Service Time Method for Open Queueing Network
Model of Disk Systems**

As we have discussed (e.g., in Section 4.3.1), queueing networks that
represent simultaneous possession of more than one resource by a customer
typically can only be analyzed approximately. An open network of this kind is
shown in Fig. 4.13. There are two types of servers, primary and secondary.

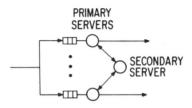

Fig. 4.13   Open queueing network model with simultaneous resource possession.

Each service center has its own primary server and there is a single secondary
server which is shared among the service centers. An arriving customer enters
one of the J service centers and requires service from the primary server. The
service at the primary server has several components, some of which require
use of the secondary server and cannot begin unless the secondary server is free.
Thus, contention for the secondary server causes delays in completing service
at the primary server. When the primary service is complete the customer
leaves the network. Such networks have been used to model disk systems
consisting of several disk drives connected to a single channel and control unit.
In the remainder of this section we shall discuss this modeling application and
the approximate analysis techniques that have been developed for this
application.

4.4.1   Description of Model

We consider several disk drives connected to a single channel and control
unit. For modeling purposes the channel and control unit are considered to be
a single device since they are essentially either both busy performing the same
service or both idle. From now on we will only refer to the channel. Requests to
transfer a record arrive at the software queue for one of the disk drives. The
requested records for a particular drive are transferred one at a time in the
order of arrival of the requests so that the queueing discipline at the drive is
FCFS. The service performed by the drive consists of several operations, i.e.
seek, latency, and transfer, each of which is either initiated by the channel
which is released once the operation starts or requires use of the channel

throughout the operation. Thus, the operations cannot begin unless the channel is free. In Fig. 4.13, each primary server represents a disk drive and the secondary server represents the channel. In Example 3.13 we assumed that the channel is always available and only modeled contention for the drive. The drive was represented as a FCFS single server queueing model whose service time is the sum of the seek, latency, and transfer times. In practice, however, contention for the channel cannot always be ignored and we must approximately analyze the network shown in Fig. 4.13.

The approach that we shall present to approximately analyze the network is to obtain an extended service time for the primary server that approximately accounts for the delays due to contention for the secondary server. Then a single server queueing model having this extended service time is analyzed. This approach is due to Wilhelm (1977) although we have modified some of the details. We will only consider disk drives (such as IBM 3330 or 3350 disk drives) that have the rotational position sensing (RPS) feature. For such disk drives the disk surface is divided into sectors whose position can be detected without using the channel.

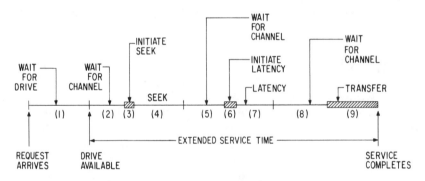

Fig. 4.14 Components of response time for an RPS disk.

In Fig. 4.14 we show the components of the response time for an RPS disk. Time intervals during which the channel is used are shown cross-hatched. We next discuss each of these components.

(1) Wait for drive. This is the time from when the request arrives until the drive is available, i.e. until the transfer operations for all previous requests for the drive have been completed.

(2) Wait for channel. This is the time from when the drive is available until the channel is available to initiate the seek.

(3) Initiate seek. The channel is used for a very short time to initiate the seek. We shall assume in the model that this time is zero. However, the channel must be available to initiate the seek.

(4)   Seek.   This is the time to move the arm from its current position to the cylinder containing the requested record. The channel is not used during the seek.

(5)   Wait for channel.   This is the time from when the seek is complete until the channel is available to initiate the latency.

(6)   Initiate latency.   The channel is used for a very short time to initiate the latency. We will assume in the model that this time is zero. However, the channel must be available to initiate the latency.

(7)   Latency.   This is the time for the sector containing the requested record to begin to pass under the head. Due to the RPS feature, the channel is not used during the latency.

(8)   Wait for channel.   With the RPS feature an attempt is made to reconnect to the channel at the end of the latency. If the channel is not available subsequent attempts to reconnect are made only when the requested sector begins to pass under the head. Thus, this time is an integral multiple (possibly zero) of the time for a complete disk rotation.

(9)   Transfer.   If records need not begin on sector boundaries, then in addition to the time to transfer the record, the transfer time includes the time to search for the record starting at the sector boundary. The channel is used throughout the transfer time.

We will denote these nine times by $X_1, \ldots, X_9$ and we assume that $X_3 = X_6 = 0$. Since X_3 and X_6 are zero, the only time the channel is busy is during the transfer operation for some drive. We define the *basic service time* for a disk drive to be the sum of the seek, latency, and transfer times and we define the *extended service time* to be the sum of the basic service time and the three channel wait times. [For some disk drives (such as the IBM 3380) initiation of the seek and latency operations is combined. In this case component (3) above becomes initiate seek and latency, and components (5) and (6) disappear so that $X_5 = 0$.]

We assume that the overall arrival process to the disk drives is a Poisson process with rate λ and that an arriving request is for disk j with probability $a_j > 0, j = 1, \ldots, J$, where $a_1 + \cdots + a_J = 1$. Then the arrival processes at the disk drives are independent Poisson processes with rates $\lambda_j = a_j \lambda, j = 1, \ldots, J$. The basic service time for drive j is given by

$$X_j = X_{4j} + X_{7j} + X_{9j}. \tag{4.55}$$

As in Example 3.13, we assume that the seek, latency, and transfer times, i.e., X_{4j}, X_{7j}, and X_{9j}, are statistically independent. We next discuss the extended service time.

A request for drive j which arrives when the drive is available can incur the first wait for channel, denoted X_{2j}. However, a request that arrives when the drive is busy will never incur this wait. This is because the drive and channel become available simultaneously at the end of a transfer operation for the drive so that the channel can immediately initiate the seek when the drive becomes available. Therefore, the extended service time for a request that arrives when the drive is busy is given by

$$S_j = X_j + X_{5j} + X_{8j}, \tag{4.56}$$

and the extended service time for a request that arrives when the drive is available is given by

$$S_j^* = S_j + X_{2j}. \tag{4.57}$$

The channel wait times X_{2j}, X_{5j}, and X_{8j} depend on the use of the channel by the other drives and, hence, on the service times of the other drives. We will assume that X_j, X_{2j}, X_{5j}, and X_{8j} are statistically independent.

4.4.2 Approximate Analysis of Model

In order to carry out the approximate analysis we represent drive j as the $M/G/1$ queueing model described in Section 3.3.3f in which the service time of a customer which arrives when the system is empty differs from the service time of a customer which arrives when the system is not empty. [This model was not used in Wilhelm (1977). Instead results from two $M/G/1$ queueing models were averaged, yielding somewhat different results.] The two service times are the extended service times S_j^* and S_j and the arrival rate is λ_j. The traffic intensity for this model is given by

$$\rho_j = \lambda_j E[S_j]. \tag{4.58}$$

Let r_j denote the steady-state response time for the model. Expressions for $E[r_j]$ and $L_{r_j}(s)$ are given by Eqs. (3.71) and (3.73). Using these equations, Eq. (4.57), and the assumption that S_j and X_{2j} are statistically independent, it is easy to show that if $\rho_j < 1$ then

$$E[r_j] = E[S_j] + \frac{\lambda_j E[S_j^2]}{2(1 - \rho_j)} + \frac{2E[X_{2j}] + \lambda_j E[X_{2j}^2]}{2(1 + \lambda_j E[X_{2j}])} \tag{4.59}$$

and

$$L_{r_j}(s) = \frac{(1 - \rho_j)L_{S_j}(s)[(\lambda_j - s)L_{X_{2j}}(s) - \lambda]}{(1 + \lambda_j E[X_{2j}])(\lambda_j - s - \lambda_j L_{S_j}(s))}. \tag{4.60}$$

These expressions for $E[r_j]$ and $L_{r_j}(s)$ are exact for the $M/G/1$ queueing model, but they are approximations for the network in Fig. 4.13. We next obtain approximate expressions for $E[X_{2j}]$, $E[X_{2j}^2]$, and $L_{X_{2j}}(s)$.

The utilization of the channel by drive j is given by $\lambda_j E[X_{9j}]$, and in addition to requiring that $\rho_j < 1$ we require that

$$\sum_{j=1}^{J} \lambda_j E[X_{9j}] < 1, \qquad (4.61)$$

i.e., that the overall channel utilization is less than one. The probability that the channel is busy with drive i, $i \neq j$, when drive j is available and a customer arrives at drive j can be approximated by

$$b_{ji} = \lambda_i E[X_{9i}]/(1 - \lambda_j E[X_{9j}]). \qquad (4.62)$$

This expression is the conditional probability that the channel is busy with drive i given that it is not busy with drive j. [In Wilhelm (1977) the unconditional probability that the channel is busy with another drive, given by the numerator in Eq. (4.62), was used instead.] If the channel is busy with drive i the request has to wait for the remainder of a transfer time for drive i. Let $\tilde{X}_{9i}$ denote the remainder of the transfer time for drive i. Then,

$$E[X_{2j}] = \sum_{i \neq j} b_{ji} E[\tilde{X}_{9i}], \qquad (4.63)$$

$$E[X_{2j}^2] = \sum_{i \neq j} b_{ji} E[\tilde{X}_{9i}^2], \qquad (4.64)$$

and

$$L_{X_{2j}}(s) = \sum_{i \neq j} [1 - b_{ji} + b_{ji} L_{\tilde{X}_{9i}}(s)]. \qquad (4.65)$$

Approximating $\tilde{X}_{9i}$ by the residual life of X_{9i} we obtain the approximations (e.g., Kleinrock, 1975, p. 406)

$$E[\tilde{X}_{9i}] = E[X_{9i}^2]/2E[X_{9i}], \qquad (4.66)$$

$$E[\tilde{X}_{9i}^2] = E[X_{9i}^3]/3E[X_{9i}], \qquad (4.67)$$

and

$$L_{\tilde{X}_{9i}}(s) = \frac{1 - L_{X_{9i}}(s)}{sE[X_{9i}]}. \qquad (4.68)$$

It follows from Eq. (4.56) that

$$E[S_j] = E[X_j] + E[X_{5j}] + E[X_{8j}] \qquad (4.69)$$

and from the statistical independence of X_j, X_{5j}, and X_{8j} that

$$\text{Var}[S_j] = \text{Var}[X_j] + \text{Var}[X_{5j}] + \text{Var}[X_{8j}] \qquad (4.70)$$

and

$$L_{S_j}(s) = L_{X_j}(s)L_{X_{5j}}(s)L_{X_{8j}}(s). \qquad (4.71)$$

We use the same approximation for the channel wait time X_{5j} as we used for the channel wait time X_{2j} so that

$$E[X_{5j}] = E[X_{2j}], \tag{4.72}$$

$$E[X_{5j}^2] = E[X_{2j}^2], \tag{4.73}$$

and

$$L_{X_{5j}}(s) = L_{X_{2j}}(s). \tag{4.74}$$

As discussed previously the channel wait time X_{8j} is an integral multiple (possibly zero) of the time for a complete disk rotation. We denote the constant disk rotation time by R and the random number of lost rotations by N_j. Then

$$X_{8j} = N_j R. \tag{4.75}$$

We assume that N_j is a geometric random variable with parameter

$$b_j = \sum_{i \neq j} b_{ji}, \tag{4.76}$$

i.e.,

$$\text{Prob}\{N_j = n\} = b_j^n(1 - b_j), \qquad n = 0, 1, \dots. \tag{4.77}$$

This is equivalent to assuming that attempts to reconnect to the channel are statistically independent and that each attempt fails with probability b_j. It follows from Eqs. (4.75) and (4.77) that

$$E[X_{8j}] = b_j R/(1 - b_j), \tag{4.78}$$

$$\text{Var}[X_{8j}] = b_j R^2/(1 - b_j)^2, \tag{4.79}$$

and

$$L_{X_{8j}}(s) = (1 - b_j)/(1 - b_j e^{-sR}). \tag{4.80}$$

Equations (4.59), (4.60), (4.62)–(4.74), (4.76), and (4.78)–(4.80) can be combined to obtain approximations for $E[r_j]$ and $L_{r_j}(s)$. In the special case where the transfer times have the same distribution for all drives, i.e., $X_{9j} = X_9$ for all j, the following equations can be combined to obtain an approximation for $E[r_j]$:

$$E[r_j] = E[S_j] + \frac{\lambda_j E[S_j^2]}{2(1 - \rho_j)} + \frac{b_j(E[X_9^2] + \lambda_j E[X_9^3]/3)}{2E[X_9] + \lambda_j b_j E[X_9^2]}, \tag{4.81}$$

$$b_j = \frac{(\lambda - \lambda_j)E[X_9]}{1 - \lambda_j E[X_9]}, \tag{4.82}$$

$$E[S_j] = E[X_j] + \frac{b_j E[X_9^2]}{2E[X_9]} + \frac{b_j R}{1 - b_j}, \tag{4.83}$$

and

$$\text{Var}[S_j] = \text{Var}[X_j] + \frac{b_j[X_9^3]}{3E[X_9]} - \frac{b_j^2(E[X_9^2])^2}{4(E[X_9])^2} + \frac{b_j R^2}{(1 - b_j)^2}. \quad (4.84)$$

The channel utilization is given by $\lambda E[X_9]$ and the utilization of drive j is given by $\lambda_j E[S_j]$ where $E[S_j]$ is a nonlinear function of λ_j. Note that the time the drive spends waiting for the channel has been included in the drive utilization. We require that both the channel and drive utilizations be less than one. In all the numerical examples we have considered the third term in Eq. (4.81) is negligible compared to the other two terms and hence can be dropped without affecting the accuracy of the approximation. If $b_j = 0$, i.e., if the channel is always available when required by the drive, then Eq. (4.81) reduces to

$$E[r_j] = E[X_j] + \frac{\lambda_j E[X_j^2]}{2(1 - \rho_j)}, \quad (4.85)$$

which is the mean response time for the standard FCFS $M/G/1$ queueing model whose service time is the basic service time X_j. This is the equation we used in Example 3.13 where we ignored channel contention.

EXAMPLE 4.4   We consider J disk drives connected to a single channel and control unit and assume that requests are equally likely to be for any of the drives. Thus, $\lambda_j = \lambda/J$ for all j. The seek, latency, and transfer times for all drives are assumed to be identical and we make the same assumptions about them as in Example 3.13. Thus, the moments of the basic service time are given by Eqs. (3.25) and (3.26), the moments of the seek time are given by Eqs. (3.27) and (3.28), the moments of the latency time are given by Eqs. (3.29) and (3.30), and the moments of the transfer time are given by Eqs. (3.31) and (3.32). In these equations X_S is the seek time, X_L is the latency time, X_T is the transfer time, C is the number of cylinders on the drive, p is the probability that the cylinder address of a requested record equals the cylinder address of the previous requested record (i.e., that the seek time is zero), B is the record length is bytes, and D is the data rate in bytes/second (the search time within a sector is assumed to be zero). Since the transfer times are equal for all drives we can use Eqs. (4.81)–(4.84) to compute $E[r_j]$.

As in Example 3.13 we will compute $E[r_j]$ for IBM's 3330-11 disk drive. For this drive $C = 808$, $R = 0.0167$ s, $D = 806 \times 10^3$ bytes/s, and the seek time characteristics can be approximated by Eq. (3.33). Also for this drive $E[X_7] = 0.00835$, $\text{Var}[X_7] = 0.0000232$, and for a fixed record size $B = 2000$ bytes, $E[X_9] = 0.00248$, $\text{Var}[X_9] = 0$, $E[X_9^3] = (E[X_9])^3$. In Fig. 4.15 we plot for $J = 4$ drives and for $J = 8$ drives $E[r_j]$ versus λ_j (the arrival rate to each drive) for $B = 2000$ bytes and $p = 0.5$. We also plot the mean response time computed as in Example 3.13 where channel contention is ignored. The maximum arrival rate to each drive for which the system is stable is 38.7 if there

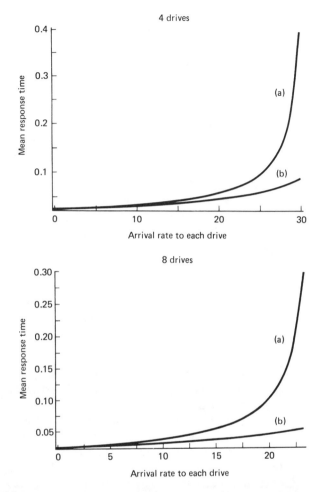

Fig. 4.15 Mean steady-state response time versus arrival rate to each drive for model of 3330-11 disk drive (record size = 2000 bytes, $p = 0.5$) — (a) channel contention included, (b) channel contention ignored.

is no channel contention. Note that due to channel contention the four drive system begins to become unstable for an arrival rate to each drive of about 30. At this arrival rate the channel utilization equals 0.31 and the drive utilization equals 0.95. The eight drive system begins to become unstable for an even smaller arrival rate. For an arrival rate equal to 23.2 the channel utilization equals 0.48 and the drive utilization equals 0.93.   △

The approximation we have presented differs somewhat from that in Wilhelm (1977). The main difference is that our expression for b_j yields larger values than Wilhelm's. Wilhelm numerically compared his approximation with simulation results for five examples in which all drives have the same parameter values. He assumed uniformly distributed latency times, exponentially distributed seek times, and exponentially distributed or constant transfer times. The comparisons were for mean queue length rather than mean response time. He found his approximation to be very accurate (relative errors of at most a few percent) at low arrival rates, and hence low mean queue lengths, and to begin to diverge from simulation results as the arrival rate increases. In four of the examples the approximation was very accurate for mean queue lengths up to three or more, but for one example (there were eight drives instead of four drives as in the other examples) the approximation underestimated the mean queue length by 25% or more for mean queue lengths less than two. Our approximation yields larger mean queue lengths than Wilhelm's, with the differences increasing as the arrival rate increases. Our approximation yields slightly larger errors than Wilhelm's in the four drive examples, but it yields much smaller errors in the eight drive example where Wilhelm's approximation broke down at small mean queue lengths. Thus, we prefer our approximation. Since most disk systems are tuned to operate with small queue lengths, the approximation presented here is practically useful.

4.4.3 Related Work

We close this section by mentioning some related work on modeling disk systems. A closely related paper is Zahorjan *et al.* (1978) from which we obtained the expression for b_j in Eq. (4.82). They conducted simulations that revealed that successive attempts to reconnect to the channel for data transfer do not have the same probability of failure b_j and in fact this probability increases on successive attempts. They then proposed an empirically based correction to b_j to be used for all attempts after the first. The model we have considered is an open model with arrivals to the disks being Poisson and having known rates. They also considered a closed central server model in which the disk system is represented. For this model the arrivals to the disks are not Poisson and the rates are not known. They proposed an iterative approximate analysis technique for this model which uses the open model approximation at each iteration. A method for the approximate analysis of models of more complex disk systems, in which a disk can be accessed via alternative channel and control unit paths and from multiple CPUs is presented in Bard (1980). The key problem here is that even if the arrival rate to the disk is known, the rates along the alternative paths are not known, and hence the channel utilizations are not known. Finally, problems that arise in obtaining parameter values for disk system models from real data are discussed in Hunter (1980) in the context of IBM 370 computers running MVS.

4.5 Other Methods for Open Networks

In this section we briefly discuss other methods that have been developed for open queueing networks. It will be necessary to consult the references for details. The networks we consider have only FCFS single server fixed capacity service centers, but have characteristics that do not allow an exact product form solution, i.e., arrival processes are not Poisson, service demands are not exponentially distributed, or service centers have finite capacity. Such networks arise in modeling communication networks where each service center represents a communication channel as in Example 3.32. In that example it was assumed that arrival processes are Poisson, message lengths are exponentially distributed, and each service center has infinite capacity. In Section 4.5.1 we consider methods for networks with non-Poisson arrival processes and nonexponential service demands, and in Section 4.5.2 we consider methods for networks with finite capacity service centers.

4.5.1 Nonexponential Interarrival Times and Service Demands

We consider open queueing networks that have only FCFS single server fixed capacity service centers. These networks are of the type defined in Section 3.6.1 except that the interarrival times from the source can have a general distribution (i.e., the arrival process is a renewal process) and the service demands at each service center can have a general distribution. We allow only one class per service center. Two methods that have been developed for the approximate analysis of such networks are the diffusion approximation (e.g., Gelenbe and Mitrani, 1980) and the decomposition approximation of Kuehn (1979).

The diffusion approximation was originally developed to approximately analyze the $G/G/1$ queue when the traffic intensity is close to one. In the approximation the integer-valued queue length random variable is approximated by a continuous random variable whose probability density function is the solution to a differential equation (the diffusion equation) subject to certain boundary conditions. The resulting density function is then discretized to approximate the queue length probability distribution. The approximate queue length distribution depends on the interarrival time and service demand distributions only through their means and variances. Different variations of the basic approach have been used to obtain somewhat different results (see Gelenbe and Mitrani, 1980, for details). For example, Kobayashi (1974) obtained the following approximation to the queue length distribution

$$\text{Prob}\{n = i\} = \begin{cases} 1 - \rho, & i = 0, \\ \rho(1 - \hat{\rho})\hat{\rho}^{i-1}, & i = 1, 2, \ldots, \end{cases} \tag{4.86}$$

where

$$\hat{\rho} = e^{-2(1-\rho)/(C^2[S] + \rho C^2[T])}, \tag{4.87}$$

ρ is the traffic intensity, and $C[T]$ and $C[S]$ are the coefficients of variation of the interarrival time and service time, respectively. The diffusion approximation is known to yield more accurate results the closer ρ is to one and the closer $C[T]$ and $C[S]$ are to one.

The approach to applying the diffusion approximation to an open network is to assume that the arrival process for each service center is a renewal process, i.e., that each service center can be treated as a $G/G/1$ queue. The arrival rate for a service center is obtained as in Section 3.6.1 from Eqs. (3.279) and (3.281), and the mean interarrival time equals the inverse of the arrival rate. The variance of the interarrival time for a service center is approximated in terms of the mean and variances of the interarrival times for the network, the means and variances of the service demands at each service center, and the routing probabilities. Different ways for doing this have been proposed. The $G/G/1$ diffusion approximation is then used to approximate the queue length distribution at a service center.

Limited accuracy assessments have been carried out (Gelenbe and Mitrani, 1980; Reiser and Kobayashi, 1974) that indicate that the diffusion approximation can yield results that are considerably more accurate than the product form solution results obtained by assuming Poisson arrivals and exponential service demands. However, large errors are possible when traffic intensities at some service centers are much less than one or the coefficients of variation of interarrival times or service demands differ substantially from one and in particular are much greater than one. Gelenbe and Mitrani (1980) discuss an extension of the diffusion approximation to networks with multiple classes at each service center. Attempts to apply the diffusion approximation to closed networks have not met with much success (Reiser and Kobayashi, 1974).

The decomposition method developed by Kuehn (1979) is also based on assuming that the arrival process for each service center is a renewal process so that each service center can be treated as a $G/G/1$ queue. The mean interarrival time for a service center is obtained as described above. A somewhat more elaborate method than the ones proposed previously is used for approximating the variance of the interarrival time for a service center given the means and variances of the interarrival times for the network, the means and variances of the service demands at each service center, and the routing probabilities. Finally, the mean response time for a service center is approximated using an expression developed for the $G/G/1$ queue that depends only on the mean and variance of the interarrival time and of the service demand. (An approximation for the queue length distribution is not obtained.) Note that Kuehn's method and the diffusion method are similar in that each service center is treated as a $G/G/1$ queue whose interarrival times are characterized only in terms of the mean and variance. Limited accuracy assessments indicated that Kuehn's method performs at least as well as the diffusion method but further assessment is required.

4.5.2 Finite Capacity Service Centers

We consider open queueing networks that have only FCFS single server fixed capacity service centers. The networks have Poisson arrivals and exponential service demands and are of the type defined in Section 3.6.1 except that each service center has finite capacity. We allow only one class per service center. In order to completely describe such a network it is necessary to describe how the network operates when a service center is full. One such mode of operation is that when a customer completes service at a service center i and is destined for a service center j which is full, the customer remains at center i and blocks the server there from serving other customers until the customer can enter center j. There may be several service centers whose servers are simultaneously blocked because center j is full. When a customer completes service at center j so that center j is no longer full, the customer that has been waiting longest to enter j does so instantaneously. If an external arrival to center j occurs when the center is full the arriving customer is lost. For such a network the throughputs cannot be determined from Eqs. (3.279) and (3.281) since the effect of blocking and lost arrivals is to decrease the throughput. However, these equations do determine the throughputs to within a common constant multiplier; i.e. they determine the relative throughputs.

Takahashi *et al.* (1980) developed a simple method for approximately analyzing such networks. Let p_j denote the probability that service center j is full. Each service center is treated as an $M/M/1$ finite capacity queue whose arrival rate and mean service time are expressed in terms of the probabilities $p_1, \ldots, p_J$. These probabilities are in turn expressed in terms of the arrival rates and mean service times yielding a set of J simultaneous nonlinear equations whose solution yields an approximation for $p_1, \ldots, p_J$. Approximations for other performance measures can be obtained from these probabilities. Only a very limited accuracy assessment was performed and further assessment is required.

Boxma and Konheim (1981) presented a more elaborate method for networks which operate somewhat differently. When a service center j fills to capacity, all servers that are serving or are about to serve customers that are next destined for center j are blocked from providing further service until center j is no longer full. When center j is no longer full, the blocked servers resume serving the customers destined for j. (It is assumed that a customer probabilistically selects the next service center to be visited prior to beginning service at the current center.) As before, external arrivals to a full center are lost. The same comments as we made above about throughputs apply here. In the method two different phases of operation are identified for a service center and the service center is treated as different $M/M/1$ finite capacity queues during the two phases. A weighted linear combination of the results from the two phases is then obtained where the weights are the probabilities of being in the phases. The method was developed for networks without feedback; i.e., a customer cannot visit a service center more than once. An extensive accuracy assessment was carried out for networks consisting of two or three centers. The relative error in approximating mean queue lengths was typically less than 10% but occasional large errors occurred. It should be possible to extend this method to networks that operate in other ways when a service center is full such as the networks considered in Takahashi *et al.* (1980).

References

Avi-Itzhak, B., and Heyman, D. P. (1973). Approximate queueing models for multiprogramming computer systems, *Oper. Res.* **21**, 1212–1229.
Balbo, G. (1979). Approximate Solutions of Queueing Network Models of Computer Systems. Ph.D. Dissertation, Computer Science Department, Purdue Univ.
Bard, Y. (1979). Some extensions to multiclass queueing network analysis, In "Performance of Computer Systems" (M. Arato, A. Butrimenko, and E. Gelenbe, eds.). North-Holland Publ., Amsterdam.
Bard, Y. (1980). A model of shared DASD and multipathing, *Comm. ACM* **23**, 564–572.
Boxma, O. J., and Konheim, A. G. (1981). Approximate analysis of exponential queueing systems with blocking, *Acta Inform.* **15**, 19–66.
Brown, R. M., Browne, J. C., and Chandy, K. M. (1977). Memory management and response time, *Comm. ACM* **20**, 153–165.
Chandy, K., and Neuse, D. (1982). Linearizer: A Heuristic Algorithm for Queueing Network Models of Computing Systems, *Comm. ACM* **25**, 126–134.
Chandy, K. M., and Sauer, C. H. (1978). Approximate methods for analysis of queueing network models of computer systems, *Comput. Surveys* **10**, 263–280.
Chandy, K. M., Herzog, U., and Woo, L. S. (1975). Parametric analysis of queueing networks, *IBM J. Res. Develop.* **19**, 43–49.
Chow, W.-M., and Yu, P. S. (1980). An Approximation Technique for Central Server Queueing Models with a Priority Dispatching Rule. IBM Research Rep. RC-8163, Yorktown Heights, New York.
Courtois, P. J. (1975). Decomposability, instabilities and saturation in multiprogramming systems, *Comm. ACM* **18**, 371–377.
Courtois, P. J. (1977). "Decomposability: Queueing and Computer System Applications." Academic Press, New York.
Gelenbe, E., and Mitrani, I. (1980). "Analysis and Synthesis of Computer Systems." Academic Press, New York.
Herzog, U., Woo, L. S., and Chandy, K. M. (1975). Solution of queueing problems by a recursive technique, *IBM J. Res. Develop.* **19**, 295–300.
Hunter, D. (1980). Modeling Real DASD Configurations. IBM Research Rep. RC8606, Yorktown Heights, New York.
Keller, T. W. (1976). Computer Systems Models with Passive Resources. Ph.D. Dissertation, Univ. of Texas, Austin, Texas.

Keller, T. W. (1977). Queueing network models of computer systems with limited parallelism in subnetworks, In "Computer Performance" (K. M. Chandy and M. Reiser, eds.), pp. 547–560. Elsevier and North-Holland Publ., Amsterdam, New York.

Kleinrock, L. (1975). "Queueing Systems, Vol. 1, Theory." Wiley, New York.

Kleinrock, L. (1976). "Queueing Systems, Vol. 2, Computer Applications." Wiley, New York.

Kobayashi, H. (1974). Application of the diffusion approximation to queueing networks I: Equilibrium queue distributions, *J. Assoc. Comput. Mach.* **21**, 316–328.

Kuehn, P. J. (1979). Approximate analysis of general queueing networks by decomposition, *IEEE Trans. Comm.* **COM-27**, 113–126.

Lavenberg, S. S., and Reiser, M. (1980). Stationary state probabilities at arrival instants for closed queueing networks with multiple types of customers, *J. Appl. Probab.* **17**, 1048–1061.

Marie, R. A. (1979). An approximate analytical method for general queueing networks, *IEEE Trans. Software Eng.* **SE-5**, 530–538.

Marie, R. A. (1980). Calculating equilibrium probabilities for $\lambda(n)/C_k/1/N$ queues, *Perform. Eval. Rev.* **9**, 117–125.

Moré, J. J., Garbow, B. S., and Hillstrom, K. E. (1980). User Guide for Minipack-1, ANL-80-74. Argonne National Laboratory, Argonne, Illinois.

Neuse, D., and Chandy, K. M. (1982). HAM: The heuristic aggregation method for solving general closed queueing network models of computer systems, *Performance Evaluation* **11**, 195–212.

Ortega, J. M., and Rheinboldt, W. C. (1970). "Iterative Solution of Nonlinear Equations in Several Variables." Academic Press, New York.

Reiser, M. (1979). A queueing network analysis of computer communication networks with window flow control, *IEEE Trans. Comm.* **COM-27**, 1199–1209.

Reiser, M., and Kobayashi, H. (1974). Accuracy of the diffusion approximation for some queueing systems, *IBM J. Res. Develop.* **18**, 110–124.

Salza, S., and Lavenberg, S. S. (1981). Approximating Response Time Distributions in Closed Queueing Network Models of Computer Performance. IBM Research Rep. RC-8735, Yorktown Heights, New York.

Sauer, C. H. (1981a). Approximate solution of queueing networks with simultaneous resource possession, *IBM J. Res. Develop.* **25**, 894–903.

Sauer, C. H. (1981b). Computational Algorithms for State-Dependent Queueing Networks. IBM Research Rep. RC-8698, Yorktown Heights, New York; to appear in *ACM Trans. Computer Systems.*

Sauer, C. H., and Chandy, K. M. (1975). Approximate analysis of central server models, *IBM J. Res. Develop.* **19**, 301–313.

Sauer, C. H., and Chandy, K. M. (1980). Approximate solution of queueing models, *Computer* **13**, (4), 25–32.

Sauer, C. H., and Chandy, K. M. (1981). "Computer Systems Performance Modeling." Prentice-Hall, Englewood Cliffs, New Jersey.

Schweitzer, P. (1979). Approximate analysis of multiclass closed networks of queues, *Internat. Conf. Stochastic Control and Optimization, Amsterdam.*

Stewart, W. J. (1978). A comparison of numerical techniques in Markov modeling, *Comm. ACM* **21**, 144–151.

Takahashi, Y., Miyahara, H., and Hasegawa, T. (1980). An approximation method for open restricted queueing networks, *Oper. Res.* **28**, 594–602.

Tripathi, S. K. (1979). On Approximate Solution Techniques for Queueing Network Models of Computer Systems, Ph.D. Dissertation, Dept. of Computer Science, Univ. of Toronto. Available as TR-106, Computer Systems Research Group, Univ. of Toronto.

Wilhelm, N. C. (1977). A general model for the performance of disk systems, *J. Assoc. Comput. Mach.* **24**, 14–31.

Zahorjan, J., Hume, J. N. P., and Sevcik, K. C. (1978). A queueing model of a rotational position sensing disk system, *Infor-Canad. J. Oper. Res. Inform. Process.* **16**, 199–216.

5

Generation Methods for Discrete Event Simulation

Gerald S. Shedler

5.1 Uniform Random Numbers

Simulation is essentially a controlled statistical sampling technique which can be used to study complex stochastic systems when analytic and/or numerical techniques do not suffice; in connection with the study of computer system models, this is often the case. By simulation we mean observation of the behavior of the stochastic system of interest by artificial sampling on a digital computer; in particular we refer to *discrete event simulation* in which stochastic changes of the system state occur only at a sequence of increasing time points.

In order to carry out a simulation of a stochastic system, we must be able to generate sample paths or realizations of the system. A necessary part of any such generation procedure is an algorithm (or algorithms) for random number generation, i.e., for the production of numbers that can be treated as instances or samples of random variables. In this section we give a brief description of uniform random number generators, concentrating on the widely used linear congruential method. A comprehensive reference on generation of uniform random numbers is the book by Ahrens and Dieter (1973a). Chapter 3 of Knuth (1969) and Chapter 6 of Kennedy and Gentle (1980) provide careful discussions of the linear congruential method. There is an extensive discussion of statistical testing of uniform random number generators in Chapter 8 of Fishman (1978).

5.1.1 Random Number Generators

Following Learmonth and Lewis (1973a), by a "random number generator" (or "pseudorandom number generator") we mean an algorithm that produces *sequences of numbers* that follow a specified *probability distribution* and possess the *appearance of randomness*. The use of "sequence of numbers" means that the algorithm is to produce many random numbers in a serial manner. Even though a particular user may need only relatively few of the numbers, we generally require that the algorithm be capable of producing many numbers. "Probability distribution" implies that we can associate a probability statement with the occurrence of each number produced by the algorithm. We usually take the probability distribution to be the uniform distribution on the interval (0, 1). If we have a source of (0, 1) uniform random numbers, then in principle it is possible to transform them by means of the inverse probability integral (see Section 5.2.1) to obtain random numbers having any desired distribution. As we shall see, however, for reasons of computational efficiency, a large amount of effort has gone into the development of methods for direct generation of nonuniform random numbers. With respect to "appearance of randomness" it may be somewhat surprising that the basis of most commonly used algorithms for uniform random number generation is a (deterministic) recurrence relation in which each succeeding number is a function of the preceding number. True randomness requires independence of successive numbers, but the algorithm produces a deterministic dependent sequence. When parameters of the recurrence relation are chosen carefully, such algorithms for uniform random number generation do yield sequences which (statistically) appear to be random. This appearance of randomness is the origin of the term "pseudorandom numbers."

Since the results of a simulation depend critically on an acceptable appearance of randomness, it is important that a proposed uniform random number generator be subjected to thorough statistical testing. Although the simulation practitioner need not necessarily be concerned with the details of the rather specialized techniques for statistical testing of random number generators, he should be convinced prior to use that an available uniform random number generator has been successfully tested.

5.1.2 *Lehmer Linear Congruential Generators*

Most available (uniform) random number generators are of a type known as *Lehmer linear congruential generators.* Such generators employ a recurrence relation of the form

$$X_n = bX_{n-1} + c \quad (\mathrm{mod}\, m). \tag{5.1}$$

Here all quantities are nonnegative integers; Eq. (5.1), read "X_n equals $bX_{n-1} + c$ modulo m," says that X_n is the remainder when $bX_{n-1} + c$ is divided by m. The quantity b is called the *multiplier*, m is the *modulus*, and c is the *increment*. Given a starting value $X_0 \geqslant 0$ along with values $b \geqslant 0, c \geqslant 0$, and m such that $m > X_0$, $m > b$, and $m > c$, successive application of Eq. (5.1) produces a sequence of integers $X_1, X_2, \ldots$ considered to be integer uniform random numbers between 0 and $m - 1$. Uniform random numbers U_n on the interval $(0, 1)$ are obtained by dividing by m, i.e., for $n = 1, 2, \ldots$,

$$U_n = X_n/m. \tag{5.2}$$

The recurrence relation of Eq. (5.1) is actually called a *mixed congruential generator*, the term "mixed" coming from the fact that it involves multiplication by a constant b along with addition of a constant c. Many random number generators are *multiplicative* or *pure congruential* in that $c = 0$, giving

$$X_n = bX_{n-1} \quad (\mathrm{mod}\, m). \tag{5.3}$$

The initial or starting value X_0 is often called the *seed* of the random number generator.

On first examination it appears that Eq. (5.1) produces m distinct numbers. This is not the case unless particular b and m are chosen. It is characteristic of generators of this type that there is ultimately a cycle of numbers that is repeated indefinitely; this repeating cycle of numbers is called the *period* of the generator. As an example, consider the linear congruential generator of Eq. (5.1) with $m = 32$. Choose $c = 0, b = 9$, and start with $X_0 = 1$:

Step n	X_{n-1}	bX_{n-1}	$bX_{n-1} \pmod{m}$
1	1	9	9
2	9	81	17
3	17	153	25
4	25	225	1
5	1	9	9
⋮			

The modulus is 32, but a period (1, 19, 17, 25) having length of only 4 is realized. This is obviously undesirable in a random number generator. If $X_0 = 2$, then $X_1 = 18$, $X_2 = 2$, $X_3 = 18$, $X_4 = 2, \ldots$, and the period has length 2. Thus, in general, the period length of a linear congruential generator depends on the starting value X_0 as well as on the parameters b, c and m.

5.1.3 Choice of Modulus and Multiplier

Our discussion follows Knuth (1969). It is clear that a congruential sequence used as a source of random numbers should have a long period. Since the period length of a congruential generator can never be greater than the modulus m, the value of m should be rather large. Note that a choice of $m = 2$ is a poor one even if only random 0s and 1s are required; at best a sequence of the form $\ldots, 0, 1, 0, 1, 0, \ldots$ is obtained. Speed of generation is another consideration in the choice of m in that we want to be able to compute $bX_n + c$ $\pmod{m}$ rapidly.

One criterion for the choice of the multiplier b is to ensure that the generated sequence has a period of maximum length; an acceptable appearance of randomness of the generated sequence, however, involves more than just a long period length. Very nonrandom sequences can have long periods; e.g., for $b = c = 1$, the sequence obtained from $X_n = X_{n-1} + 1$ (mod m) has a period of (maximum) length m, but certainly does not have an acceptable appearance of randomness. This example shows that it is always possible in a mixed congruential generator with modulus m to achieve the maximum period length m. Note that the choice of the starting value X_0 does not affect the period length when the period has length m since every number from 0 through $m - 1$ occurs exactly once in the period.

Number-theoretic results are available for characterizing the values of b and c which provide a maximum period length; see Knuth (1969, Chapter 3, pp. 15–18). For the special case of multiplicative congruential generators ($c = 0$), the basic result concerning maximum period length says that the maximum period length (m) cannot be achieved. It is possible, however, to obtain multiplicative congruential generators with very long periods. Based on involved number-theoretic considerations, results pertaining to the maximum period for this multiplicative case are available.

If the modulus m in a multiplicative congruential generator is prime, i.e., has no divisors other than 1 and itself, it is possible to achieve a period of length $m - 1$. Such a period length, of course, is just one less than the maximum possible length. Moreover, if we choose a multiplier b satisfying an appropriate sufficient number-theoretic condition with respect to (prime) m, then for any starting value $X_0 < m$, a period of length $m - 1$ is achieved. The determination of values for multipliers b that satisfy the condition for maximum period length in a multiplicative congruential generator in general involves lengthy calculations. Further details are in Knuth (1969, Chapter 3).

5.1.4 System/360 Uniform Random Number Generator

Although there are an infinite number of positive integers, only a finite number of positive integers are representable in any particular digital computer system, the limitation being the word size of the system. We present in this section a particular (multiplicative congruential) uniform random number generator which utilizes the full word size of IBM System/360 (370) computer systems. In the System/360, the word size is 32 bits with 1 bit reserved for algebraic sign; an obvious choice for m is thus 2^{31}.

A multiplicative linear congruential generator ($c = 0$) with $m = 2^k$ (for some positive integer k) can have a maximum period length of $m/4$. Accordingly, for System/360 computer systems with $m = 2^{31}$, the maximum period length is $2^{31}/4 = 2^{29}$ and the period length may also depend on the starting value. When the modulus m is prime, the maximum possible period length is $m - 1$. It happens (fortuitously) that the largest prime less than or equal to 2^{31} is $2^{31} - 1$, and by choosing $m = 2^{31} - 1$, uniform random number generators having a period length of $m - 1 = 2^{31} - 2$ can be implemented on System/360 computer systems.

Note that the conditions ensuring maximum period length do not necessarily guarantee good statistical properties for the generator, although the choice of the particular multiplier $b = 7^5$ does satisfy some known conditions regarding the statistical performance of the generated sequence. These, however, are beyond the scope of this discussion.

System/360 Generator.   Let $X_0 > 0$. Then for $n \geqslant 1$, set

$$X_n = 7^5 X_{n-1} \pmod{2^{31} - 1} = 16807 X_{n-1} \pmod{2^{31} - 1} \qquad (5.4)$$

and

$$U_n = X_n/(2^{31} - 1). \qquad (5.5)$$

The System/360 uniform random number generator has been tested extensively, and the results of the statistical tests indicate that it is very satisfactory; see Lewis *et al.* (1969) and Learmonth and Lewis (1973b). Versions of this generator are used in the IBM SL/MATH package, the IBM version of APL, the Naval Postgraduate School random number generator package LLRANDOM (Learmonth and Lewis, 1973a), and the International Mathematics and Statistics Library (IMSL) package. The generator is also used in the IBM simulation programming language SIMPL/I. There are System/360 basic assembler language implementations of this generator (with FORTRAN linkage) in Lewis *et al.* (1969) and Learmonth and Lewis (1973a). The assembly language subroutines GGL1 and GGL2 in the IBM Mathematics Subroutine Library (IBM, 1974) also implement this generator, as does the FORTRAN subroutine GGL therein.

In addition to having an acceptable appearance of randomness, the integers in the sequence generated by Eq. (5.4) have the property that their low-order (right-most) bits are uniformly distributed. It is possible to exploit this property for efficiency in assembler language implementations of algorithms for generation of nonuniform random numbers; see, e.g., Robinson and Lewis (1975). Note that only certain congruential generators have uniformly distributed low-order bits; see Knuth (1969, pp. 12, 14) for a discussion.

Multipliers other than 16807 have been proposed and are used in linear congruential generators having modulus $2^{31} - 1$. In particular, the implementation of the simulation programming language SIMSCRIPT II for System/360 uses the multiplier 630360016. See Hoaglin (1976) for a report of statistical tests of several such multipliers.

There are other practical considerations in uniform random number generators. A generator should be fast and without excessive memory requirements. Generators of uniform random numbers are frequently available as subroutine or function subprograms written in assembler or machine language. A variety of programming tricks are used to speed up routines, e.g., division simulation (cf. Payne *et al.*, 1969, and Gustavson and Liniger, 1970) rather than division operation, but care must be used in the selection of such tricks. There are examples in the literature where the result of choosing a multiplier having a binary representation containing many zeros (to speed up multiplication) has been an unacceptable period length.

5.1.5 Shuffling in Linear Congruential Generators

For most simulation purposes the sequence of numbers produced by the multiplicative congruential generator based on Eq. (5.4) has an acceptable appearance of randomness; i.e., it does appear to consist of independent, uniformly distributed numbers on (0, 1). Of course, due to the procedure used to produce them, the numbers are not actually independent, and it is possible to consider that a sequence of such numbers might be "shuffled" or further randomized to yield a better appearance of randomness. From the point of view of statistical tests, some results of shuffling have been encouraging. In particular, the widely available congruential generator RANDU, based on the recurrence relation

$$X_n = (2^{16} + 3)X_{n-1} \pmod{2^{31}} = 65539X_{n-1} \pmod{2^{31}} \qquad (5.6)$$

and known to have some deficiencies, has been improved by shuffling. [In the absence of shuffling, all triples (U_n, U_{n+1}, U_{n+2}), produced by RANDU and interpreted as coordinates of points in three-dimensional space (with $0 \leqslant x, y, z \leqslant 1$), lie on precisely 15 planes; for a proper appearance of randomness, these points should fill the three-dimensional space. This property of RANDU illustrates the need for proper selection of the multiplier in a congruential generator.]

The implementation of the System/360 generator in the random number generator package LLRANDOM at the Naval Postgraduate School incorporates a shuffling mechanism. The LLRANDOM package maintains a table of 128 random integers, initial values in the table being elements of the sequence produced from Eq. (5.4) lagged by one million integers starting with an arbitrary seed. When a new integer is generated according to Eq. (5.4), its right-most (low-order) seven bits are masked off to form an index into the table ($2^7 = 128$). The integer in the table indexed by the right-most seven bits is returned as output, and that table entry is replaced by the integer just generated. Note that this particular shuffling scheme is dependent on the choice of the modulus m. For a modulus of 2^{31} the right-most bits of a congruential sequence are nonuniform and their use in this scheme would defeat the purpose of shuffling. With a modulus of $m = 2^{31} - 1$ and the multiplier $b = 7^5$, however, the right-most bits are uniform and the desired results are obtained.

5.2 Nonuniform Random Numbers

The problem of generating random numbers from a specified nonuniform distribution is in principle solved by having a source of uniform random numbers and transforming them by means of the inverse probability integral as we shall discuss in Section 5.2.1. Because it is not always possible to compute or to compute efficiently the inverse of a given distribution function, it is of interest to have methods for direct generation of nonuniform random numbers. Desirable properties of such direct methods are that they be exact, very fast, easy to implement, and economical of computer storage. The property of exactness is that any deviation from the specified distribution results from computer round-off error rather than a defect in the method itself. Comparisons are hard to make among particular methods, partly because of machine dependencies. It is often true that, with very little cost in complexity, it is possible to improve on the inverse probability integral transformation by an order of magnitude in execution time; the fastest available algorithms for nonuniform random number generation, however, are often quite complex.

Apart from use of the inverse probability integral transformation, techniques for generation of nonuniform random numbers can be put in five classes (with overlapping boundaries) as follows:

    (i)   composition,
    (ii) rejection–acceptance,
    (iii) decomposition,
    (iv) characterization, and
    (v) comparison.

Methods (ii) and (iii) are systematic, and allow the generation of most types of nonuniform random numbers simply, if not with full efficiency. The book by Ahrens and Dieter (1973b) is a thorough treatment of techniques for producing nonuniform random numbers. Schmeiser (1980) gives a survey of recent advances and an extensive bibliography. Chapter 3 of Knuth (1969) is also a useful reference, in particular for application of decomposition to the normal distribution. There is a general discussion of methods for nonuniform random numbers in Chapter 9 of Fishman (1978) and in Chapter 6 of Kennedy and Gentle (1980).

5.2.1 *Inverse Probability Integral Transformation*

Generation of nonuniform random numbers by inverse transformation of a uniform random number is based on the observation that if U is uniformly distributed on the unit interval and $F(x)$ is a strictly increasing distribution function, then the random variable $X = F^{-1}(U)$ has distribution $F(x)$. Here $F^{-1}(\cdot)$ represents the inverse function corresponding to F, i.e., $x = F^{-1}(y)$ when $y = F(x)$. It follows that to produce samples of a random variable X having distribution $F(x)$ by transformation of a uniform random number U, we must be able to solve the equation $F(x) = y$, $0 \leqslant y \leqslant 1$; see Fig. 5.1.

Inverse transformation can be used to produce exponential random numbers. A random variable X has an exponential distribution (with rate parameter $\lambda > 0$ and mean λ^{-1}) if for $t \geqslant 0$,

$$\text{Prob}\{X \leqslant t\} = 1 - e^{-\lambda t}. \tag{5.7}$$

ALGORITHM 5.1   EXPONENTIAL DISTRIBUTION (INVERSE TRANSFORMATION)

1. Generate U uniformly distributed between 0 and 1.
2. Return $X = -\lambda^{-1} \ln U$.

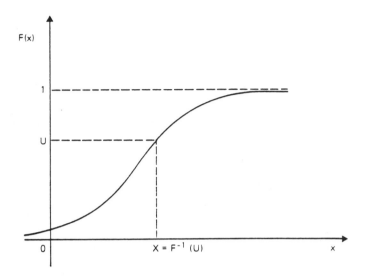

Fig. 5.1 Inverse probability integral transformation.

The transformation $X = -\lambda^{-1} \ln U$ is obtained by solving the equation $U = F(X)$ for X, yielding $X = -\lambda^{-1} \ln(1 - U)$, and observing that if U is uniformly distributed on the unit interval, so is $1 - U$. It is easy to verify that X obtained in step 2 of Algorithm 5.1 is exponentially distributed. Note that Algorithm 5.1 can be modified to produce samples of a geometric random variable. The (discrete) random variable N has a geometric distribution [with parameter $0 < p < 1$ and mean $p/(1 - p)$] if for $k = 0, 1, \ldots$,

$$\text{Prob}\{N = k\} = p^k(1 - p). \tag{5.8}$$

It is easy to show that if U is a uniform random number between 0 and 1, and if $\lambda = -\ln p$, then $N = \lfloor -\lambda^{-1} \ln U \rfloor$ is a sample from the geometric distribution defined by Eq. (5.8). Here $\lfloor x \rfloor$ denotes the integer part of x.

ALGORITHM 5.2   GEOMETRIC DISTRIBUTION (INVERSE TRANSFORMATION)

1. Generate U uniformly distributed between 0 and 1.
2. Return $N = \lfloor -\lambda^{-1} \ln U \rfloor$.

The inverse transformation can also be used to produce samples from a specified discrete distribution. A random variable X taking values 0 and 1 has a Bernoulli distribution (with parameter $0 < p < 1$) if

$$\text{Prob}\{X = 1\} = p \quad \text{and} \quad \text{Prob}\{X = 0\} = 1 - p. \tag{5.9}$$

ALGORITHM 5.3   BERNOULLI DISTRIBUTION (INVERSE TRANSFORMATION)

1. Generate U uniformly distributed between 0 and 1.
2. Return

$$X = \begin{cases} 1 & \text{if} \quad U \leqslant p, \\ 0 & \text{if} \quad U > p. \end{cases}$$

With this algorithm, in effect the unit interval is partitioned into subintervals of length p and $1 - p$; the subinterval (in which a generated uniform random number lies) determines the value of the Bernoulli random variable.

In principle, this technique can be used for any discrete random variable. As an example, consider the Poisson distribution. A random variable N has the Poisson distribution (with parameter and mean $\lambda > 0$) if for $n = 0, 1, \ldots$,

$$\text{Prob}\{N = n\} = e^{-\lambda}\lambda^n/n!. \tag{5.10}$$

To obtain Poisson random numbers, we compute the Poisson probabilities

$$\begin{aligned} p_0 &= \text{Prob}\{N = 0\} = e^{-\lambda}, \\ p_1 &= \text{Prob}\{N = 1\} = \lambda e^{-\lambda}, \\ p_2 &= \text{Prob}\{N = 2\} = \tfrac{1}{2}\lambda^2 e^{-\lambda}, \\ &\quad\vdots \end{aligned} \tag{5.11}$$

and partition the unit interval into nonoverlapping intervals of length p_0, $p_1, \ldots$.

ALGORITHM 5.4   POISSON DISTRIBUTION (INVERSE TRANSFORMATION)

1. Generate U uniformly distributed between 0 and 1.
2. Return

$$N = \begin{cases} 0 & \text{if} \quad U \leqslant e^{-\lambda}, \\ 1 & \text{if} \quad e^{-\lambda} < U \leqslant e^{-\lambda} + \lambda e^{-\lambda}, \\ 2 & \text{if} \quad e^{-\lambda} + \lambda e^{-\lambda} < U \leqslant e^{-\lambda} + \lambda e^{-\lambda} + \tfrac{1}{2}\lambda^2 e^{-\lambda}, \\ \vdots \end{cases}$$

Note that since we can compute the Poisson probabilities recursively; i.e. (according to $p_0 = e^{-\lambda}$ and $p_n = (\lambda/n)p_{n-1}$, $n = 1, 2, \ldots$), it is fairly simple to generate N by inverse transformation. If a linear search starting from zero is used to find n such that $p_0 + \cdots + p_{n-1} < U \leqslant p_0 + \cdots + p_n$, where $p_{-1} = 0$, U is uniformly distributed between 0 and 1, and $n = 0, 1, \ldots$, on the average $\lambda + 1$ comparisons, multiplications, and divisions are required. This assumes that we are not prepared to use some memory to store some of the p_n, e.g., for $n = 0$ up to $n = \lfloor 2\lambda \rfloor$. It is also possible to use searches that start at other than zero, e.g., at the value k for which $\text{Prob}\{N = k\}$ is maximum. This technique is very fast if the mean λ is small, and it has the property that only one uniform random number U is required for each Poisson random number produced.

We give one more application of inverse transformation. For $a < b$, a triangular random variable X on the interval $[2a, 2b]$ has density function

$$f_X(x) = \begin{cases} 0 & \text{if } x < 2a \text{ or } x > 2b, \\ (x - 2a)/(b - a)^2 & \text{if } 2a \leqslant x < a + b, \\ (2b - x)/(b - a)^2 & \text{if } a + b \leqslant x \leqslant 2b, \end{cases} \quad (5.12)$$

and equivalently, the distribution function

$$F_X(x) = \begin{cases} 0 & \text{if } x < 2a, \\ [(x - 2a)^2]/2(b - a)^2 & \text{if } 2a \leqslant x < a + b, \\ 1 - [(2b - x)^2]/2(b - a)^2 & \text{if } a + b \leqslant x \leqslant 2b, \\ 1 & \text{if } x > 2b. \end{cases} \quad (5.13)$$

This random variable arises as the sum of two independent random variables uniformly distributed on the interval $[a, b]$. To produce samples of the triangular random variable X by inverse transformation, we solve the equation $U = \{(X - 2a)^2\}/2(b - a)^2$ for $0 \leqslant U < \frac{1}{2}$ (i.e., $2a \leqslant X < a + b$), and then solve $U = 1 - \{(2b - X)^2\}/2(b - a)^2$ for $\frac{1}{2} \leqslant U \leqslant 1$ (i.e., $a + b \leqslant X \leqslant 2b$).

ALGORITHM 5.5   TRIANGULAR DISTRIBUTION (INVERSE TRANSFORMATION)

1. Generate U uniformly distributed between 0 and 1.
2. Return

$$X = \begin{cases} 2a + (b - a)\sqrt{2U} & \text{if } 0 \leqslant U < \frac{1}{2}, \\ 2b + (a - b)\sqrt{2(1 - U)} & \text{if } \frac{1}{2} \leqslant U < 1. \end{cases}$$

5.2.2   Composition

Composition techniques can be used to produce samples of a random variable X which has a representation as a sum of independent random variables with a common distribution, i.e., as $X = T_1 + T_2 + \cdots + T_n$ for some $n > 1$, where the $\{T_i\}$ are independent, identically distributed random variables.

An Erlang random variable X (with scale parameter $\lambda > 0$ and integral shape parameter $k > 0$) has density function

$$f_X(x) = e^{-\lambda x}\lambda^k x^{k-1}/(k - 1)! \quad (5.14)$$

concentrated on $x \geqslant 0$. This random variable has the representation $X = T_1 + T_2 + \cdots + T_k$, where the $\{T_i\}$ are independent and exponentially distributed with mean $E[T_i] = \lambda^{-1}$; thus, $E[X] = k\lambda^{-1}$ and $\text{Var}[X] = k\lambda^{-2}$.

ALGORITHM 5.6   ERLANG DISTRIBUTION (COMPOSITION)

1. Generate $U_1, U_2, \ldots, U_k$ (mutually) independent and uniformly distributed between 0 and 1.
2. Set $X = -\lambda^{-1}\ln(U_1 U_2 \cdots U_k)$.

The expression for X in step 2 results from algebraic manipulation of $X = T_1 + T_2 + \cdots + T_k$, where

$$T_j = -\lambda^{-1}\ln U_j$$

for $j = 1, 2, \ldots, k$. As a result, the logarithm need be taken only once, but $k - 1$ multiplications instead of $k - 1$ additions are required.

We can also use composition to produce samples from the gamma distribution. A gamma random variable (with scale parameter $\lambda > 0$ and shape parameter $k > 0$) has density function given by Eq. (5.14), with the factorial $(k - 1)!$ replaced by $\Gamma(k)$, the gamma function defined for $k > 0$ by

$$\Gamma(k) = \int_0^\infty t^{k-1}e^{-t}\,dt. \tag{5.15}$$

The gamma function interpolates the factorials in the sense that $\Gamma(k + 1) = k!$ for $k = 0, 1, \ldots$; for all $k > 0$, $\Gamma(k + 1) = k\Gamma(k)$. As before, $E[X] = k\lambda^{-1}$ and $\operatorname{Var}[X] = k\lambda^{-2}$.

The sum of two independent gamma random variables, each with scale parameter m, and shape parameters k_1 and k_2, respectively, is a gamma random variable with scale parameter m and shape parameter $k = k_1 + k_2$. It is convenient to generate samples of the gamma distribution with arbitrary shape parameter k as the sum of a random number gamma, distributed with shape parameter k_1 equal to the integer part of k, and a random number gamma, distributed with shape parameter $k_2 = k - k_1$. Generation of the latter is fairly difficult and is done by a special, carefully written program; see Ahrens and Dieter (1974) and Robinson and Lewis (1975). The idea is to use a rejection–acceptance technique (see Section 5.2.3) based on the observation that the function

$$g(x) = \begin{cases} x^{k-1}/\Gamma(k) & \text{if } 0 \leqslant x \leqslant 1, \\ e^{-x}/\Gamma(k) & \text{if } 1 < x \end{cases} \tag{5.16}$$

majorizes the gamma density function

$$f(x) = e^{-x}x^{k-1}/\Gamma(k). \tag{5.17}$$

To illustrate the use of composition for a discrete random variable, we consider the binomial distribution. For a positive integer n and $0 < p < 1$, the random variable X has a binomial distribution (with mean np) if for

$k = 0, 1, \ldots, n$,

$$\text{Prob}\{X = k\} = \binom{n}{k} p^k (1 - p)^{n-k}. \tag{5.18}$$

Random numbers having this binomial distribution can be obtained by observing that X has the representation $X = Y_1 + Y_2 + \cdots + Y_n$, where the $\{Y_i\}$ are independent Bernoulli random variables; i.e., $\text{Prob}\{Y_i = 1\} = p$ and $\text{Prob}\{Y_i = 0\} = 1 - p$ for $i = 1, 2, \ldots, n$.

ALGORITHM 5.7   BINOMIAL DISTRIBUTION (COMPOSITION)

1. Generate $U_1, U_2, \ldots, U_n$ mutually independent and uniformly distributed between 0 and 1.
2. For $i = 1, 2, \ldots, n$ set

$$Y_i = \begin{cases} 1 & \text{if} \quad U_i \leqslant p, \\ 0 & \text{if} \quad U_i > p. \end{cases}$$

3. Return $X = Y_1 + Y_2 + \cdots + Y_n$.

This technique for producing binomial random numbers is costly computationally when n is large, and other methods are worth considering.

5.2.3   Rejection–Acceptance

Like decomposition to be described in Section 5.2.5, rejection–acceptance is a systematic way of generating nonuniform random numbers. Rejection–acceptance techniques are often used in conjunction with decomposition techniques, and are applicable to discrete as well as continuous random variables.

Let X be a random variable having a density function $f_X(x)$ that is bounded and concentrated on a finite interval (which we take to be the unit interval). Thus, we suppose that for some $\alpha < \infty$,

$$f_X(x) \leqslant \alpha \qquad \text{if} \quad 0 \leqslant x \leqslant 1$$

and

$$f_X(x) = 0 \qquad \text{otherwise.} \tag{5.19}$$

ALGORITHM 5.8   REJECTION-ACCEPTANCE (UNIFORM MAJORIZING DENSITY FUNCTION)

1. Generate U_1 and U_2 independent and uniformly distributed between 0 and 1.
2. Compute $\alpha^{-1} f_X(U_1)$. If $U_2 \leqslant \alpha^{-1} f_X(U_1)$, return $X = U_1$. Otherwise, reject the pair U_1, U_2 and repeat 1.

Note that not all pairs U_1, U_2 of uniform random numbers produce a sample of the random variable X; see Fig. 5.2. It is easy to show [cf. Gaver and Thompson (1974), pp. 568–569] that Algorithm 5.8 produces a random sample from the density function $f_X(x)$.

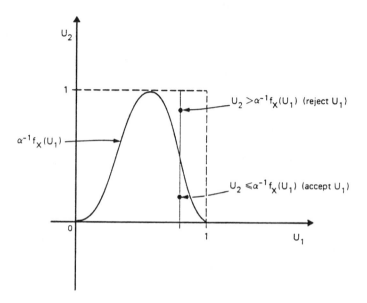

Fig. 5.2   Rejection–acceptance.

A uniform majorizing density function can be used to produce samples of a triangular random variable X on the unit interval, i.e., having density function

$$f_X(x) = \begin{cases} 4x & \text{if } 0 \leqslant x \leqslant \frac{1}{2}, \\ 4 - 4x & \text{if } \frac{1}{2} \leqslant x \leqslant 1. \end{cases} \tag{5.20}$$

The density function $f_X(x)$ satisfies $f_X(x) \leqslant 2$ for $0 \leqslant x \leqslant 1$.

Algorithm 5.9 provides a rejection–acceptance procedure which uses a general majorizing density function to produce samples of a random variable X having a density function $f_X(x)$. We assume that $f_X(x)$ is concentrated on the interval $[a, b]$, where $-\infty \leqslant a < b \leqslant +\infty$. Let $g(x)$ be a function such that for $a \leqslant x \leqslant b$,

$$f_X(x) \leqslant g(x)$$

and

$$\alpha = \int_a^b g(x)\,dx < \infty. \tag{5.21}$$

Then $h(x) = g(x)/\alpha$ is a density function concentrated on $[a, b]$.

ALGORITHM 5.9   REJECTION-ACCEPTANCE (GENERAL MAJORIZING DENSITY FUNCTION)

1. Generate Y having density function $h(x)$.
2. Generate U uniformly distributed between 0 and 1.
3. If $U \leqslant f_X(Y)/g(Y)$, return $X = Y$. Otherwise, reject the pair U, Y and repeat 1.

Note that in step 3 the probability of acceptance is α^{-1}. For each sample X, the number of comparisons required has a geometric distribution (starting at one), since it arises as a sequence of independent (Bernoulli) trials with probability of success equal to α^{-1}. Therefore, the average number of comparisons is α. This means that for an efficient algorithm we would like α to be close to 1; this is accomplished by choosing $g(x)$ to fit $f_X(x)$ as closely as possible over the interval $[a, b]$. There is of course the basic requirement that the random variable Y with density function $h(x)$ be easy to generate (and in particular be easier to generate than X). Examples of useful random variables Y are

(i)   uniform random variables;
(ii)   "wedges" generated by maxima and minima of pairs of independent uniform random variables on the unit interval, i.e., for which, respectively,

$$f_Y(x) = h(x) = \begin{cases} 2x & \text{if } 0 \leqslant x \leqslant 1, \\ 0 & \text{otherwise,} \end{cases} \tag{5.22}$$

and

$$f_Y(x) = h(x) = \begin{cases} 2(1 - x) & \text{if } 0 \leqslant x \leqslant 1, \\ 0 & \text{otherwise;} \end{cases} \tag{5.23}$$

(iii)   exponential random variables; and
(iv)   random variables Y of the form $Y = 1/U$ [where U is a uniform random variable on the interval $(0, 1)$] for which

$$f_Y(x) = h(x) = \begin{cases} 1/x^2 & \text{if } x \geqslant 1, \\ 0 & \text{if } x < 1. \end{cases} \tag{5.24}$$

By way of comparison with the inverse probability integral transformation, rejection–acceptance requires evaluation of the density function $f_X(x)$, but this is almost always easier (e.g., for a normal distribution) than the inverse distribution function.

A normal random variable X (with mean μ and standard deviation $\sigma > 0$) has density function

$$f_X(x) = (2\pi\sigma^2)^{-1/2} e^{-(x-\mu)^2/2\sigma^2} \tag{5.25}$$

on $-\infty < x < +\infty$. Algorithm 5.10, which provides standardized (mean 0, standard deviation 1) normal random numbers X, uses a rejection–acceptance technique to produce the absolute value of a normal random number; a true normal random number is then obtained by attaching a random sign (i.e., $+$ with probability $\frac{1}{2}$ or $-$ with probability $\frac{1}{2}$).

ALGORITHM 5.10   NORMAL DISTRIBUTION (REJECTION–ACCEPTANCE)

1. Generate U_1 and U_2 independent and uniformly distributed between 0 and 1.
2. Set $X = -\ln U_1$.
3. If $U_2 \leqslant e^{-(X-1)^2/2}$, accept X. Otherwise, reject the pair U_1, U_2 and repeat 1.
4. Generate a random sign ($+$ or $-$), attach it to X, and return X.

This technique for generating normal random numbers (like the polar method given below) has essentially perfect accuracy. Note that if X is a mean 0, standard deviation 1 random number, then $\sigma X + \mu$ is a mean μ, standard deviation σ random number.

For generating samples of discrete random variables with a finite number of points of support, there is a simple, fast general technique (Walker, 1977) known as the "alias method." The technique is related to rejection–acceptance but it is superior because instead of being discarded, "rejected" random numbers are replaced by "aliases." Two tables of stored constants are used. For a specified discrete distribution, these must be computed once. A derivation and detailed discussion of the alias method is in Kronmal and Peterson (1979).

The "ratio-of-uniforms method" for generating nonuniform random numbers provides another context for rejection–acceptance techniques; see Kinderman and Monahan (1977) for a discussion. The idea is as follows. Let X be a random variable with density function $f(x)$ and define a region $C(f)$ of the plane according to

$$C(f) = \{(u,v): 0 \leqslant u < [f(v/u)]^{1/2}\}. \tag{5.26}$$

The underlying result is that if (U, V) is a pair of random variables uniformly distributed over $C(f)$, then $X = V/U$ has density function $f(x)$. For most standard distributions it is necessary to use a rejection–acceptance technique to obtain (U, V) uniformly distributed over $C(f)$. Algorithms based on the ratio-of-uniforms method tend to be short and are often relatively efficient.

5.2.4   Characterization

Given a source of uniform random numbers, it is sometimes possible to generate nonuniform random numbers by drawing on transformations, characterizations, and other special results of applied probability. As an illustration, we consider the Poisson distribution and a technique based on properties of a (homogeneous) Poisson process.

By definition, a (homogeneous) Poisson process of rate $\lambda > 0$ is a series of point events in which the numbers of events in nonoverlapping intervals are independent random variables (independent increments) and the number of events in an interval has a Poisson distribution with parameter λ times the length of the interval. Denote by $N(t)$ the number of events in $(0, t]$ and let X_1 be the time to the first event after 0. Observe that $N(t) = 0$ if and only if $X_1 > t$. Therefore

$$\text{Prob}\{N(t) = 0\} = (\lambda t)^0 e^{-\lambda t}/0! = e^{-\lambda t} = \text{Prob}\{X_1 > t\} = 1 - F_{X_1}(t). \quad (5.27)$$

Thus, the time to the first event is exponentially distributed (rate parameter λ), and because the Poisson process has independent increments, all times-between-events $X_1, X_2, \ldots$ are independent and identically distributed exponential random variables.

There is a fundamental identity for any series of events that relates counts of events to times-between-events: for $t \geqslant 0$ and $n = 0, 1, 2, \ldots,$

$$N(t) = n \quad \text{if and only if} \quad X_1 + \cdots + X_n \leqslant t \quad \text{and} \quad X_1 + \cdots + X_{n+1} > t. \quad (5.28)$$

This identity (for $t = 1$) suggests a procedure for obtaining samples of a Poisson random variable with parameter λ. From mutually independent and uniformly distributed (between 0 and 1) random numbers $U_1, U_2, \ldots,$ we can obtain exponential (rate parameter λ) random numbers $X_1, X_2, \ldots$ by logarithmic transformation; then we take $N = k$, where k is defined by the joint condition $X_1 + \cdots + X_k \leqslant 1$ and $X_1 + \cdots + X_k + X_{k+1} > 1$. According to this scheme,

$$N = \begin{cases} 0 & \text{if } X_1 > 1, \\ 1 & \text{if } X_1 \leqslant 1 \quad \text{and} \quad X_1 + X_2 > 1, \\ 2 & \text{if } X_1 \leqslant 1, \quad X_1 + X_2 \leqslant 1, \quad \text{and} \quad X_1 + X_2 + X_3 > 1, \\ \vdots \end{cases} \quad (5.29)$$

Note that with this scheme it may be necessary to generate more than one uniform random number in order to produce a single sample of the Poisson random variable N. There is also the following computational consideration. The event $N = k$ occurs if and only if $X_1 + \cdots + X_k \leqslant 1$ and $X_1 + \cdots + X_k + X_{k+1} > 1$, and the latter occurs if and only if $U_1 U_2 \cdots U_k > e^{-\lambda}$ and $U_1 U_2 \cdots U_{k+1} \leqslant e^{-\lambda}$. Thus,

$$N = \begin{cases} 0 & \text{if } U_1 \leqslant e^{-\lambda}, \\ 1 & \text{if } U_1 > e^{-\lambda} \quad \text{and} \quad U_1 U_2 \leqslant e^{-\lambda}, \\ 2 & \text{if } U_1 > e^{-\lambda}, \quad U_1 U_2 > e^{-\lambda}, \quad \text{and} \quad U_1 U_2 U_3 \leqslant e^{-\lambda}, \\ \vdots \end{cases} \quad (5.30)$$

and by computing $e^{-\lambda}$ once we avoid the necessity of taking logarithms and dividing by λ each time a uniform random number U is generated; it is necessary, however, to multiply rather than add the uniform random numbers.

ALGORITHM 5.11   POISSON DISTRIBUTION (MULTIPLICATION METHOD)

1. Set $N = 0$ and $W = 1$.
2. Generate U uniformly distributed between 0 and 1 and set W equal to WU.
3. If $W > e^{-\lambda}$, set $N = N + 1$ and go to 2; otherwise, return N.

This technique for producing Poisson random numbers is generally a little faster than inverse transformation, but requires more uniform random numbers; with the random number generator package LLRANDOM (Learmonth and Lewis, 1973a), generation of a uniform random number on an IBM System 360/65 takes about 13 μs, multiplication 7 μs, and division 30 μs. Note that as $e^{-\lambda}$ decreases (i.e., as $E[N]$ increases), more uniform random numbers must be generated and multiplied before the product is smaller than $e^{-\lambda}$. In fact

E[number of uniform random numbers per Poisson random number]

  $= E$[number of comparisons per Poisson random number] $= \lambda + 1$

  $= E$[number of multiplications per Poisson random number] $+ 1$.

Sophisticated decomposition techniques for generation of Poisson random numbers whose timing does not go up with λ have been developed by Ahrens and Dieter (1974).

As another example, consider the so-called "polar method" (cf. Knuth, 1969, pp. 104–105) for producing normal random numbers. The polar method uses a rejection–acceptance technique based on the result that if two independent normal (mean 0, standard deviation 1) random variables X_1 and X_2 are transformed to polar coordinates R and θ according to

$$R^2 = X_1^2 + X_2^2 \qquad \text{and} \qquad \theta = \tan^{-1}(X_2/X_1), \qquad (5.31)$$

then R^2 is exponentially distributed (mean 2), and θ is uniformally distributed (between 0 and 2π), independent of R. Algorithm 5.12 produces a pair X_1, X_2 of independent, standardized normal random numbers.

ALGORITHM 5.12   NORMAL DISTRIBUTION (POLAR METHOD)

1. Generate U_1 and U_2 independent and uniformly distributed between 0 and 1.
2. Set $V_1 = 2U_1 - 1$ and $V_2 = 2U_2 - 1$.
3. Set $S = V_1^2 + V_2^2$. If $S \geqslant 1$, reject the pair U_1, U_2 and repeat 1. Otherwise, return

$$X_1 = V_1[(-2\ln S)/S]^{1/2} \qquad \text{and} \qquad X_2 = V_2[(-2\ln S)/S]^{1/2}.$$

Note that the polar method is exact, whereas a procedure based on obtaining the inverse of the normal probability integral numerically usually is not. On an IBM System 360/65 the polar method requires approximately 300 μs for each normal random number, and the fastest decomposition technique requires about 45 μs; see Learmonth and Lewis (1973a).

Characterization techniques can be used to obtain samples from the beta distribution. A beta random variable X takes on values in the unit interval and has density function of the form

$$f_X(x) = \begin{cases} x^{a-1}(1-x)^{b-1}/B(a,b) & \text{if } 0 \leqslant x \leqslant 1, \\ 0 & \text{otherwise,} \end{cases} \tag{5.32}$$

where $a, b > 0$. The quantity $B(a,b)$ in Eq. (5.32) is the beta function

$$B(a,b) = \int_0^1 x^{a-1}(1-x)^{b-1}\,dx = \frac{\Gamma(a)\Gamma(b)}{\Gamma(a+b)} \tag{5.33}$$

and $\Gamma(\cdot)$ is the gamma function. The random variable X defined by Eqs. (5.32) and (5.33) has mean $a/(a+b)$ and standard deviation

$$[ab/(a+b+1)]^{1/2}/(a+b).$$

Note that when $a = b = 1$, the beta distribution reduces to the uniform distribution on the unit interval. The beta density function is a two-parameter family on the unit interval which can assume a variety of different shapes and is one of the most frequently used to fit data; see Johnson and Kotz (1970, pp. 42–43).

Sampling from the beta distribution reduces to sampling from two gamma distributions. This is because the random variable $Y/(Y+Z)$ has a beta distribution with parameters a and b when Y and Z are independent random variables having gamma distributions [defined by Eq. (5.14) with $(k-1)!$ replaced by $\Gamma(k)$] with scale parameter 1 and shape parameters a and b, respectively; see, e.g., Fishman (1973, pp. 204–205).

ALGORITHM 5.13   BETA DISTRIBUTION (GAMMA SAMPLING; ARBITRARY a, b)

1. Generate Y having a gamma distribution with scale parameter 1 and shape parameter a.
2. Generate Z having a gamma distribution with scale parameter 1 and shape parameter b.
3. Return $X = Y/(Y+Z)$.

It is also possible to produce samples of a beta random variable by using a rejection–acceptance technique based on the following characterization. Define Y_1 and Y_2 according to $Y_1 = U_1^{1/a}$ and $Y_2 = U_2^{1/b}$, where U_1 and U_2 are independent random variables, uniformly distributed on the unit interval.

Then, given that $Y_1 + Y_2 \leqslant 1$, the random variable $X = Y_1/(Y_1 + Y_2)$ has a beta distribution with parameters a and b; see Fishman (1973, pp. 206–207).

ALGORITHM 5.14   BETA DISTRIBUTION (ARBITRARY a, b)

1. Generate U_1 and U_2 independent and uniformly distributed between 0 and 1.
2. Set $Y_1 = U_1^{1/a}$ and $Y_2 = U_2^{1/b}$.
3. If $Y_1 + Y_2 \leqslant 1$, return $X = Y_1/(Y_1 + Y_2)$; otherwise go to 1.

When a and b are both greater than 1, beta random numbers can also be produced by using rejection–acceptance techniques and sampling from the normal distribution; see Ahrens and Dieter (1973b, Chapter 10).

When both parameters of the beta distribution are integers, we can proceed as follows.

ALGORITHM 5.15   BETA DISTRIBUTION (ORDERING, INTEGRAL a, b)

1. Generate $U_1, U_2, \ldots, U_{a+b-1}$ mutually independent and uniformly distributed between 0 and 1.
2. Set X equal to the ath smallest of the $\{U_i\}$ and return X.

The validity of this procedure follows from the observations that the density function of the kth smallest of n independent samples from the uniform distribution on the unit interval is

$$f(x) = n\binom{n-1}{k-1}x^{k-1}(1-x)^{n-k} \tag{5.34}$$

for $0 \leqslant x \leqslant 1$, and 0 otherwise, and that (when a and b are positive integers) the beta function $B(a, b)$ in Eq. (5.33) can be expressed in terms of binomial coefficients according to

$$[B(a,b)]^{-1} = (a+b-1)\binom{a+b-2}{a-1} = (a+b-1)\binom{a+b-2}{b-1}. \tag{5.35}$$

Finding the ath smallest uniform random number in step 2 can be accomplished efficiently by partial sorting; see Ahrens and Dieter (1973b, Chapter 10).

5.2.5   Decomposition

We now consider a very powerful, systematic way of generating nonuniform random numbers which is applicable to discrete as well as continuous random variables. Decomposition (mixing) techniques are based on viewing samples of the specified random variable X as coming from several populations. The essential idea is to represent the distribution function of X as a convex linear mixture of distributions in such a way that most of the time X is realized as a sample of random variable that is easy to generate. Specific decomposition procedures are usually complex and often incorporate rejection–acceptance techniques.

Let X be a random variable having a density function $f_X(x)$ which can be represented as

$$f_X(x) = p_1 f_1(x) + \cdots + p_k f_k(x), \qquad (5.36)$$

where the $\{p_j\}$ are nonnegative and sum to one, and the $\{f_j(x)\}$ are probability density functions. Also define a discrete random variable Z according to

$$\text{Prob}\{Z = j\} = p_j, \qquad (5.37)$$

for $j = 1, 2, \ldots, k$.

ALGORITHM 5.16 DECOMPOSITION

1. Generate Z having the discrete distribution given by Eq. (5.37).
2. Generate and return X having density function $f_Z(x)$.

Algorithm 5.16 applies directly to mixed distributions. A simple example is the hyperexponential distribution defined for $t \geqslant 0$ by

$$\text{Prob}\{X \leqslant t\} = p(1 - e^{-\lambda t}) + (1 - p)(1 - e^{-\mu t}), \qquad (5.38)$$

where $0 < p < 1$, λ, $\mu > 0$, and $\lambda \neq \mu$.

The fastest methods available at present for normal and exponential random numbers use decomposition based on the ideas of Marsaglia *et al.* (1964). The approach is to divide the density function (of the normal or exponential) random variable into a tail and a large number of rectangles and wedges; see Knuth (1969, pp. 105–112) for a detailed discussion of the generation of normal random numbers by decomposition. The Naval Postgraduate School random number generator package LLRANDOM (Learmonth and Lewis, 1973a) contains System/360 Basic Assembler Language implementations of decomposition techniques for normal and exponential random numbers.

There are many ways of decomposing a specified density function. In selecting a decomposition we are guided by geometric considerations. Triangular density functions, i.e., corresponding to $U_1 + U_2$ where U_1 and U_2 are independent and identically distributed uniform random variables are frequently used in decomposition techniques. Also useful are wedges corresponding to $\max(U_1, U_2)$, i.e., having density function

$$f(x) = \begin{cases} 2x & \text{if } 0 \leqslant x \leqslant 1, \\ 0 & \text{otherwise,} \end{cases} \qquad (5.39)$$

and min(U_1, U_2), i.e.,

$$f(x) = \begin{cases} 2(1 - x) & \text{if } 0 \leqslant x \leqslant 1, \\ 0 & \text{otherwise.} \end{cases} \tag{5.40}$$

In connection with Algorithm 5.16, note that if U [a uniform random number on $(0, 1)$] is used to select the value of Z, it may be scaled and reused to generate the population random variable X_Z; i.e., given that $P_{j-1} = p_1 + \cdots + p_{j-1} < U \leqslant P_j = p_1 + \cdots + p_j, (U - P_{j-1})/p_j$ may be used as an independent $(0, 1)$ uniform random number.

Although the Cauchy distribution is not of great importance in computer system modeling, it serves well to illustrate decomposition. A Cauchy random variable X has density function

$$f_X(x) = \pi^{-1}(1 + x^2)^{-1} \tag{5.41}$$

on $-\infty < x < +\infty$. Robinson and Lewis (1975) use decomposition together with a rejection–acceptance technique to produce a sample of the absolute value of X and then attach a random sign. Decompose the area under $f_{|X|}(x)$ into three areas by a vertical line $x = a$ and a horizontal line $f_{|X|}(x) = f_{|X|}(a)$. Call the area between the horizontal and vertical lines region 1, the area above the horizontal line region 2, and the area to the right of $x = a$ region 3; see Fig. 5.3. We choose $a = 1$ so as to make region 1 as large as possible (thereby sampling from a uniform distribution as often as possible). The areas of regions 1, 2, and 3 are equal, respectively, to p_1, p_2, and p_3, and $f_1(x), f_2(x)$, and $f_3(x)$ are the corresponding uniform, wedge-shaped, and long-tailed density functions.

Specifically, for $0 \leqslant x < \infty$ we represent $f_{|X|}(x)$ as

$$f_{|X|}(x) = p_1 f_1(x) + p_2 f_2(x) + p_3 f_3(x), \tag{5.42}$$

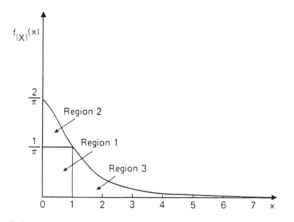

Fig. 5.3 Density function decomposition for Cauchy random variable.

where

$$f_1(x) = \begin{cases} 1 & \text{if} \quad 0 \leqslant x \leqslant 1, \\ 0 & \text{if} \quad x > 1, \end{cases} \tag{5.43}$$

$$f_2(x) = \begin{cases} [(2/\pi)(1 + x^2)^{-1} - (1/\pi)]/[\tfrac{1}{2} - (1/\pi)] & \text{if} \quad 0 \leqslant x \leqslant 1, \\ 0 & \text{if} \quad x > 1, \end{cases} \tag{5.44}$$

and

$$f_3(x) = \begin{cases} (4/\pi)(1 + x^2)^{-1} & \text{if} \quad x > 1, \\ 0 & \text{if} \quad 0 \leqslant x \leqslant 1, \end{cases} \tag{5.45}$$

with $p_1 = 1/\pi$, $p_2 = \tfrac{1}{2} - (1/\pi)$, and $p_3 = \tfrac{1}{2}$.

Samples from the uniform density function $f_1(x)$ can be obtained directly, and samples from the tail density function $f_3(x)$ can be obtained by a rejection–acceptance technique. The latter is accomplished by choosing $h(x) = 1/x^2$ as a majorizing density function and recalling that this is the density function of the reciprocal of a random variable uniformly distributed on the interval $(0, 1)$. The remaining wedge-shaped density function $f_2(x)$ is a so-called "nearly linear" density function for which there is an efficient rejection–acceptance technique due to Marsaglia (1964); also see Knuth (1969, pp. 108–109).

It is also possible to use decomposition with continuous mixtures of distributions. As an example, consider the negative binomial random variable. The discrete random variable X has a negative binomial distribution [with parameters $0 < p < 1$ and $r > 0$, and mean $rp/(1 - p)$] if for $k = 0, 1, \ldots,$

$$\text{Prob}\{X = k\} = \Gamma(r + k)/[\Gamma(k + 1)\Gamma(r)]p^k(1 - p)^r. \tag{5.46}$$

Here r need not be restricted to the positive integers. If $r = 1$ the negative binomial reduces to the geometric distribution given by Eq. (5.8). For positive integral r, X is the number of successes (occurring with probability p) encountered in a sequence of independent Bernoulli trials before the rth failure; in this case, X is the sum of r independent geometric random variables with parameter p. Using Algorithm 5.7, we can produce samples of the negative binomial random variable by composition.

We can also produce samples of X (even for nonintegral r) by observing that a negative binomial random variable is obtained by randomizing a Poisson random variable having parameter Y, where Y is a random variable having a gamma distribution with parameters r and $p/(1 - p)$. Specifically, if for $k = 0, 1, \ldots,$

$$\text{Prob}\{X = k \mid Y = y\} = e^{-y}y^k/k!, \tag{5.47}$$

where for $0 \leqslant y < \infty$,

$$f_Y(y) = \lambda^r y^{r-1} e^{-\lambda y}/\Gamma(r) \tag{5.48}$$

and $\lambda = (1 - p)/p$, then X has the negative binomial distribution given by Eq. (5.46).

Algorithm 5.17 Negative Binomial (Decomposition)

1. Generate Y having a gamma distribution with parameters r and $p/(1 - p)$.
2. Generate and return X having a Poisson distribution with parameter Y.

Implementations of efficient algorithms for producing gamma random numbers (nonintegral shape parameter) are described by Robinson and Lewis (1975); see Schmeiser (1980) for references to recent work.

5.2.6 Comparison

Techniques involving generalizations of a scheme due to Von Neumann (1951) for producing exponential random numbers have been developed for certain kinds of random numbers. The Von Neumann technique is based on comparisons among uniform random numbers. In particular, these comparison techniques lead to a simple algorithm for producing samples from density functions of the form $\alpha e^{-G(x)}$. A complete description of the theory and application of comparison techniques is in Chapter 6 of Ahrens and Dieter (1973b).

The basic comparison procedure (Forsythe, 1972) produces samples of a random variable X having a density function of the form

$$f_X(x) = \left(\int_a^b e^{-G(y)} dy \right)^{-1} e^{-G(x)} \qquad (5.49)$$

concentrated on a fixed interval $[a, b]$, where $0 \leqslant G(x) \leqslant 1$. To accomplish this, a sequence of mutually independent random numbers $T, U_1, U_2, \ldots$ is generated, the $\{U_j\}$ being uniformly distributed between 0 and 1; the distribution function $F(t)$ of T is assumed to be invertible in the interval $[a, b]$ and such that $G(\cdot) = F^{-1}(\cdot)$. With probability 1, either $T < U_1$ or there is a finite integer K such that $T \geqslant U_1 \geqslant \cdots \geqslant U_{K-1} < U_K$. Sequences of random numbers $T, U_1, \ldots, U_K$ are generated until an odd stopping subscript is encountered.

Algorithm 5.18 Comparison (Sampling on an Interval $[a, b]$)

1. Generate U uniformly distributed between 0 and 1. Set $X = a + (b - a)U$ and $T = G(X)$.
2. Generate $U_1, U_2, \ldots, U_K$, mutually independent and uniformly distributed between 0 and 1, with K determined by $T \geqslant U_1 \geqslant \cdots \geqslant U_{K-1} < U_K$ ($K = 1$ if $T < U_1$).

3. If K is even, reject X and repeat 1.
4. If K is odd, return X.

Refinements of the basic comparison procedure yield a range of short, medium-speed to long, high-speed algorithms for normal random numbers; cf. Chapter 8 of Ahrens and Dieter (1973b). To illustrate the application of comparison, we give a procedure for generating unit exponential random numbers. In the algorithm, all uniform random numbers U and V are independent.

ALGORITHM 5.19   EXPONENTIAL DISTRIBUTION (COMPARISON)

1. Set $C = 0$.
2. Generate U uniformly distributed between 0 and 1 and set $T = U$.
3. Generate V uniformly distributed between 0 and 1. If $U < V$, go to 6.
4. Generate U uniformly distributed between 0 and 1. If $U < V$, go to 3.
5. Set $C = C + 1$ and go to 2.
6. Return $X = C + T$.

5.3   Discussion

In the foregoing exposition of some of the basic principles of uniform and nonuniform random number generation, we have not dwelled on details of implementations nor to any degree on subtle refinements of particular methods. The former are certainly important; the latter almost always occur and are often critical with respect to speed considerations. Rather, the attempt has been to place in perspective the several classes of generation methods that are available. It is of course highly desirable that a library of carefully implemented, fast routines for nonuniform random number generation be at the disposal of the simulation analyst. The intent here is to provide enough detail so that, faced with a distribution for which no generator is available, the analyst can develop an algorithm that produces samples correctly, if not with full efficiency.

5.3.1   Selection of Random Number Generators

The responsibility for selecting appropriate random number generators for an application lies with the simulation analyst. Regrettably, some rather poor (uniform and nonuniform) random number generators are readily available in certain subroutine packages, as well as in connection with some simulation programming languages. In the case of a uniform random number generator, the analyst should ensure not only that an available generator is acceptably fast, but also that it has been subjected successfully to thorough statistical testing. For nonuniform random number generators, the analyst should be aware of the tradeoffs that exist among methods so that a reasonable choice can be made.

There are four primary considerations in selection of a method for generating samples from a specified distribution: exactness, ease of implementation, speed of execution, and storage requirement. With respect to exactness,

TABLE 5.1

Generation of Nonuniform Random Numbers (Continuous Distributions)[a]

Exponential (5.7)	inverse transformation 5.1	relatively slow, easy to implement
	decomposition	fast, relatively hard to implement; see Learmonth and Lewis (1973a)
	comparison 5.19	suitable for small machines; see Ahrens and Dieter (1973b) for refinements
Hyperexponential (5.38)	decomposition 5.16	all methods for exponential random numbers available
Normal (5.25)	characterization 5.12	polar method; relatively slow, easy to implement
	decomposition	fast, relatively hard to implement; see Learmonth and Lewis (1973a) and Knuth (1969)
	comparison	fast, reasonably easy to implement; see Ahrens and Dieter (1973b)
Erlang (5.14)	composition 5.6	easy to implement
Gamma (5.14)	rejection–acceptance	shape parameter determines best methods; see Atkinson and Pearce (1976), Fishman (1976a), Marsaglia (1977), and Schmeiser and Lal (1980a)
Beta (5.32)	characterization 5.13	gamma sampling; arbitrary a, b; easy to implement
	characterization 5.14	uses rejection–acceptance; arbitrary a, b; easy to implement
	characterization 5.15	ordering; a, b integers; uses partial sorting
	characterization	uses rejection–acceptance, normal sampling, $a, b > 1$; fast for $a = b$; see Ahrens and Dieter (1973b)
	rejection–acceptance	arbitrary a, b; speed largely independent of parameter values; see Cheng (1979)
	rejection–acceptance	$a, b > 1$; uses exponential majorizing functions; see Schmeiser and Babu (1980)

[a] In Tables 5.1 and 5.2, citations in parentheses, e.g., (5.7), refer to equations in Section 5.2; citations without parentheses, e.g., 5.8, refer to algorithms of Section 5.2.

recall first that this refers to the property that any deviation from the specified distribution results from computer round-off error rather than a defect in the method itself. Algorithms that are not exact have been proposed for nonuniform random number generation. For example, these are methods for producing random numbers that are approximately normally distributed. These call for the summation of several (e.g., 12) uniform random numbers or the use of inverse transformation with an approximate inverse. The potential problems, with respect to analysis of simulation output, are readily apparent. Moreover, we are not aware of any (univariate) probability distribution for which a reasonable (in the sense of speed and ease of implementation) exact method cannot be obtained. We recommend avoidance of random number generators that are not exact.

With exact generators, it is usually the case that tradeoffs must be made among ease of implementation, length of the resulting program, and speed of execution. We have already noted that comparisons of the speed of various methods are hard to make, partly because of machine dependencies; for discussion of these matters, and timing results for particular generators, see Ahrens and Dieter (1973b). We attempt in Tables 5.1 and 5.2 to summarize

TABLE 5.2

Generation of Nonuniform Random Numbers (Discrete Distributions)

Geometric (5.8)	inverse transformation 5.2	easy to implement
Poisson (5.10)	inverse transformation 5.4	time proportional to mean; fast if mean is small
	characterization 5.11	time proportional to mean; somewhat simpler than inverse transformation
	decomposition	"center-triangle" method, see Ahrens and Dieter (1973b); very fast for moderate to large mean
	rejection–acceptance	uses Poisson majorizing density function; see Fishman (1979)
Bernoulli (5.9)	inverse transformation 5.3	easy to implement
Binomial (5.15)	composition 5.7	computationally costly when n large
	characterization	beta sampling; uses rejection–acceptance; see Ahrens and Dieter (1973b); much faster than composition for large n
	rejection–acceptance	finite execution time for any mean; see Atkinson (1979a)
Negative binomial (5.46)	composition	r must be positive integer
	decomposition 5.17	superior for moderate and large r; requires gamma and Poisson generators

available techniques for certain common nonuniform distributions, both continuous and discrete. In the tables, citations in parentheses, e.g., (5.7), refer to equations in Section 5.2 where these particular distributions are defined; citations without parentheses, e.g., 5.8, refer to algorithms of Section 5.2. We have observed that the speed of execution of many of the best available nonuniform random number generators depends in many cases on refinements not discussed here of the basic generation methods of Section 5.2. For this reason Tables 5.1 and 5.2 also contain appropriate references.

5.3.2 Single and Multiple Random Number Streams

It is typically the case for simulation that several streams of random numbers are needed. For example, when simulating a network of queues, random service times for each of several servers may be required. Since, as we have seen in Section 5.2, many algorithms for producing nonuniform random numbers require generation of one or more uniform random numbers, the question arises as to whether single or multiple streams should be used. When a single stream of uniform random numbers is used, the course of the simulation determines (usually in a complex manner) how individual uniform random numbers are used; thus, e.g., in a single server queueing system with Poisson arrivals and exponential service times, a random subsequence of the generated uniform random numbers could be transformed to give the interarrival times, with the remaining random numbers used to generate the service times. Alternatively, if appropriate seeds are available, nonoverlapping portions of the uniform random number sequence could be used to generate the interarrival times and the service times, respectively. The concern is that when a single stream of uniform random numbers is used, we are in effect assuming that particular random subsequences of the original uniform random number sequence will have an acceptable appearance of randomness, and this may not be the case. There are examples of simulations where the use of a single stream of uniform random numbers has led to rather bizarre results. Although this aspect of random number generation is not well understood, in many cases it is probably good practice to use separate streams. Some additional bookkeeping is required to handle the separate streams, and judgment is needed as to what extent multiple streams should be used for simulation of a complex stochastic system. When simulating a network of queues, it is probably advisable to use separate random number streams for the interarrival times, service times, and routing of jobs from a particular service center.

In Table 5.3 we give values of seeds that can be used to generate independent streams of uniform random numbers from the System/360 uniform random number generator of Eqs. (5.4) and (5.5). These seeds are values of X_n which are 100000 apart in the sequence, i.e., if $X_0 = 377003613$, then $X_{100000} = 648473574$, $X_{200000} = 1396717869$, etc. It is necessary when using multiple streams of random numbers to keep in mind approximately how many random numbers are going to be needed; undesired dependence among random numbers will result if portions of the original sequence overlap inadvertently.

TABLE 5.3

Seeds for System/360 Uniform Random Number Generator
Values of X_n 100000 Apart in $X_n = 7^5 X_{n-1}$ (mod $2^{31} - 1$)[a]

377003613	648473574	1396717869	2027350275	1356162430
1752629996	645806097	201331468	1393552473	1966641861
711072531	769795447	1074543187	1933483444	625102656
1116874679	1442211901	989455196	1996695068	1850124212
1267310126	1741371275	886499692	1014119573	933913228
2082204497	920168983	1079618777	1888797415	1002901030
1582733583	254293472	1095895189	219529399	1706847402
1951007719	1169002398	1482199345	1976077334	775245191
1976418161	35067978	400884188	1895732964	1904749580
1301700180	63685808	936615625	110322717	1029730003
251900732	725094089	828842333	1471230052	1703522097
1356420548	1670372925	437765009	39279049	2123613511
150006407	1633650593	751601611	1410990605	1262214427
645360044	1504645702	1063375004	941885586	1753135176
253642018	1701685042	1448665492	1034856864	428280431
259758456	6007372272	704726097	398944698	114386769
288727775	1499601820	2136214308	1197972807	1888007825
686553263	747119178	154337000	136758808	9182540
303111010	154232008	921093990	1684263351	1166344707
1167753617	1374693082	1812641667	502455872	857532898

[a] Table is to be read across.

It is fundamental for simulation, since results are based on observation of a stochastic system, that some assessment of the precision of reported results be provided. The most obvious (but not the only) means of assessing the variability of a point estimate obtained by simulation is replication; the idea is to obtain (from independent random number streams) a set of independent observations of the quantity of interest, and compute from these observations a valid confidence interval or other measure of the precision of the results. (Chapter 6 discusses replication and other methods for assessing the variability of simulation results.) Having selected (in accordance with the discussion of Section 5.3.2) one or more seeds to be used in a single replication, it is easy to carry out additional independent replications. In a subsequent replication, we can use as seed for each of the uniform random number streams of the simulation the value [of X_n in Eq. (5.4)] left behind by the previous replication. Thus, for additional independent replications, we need only re-establish the initial state of the system and continue the simulation.

For some stochastic systems particular random number streams can be transformed and/or re-used in certain ways so that the resulting estimates have smaller variance than otherwise would be the case. Indeed, this is the basis for certain *variance reduction* techniques, e.g., the method of antithetic variables proposed by Page (1965) in the context of queueing systems; see Gaver and Thompson (1974, pp. 584–586). Here pairs of correlated observations are employed; when a uniform random number U is generated in a realization, the uniform random number $1 - U$ is used in a companion realization. Further details of this and related variance reduction techniques are outside the scope of the present discussion. The point here is the observation that for reasons of statistical efficiency, the simulation analyst may wish to re-use and/or transform particular sequences of (uniform) random numbers that arise during the simulation; to do so, the analyst must have knowledge of and be able to control the random number generator seeds that are used. A simulation programming language should facilitate this aspect of simulation, but some do not.

5.4 Sample Paths for Stochastic Processes

In the previous sections, we have considered the generation and use of random number streams. Implicit in all of this is the notion that each stream of numbers should appear to consist of independent samples of a specified random variable. We have not considered the problem of sampling from multivariate distributions, e.g., producing samples of a pair of dependent random variables. Systematic methods for producing samples of jointly distributed random variables are not generally available, although there are methods for particular situations, e.g., involving exponential, gamma, and normal random variables; see Chapter 8 of Fishman (1973) and Schmeiser and Lal (1980b).

The remaining sections deal with generating realizations or sample paths for stochastic processes. This is pertinent to the simulation of any stochastic system, in connection with the process which constitutes the "state vector" of the system. The problem also arises when, as in the case of an arrival process to an open queueing system, a stochastic process is part of the specification of the model. The emphasis here is on the latter situation.

5.4.1 State Vector Processes

When simulating a stochastic system, we observe the behavior of the system as it evolves in time. Implicit in any implementation of a simulation is the definition of an appropriate system state vector. This "state of the system at time t" constitutes a stochastic process (in continuous or discrete time), and to obtain estimates of quantities of interest, we must somehow generate realizations or sample paths of this stochastic process. For complex stochastic systems usually it is necessary to generate the process (e.g., using an event scheduling approach) by means of timing routines applicable to a general discrete event simulation. Typically such routines are provided by a high level simulation programming language such as GPSS, SIMPL/I, or SIMSCRIPT.

For some systems that we wish to simulate, it will be possible to characterize the state vector process as a familiar stochastic process (e.g., the process of numbers-in-queue in certain closed queueing networks with exponential service times as a continuous time Markov chain). When this can be done, it may be possible to generate the process directly and more efficiently than by using all of the apparatus for timing which is necessary for a general discrete event simulation. See Appendix 4 of Iglehart and Shedler (1980) for an example.

For some stochastic processes of relatively simple structure (e.g., a homogeneous Poisson process in which the times-between-events are independent, exponentially distributed random variables, or a discrete time Markov chain where we sample independently but from different distributions determined by the state of the process), the methods of Section 5.2 for generation of (independent) nonuniform random numbers can be applied rather directly. Generation of most stochastic processes, however, requires new methods since sequences of correlated random numbers must be produced. Systematic generation methods for stochastic processes are not available, although for some particular processes (e.g., continuous time Markov chains and semi-Markov processes), there are efficient methods based on special characterizations.

Let $\{X(t): t \geqslant 0\}$ be a (time-homogeneous) continuous time Markov chain with finite state space E. This means that for any $t, s \geqslant 0$ and $j \in E$,

$$\text{Prob}\{X(t + s) = j \,|\, X(u); u \leqslant t\} = \text{Prob}\{X(t + s) = j \,|\, X(t)\} \quad (5.50)$$

and that the conditional probability

$$\text{Prob}\{X(t + s) = j \,|\, X(t) = i\} = P_{ij}(s) \quad (5.51)$$

is independent of $t \geqslant 0$ for all $i, j \in E$ and $s \geqslant 0$. The Markov chain is specified by a matrix $Q = (q_{ij})$, called the generator, such that $q_{ij} \geqslant 0$ for $i, j \in E$ with $i \neq j$, and for all i,

$$\sum_{j \in E} q_{ij} = 0.$$

The quantity q_{ij} is the derivative $dP_{ij}(t)/dt$ evaluated at $t = 0$.

Denote by $\{\tau_n : n \geqslant 0\}$ the times at which the process changes state, and for $n = 0, 1, \ldots$, set $X_n = X(\tau_n)$. Generation of the continuous time Markov chain can be based on the following characterization. For any $j \in E$, $u > 0$, and $n = 0, 1, \ldots$,

$$\text{Prob}\{X_{n+1} = j, \tau_{n+1} - \tau_n > u \mid X_0, \ldots, X_n; \tau_0, \ldots, \tau_n\} = r_{ij} \exp(-q_i u)$$

$$(5.52)$$

if $X_n = i$. In this equation $q_i = -q_{ii}$ and

$$r_{ij} = \begin{cases} q_{ij}/q_i & \text{if } i \neq j, \\ 0 & \text{if } i = j. \end{cases}$$

Thus, given a jump to state i, the process remains in state i for an exponentially distributed (rate parameter q_i) amount of time, and then jumps to state j with independent probability r_{ij}. It follows that generation of a sample path for the Markov chain can be accomplished by producing a pair of independent random numbers. This pair consists of an exponential random number and a sample from a discrete distribution specified by the jump probabilities.

Formal definition of a semi-Markov process is in terms of a Markov renewal process: see Çinlar (1975, pp. 313–316). Denote by E the finite state space of a discrete time stochastic process $\{Y_n : n \geqslant 0\}$ and let $\{T_n : n \geqslant 0\}$ be an increasing sequence of random variables with $T_0 = 0$. The process $\{(Y_n, T_n) : n \geqslant 0\}$ is a *Markov renewal process* with state space E if for all $n \geqslant 0, j \in E$, and $t \geqslant 0$,

$$\text{Prob}\{Y_{n+1} = j, T_{n+1} - T_n \leqslant t \mid Y_0, \ldots, Y_n; T_0, \ldots, T_n\}$$

$$= \text{Prob}\{Y_{n+1} = j, T_{n+1} - T_n \leqslant t \mid Y_n\}. \tag{5.53}$$

Then the stochastic process $\{Y(t) : t \geqslant 0\}$ given by

$$Y(t) = Y_n \qquad \text{for} \quad T_n \leqslant t < T_{n+1} \tag{5.54}$$

is a *semi-Markov process*.

Semi-Markov processes are continuous time stochastic processes in which jumps from state to state occur in accordance with a discrete time Markov chain, but the time spent in a state prior to the next jump (the holding time) is random. Following a jump into a state, the holding time in the state is independent of the past history of the process, and may depend on the current state as well as on the next state. It follows from this conditional independence of the holding times that a semi-Markov process can be generated as follows. Given a jump to some state, generate the next state according to the given discrete time Markov chain. Then, given the current state and the next state, generate an independent sample from the appropriate holding time distribution as the time until the jump to the next state. Observe that a continuous time Markov chain can be thought of as a semi-Markov process in which there are no jumps from a state to itself and the holding times in a state are exponentially distributed with rate parameter dependent only on the current state.

5.4.2 Series of Events

We now consider the situation in which the specification of the stochastic system includes one or more stochastic processes. For computer system simulation, the most familiar example is probably an arrival process to a network of queues. In this situation, it is necessary to generate a stochastic process even if a simulation programming language with built-in timing routines is used.

The most apparent methodological advantage of simulation is that it is applicable in principle to systems of arbitrary complexity. Thus, in particular, there is no need to restrict attention to simple arrival patterns (e.g., Poisson arrivals) in situations where they are known to be inconsistent with available data or are intuitively suspect. There are many ways to model departures from a Poisson pattern; see, e.g., the Markov arrival processes defined in Section 6 of Iglehart and Shedler (1980). The following sections deal with generation methods for series of events, i.e., particular stochastic processes that are appropriate models for arrival processes in networks of queues.

A series of events is specified by a continuous time stochastic process called its *counting process*; we shall denote the counting process by $\{N(t): t \geqslant 0\}$, where $N(t)$ is the total number of events in $(0, t]$. Equivalently, the series of events is specified by a discrete time stochastic process, the *interval process* $\{X_i: i \geqslant 1\}$, where X_i is the time between the $(i-1)$st and ith events. Related to the times-between-events are the times-to-events, $\{T_i: i \geqslant 1\}$, defined by $T_1 = X_1$ and $T_i = T_{i-1} + X_i$ for $i > 1$; see Fig. 5.4. The equivalence between

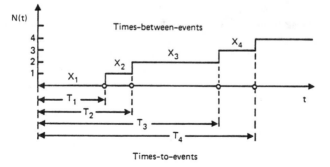

Times-to-events

Fig. 5.4 Series of events.

the counting and interval specifications of a series of events is given by Eq. (5.28). A series of events is often referred to as a *stochastic point process.*

5.4.3 Nonhomogeneous Poisson Processes

The nonhomogeneous Poisson process (cf. e.g., Çinlar, 1975, pp. 94–101) is a widely used model for a series of events having time-varying rate. This process is often used to model event streams when there is gross inhomogeneity in a system, e.g., time of day effect or long-term growth in the use of a facility. The nonhomogeneous Poisson process has the characteristic properties that the numbers of events in any finite set of nonoverlapping intervals are independent random variables and that the number of events in any interval has a Poisson distribution. The nonhomogeneous Poisson process can be defined in terms of a monotone, nondecreasing function $\Lambda(t)$ which is bounded in any finite interval. Then the number of events in a finite interval, e.g., $(0, t_0]$, has a Poisson distribution with parameter $\Lambda(t_0) - \Lambda(0)$. The derivative $\lambda(t)$ of $\Lambda(t)$ is the *rate function* for the process; the *integrated rate function* $\Lambda(t)$ has the interpretation that for $t \geqslant 0$, $\Lambda(t) - \Lambda(0) = E[N(t)]$, where $N(t)$ is the total number of events in $(0, t]$. In contrast to the homogeneous Poisson process, i.e., $\lambda(t)$ constant, the times-between-events in a nonhomogeneous Poisson process are neither independent nor identically distributed.

The nonhomogeneous Poisson process has been used (Lewis and Shedler, 1976) as a model for the series of transaction initiation events in a running IMS (Information Management System) data base management system. The process may also be of interest as a model for arrivals of messages from computer terminals, etc.

Generation of the nonhomogeneous Poisson process in a fixed interval $(0, t_0]$ is more natural than generation for a fixed number of events since time, not event serial number, is the basic parameter of the inhomogeneity. Thus the algorithms here for generation of the nonhomogeneous Poisson process produce a sequence of times-to-events in a fixed interval. Although such methods require more memory than successive generation of individual times until the next event, in general they are far more efficient with respect to speed. Note that when simulating nonhomogeneous systems of this kind, estimates of quantities of interest will be based on multiple replications. For a review of methods for generation of the nonhomogeneous Poisson process, see Lewis and Shedler (1978).

Time-scale transformation of a homogeneous (rate one) Poisson process via the inverse of the integrated rate function $\Lambda(t)$ constitutes a general method (cf. Çinlar, 1975, pp. 98–99) for generation of the nonhomogeneous Poisson process. This method is based on the result that $T_1, T_2, \ldots$ are the times-to-events in a nonhomogeneous Poisson process with integrated rate function

$\Lambda(t)$ if and only if $T'_1 = \Lambda(T_1)$, $T'_2 = \Lambda(T_2), \ldots$ are the times-to-events in a homogeneous Poisson process of rate one; see Fig. 5.5. The time-scale transformation method is a direct analogue of inverse transformation for nonuniform random numbers. For many rate functions, inversion of $\Lambda(t)$ is not simple and must be done numerically. The resulting algorithm for generation of the nonhomogeneous Poisson process may be far less efficient than generation based on other methods.

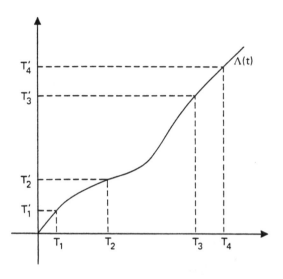

Fig. 5.5 Time-scale transformation.

A second general method is to generate the times-between-events individually, an approach which may seem more natural in the context of the event scheduling approach to simulation. Thus, given the times of the previous events $T_1 = t_1, T_2 = t_2, \ldots, T_i = t_i$, the time to the next event, $X_i = T_{i+1} - T_i$, is independent of $t_1, t_2, \ldots, t_{i-1}$ and has distribution function $F_{X_i}(x) = 1 - \exp[-\{\Lambda(t_i + x) - \Lambda(t_i)\}]$. It is possible to find the inverse distribution function $F_{X_i}^{-1}(U_i)$, usually numerically, and to generate X_i according to $X_i = F_{X_i}^{-1}(U_i)$, where U_i is a uniform random number on the interval $(0, 1)$. Note, however, that this not only involves computing the inverse distribution function for each X_i but that each distribution has different parameters and possibly a different form. An additional complication is that X_i is not necessarily a proper random variable; i.e., there may be positive probability that X_i is infinite. It is necessary to take this into account for each X_i before the inverse probability integral transformation is applied. The method is therefore very inefficient with respect to speed, more so than the time scale transformation method.

Generation of the nonhomogeneous Poisson process in a fixed interval $(0, t_0]$ can be reduced to the generation of a Poisson number of "order statistics" from a fixed density function by the following result. If $T_1, T_2, \ldots, T_n$ denote times-to-events for the nonhomogeneous Poisson process in $(0, t_0]$, and if $N(t_0) = n$, then conditional on having observed n (> 0) events in $(0, t_0]$, the $\{T_i\}$ are distributed as the order statistics from a sample with distribution function

$$F(t) = \{\Lambda(t) - \Lambda(0)\}/\{\Lambda(t_0) - \Lambda(0)\} \tag{5.55}$$

on $0 \leqslant t \leqslant t_0$. This means that given n, the joint distribution of the times-to-events in the interval $(0, t_0]$ is the same as that of n independent samples from the distribution $F(t)$, arranged in nondecreasing order.

The order statistics method for generation of the nonhomogeneous Poisson process is in general more efficient (with respect to speed) that either of the previous two methods. Of course, a price is paid for this greater efficiency; namely, more memory is needed to store the sequence of times-to-events. Enough memory must be provided so that with very high probability the random number of events generated in the interval can be stored. Recall that the number of events in the interval $(0, t_0]$ is Poisson distributed and let μ_0 denote its mean. Memory of size equal to $\mu_0 + 4\mu_0^{1/2}$ will ensure that overflow will occur on the average in only one out of approximately every 40,000 realizations. This probability is small enough so that in the case of overflow, the realization of the process generally can be discarded. Note that the order statistics method transforms the problem of generating a nonhomogeneous Poisson process into the problem of generating nonuniform random numbers; hence, all methods for nonuniform random number generation can be used.

Finally, there is a simple and relatively efficient new method (Lewis and Shedler, 1979) for generation of the nonhomogeneous Poisson process. The method is applicable for any given rate function $\lambda(t)$ and is based on controlled deletion of events in a Poisson process with a rate function $\lambda^*(t)$ that dominates $\lambda(t)$. In its simplest implementation, this thinning method obviates the need for numerical integration of the rate function, for ordering of events, and for generation of Poisson random numbers. Specifically, suppose that $\lambda(t) \leqslant \lambda^*(t)$ in the fixed interval $(0, t_0]$. The basis for the thinning method is that if T_1^*, $T_2^*, \ldots, T_n^*$ are events of the nonhomogeneous Poisson process with rate function $\lambda^*(t)$ in $(0, t_0]$, and if the event T_i^* is deleted with (independent) probability $1 - \lambda(T_i^*)/\lambda^*(T_i^*)$, then the remaining events form a nonhomogeneous Poisson process with rate function $\lambda(t)$ in $(0, t_0]$.

To illustrate, we consider as a parametric model for the rate function $\lambda(t)$ the so-called exponential polynomial of degree r; i.e., for $0 \leqslant t \leqslant t_0$

$$\lambda(t) = \exp(a_0 + a_1 t + \cdots + a_r t^r). \tag{5.56}$$

Note that with this model, $\lambda(t)$ is nonnegative for all values of the coefficients

$a_0, a_1, \ldots, a_r$. In addition, the exponential polynomial model is convenient because it leads to simple statistical procedures for rate function estimation; cf. Chapter 2 of Cox and Lewis (1966). The simplest case ($r = 1$) is

$$\lambda(t) = \exp(a_0 + a_1 t) = \lambda \exp(a_1 t). \tag{5.57}$$

Here the rate function is monotonically increasing or decreasing, depending on whether a_1 is greater than or less than 0, with $a_1 = 0$ giving a homogeneous Poisson process.

For the degree-one exponential polynomial rate function, $\Lambda(t) - \Lambda(0) = \lambda(e^{a_1 t} - 1)/a_1$, and the inverse of the integrated rate function can be obtained explicitly. It is therefore easy to use time-scale transformation to generate this nonhomogeneous Poisson process in the fixed interval $(0, t_0]$.

ALGORITHM 5.20   NONHOMOGENEOUS POISSON (TIME SCALE
                 TRANSFORMATION, $a_1 \neq 0$)

1. Generate a homogeneous Poisson process of rate 1 in the time interval $(0, \Lambda(t_0)] = (0, \lambda(e^{a_1 t_0} - 1)/a_1]$, with events at times $T'_1, T'_2, \ldots, T'_n$. If there are no events in the homogeneous Poisson process in $(0, \Lambda(t_0)]$, exit (there are no events in $(0, t_0]$).
2. Return $T_1 = a_1^{-1} \ln(1 + a_1 T'_1/\lambda), \ldots, T_n = a_1^{-1} \ln(1 + a_1 T'_n/\lambda)$.

In the case of the degree-one exponential polynomial rate function, inverse transformation can be used to obtain samples from distribution $F(t)$ of Eq. (5.55). The following algorithm for generating the nonhomogeneous Poisson process (in a fixed interval) is based on order statistics and is more efficient than Algorithm 5.20.

ALGORITHM 5.21   NONHOMOGENEOUS POISSON PROCESS (ORDER
                 STATISTICS, $a_1 \neq 0$)

1. Generate n as a Poisson random number with parameter $(e^{a_1 t_0} - 1)\lambda/a_1 = c/a_1$. If $n = 0$, exit (there are no events in $(0, t_0]$).
2. Otherwise, generate n uniform random numbers and order them to get $U_{(1)} \leqslant \cdots \leqslant U_{(n)}$.
3. Return $T_i = a_i^{-1} \ln(1 + cU_{(i)})$ for $i = 1, 2, \ldots, n$.

This algorithm uses a Poisson random number, n uniform random numbers, n logarithms, and a costly ordering of the n uniform random numbers if these are not available directly from a generator. The algorithm can be improved by using the Von Neumann comparison technique of Section 5.2.6 to sample from the distribution $F(t)$; in general it will be unnecessary to take logarithms.

The following scheme, based on generation of "gap statistics" from a random number of exponential random numbers with suitably chosen parameters, is even more efficient than generation using order statistics. The gap statistics $\{Y_i\}$ associated with independent, identically, and exponentially distributed random variables (rate parameter $\beta > 0$) are the quantities $D_1 = Y_{(1)}$, $D_2 = Y_{(2)} - Y_{(1)}, \ldots, D_m = Y_{(m)} - Y_{(m-1)}$, where $Y_{(1)}, Y_{(2)}, \ldots, Y_{(m)}$ are the $\{Y_i\}$ arranged in nondecreasing order. The gap statistics procedure is based on the result that if m is a realization of a Poisson random variable with parameter $-\lambda/a_1$ and if $\beta = -a_1$, then the gap process is a nonhomogeneous Poisson process with rate function $\lambda(t) = \lambda \exp(a_1 t)$.

The gap statistics procedure uses standard packages for exponential random numbers and obviates the need for ordering of the random numbers. We assume the availability of a source of unit exponential random numbers $E_1, E_2, \ldots$ obtained by logarithms or other methods.

ALGORITHM 5.22   NONHOMOGENEOUS POISSON PROCESS (GAP STATISTICS, $a_1 < 0$)

1. Generate m as a Poisson random number with mean $-\lambda/a_1$. If $m = 0$, exit (there are no events in $(0, t_0]$).
2. For $m > 0$, if $E_1/(-a_1 m) > t_0$, exit. Otherwise, set it equal to T_1.
3. If $T_1 + E_2/\{-a_1(m - 1)\} > t_0$, then return T_1 and exit. Otherwise, set it equal to T_2.
4. Continue, possibly for m times. If $T_{m-1} + E_m/(-a_1) > t_0$, return $T_1, T_2, \ldots, T_{m-1}$ and exit. Otherwise, set it equal to T_m and return $T_1, T_2, \ldots, T_m$.

The case $a_1 > 0$ is handled the same way as $a_1 < 0$ by using a time reversal technique. Generate times-to-events according to the gap statistics algorithm with $\lambda(t) = \lambda^* \exp(a_1^* t)$, where $\lambda^* = \exp(a_0 + a_1 t_0)$ and $a_1^* = -a_1$; the output is a sequence $T_1^*, T_2^*, \ldots, T_n^*$. Then set $T_1 = t_0 - T_n^*, \ldots, T_n = t_0 - T_1^*$. These $\{T_i\}$ are the required times-to-events in the nonhomogeneous Poisson process for $a_1 > 0$.

5.4.4 Semi-Markov Generated Point Processes

A semi-Markov process [defined by Eqs. (5.53) and (5.54)] gives rise to a series of events if a jump in the semi-Markov process is considered to be the occurrence of an event. If we distinguish *types* of events in accordance with the state into which the process jumps, *multivariate series of events* is obtained. Otherwise the series of events is *univariate*. The univariate two-state semi-Markov generated point process has been used (Lewis and Shedler, 1973) as a model for page exceptions in a demand paged computer system having a two-level memory; observed departures from a Poisson pattern of page exceptions are a consequence of locality of reference.

The two-state semi-Markov generated point process can be specified by a matrix of one-step transition probabilities

$$P = \begin{bmatrix} p_1 & 1 - p_1 \\ 1 - p_2 & p_2 \end{bmatrix} \tag{5.58}$$

with $0 < p_1, p_2 < 1$, and a matrix of conditional holding time distributions

$$F = \begin{bmatrix} F_{11}(\cdot) & F_{12}(\cdot) \\ F_{21}(\cdot) & F_{22}(\cdot) \end{bmatrix}. \tag{5.59}$$

The probability that the next transition is to state 1, given that there has just been a transition to state 1 (resp., state 2) is p_1 (resp., $1 - p_2$), etc. Similarly, the holding time in state 1, given that there has just been a transition to state 1 (resp., state 2) and that the next transition is to state 1, is an independent sample from distribution $F_{11}(\cdot)$ [resp., $F_{21}(\cdot)$], etc. We also prescribe stationary initial conditions, i.e., take

$$\text{Prob}\{Y_0 = 1\} = \pi_1 = (1 - p_2)/(2 - p_1 - p_2)$$

and $\text{Prob}\{Y_0 = 2\} = 1 - \pi_1$. Note that the times-between-events in this stationary univariate point process are correlated; cf. Cox and Lewis (1966, pp. 195–196). Algorithm 5.23 produces n times-between-events for the point process.

ALGORITHM 5.23   STATIONARY UNIVARIATE TWO-STATE SEMI-MARKOV
GENERATED POINT PROCESS

1. Put $k = 1$ and generate U, uniformly distributed between 0 and 1. Set

$$Y_0 = \begin{cases} 1 & \text{if} \quad U \leqslant \pi_1, \\ 2 & \text{if} \quad U > \pi_1. \end{cases}$$

2. Generate V, uniformly distributed between 0 and 1. If $V \leqslant p_{Y_{k-1}}$, set $Y_k = Y_{k-1}$. Otherwise, set

$$Y_k = \begin{cases} 1 & \text{if} \quad Y_{k-1} = 2, \\ 2 & \text{if} \quad Y_{k-1} = 1. \end{cases}$$

3. Generate X_k, a random sample having distribution $F_{Y_{k-1}Y_k}(\cdot)$.
4. Put $k = k + 1$. If $k > n$, return $X_1, X_2, \ldots, X_{k-1}$. Otherwise, go to 2.

Observe that in successive executions of step 2 of the algorithm, a sample path of the imbedded discrete-time Markov chain $\{Y_n : n \geqslant 0\}$ is generated. Generalization of the algorithm to generate an N state semi-Markov point process is straightforward. Note also that if the generation of X_k in step 3 involves one or more uniform random numbers, the question arises as to whether such random numbers should be taken from a single stream also used to generate the random numbers in step 2. The alternative is to use several streams of uniform random numbers obtained from different seeds. In this case, it is advisable to use separate streams.

5.4.5 Branching Poisson Processes

The branching Poisson process is a model for a clustered (univariate) series of events and is constructed as follows. There is a series of *primary events* which form a Poisson process, and each of these primary events gives rise to a subsidiary series of events. In each subsidiary process there is a random number S of *subsidiary events* separated in time by the random variables $Y_1, Y_2, \ldots, Y_S$. The random variable S may take the value 0, in which case there are no subsidiary events associated with a particular primary event. The times-between-events in a subsidiary process are independent and identically distributed as a (positive) random variable Y. The subsidiary processes are assumed to have identical stochastic structure and to be mutually independent. The usual assumptions are that the two types of events (primary and subsidiary) are indistinguishable, and that the complete process is the superposition of the events in the primary and subsidiary processes; see Fig. 5.6.

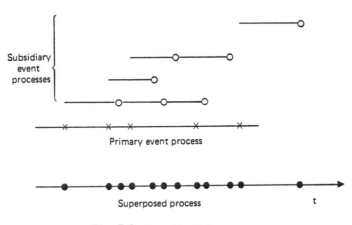

Fig. 5.6 Branching Poisson process.

The branching Poisson process has been used (Lewis, 1964) as a model for the analysis of computer failure patterns, and it accounts for observed departures from a Poisson pattern. Physically, the observed clustering of failures arises from imperfect repair, i.e., because failed components are not always located and removed the first time they cause system failure, nor are the failed components always needed for correct system operation. The branching Poisson process may also be of interest as a model for a clustered request stream, e.g., to a storage subsystem.

We now consider generation of the branching Poisson process in which the number of events in a subsidiary process is conditionally geometric (parameter

p), an assumption that greatly facilitates simulation of the process. This branching Poisson process is specified by

λ, the rate parameter of the Poisson process of primary events;

r, the probability that a subsidiary process starts;

p, the probability that after a particular subsidiary event, the subsidiary process does not terminate; and

$F_Y(\cdot)$, the distribution function for Y, the time-between-events in a subsidiary process.

In applications of the branching Poisson process, it is often difficult to make plausible assumptions about the most appropriate distribution for Y. However, distributions such as the exponential, Erlang (gamma with integral shape parameter), and hyperexponential are convenient for analytical and statistical work, and such assumptions also facilitate generation of the process. We shall suppose that Y has an exponential distribution with parameter μ. An algorithm for generating this branching Poisson process, which avoids costly sorting of times-to-events, can be based on the idea of competing Poisson processes.

Denote the times-to-events of the branching Poisson process by $T_1, T_2, \ldots$, and let Z be the exponentially distributed (mean λ^{-1}) time between primary events. The idea is to keep track of a nonnegative count $N(\cdot)$, the number of operative subsidiary processes. The key observation is that for all (primary or subsidiary) event times T_k, given the count $N(T_k) = n$, the time $T_{k+1} - T_k$ until the next (primary or subsidiary) event is determined by the occurrence of the first event in n competing processes:

n Poisson processes of rate μ (for subsidiary event processes) and
1 Poisson process of rate λ (for the primary event process).

The interval $T_{k+1} - T_k$ has an exponential distribution with rate parameter $\lambda + n\mu$ and e.g., can be generated by taking

$$T_{k+1} - T_k = -(\lambda + n\mu)^{-1} \ln U. \tag{5.60}$$

Next we observe that the type of event at time T_{k+1} can be determined independently of $T_{k+1} - T_k$ according to

$$\text{Prob\{event at } T_{k+1} \text{ is primary} \,|\, N(T_k) = n\} = \lambda/(\lambda + n\mu)$$

and

$$\text{Prob\{event at } T_{k+1} \text{ is subsidiary} \,|\, N(T_k) = n\} = n\mu/(\lambda + n\mu). \tag{5.61}$$

Given λ, $\mu > 0$, $0 < p$, $r < 1$, and a positive integer m, Algorithm 5.24 returns n times-to-events $T_1, T_2, \ldots, T_n$ in the superposed process.

ALGORITHM 5.24   BRANCHING POISSON PROCESS (S GEOMETRIC, Y EXPONENTIAL)

1. Initialize $k = 1$ and set $T = N = 0$.
2. Generate X exponentially distributed with mean $(\lambda + N\mu)^{-1}$. Set $T = T + X$.
3. Generate U uniformly distributed between 0 and 1. Set

$$V = \begin{cases} 0 & \text{if } 0 < U \leqslant \lambda/(\lambda + N\mu), \\ 1 & \text{if } \lambda/(\lambda + N\mu) < U \leqslant 1. \end{cases}$$

4. If $V = 1$, go to 5; otherwise, there is a primary event at T. Set $T_k = T$ and generate W uniformly distributed between 0 and 1. If $W \leqslant r$, set $N = N + 1$. Go to 6.
5. Set $T_k = T$; there is a subsidiary event at T. Generate W uniformly distributed between 0 and 1. If $W \geqslant p$, set $N = N - 1$. Go to 6.
6. Set $k = k + 1$. If $k > m$, return $T_1, T_2, \ldots, T_k$. Otherwise, go to 2.

This algorithm can be modified to generate branching Poisson processes in which the time Y between events in a subsidiary process has an Erlang distribution (gamma distribution with integral shape parameter). The basic idea for the case of shape parameter 2 is to represent Y as $Y = Y_1 + Y_2$, where Y_1 and Y_2 are independent, identically distributed exponential random variables. To generate this branching Poisson process, the evolution of a subsidiary process is viewed as a sequence of phases, consisting (in pairs) of *null subsidiary* and *real subsidiary events*. An operative subsidiary process is considered to be in the null phase if an interval Y_1 is in progress, and considered to be in the real phase if an interval Y_2 is in progress. Then we keep track of two nonnegative counts $N_1(\cdot)$ and $N_2(\cdot)$, respectively, the number of operative subsidiary processes that are in the null subsidiary and real subsidiary phase. If T_k^* is a time at which an event (primary, null subsidiary, or real subsidiary) occurs, given the counts $N_1(T_k^*)$ and $N_2(T_k^*)$, the time $T_{k+1}^* - T_k^*$ until the next (primary, null subsidiary, or real subsidiary) event is determined by the occurrence of the first event in $N_1(T_k^*) + N_2(T_k^*) + 1$ competing Poisson processes. The algorithm returns only the primary and real subsidiary events.

References

Ahrens, J., and Dieter, U. (1973a). "Uniform Random Numbers." Institut für Mathematische Statistik. Technische Hochschule in Graz, Graz, Austria.
Ahrens, J., and Dieter, U. (1973b). "Nonuniform Random Numbers." Institut für Mathematische Statistik. Technische Hochschule in Graz, Graz, Austria.
Ahrens, J., and Dieter, U. (1974). Computer methods for sampling from the gamma, beta, Poisson and binomial distributions. *Computing* **12**, 223–246.

Atkinson, A. C. (1979a). The computer generation of Poisson random variables. *Appl. Statist.* **28**, 29–35.

Atkinson, A. C. (1979b). Recent developments in the computer generation of Poisson random varibles. *Appl. Statist.* **28**, 260–263.

Atkinson, A. C., and Pearce, M. C. (1976). The computer generation of beta, gamma and normal random variables. *J. Roy. Statist. Soc. Ser. A* **139**, 431–461.

Cheng, R. C. H. (1979). Generating beta variates with nonintegral shape parameter, *Comm. ACM* **21**, 317–322.

Çinlar, E. (1975). "Introduction to Stochastic Processes." Prentice-Hall, Englewood Cliffs, New Jersey.

Cox, D. R., and Lewis, P. A. W. (1966). "The Statistical Analysis of Series of Events." Methuen, London, and Barnes and Noble, New York.

Fishman, G. S. (1973). "Concepts and Methods in Discrete Event Simulation." Wiley, New York.

Fishman, G. S. (1976a). Sampling from the gamma distribution on a computer, *Comm. ACM* **19**, 407–409.

Fishman, G. S. (1978). "Principles of Discrete Event Simulation." Wiley, New York.

Fishman, G. S. (1979). Sampling from the binomial distribution on a computer. *J. Amer. Statist. Assoc.* **74**, 418–423.

Forsythe, G. E. (1972). Von Neumann's comparison method for random sampling from the normal and other distributions. *Math. Comp.* **26**, 817–826.

Gaver, D. P., and Thompson, G. L. (1973). "Programming and Probability Models in Operations Research." Brooks-Cole, Monterey, California.

Gustavson, F. G., and Liniger, W. (1970). A fast random number generator with good statistical properties. *Computing* **6**, 221–226.

Hoaglin, D. (1976). Theoretical Properties of Congruential Random-Number Generators: An Empirical View, Memorandum NS-340. Department of Statistics, Harvard Univ., Cambridge, Massachusetts.

IBM (1974). IBM Subroutine Library-Mathematics, User's Guide SH12-5300-1. IBM Corp., Data Processing Division, White Plains, New York.

Iglehart, D. L., and Shedler, G. S. (1980). "Regenerative Simulation of Response Times in Networks of Queues," Lecture Notes in Control and Information Sciences, Vol. 26. Springer-Verlag, Berlin and New York.

Johnson, N. L., and Kotz, S. (1970). "Distributions in Statistics, Continuous Univariate Distributions-2." Houghton-Miflin, Boston, Massachusetts.

Kennedy, W. J., and Gentle, J. E. (1980). "Statistical Computing." Dekker, New York.

Kinderman, A. J., and Monahan, J. F. (1977). Computer generation of random variables using the ratio of uniform deviates. *ACM Trans. Math. Software* **3**, 257–260.

Knuth, D. E. (1969). "The Art of Computer Programming," *Vol. 2*, Semi-Numerical Algorithms. Addison-Wesley, Reading, Massachusetts.

Kronmal, R. A., and Peterson, A. V. (1979). On the alias method for generating random variables from a discrete distribution. *Amer. Statist.* **33**, 214–218.

Learmonth, G. P., and Lewis, P. A. W. (1973a). Naval Postgraduate School Random Number Generator Package LLRANDOM. Naval Postgraduate School Report NPS55Lw73061A, Monterey, California.

Learmonth, G. P., and Lewis, P. A. W. (1973b). Statistical tests of some widely used and recently proposed uniform random number generators. *Proc. Conf. Comput. Sci. Statist., 7th, Ann. Symp. Interface* 163–171. Iowa State Univ.

Lewis, P. A. W. (1964). A branching Poisson process model for the analysis of computer failure patterns. *J. Roy. Statist. Soc. B* **26**, 398–456.

Lewis, P. A. W., and Shedler, G. S. (1973). Empirically derived micromodels for sequences of page exceptions, *IBM J. Res. Develop.* **17**, 86–100.

Lewis, P. A. W., and Shedler, G. S. (1976). Statistical analysis of nonstationary series of events in a data base system, *IBM J. Res. Develop.* **20**, 465–482.

Lewis, P. A. W., and Shedler, G. S. (1978). Simulation methods for Poisson processes in nonstationary systems. *Proc. Winter Simulation Conf., Miami Beach, Florida* **1**, 154–163. Published by IEEE (Catalogue No. 78CH1415-9), New York.

Lewis, P. A. W., and Shedler, G. S. (1979). Simulation of nonhomogeneous Poisson processes by thinning. *Naval Logist. Res. Quart.* **26**, 403–413.

Lewis, P. A. W., Goodman, A. S., and Miller, J. M. (1969). A pseudo-random number generator for the System/360. *IBM Syst. J.* **8**, 136–146.

Marsaglia, G. (1964). Random variables and computers. *Trans. Prague Conf. Informat. Theory. Statist. and Decision Functions, 3rd, Prague, Czechoslovakia.*

Marsaglia, G. (1977). The squeeze method for generating gamma variates. *Comput. Math. Appl.* **3**, 321–325.

Marsaglia, G., MacLaren, M. D., and Bray, T. A. (1964). A fast procedure for generating normal random variables. *Comm. ACM* **7**, 4–10.

Page, E. (1965). On Monte Carlo methods in congestion problems: II. Simulation of queueing systems. *Oper. Res.* **13**, 300–305.

Payne, W. H., Rabung, I. R., and Bogyo, T. P. (1969). Coding the Lehmer pseudo-random number generator. *Comm. ACM* **12**, 85–86.

Robinson, D. W., and Lewis, P. A. W. (1975). Generating Gamma and Cauchy Random Variables: An Extension to the Naval Postgraduate School Random Number Package. Naval Postgraduate School Rep. NPS72Ro75041, Monterey, California.

Schmeiser, B. W. (1980). Random variate generation: A survey. *Proc. Winter Simulation Conf., Orlando, Florida.*

Schmeiser, B. W., and Babu, A. J. G. (1980). Beta variate generation using exponential majorizing functions. *Oper. Res.* **28**, 917–926.

Schmeiser, B. W., and Lal, R. (1980a). Squeeze methods for generating gamma variates. *J. Amer. Statist. Assoc.* **75**, 679–682.

Schmeiser, B. W., and Lal, R. (1980b). Multivariate modeling in simulation: A survey, *ASQC Tech. Conf. Trans.* 252–261.

Von Neumann, J. (1951). "Various techniques used in connection with random digits." Collected Works V (1963), 768–70, Pergamon Press, New York.

Walker, A. J. (1977). An efficient method for generating discrete random variables with general distributions. *ACM Trans. Math. Software* **3**, 253–256.

For further reading the following articles deal with topics covered in this chapter.

Cheng, R. C. H. (1977). The generation of gamma variables with non-integral shape parameter. *Appl. Statist.* **26**, 71–75.

Cheng, R. C. H., and Feast, G. M. (1980). Gamma variate generators with increased shape parameter range. *Comm. ACM* **23**, 389–394.

Fishman, G. S. (1976b). Sampling from the Poisson distribution on a computer. *Comm. ACM* **19**, 407–409.

Marsaglia, G. (1968). Random numbers fall mainly in the planes. *Proc. Nat. Acad. Sci. USA* **60**, 25–28.

Marsaglia, G. (1972). The structure of linear congruential sequences. In "Applications of Number Theory to Numerical Analysis" (S. K. Zaremba, ed.). Academic Press, New York.

Marsaglia, G., and Bray, T. A. (1968). One-line random number generators and their use in combinations. *Comm. ACM* **11**, 757–759.

Payne, W. H. (1977). Normal random numbers: Using machine analysis to choose the best algorithm. *ACM Trans. Math. Software* **3**, 346–358.

Tadikamalla, P. R. (1978). Computer generation of gamma random variables II. *Comm. ACM* **21**, 925–927.

6

The Statistical Analysis
of Simulation Results

Peter D. Welch

6.1   The Random Nature of Simulation Outputs

6.1.1   Introduction

In this chapter we shall discuss certain basic problems of statistical inference arising from the simulation of the type of computer system models treated in this handbook. These models have a random input that consists of a set of sequences of random variables whose distributions are specified. These random variables represent features of the work load or features of the system such as think times, branching or routing indicators, device service times, memory requirements, etc. Correspondingly, the models have a random output that consists of a set of sequences of random variables such as system response times, subsystem response times, device utilizations, etc., whose distributions are unknown. The reason for constructing and running the simulation is to estimate certain characteristics of these output distributions.

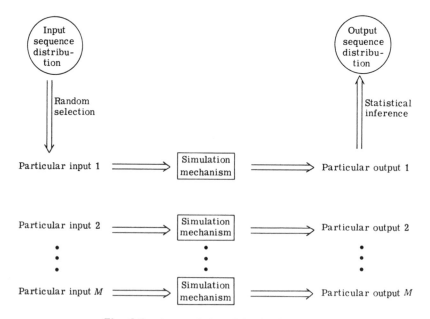

Fig. 6.1   A general view of the simulation process.

The model is simulated because these characteristics cannot be computed from analytic results.

To accomplish this estimation the experimenter follows the general procedure diagrammed in Fig. 6.1. He generates (according to the specified distributions) a particular realization of the set of input sequences. He runs the simulation with this realization as input and thereby generates a particular realization of the set of output sequences. He repeats this process M times generating M distinct realizations of the set of output sequences. (We shall see that in certain circumstances M can be equal to one.) Using these M realizations he estimates the required characteristics of the output distributions. This estimation is a statistical process. It has most of the problems common to the application of statistics to natural phenomena where, again, characteristics of probability distributions of random variables are estimated from a set of realizations or samples of the random variables.

EXAMPLE: A CLOSED QUEUEING NETWORK WITH BLOCKING   As an example we consider the simple closed queueing network model of a computing system diagrammed in Fig. 6.2. This is a model of the same general form discussed in Chapters 1, 4, and 8. We shall use this same example in many of our subsequent discussions to illustrate problems and techniques.

We suppose there are 25 customers in the network. These customers represent 25 users at terminals. There is no queueing at the terminals but there is a random think time. At the queues indicated, service is on a first come, first served basis. We assume a central processing facility with a maximum multiprogramming level of 5. This is represented in Fig. 6.2 by the dashed enclosure. Hence, the number of customers in this dashed enclosure

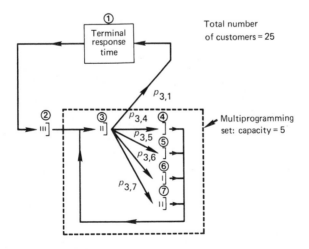

Fig. 6.2 A closed queueing model with blocking.

cannot exceed 5. Customers wait in Queue 2 for entry into the multiprogramming set. Queue 3 is in front of the processor and Queues 4–7 are in front of backing store devices. When customers depart from the processor, Queue 3, they choose a route according to the branching probabilities indicated.

The input to the simulation of this system is a set of seven independent sequences of independent, identically distributed random variables. They are

$$\{S_{1,n} : n = 1, 2, \ldots\}: \quad \text{the think times,} \tag{6.1}$$

$$\{S_{3,n} : n = 1, 2, \ldots\}: \quad \text{the service times at the processor,} \tag{6.2}$$

$$\{S_{i,n} : n = 1, 2, \ldots\}: \quad i = 4, \ldots, 7, \text{ the service times at the backing store devices,} \tag{6.3}$$

and

$$\{\theta_n : n = 1, 2, \ldots\}: \quad \text{the branching indicators after departure from the processor.} \tag{6.4}$$

The random variables θ_n are discrete random variables with the probability distribution

$$\text{Prob}\{\theta_n = k\} = p_{3,k}, \qquad k = 1, 4, 5, 6, 7. \tag{6.5}$$

When we run a simulation of this system, as we discussed earlier, we generate a particular realization of the sequences $\{S_{1,n}\}$; $\{S_{i,n}\}$, $i = 3, \ldots, 7$; and $\{\theta_n\}$. We do this from a recursively generated random number sequence as is discussed in Chapter 5. This particular realization of the input random sequences produces, through the simulation, a particular realization of the output random sequences. If we generate a *second* independent realization of the input sequences we will produce, through the simulation, a *second* independent realization of the output sequences. This second set of independent input sequences is derived again from the random number generator through the choice of a second set of seeds as described in Chapter 5. Through this process we generate random, independent realizations of the input sequences and hence, through the simulation, produce random, independent realizations of the output sequences.

To illustrate this, the model of Fig. 6.2 was simulated for exponential service times and exponential terminal think times. The following specific parameters were used.

$$E[S_{1,n}] = 10, \quad E[S_{3,n}] = 0.1, \quad E[S_{4,n}] = E[S_{5,n}] = 0.2778,$$

$$E[S_{6,n}] = E[S_{7,n}] = 2.5, \tag{6.6}$$

$$p_{3,1} = 0.2, \quad p_{3,4} = p_{3,5} = 0.36, \quad p_{3,6} = p_{3,7} = 0.04.$$

In the manner described above, five independent runs of the simulation were made and, as an example, the output sequence of waiting times in the queue in front of the multiprogramming set were recorded. This is Queue 2 in Fig. 6.2. Formally, we recorded five particular sample realizations of the random sequence $\{W_{2,n}: n = 1, 2, \ldots, 300\}$ where

$$W_{2,n} = \text{waiting time for the } n\text{th departing customer}$$
$$\text{in the queue in front of the multiprogramming set.} \quad (6.7)$$

The sample realizations are plotted in Fig. 6.3. Notice their random appearance and the variation from sequence to sequence. *The characteristics of the distributions of random sequences such as these are what we are interested in estimating. These characteristics must be estimated from sets of sample sequences such as are depicted in Fig. 6.3.*

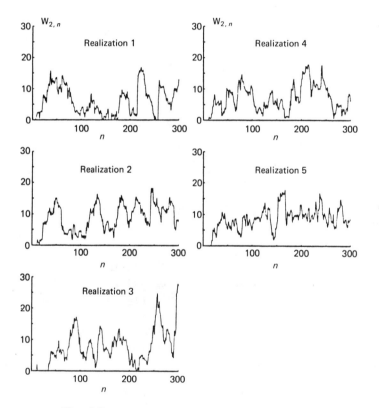

Fig. 6.3　Five sample realizations of the sequence $\{W_{2,n}\}$.

Examples of other random sequences of interest would be waiting time sequences in other queues; queue length sequences such as $\{Q_{2,n}: n = 1, 2, \ldots\}$

where

$Q_{2,n} =$ the time average of the number waiting in the queue in
front of the multiprogramming set or in the
multiprogramming set during the time $(n - 1)\delta \leqslant t \leqslant n\delta$
where δ is a specified sampling period;   (6.8)

utilization sequences such as $\{U_{3,n}: n = 1, 2, \ldots\}$ where

$U_{3,n} =$ the proportion of time the processor was busy during the
period $(n - 1)\delta \leqslant t \leqslant n\delta$ where δ is a specified sampling
period;   (6.9)

and system or subsystem response time sequences such as $\{R_n: n = 1, 2, \ldots\}$
where

$R_n =$ the time from completion of the previous think time to
the initiation of the next think time
for the nth customer arriving at the terminals.   (6.10)

In all these cases, the problem is as described for the waiting time sequence
$\{W_{2,n}: n = 1, 2, \ldots\}$; i.e., characteristics of the distribution must be estimated
from a set of sample realizations of the sequences.

Now the outputs of simulations are always random sequences but
frequently they can be viewed as samples of random processes defined on
continuous time or as functions or integrals of such processes. For example, if
we let

$Q_2(t) =$ number of customers waiting in the queue in front of the
multiprogramming set or in the multiprogramming set
at time t,   (6.11)

then $\{Q_2(t): t \geqslant 0\}$ is a random process with a continuous parameter t. It is
called a continuous parameter process. For each $t \geqslant 0$, $Q_2(t)$ is a random
variable. The sequence $Q_{2,n}$ defined in Eq. (6.8) above can be expressed as

$$Q_{2,n} = \frac{1}{\delta} \int_{(n-1)\delta}^{n\delta} Q_2(t)\, dt. \qquad (6.12)$$

Similarly if we let

$Q_3(t) =$ number of customers waiting or being served
in Queue 3, the queue in front of the processor,   (6.13)

then we can define the continuous parameter utilization process

$$U_3(t) = \begin{cases} 1 & \text{if } Q_3(t) \geqslant 1, \\ 0 & \text{if } Q_3(t) = 0. \end{cases} \qquad (6.14)$$

With this definition the sequence $U_{3,n}$ defined by Eq. (6.9) can be expressed as

$$U_{3,n} = \frac{1}{\delta} \int_{(n-1)\delta}^{n\delta} U_3(t)\, dt. \qquad (6.15)$$

6.1.2 Transient Behavior of a Random Sequence

As we saw in Section 6.1.1, the outputs of simulations are random sequences. For purposes of discussion we again consider a sequence drawn from the queueing network example of Section 6.1.1. We consider

$W_{2,n} =$ waiting time, for the nth departing customer, in the
  queue in front of the multiprogramming set.   (6.16)

Now $\{W_{2,n} : n = 1, 2, \ldots\}$ is a sequence of random variables. Hence if we fix n, say at $n = 20$, we have a single random variable

$W_{2,20} =$ waiting time, for the 20th departing customer, in the
  queue in front of the multiprogramming set.   (6.17)

Random variables such as $W_{2,20}$ were discussed in Chapter 2. They are quantities whose value depends upon the outcome of a random experiment;

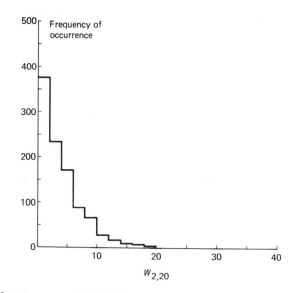

Fig. 6.4 Histogram of 1000 independent samples of $W_{2,20}$: all customers initially beginning terminal response times.

in this case, the simulation. The random variable $W_{2,20}$ has a probability distribution associated with it. If we repeat the simulation with independent samples from the input population, we will generate independent samples of $W_{2,20}$. This was done and a set of 1000 independent samples of $W_{2,20}$ were generated. The histogram of these 1000 samples is plotted in Fig. 6.4. This histogram is an estimate of the probability distribution of $W_{2,20}$ and approximates the shape of that distribution.

When we run the simulation we run it given a set of initial conditions. In the example under discussion these conditions involve the location of customers in the system. (We assume that customers initially in service at a service center are just beginning their service time.) The distribution of $W_{2,20}$ depends upon these initial conditions and the samples generated for the histogram of Fig. 6.4 were generated with all customers initially in front of the terminals (i.e., beginning a think time). These were also the initial conditions for the five sample sequences illustrated in Fig. 6.3. To illustrate the dependence of the distribution of $W_{2,20}$ on the initial conditions we generated 1000 independent samples of $W_{2,20}$ with different initial customer locations; 5 customers were in front of the processor (Queue 3) and the remaining 20 customers were in the queue in front of the multiprogramming set (Queue 2). The histogram of these 1000 samples is plotted in Fig. 6.5. Notice the difference in the histograms of Figs. 6.4 and 6.5.

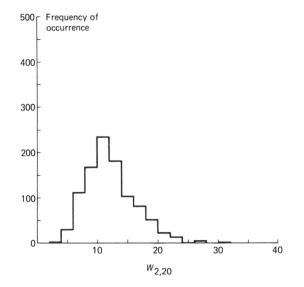

Fig. 6.5 Histogram of 1000 independent samples of $W_{2,20}$: 5 customers initially in front of the processor, 20 customers initially in front of the multiprogramming set.

The distributions of the random variables $\{W_{2,n} : n = 1, 2, \ldots\}$ also depend upon the location n in the sequence. Thus the distribution of $W_{2,40}$ will in general be different from the distribution of $W_{2,20}$. Again, for the case where all the customers are initially beginning think times we generated 1000 independent samples of the random variable $W_{2,40}$. The histogram of these samples is plotted in Fig. 6.6. Comparison of Figs. 6.4 and 6.6 shows the dependence of the distributions on the location in the sequence.

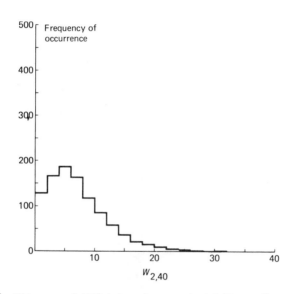

Fig. 6.6 Histogram of 1000 independent samples of $W_{2,40}$: all customers initially beginning terminal response times.

Characteristics of the output of the simulation such as the distribution of $W_{2,20}$, that depend upon the initial conditions and upon the point at which they occur either in a sequence or in time, we call transient characteristics. They are contrasted with steady-state characteristics which we shall discuss in the next section. Transient characteristics could be characteristics of elements in the basic output sequences such as $W_{2,20}$ or they could be characteristics of functions of these elements such as the average of the first 100 waiting times in the queue in front of the multiprogramming set; i.e.,

$$\bar{W}_2 = \frac{1}{100} \sum_{n=1}^{100} W_{2,n}. \qquad (6.18)$$

For purposes of discussion we have considered a particular waiting time sequence, $\{W_{2,n} : n = 1, 2, \ldots\}$. All our remarks apply equally well to other waiting time sequences or to sequences of queue sizes, utilizations, or subsystem response times.

6.1.3 Steady-State Behavior of a Random Sequence

In many simulations the distributions associated with the random variables in an output sequence converge to what we call a limiting or steady-state distribution. For example consider the sequence $\{W_{2,n} : n = 1, 2, \ldots\}$ discussed above. As n gets large the distributions of $W_{2,n}$ converge to a limiting distribution. This is illustrated in Fig. 6.7 where we have plotted histograms of 1000 independent samples of $W_{2,20}$, $W_{2,40}$, $W_{2,60}$, $W_{2,80}$, $W_{2,100}$, and $W_{2,120}$. Notice that the distributions converge and that the histograms corresponding to $W_{2,100}$ and $W_{2,120}$ are approximately the

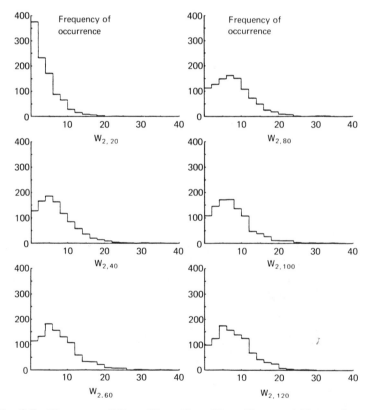

Fig. 6.7 Histograms of $W_{2,20}$, $W_{2,40}$, $W_{2,60}$, $W_{2,80}$, $W_{2,100}$, and $W_{2,120}$: all customers initially beginning terminal response times.

same. Thus, in this case, as n gets large the distributions of $W_{2,n}$ for all n are essentially identical.

Furthermore, the $W_{2,n}$ converge to this same limiting distribution for any set of initial conditions. To illustrate this we have plotted histograms of $W_{2,20}$, $W_{2,40}$, $W_{2,60}$, $W_{2,80}$, $W_{2,100}$, and $W_{2,120}$ in Fig. 6.8 for a different set of initial conditions from those of Fig. 6.7. Notice the convergence of the histograms to the same limiting shape.

Hence, in the situations where a sequence has a limiting distribution it goes through a transient phase which depends upon the initial conditions, and thereafter, it has an essentially unchanging distribution which is independent of the initial conditions. In the case of this example such limiting distributions exist for all the output sequences we have discussed: waiting times, queue lengths, utilizations, and subsystem response times. The convergence behavior during the transient phase depends upon the initial conditions and the particular output sequence. The transient phase, of course, does not end at

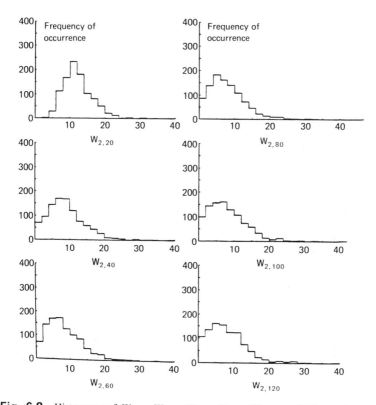

Fig. 6.8   Histograms of $W_{2,20}$, $W_{2,40}$, $W_{2,60}$, $W_{2,80}$, $W_{2,100}$, and $W_{2,120}$: 5 customers initially in front of the processor, 20 customers initially in front of the multiprogramming set.

a particular point but the behavior of the sequence gradually converges to the steady-state behavior.

In the steady-state phase it is possible to generate an arbitrarily long sequence of random variables all of which have, approximately, the steady-state distribution. Hence one can obtain repeated observations from the distribution of interest without repeating the simulation. Thus, in this case, it is possible to make statistical inferences from a single output sequence. However, these repeated observations are not, in general, independent. We shall see that coping with this dependence in a valid and effective way is the central statistical problem of estimating steady-state characteristics.

Usually, in computing system simulation, the experimenter is interested in the steady-state characteristics of the output sequences. However, there are times when transient characteristics are the major or only concern, and in many situations there is interest in the transient phase for the purpose of controlling its effect on the estimation of steady-state characteristics. In some simulations only transient behavior exists.

6.1.4 Point Estimators and Confidence Intervals

As we have discussed above, the outputs of a simulation are sequences of random variables. The experimenter is interested in certain characteristics of the probability distributions of these random variables. These characteristics are unknown and cannot be computed from any theoretical analysis. To estimate them is the reason for the simulation.

The experimenter might be interested in the probability distribution functions themselves but more typically he is interested in measures of their location, such as the mean or median, or in measures of their spread, such as the variance or 95% point. These characteristics must be estimated from the outputs of one or more runs of the simulation. Some function of the output sequences must be defined and evaluated to provide the estimate. Now the output sequences consist of random variables. Hence, any function of them is also a random variable. *Thus, any estimate will be a random variable. Consequently a fixed, deterministic quantity must be estimated by a random quantity.* Methods of dealing meaningfully with this are the subject of this chapter of the handbook.

As an example, consider again the queueing network diagrammed in Fig. 6.2. Suppose we are interested in estimating the steady-state mean waiting time in front of the multiprogramming set. That is, we are interested in

$$\mu_2 = \lim_{n \to \infty} E[W_{2,n}], \qquad (6.19)$$

where $W_{2,n}$ is defined by Eq. (6.7). Suppose we make a single run and observe a sample sequence of $W_{2,n}$ of length 1000, i.e., $W_{2,1}, \ldots, W_{2,1000}$. Now, judging from the histograms of Fig. 6.7, a reasonable estimator to use for μ_2 would be the average over the last 900 samples. The first 100 samples would not be used because they reflect the transient phase. We designate this estimator as

$$\hat{\mu}_2 = \frac{1}{900} \sum_{n=101}^{1000} W_{2,n}. \tag{6.20}$$

Since the $W_{2,n}$ are random variables, so is $\hat{\mu}_2$. Hence, $\hat{\mu}_2$ has a probability distribution. Now, for $\hat{\mu}_2$ to be a good estimator of μ_2, its distribution must be centered about μ_2. Further, the distribution of $\hat{\mu}_2$ must be narrow enough so that it is very likely that $\hat{\mu}_2 - \mu_2$ be within the accuracy requirements of the experimenter. Finally, this information about the distribution of $\hat{\mu}_2$ must be obtained from the simulation run or runs. *Hence the experimenter must generate from the simulation not only an estimate $\hat{\mu}_2$ but also enough information about the probability distribution of $\hat{\mu}_2$ so that he can be reasonably sure that it is close enough to the unknown quantity μ_2 for his purposes.*

A common way of accomplishing this is to have an estimator that is approximately unbiased, i.e., an estimator $\hat{\mu}_2$ such that

$$E[\hat{\mu}_2] \approx \mu_2 \tag{6.21}$$

and to generate an estimate of the variance $\sigma^2(\hat{\mu}_2)$ of $\hat{\mu}_2$. Call this latter estimate $\hat{\sigma}^2(\hat{\mu}_2)$. Then $\hat{\sigma}(\hat{\mu}_2)$ is an estimate of the standard deviation of $\hat{\mu}_2$, and under a wide set of conditions, we are fairly sure that

$$\hat{\mu}_2 - 2\hat{\sigma}(\hat{\mu}_2) \leqslant \mu_2 \leqslant \hat{\mu}_2 + 2\hat{\sigma}(\hat{\mu}_2) \tag{6.22}$$

and almost certain that

$$\hat{\mu}_2 - 3\hat{\sigma}(\hat{\mu}_2) \leqslant \mu_2 \leqslant \hat{\mu}_2 + 3\hat{\sigma}(\hat{\mu}_2). \tag{6.23}$$

Generally there is theory that relates the choice of the multiplier of the estimated standard deviation [2 and 3 in Eqs. (6.22) and (6.23), respectively] to the probability that the bounds are correct. That is, we have supporting statistical theory that provides us with a multiplier $c(\alpha)$ such that

$$\text{Prob}\{\hat{\mu}_2 - c(\alpha)\hat{\sigma}(\hat{\mu}_2) \leqslant \mu_2 \leqslant \hat{\mu}_2 + c(\alpha)\hat{\sigma}(\hat{\mu}_2)\} \approx 1 - \alpha. \tag{6.24}$$

The random variable $\hat{\mu}_2$ is called a point estimator of μ_2. The interval

$$(\hat{\mu}_2 - c(\alpha)\hat{\sigma}(\hat{\mu}_2), \hat{\mu}_2 + c(\alpha)\hat{\sigma}(\hat{\mu}_2)) \tag{6.25}$$

is called a confidence interval. It is associated with the confidence level, $1 - \alpha$. (We state the confidence level as one minus the parameter α for convenience in specific situations later on.) This confidence interval is a random interval. It has a center $\hat{\mu}_2$, which is a random variable, and a width $2c(\alpha)\hat{\sigma}(\hat{\mu}_2)$, which is a random variable. Hence if we were to repeat the experiment with different input sequences we would obtain a different interval. The meaning of Eq. (6.24) is that if we repeat the experiment in an independent fashion a number of times generating a set of these random intervals, on the average a proportion of them equal to $1 - \alpha$ will cover the true value.

Confidence intervals need not be generated through an estimate of the variance of an unbiased estimator. In general a confidence interval on an unknown characteristic μ is established by generating, from the output sequences, two random variables $L(\alpha)$ and $U(\alpha)$ such that

$$\text{Prob}\{L(\alpha) \leqslant \mu \leqslant U(\alpha)\} = 1 - \alpha. \tag{6.26}$$

We shall consider the requirement that an experimenter generate an estimate plus information as to the accuracy of that estimate to be met by producing a confidence interval or a set of confidence intervals at different confidence levels. Consequently, the discussion in the sections that follow will be specifically concerned with methods for generating valid confidence intervals for important characteristics of the probability distributions of output random sequences.

6.2   Estimating Transient Characteristics

6.2.1   Independent Replications of a Simulation

To estimate characteristics of the probability distribution of a random variable, repeated observations of the random variable must be made and an inference drawn from the resulting set of sample values. Most statistical theory assumes that these observations are independent and consequently, in general, more reliable inferences can be drawn more easily from independent than nonindependent observations.

When estimating a transient characteristic usually the only efficient way to get repeated observations is to repeat the simulation. Hence fundamental to the estimation of transient characteristics is the understanding of, and the ability to make, repeated, independent runs of the simulation. We shall see later that this is also one basic approach to the estimation of steady-state characteristics.

To obtain independent replications of a simulation, the experimenter has to generate independent realizations of the input sequences of random variables which drive the simulation. These sequences are generated, as is discussed in Chapter 5, from a recursively generated random number stream. Hence the experimenter must know how to control the seed of the random number generator so as to produce effectively independent sets of input sequences. This choice of seeds for independent replications is discussed in Chapter 5.

6.2.2 Definitions and Notation

We assume we are interested in a transient random variable which we designate as X. The random variable X could be any function of the basic output sequences of the simulation. For example, considering the system diagrammed in Fig. 6.2 possibilities for X include:

$W_{2,20}$:   the waiting time of the 20th departing customer in the queue in front of the multiprogramming set,

$(1/40) \sum_{n=11}^{50} W_{3,n}$: the average waiting time of the 11th through 50th departing customers in the queue in front of the processor,

$Q_{2,10}$:   the time average of the number waiting in the queue in front of the multiprogramming set or in the multiprogramming set during the time $9\delta \leqslant t \leqslant 10\delta$ where δ is a specified sampling period,

$(1/100) \sum_{n=1}^{100} U_{3,n}$: the proportion of the time the processor was busy during the period $0 \leqslant t \leqslant 100\delta$, and

R_{30}:   the time from completion of the previous think time to the initiation of the next think time for the 30th customer arriving at the terminals.

The transient random variable X has an unknown probability distribution whose characteristics we are trying to estimate. We let $F(x)$ be its distribution function; i.e.,

$$F(x) = \text{Prob}\{X \leqslant x\} \tag{6.27}$$

and μ and σ^2 be its mean and variance, respectively; i.e.,

$$\mu = E[X], \tag{6.28}$$

$$\sigma^2 = E[(X - \mu)^2]. \tag{6.29}$$

We assume that we generate M replications of the simulation and obtain M independent observations of X which we designate as $X_1, X_2, \ldots, X_M$. Thus,

$$X_m = \text{value of the random variable } X \text{ on the } m\text{th replication of the simulation.} \tag{6.30}$$

All the estimators including the limits of the confidence intervals will be functions of these M observations.

6.2.3 Estimating the Mean Value of a Transient Random Variable

We assume we have M independent observations $X_1, \ldots, X_M$ of a transient random variable and we wish to estimate its mean value

$$\mu = E[X]. \tag{6.31}$$

The standard point estimator of μ is the sample mean

$$\hat{\mu} = \bar{X} = \frac{1}{M} \sum_{m=1}^{M} X_m. \tag{6.32}$$

The estimator $\hat{\mu}$ is a random variable with

$$E[\hat{\mu}] = \mu; \tag{6.33}$$

i.e., it is unbiased, and

$$\text{Var}[\hat{\mu}] = \sigma^2/M \tag{6.34}$$

where

$$\sigma^2 = \text{Var}[X]. \tag{6.35}$$

Thus the distribution of $\hat{\mu}$ is "centered" about the unknown mean with a variance which gets smaller as M increases. Hence, $\hat{\mu}$ becomes more likely to provide a better estimator of μ as the sample size M gets larger.

A confidence interval for μ is provided through the t-statistic as follows. The sample variance is defined as

$$s^2 = \hat{\sigma}^2 = \frac{1}{M-1} \sum_{m=1}^{M} (X_m - \bar{X})^2 = \frac{1}{M-1} \sum_{m=1}^{M} X_m^2 - \frac{M}{M-1} (\bar{X})^2 \tag{6.36}$$

where $\bar{X}$, the sample mean, is given by Eq. (6.32). The sample variance s^2 is an unbiased estimate of the variance σ^2 of X. The quantity s^2/M is an estimate of the variance of $\hat{\mu}$. The sample standard deviation $\hat{\sigma} = s$ is the square root of the sample variance. Given these definitions the random variable

$$\frac{\hat{\mu} - \mu}{s/M^{1/2}} \tag{6.37}$$

has approximately a t-distribution with $M - 1$ degrees of freedom. (The t-distribution is approximately a normal distribution with zero mean and unit variance for large M, say $M > 25$.) Hence, if we let

$$t_n(x) = 100x\text{th percentile of the } t\text{-distribution with } n \text{ degrees of freedom,} \tag{6.38}$$

we have

$$\text{Prob}\left\{ t_{M-1}\left(\frac{\alpha}{2}\right) \leq \frac{\hat{\mu} - \mu}{s/M^{1/2}} \leq t_{M-1}\left(1 - \frac{\alpha}{2}\right) \right\} = 1 - \alpha. \tag{6.39}$$

The t-distribution is symmetric about zero and hence

$$t_{M-1}(\alpha/2) = -t_{M-1}(1 - \alpha/2). \tag{6.40}$$

Substituting Eq. (6.40) into Eq. (6.39) and reworking the inequalities we obtain the confidence interval and statement

$$\text{Prob}\{\hat{\mu} - t_{M-1}(1 - \alpha/2)s/M^{1/2} \leqslant \mu \leqslant \hat{\mu} + t_{M-1}(1 - \alpha/2)s/M^{1/2}\} \approx 1 - \alpha.$$

$$\tag{6.41}$$

Curves of $t_n(1 - \alpha/2)$ are given in Fig. 6.9 for $1 - \alpha = 0.9$ and $1 - \alpha = 0.95$. Notice that for large n these are the usual multipliers 1.64 and 1.96 of the normal distribution with zero mean and unit variance.

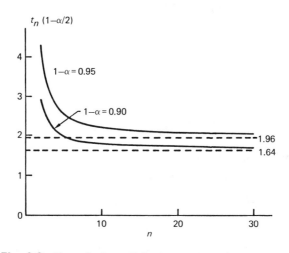

Fig. 6.9 Plots of $t_n(1 - \alpha/2)$ for $1 - \alpha = 0.9$ and $1 - \alpha = 0.95$.

This method of generating confidence intervals using the t-distribution is very important and will find application to the estimation of steady-state as well as transient characteristics. It is exact if the X_m are normally distributed and is a useful approximation under very general conditions.

6.2.4 Estimating the Variance of a Transient Random Variable

Again as in Section 6.2.3, we assume we have M independent observations of a transient random variable X. As before these are obtained from M independent replications of the simulation. We designate the observations as $X_1, \ldots, X_M$. We wish to estimate and place a confidence interval on the unknown variance σ^2 of the distribution of X.

The recommended point estimator of σ^2 is the sample variance $\hat{\sigma}^2$ given by Eq. (6.36). This estimator is unbiased; i.e.,

$$E[\hat{\sigma}^2] = \sigma^2. \tag{6.42}$$

This is the reason for the divisor $M - 1$ rather than M in Eq. (6.36). A confidence interval can be obtained for σ^2 under the assumption that the X_m are normally distributed. Unfortunately however, unlike the result for the mean value, its validity is quite sensitive to deviations from the normal assumption. Hence, we will develop a confidence interval based on a technique, called jackknifing, which is much less sensitive to the form of the distribution of the X_m. For a general discussion of this technique see Miller (1974).

We let $\hat{\sigma}^2$ be the sample variance defined by Eq. (6.36). We let $\hat{\sigma}_j^2$: $j = 1, \ldots, M$ be the sample variance of the X_m: $m = 1, \ldots, M$ with the observation X_j removed. That is,

$$\hat{\sigma}_j^2 = \frac{1}{M-2} \sum_{m \neq j} X_m^2 - \frac{M-1}{M-2} (\bar{X}_j)^2, \tag{6.43}$$

where

$$\bar{X}_j = \frac{1}{M-1} \sum_{m \neq j} X_m. \tag{6.44}$$

Next we define "pseudovalues"

$$Z_j = M\hat{\sigma}^2 - (M-1)\hat{\sigma}_j^2, \qquad j = 1, \ldots, M. \tag{6.45}$$

Notice that

$$E[Z_j] = \sigma^2. \tag{6.46}$$

Hence the distribution of the Z_j is centered about σ^2. Now we let $\bar{Z}$ be the sample mean of the Z_j, $j = 1, \ldots, N$, and s_z^2 be the sample variance, i.e.,

$$\bar{Z} = \frac{1}{M} \sum_{j=1}^{M} Z_j \tag{6.47}$$

and

$$s_z^2 = \frac{1}{M-1} \sum_{j=1}^{M} (Z_j - \bar{Z})^2. \tag{6.48}$$

Given these definitions

$$\frac{\bar{Z} - \sigma^2}{s_z/M^{1/2}} \tag{6.49}$$

has approximately a t-distribution with $M - 1$ degrees of freedom. Hence, in an exactly parallel fashion to the development of Section 6.2.3, we have the confidence interval and statement

$$\text{Prob}\{\bar{Z} - t_{M-1}(1 - \alpha/2)s_z/M^{1/2} \leqslant \sigma^2 \leqslant \bar{Z} + t_{M-1}(1 - \alpha/2)s_z/M^{1/2}\}$$

$$\approx 1 - \alpha. \tag{6.50}$$

Curves of $t_n(1 - \alpha/2)$ are given in Fig. 6.9 for $1 - \alpha = 0.9$ and $1 - \alpha = 0.95$.

6.2.5 Estimating the Probability that a Transient Random Variable Lies in Some Fixed Interval

Many times an experimenter is interested in the probability that a random variable has a value that lies in some prespecified interval. For example, there is frequently interest in the probability that the response time of a system or subsystem is less than some specified amount. Often system specifications place a lower limit on such a probability. Other examples would be the probability that a queue size is less than some value, that a waiting time is greater than zero, etc.

Hence we have independent observations $X_1, \ldots, X_M$ of the transient random variable and a prespecified interval I. We wish to estimate

$$p = \text{Prob}\{X \in I\}. \tag{6.51}$$

We let n be the number of X_m in the sample that are within the interval I. Then n/M is the proportion in the sample that are within I and is the recommended point estimate of p; i.e.,

$$\hat{p} = n/M. \tag{6.52}$$

As with earlier point estimates, $\hat{p}$ is unbiased; i.e.,

$$E[\hat{p}] = p. \tag{6.53}$$

The quantity n, the number of the X_m within the interval I, is a random variable with a binomial distribution with parameter p. Specifically,

$$\text{Prob}\{n = k\} = \frac{M!}{k!(M-k)!} p^k(1 - p)^{M-k}. \tag{6.54}$$

Hence estimating the probability p is equivalent to estimating the parameter of the binomial distribution where $X_m \in I$ is defined as a success and $\text{Prob}\{X_m \in I\} = p$ is the probability of success. An exact confidence interval for p is given by

$$\text{Prob}\{\hat{p}_L \leqslant p \leqslant \hat{p}_U\} \geqslant 1 - \alpha, \tag{6.55}$$

where we distinguish three cases:

Case 1: $n = 0$

Then

$$\hat{p}_L = 0, \tag{6.56}$$

and $\hat{p}_U$ is the solution of

$$(1 - \hat{p}_U)^M = \alpha/2. \tag{6.57}$$

Case 2: $0 < n < M$

Then $\hat{p}_L$ is the solution of

$$\sum_{k=n}^{M} \frac{M!}{k!(M-k)!} \hat{p}_L^k (1 - \hat{p}_L)^{M-k} = \frac{\alpha}{2}, \tag{6.58}$$

and $\hat{p}_U$ is the solution of

$$\sum_{k=0}^{n} \frac{M!}{k!(M-k)!} \hat{p}_U^k (1 - \hat{p}_U)^{M-k} = \frac{\alpha}{2}. \tag{6.59}$$

Case 3: $n = M$

Then $\hat{p}_L$ is the solution of

$$\hat{p}_L^M = \alpha/2, \tag{6.60}$$

and

$$\hat{p}_U = 1. \tag{6.61}$$

This problem is discussed in many statistical texts; see, e.g., Hald (1952a) or Bradley (1968). Tables of $(\hat{p}_L, \hat{p}_U)$ are given in Hald (1952b) and graphs of $(\hat{p}_L, \hat{p}_U)$ are plotted in Clopper and Pearson (1934). The left-hand sides of Eqs. (6.57)–(6.60) are monotonic functions of $\hat{p}_L$ and $\hat{p}_U$ and hence they can be solved by consulting available tables (see e.g. Harvard Computation Laboratory, 1955) of sums over the binomial distribution. An experimenter could write a computer program to yield $(\hat{p}_L, \hat{p}_U)$ given n and M. Recursive relationships for calculating binomial coefficients are available but care has to be taken to prevent underflow problems.

If the quantity $Mp(1 - p)$ is large then the left-hand sides of Eqs. (6.58) and (6.59) can be approximated using the normal approximation to the binomial distribution. If we let $\Phi(x)$ be the $100x$th percentile of the normal random variable with zero mean and unit variance then Eqs. (6.58) and (6.59) become

$$\frac{n - \frac{1}{2} - M\hat{p}_L}{[M\hat{p}_L(1 - \hat{p}_L)]^{1/2}} \approx \Phi\left(1 - \frac{\alpha}{2}\right), \tag{6.62}$$

$$\frac{n + \frac{1}{2} - M\hat{p}_U}{[M\hat{p}_U(1 - \hat{p}_U)]^{1/2}} \approx \Phi\left(\frac{\alpha}{2}\right). \tag{6.63}$$

The solutions of these equations yield

$$\hat{p}_L \approx \frac{n - \frac{1}{2} + \Phi^2(1, -\alpha/2)/2 - \Phi(1 - \alpha/2)[\Phi^2(1 - \alpha/2)/4 + (n - \frac{1}{2})(M - n + \frac{1}{2})/M]^{1/2}}{M + \Phi^2(1 - \alpha/2)}$$

(6.64)

and

$$\hat{p}_U \approx \frac{n + \frac{1}{2} + \Phi^2(\alpha/2)/2 - \Phi(\alpha/2)[\Phi^2(\alpha/2)/4 + (n + \frac{1}{2})(M - n - \frac{1}{2})/M]^{1/2}}{M + \Phi^2(\alpha/2)}.$$

(6.65)

For a 90% confidence level

$$\Phi(0.95) = -\Phi(0.05) = 1.64,$$

(6.66)

while for a 95% confidence level

$$\Phi(0.975) = -\Phi(0.025) = 1.96.$$

(6.67)

An often quoted rule of thumb for the normal approximation to the binomial to be reasonable is $Mp(1 - p) > 9$ although this may be too conservative for some simulation work. For a discussion of this question see Parzen (1960, pp. 239–245).

6.2.6 Estimating a Percentile (Quantile) of the Probability Distribution of a Transient Random Variable

Associated with any random variable X there is a distribution function $F(x)$ defined by

$$F(x) = \text{Prob}\{X \leqslant x\}.$$

(6.68)

The 100βth percentile x_β is defined as the smallest value of x such that

$$F(x) \geqslant \beta.$$

(6.69)

If X has a nonzero probability density function in the region of x_β then there is only one x with this property. Frequently in simulation experiments there is interest in $x_{0.50}$, the median, as an alternative to the mean as a measure of the location of a distribution. Further there is often interest in points such as $x_{0.90}$ or $x_{0.95}$, the 90th or 95th percentiles, as measures of the spread or range of a distribution.

Given the set $X_1, \ldots, X_M$ of M independent observations of X we wish to estimate x_β. We define $Y_1, Y_2, \ldots, Y_M$ to be a reordering of the X_m such that

$$Y_m \leqslant Y_{m+1}.$$

(6.70)

The Y_m are called order statistics. We let, for any real number y,

$$[y] = \text{largest integer less than or equal to } y.$$

(6.71)

Then the recommended estimator of x_β is

$$\hat{x}_\beta = \begin{cases} Y_{[M\beta]} & \text{if } M\beta \text{ in an integer,} \\ Y_{[M\beta]+1} & \text{if } M\beta \text{ is not an integer.} \end{cases} \tag{6.72}$$

This estimator $\hat{x}_\beta$ is called the sample 100βth percentile.

A confidence interval can be placed on x_β using

$$\text{Prob}\{Y_r \leqslant x_\beta \leqslant Y_s\} \geqslant \sum_{k=r}^{s-1} \frac{M!}{k!(M-k)!} \beta^k(1-\beta)^{M-k}. \tag{6.73}$$

To get a confidence interval at a confidence level of at least $1-\alpha$ we would sum the binomial distribution symmetrically about $M\beta$ until the right-hand side of Eq. (6.73) first exceeded $1-\alpha$. This would yield an r and an s which would give the confidence interval on the left. Available tables of binomial probabilities and their sums can be used to accumulate the right-hand side (see, e.g., Harvard Computation Laboratory, 1955).

For $M\beta(1-\beta)$ large (say greater than 9) the normal approximation to the binomial can be used to obtain approximate values of s and r. Using this approximation we have

$$\sum_{k=r}^{s-1} \frac{M!}{k!(M-k)!} \beta^k(1-\beta)^{M-k} \approx N\left\{\frac{s-\tfrac{1}{2}-M\beta}{[M\beta(1-\beta)]^{1/2}}\right\} - N\left\{\frac{r-\tfrac{1}{2}-M\beta}{[M\beta(1-\beta)]^{1/2}}\right\}, \tag{6.74}$$

where $N(x)$ is the cumulative distribution function of the normal random variable with zero mean and unit variance. Hence, to have a confidence interval at level at least $1-\alpha$, s would be the smallest integer greater than or equal to $s_{\alpha/2}$ where

$$\frac{s_{\alpha/2}-\tfrac{1}{2}-M\beta}{[M\beta(1-\beta)]^{1/2}} = \Phi\left(1-\frac{\alpha}{2}\right), \tag{6.75}$$

and r would be the largest integer less than or equal to $r_{\alpha/2}$ where

$$\frac{r_{\alpha/2}-\tfrac{1}{2}-M\beta}{[M\beta(1-\beta)]^{1/2}} = \Phi\left(\frac{\alpha}{2}\right). \tag{6.76}$$

The function $\Phi(x)$ is the $100x$th percentile of the normal random variable with zero mean and unit variance. [$\Phi(x)$ is the inverse function of $N(x)$.]

6.3 Estimating Steady-State Characteristics

6.3.1 Introduction

As we discussed in Section 6.1.3, in many simulations the distributions associated with the random variables in an output sequence converge to what we call a steady-state distribution. Examples would be the waiting time, queue length, utilization, and subsystem response time sequences as defined in Eqs. (6.7)–(6.10) in the example of Section 6.1.1.

In our discussion we designate a generic sequence of this type as $\{V_n : n = 1, 2, 3, \ldots\}$. Hence

$$\lim_{n \to \infty} \text{Prob}\{V_n \leqslant x\} = F(x), \tag{6.77}$$

where $F(x)$ is the steady-state distribution function. We are interested here in estimating characteristics of this steady-state distribution, such as its mean and variance, as we were interested in estimating characteristics of the transient distribution in Section 6.2.

This situation is basically different from the transient case in that from a single run of the simulation, we can get repeated observations whose distributions are approximately the unknown distribution in which we are interested. That is, if we have an output sequence $\{V_n : n = 1, 2, \ldots, N\}$ then from some point n_0 onward the random variables $V_{n_0+1}, \ldots, V_N$ all have approximately the steady-state distribution. In the transient case we could generally achieve this only by repeating the simulation. However, there are two problems in this situation that were not present in the transient case. First the nature and hence, the extent, of the transient phase is not known a priori. Hence we do not know the location of a point n_0 after which the random variables of the sequence have approximately the steady-state distribution. Second, in general, the V_n are correlated and hence are not independent. Thus, the standard statistical techniques for repeated *independent* observations from the same distribution cannot be applied directly.

There are a number of procedures available which deal with these two difficulties. Each, as we shall point out, has advantages and disadvantages in various situations. Hence, from the standpoint of the practical experimenter who wants to know what to do without any complications, the situation is not ideal. However, in many situations the adequacy of one or more of the methods is clear cut. Further, this discussion should give the experimenter perspective on methods that may be built in as part of the simulation package he is using. For example, the regenerative method, the spectral method, and the method of independent replications are built into the RESearch Queueing package (RESQ) which is discussed in Chapter 8 of this handbook.

6.3.2 Estimating the Extent of the Transient Phase

In three of the steady-state estimation procedures to be discussed below it is good practice to eliminate from consideration the early observations of the sequence $\{V_n : n = 1, 2, \ldots\}$ whose distributions do not approximate the steady-state distribution. In the fourth procedure the experimental protocol is such that this is not necessary. How many of these observations to ignore depends upon the transient behavior of the sequence which, along with the steady-state behavior, is unknown a priori.

One way to proceed is to estimate the transient behavior using the methods discussed in Section 6.2. This means we must make preliminary, short, independent replications of the simulation. Again consider $\{V_n : n = 1, 2, \ldots\}$. For each V_n there is a probability distribution function

$$F_n(x) = \text{Prob}\{V_n \leqslant x\}. \tag{6.78}$$

These $F_n(x)$ converge, as n increases, to the steady-state distribution function $F(x)$. We are concerned with removing from consideration those early members of the sequence X_n such that

$$F_n(x) \not\approx F(x). \tag{6.79}$$

The most straightforward procedure would be to estimate $F_n(x)$, as a function of n and x, as we did via the histograms in the example of Section 6.1.2. This would be done over a range of n sufficient to observe the convergence of $F_n(x)$. In practice, however, such an investigation would usually require more computing time than would be reasonable. Hence, instead of estimating $F_n(x)$, one or more of the important characteristics of $F_n(x)$ are estimated and observed as functions of n.

The simplest procedure is to test the convergence of the mean of the distribution. We let

$$\mu_n = E[V_n]. \tag{6.80}$$

Then the sequence $\{\mu_n : n = 1, 2, \ldots\}$ will converge to the mean of the steady-state distribution. A necessary condition that $F_n(x) \approx F(x)$ is that $\mu_n \approx \mu$. The sequence μ_n can be estimated by repeating the simulation and generating the sequence of sample means. Suppose we repeat the simulation M times and generate the observations

$$V_{1n}, \qquad n = 1, \ldots, N,$$
$$V_{2n}, \qquad n = 1, \ldots, N,$$
$$\vdots$$
$$V_{Mn}, \qquad n = 1, \ldots, N. \tag{6.81}$$

Then

$$\hat{\mu}_n = \bar{V}_n = \frac{1}{M} \sum_{m=1}^{M} V_{mn}, \qquad n = 1, \ldots, N, \tag{6.82}$$

is the sequence of sample means. The sequence $\hat{\mu}_n$ is a random sequence. Since

$$E[\hat{\mu}_n] = \mu_n, \tag{6.83}$$

it fluctuates about the converging sequence of means. The larger the value of M the narrower the fluctuations and the closer the approximation to the sequence $\{\mu_n\}$. Hence, by taking M large enough, a reasonable estimate can be made of a convergence point for the sequence $\{\mu_n\}$.

To illustrate this we return again to the example of Section 6.1.1 which is a simulation of the queueing network diagrammed in Fig. 6.2. For this network we consider the output sequence $\{W_{2,n}: n = 1, 2, \ldots\}$, where

$$W_{2,n} = \text{waiting time, for the } n\text{th departing customer, in the queue in front of the multiprogramming set,} \qquad (6.84)$$

and we let

$$V_{mn} = \text{value assumed by } W_{2,n} \text{ during the } m\text{th repetition of the simulation; } m = 1, \ldots, M \text{ and } n = 1, \ldots, N. \qquad (6.85)$$

A sample set V_{mn} for $M = 5$ and $N = 300$ is plotted in Fig. 6.3. For this set of data we calculated the sequence $\{\hat{\mu}_n\}$ and have plotted it in Fig. 6.10. Notice that a reasonable judgement can be made as to the extent of the transient phase

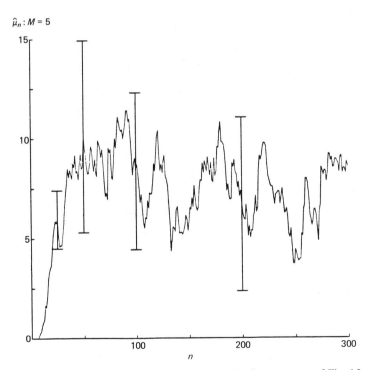

Fig. 6.10   A realization of $\{\hat{\mu}_n\}$ obtained from the five sequences of Fig. 6.3.

from the average of 5 output sequences whereas this would be impossible from any individual output sequence. In this case a reasonable estimate of the end of the transient phase would be 50 waiting times. This is consistent with the behavior of the histograms of Fig. 6.7.

As we mentioned above the larger M, the more stable is the sequence $\{\hat{\mu}_n\}$ and hence, the more reliable the judgement as to the point of convergence. We illustrate this in Fig. 6.11 where we have averaged over $M = 25$ and $M = 100$ output sequences.

Some notion as to the significance of the convergence features of the sequence $\{\hat{\mu}_n\}$ can be obtained by plotting confidence intervals for a selected set of the μ_n. These confidence intervals can be obtained via the t-distribution as we have detailed in Section 6.3.2 [see Eq. (6.41)]. A set of 90% confidence intervals were calculated and are plotted in Figs. 6.10 and 6.11. They were done for μ_{25}, μ_{50}, μ_{100}, and μ_{200}. It is important to realize that these individual confidence intervals can only be used as a rough guideline for the sequence $\{\mu_n\}$. They are only valid 90% confidence intervals when taken individually. A

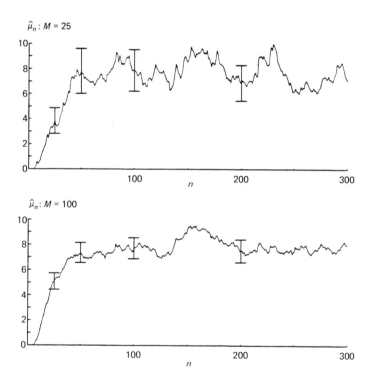

Fig. 6.11 Realizations of $\{\hat{\mu}_n\}$ obtained from 25 and 100 independent realizations of $\{W_{2,n}\}$.

much weaker confidence statement holds on the joint coverage of all the confidence intervals. Specifically, the probability that the sequence $\{\mu_n\}$ passes through all four intervals is greater than 0.6. This follows from the Bonferroni inequality that for any events $A_1, \ldots, A_N$

$$\text{Prob}\left\{\bigcap_{n=1}^{N} A_n\right\} \geq 1 - \sum_{n=1}^{N} \text{Prob}\{\text{not } A_n\}, \tag{6.86}$$

where the left-hand side of the inequality is the probability that all N events occur.

Finally, sometimes these judgments about the long term trends in $\{\mu_n\}$ are easier to make if an explicit attempt is made to smooth out the short term (high frequency) fluctuations in $\{\hat{\mu}_n\}$. The simplest way to do this is to take a moving average over an interval long enough to remove short term fluctuations but not so long as to distort the long term trend. A moving average of length $2K + 1$ is

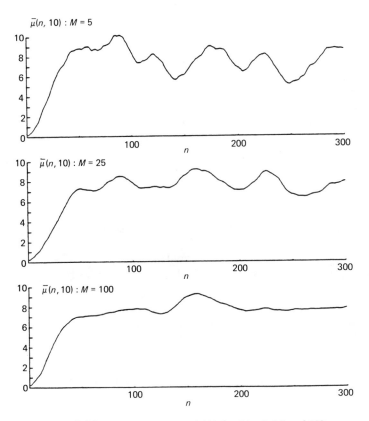

Fig. 6.12 Moving averages of $\hat{\mu}(n)$ for $M = 5$, 25, and 100.

defined as

$$
\bar{\mu}(n;K) = \begin{cases} (2K+1)^{-1}\sum_{k=-K}^{K}\hat{\mu}_{n+k} & \text{if } n \geqslant K+1, \\ (2n-1)^{-1}\sum_{k=-(n-1)}^{n-1}\hat{\mu}_{n+k}. & \text{if } n < K+1. \end{cases} \tag{6.87}
$$

In Fig. 6.12 we plot $\bar{\mu}(n, 10)$ for the $\{\hat{\mu}_n\}$ of Figs. 6.10 and 6.11.

As we remarked earlier, the convergence of μ_n to μ is a necessary but not sufficient condition for the convergence of $F_n(x)$ to $F(x)$. If the mean of the steady-state distribution was what the experimenter was ultimately interested in estimating then the convergence of μ_n would be adequate. However if he were interested in say the variance or the 90th percentile then he might choose to study the transient behavior of these quantities in exactly the same fashion as we have indicated for the mean. Consider, for example, the variance sequence $\{\sigma_n^2\}$. The simulation would be repeated obtaining the observations V_{mn} of Eqs. (6.81). Following the discussion of Section 6.2.4 the sample variance

$$
\hat{\sigma}_n^2 = \frac{1}{M-1}\sum_{m=1}^{M}(V_{mn}-\hat{\mu}_n)^2 \tag{6.88}
$$

would be calculated and observed as a function of n. Again M would have to be increased to the point where the long term convergence of $\sigma_n^2 = \text{Var}[V_n]$ could be judged despite the random fluctuations in $\{\hat{\sigma}_n^2\}$. As with μ_n, confidence intervals could be placed on σ_n^2 for some values of n. Further $\hat{\sigma}_n^2$ could be smoothed using the same moving average technique described in Eqs. (6.87) for $\hat{\mu}_n$. A percentile or the probability that the random variable lies in some interval would be handled in a similar fashion.

Other techniques for handling the problem of the initial transient have been suggested. See, e.g., Schruben (1982) and Kelton (1980).

6.3.3 The Method of Independent Replications

We saw in the introductory discussion of Section 6.3.1 that there were two basic problems in estimating any characteristic of the steady-state distribution of an output sequence $\{V_n : n = 1, 2, \ldots\}$. First, the sequence goes through a transient phase of unknown duration during which the distribution does not approximate the steady-state distribution. Second, in general, the observations are correlated and, hence, do not satisfy the independence assumption which underlies standard statistical methods. Such methods were applied to the estimation of the characteristics of transient distributions in Sections 6.2.3–6.2.6. There the independence was achieved by making independent replications of the simulation.

In this section we shall consider the most direct, and easiest to understand, approach to the estimation of the characteristics of steady-state distributions.

It is called the method of independent replications. In this approach the extent
of the transient phase is estimated using a technique such as that described in
the previous section. Using this transient phase estimate, a set of independent
simulation runs is partitioned into "transient" phases and "steady-state"
phases. From the observations in each steady-state phase a standard point
estimate of the characteristic of interest is formed. These point estimates are
independent because of the independence of the simulation runs from which
they are derived. The final point estimate is the average of these independent
estimates. A confidence interval is generated by applying standard arguments
based on the t-distribution. The treatment of the variance is slightly different.

Given this introduction we now consider in detail the estimation of the
mean of the steady-state distribution.

a. Estimating the Mean Value of a Steady-State Distribution

We assume an output sequence of random variables $\{V_n: n = 1, 2, \ldots\}$
where

$$\text{Prob}\{V_n \leqslant x\} = F_n(x) \to F(x). \tag{6.89}$$

We wish to generate a point estimate and a confidence interval for the mean
value μ associated with $F(x)$.

In the method we shall now describe, the method of independent
replications, it is very important that the duration of the transient phase be
estimated and that the early elements of the sequence, whose mean is not
approximately equal to μ, be removed from consideration. This could be done
by estimating the transient mean $\mu_n = E[X_n]$ and observing the behavior of the
estimate $\hat{\mu}_n$ as a function of n. This process was discussed in detail in Section
6.3.2.

Hence we assume that we have an estimate $\hat{n}_0$ of a point beyond which the
random variables of the sequence all have a mean value that is approximately
equal to μ; i.e.,

$$E[V_{\hat{n}_0+n}] \approx \mu, \qquad n = 1, 2, \ldots. \tag{6.90}$$

Given $\hat{n}_0$, if we make a run of the simulation which generates $\{V_1, \ldots, V_N\}$
where $N > \hat{n}_0$ then $\{V_1, \ldots, V_{\hat{n}_0}\}$ can be considered the transient part and
$\{V_{\hat{n}_0+1}, \ldots, V_N\}$, the steady-state part. Considering only the steady-state part,
a reasonable estimator of μ would be the sample mean

$$\bar{V} = \frac{1}{N - \hat{n}_0} \sum_{n=\hat{n}_0+1}^{N} V_n. \tag{6.91}$$

From (6.90) we have that $\bar{V}$ is an approximately unbiased estimator of μ; i.e.,

$$E[\bar{V}] \approx \mu. \tag{6.92}$$

However, because of the correlation between the V_n we cannot apply standard statistical methods to obtain an estimate of the variance of $\bar{V}$ and hence generate a confidence interval for μ. Specifically, for correlated observations, $\text{Var}[\bar{V}] \neq \text{Var}[V]/(N - n_0)$. This difficulty is discussed further in Section 6.3.4. The method of independent replications circumvents the problem by working with independent runs of the simulation.

In the method of independent replications, independent sample means are generated from independent simulation runs. A point estimate and a confidence interval are generated from these sample means as we shall now describe. M independent runs of the simulation are made, each generating an output sequence of length N. Hence we have a set of observations

$$
\begin{aligned}
V_{mn} = {}&\text{nth member of the output sequence from the mth} \\
&\text{independent replication of the simulation,} \\
&m = 1, \ldots, M, n = 1, \ldots, N.
\end{aligned}
\tag{6.93}
$$

On each replication we form the sample mean

$$
\hat{\mu}_m = \frac{1}{N - \hat{n}_0} \sum_{n = \hat{n}_0 + 1}^{N} V_{mn}.
\tag{6.94}
$$

Now the $\hat{\mu}_m$, $m = 1, \ldots, M$, are independent and

$$
E[\hat{\mu}_m] \approx \mu,
\tag{6.95}
$$

hence a reasonable, approximately unbiased estimate of μ is

$$
\hat{\mu} = \frac{1}{M} \sum_{m=1}^{M} \hat{\mu}_m.
\tag{6.96}
$$

Moreover, if we let

$$
s^2(\hat{\mu}_m) = \frac{1}{M - 1} \sum_{m=1}^{M} (\hat{\mu}_m - \hat{\mu})^2 = \frac{1}{M - 1} \sum_{m=1}^{M} \hat{\mu}_m^2 - \frac{M}{M - 1} \hat{\mu}^2
\tag{6.97}
$$

be the sample variance of the $\hat{\mu}_m$ then

$$
\frac{\hat{\mu} - \mu}{s(\hat{\mu}_m)/M^{1/2}}
\tag{6.98}
$$

has approximately a t-distribution with $M - 1$ degrees of freedom. Hence, in a fashion exactly parallel to the discussion in Section 6.2.3 we obtain the confidence interval and statement

$$
\text{Prob}\{\hat{\mu} - t_{M-1}(1 - \alpha/2)s(\hat{\mu}_m)/M^{1/2} \leqslant \mu \leqslant \hat{\mu} + t_{M-1}(1 - \alpha/2)s(\hat{\mu}_m)/M^{1/2}\}
$$

$$
\approx 1 - \alpha,
\tag{6.99}
$$

where $t_n(x)$ is the $100x$th percentile of the t-distribution with n degrees of freedom. Curves of $t_n(1 - \alpha/2)$ are given in Fig. 6.9 for $1 - \alpha = 0.9$ and $1 - \alpha = 0.95$.

In Section 6.3.6 we show that the expectation of the standard deviation of the $\hat{\mu}_m$ is proportional to $(N - \hat{n}_0)^{-1/2}$. Now for $M \geqslant 10$ the function $t_{M-1}(1 - \alpha/2)$ is approximately constant. Hence the expected width of the confidence interval given by Eq. (6.99) is approximately proportional to $\{M(N - \hat{n}_0)\}^{-1/2}$; i.e.,

$$E[2t_{M-1}(1 - \alpha/2)s(\hat{\mu}_m)/M^{1/2}] \approx \text{const}/\{M(N - \hat{n}_0)\}^{1/2}. \quad (6.100)$$

Thus we can decrease the expected width of the confidence interval by increasing either M, the number of replications, or N, the length of each replication. Generally it is best practice to keep M small, say of the order of 10, and let N be large. This minimizes the amount of unused data, $M\hat{n}_0$, and minimizes any residual bias caused by the slow convergence to μ of $\{\mu_n\}$ for $n > \hat{n}_0$.

b. Estimating the Probability that a Steady-State Random Variable Lies in Some Fixed Interval

The case where we are interested in estimating the probability that a steady-state random variable lies in some prespecified fixed interval is handled in exactly the same fashion as was the mean. We designate the interval as I and let

$$p_n = \text{Prob}\{V_n \in I\} \quad (6.101)$$

and

$$p = \lim_{n \to \infty} p_n. \quad (6.102)$$

We are interested in placing a confidence interval on p. Again we must estimate the extent of the transient phase; i.e., we must produce an estimate $\hat{n}_0$ such that

$$p_n \approx p \quad \text{for} \quad n > \hat{n}_0. \quad (6.103)$$

If the interval I is near the center of the steady-state distribution then it would be reasonable to obtain $\hat{n}_0$ by observing estimates of the transient mean μ_n. However if I is at the extremes of the steady-state distribution it would be best to observe estimates of the transient probability p_n. This issue was discussed in Section 6.3.2. For our purposes now we assume an $\hat{n}_0$ satisfying Eq. (6.103) has been obtained.

Given $\hat{n}_0$ we generate M independent replications of the simulation. These generate the set $\{V_{mn} : m = 1, \ldots, M, n = 1, \ldots, N\}$ of observations described in Eq. (6.93). We assume that $N \gg \hat{n}_0$. For each replication we form the estimate

$$\hat{p}_m = v_m/(N - \hat{n}_0), \quad (6.104)$$

where

$$v_m = \text{number of } V_{mn} \text{ for } n > \hat{n}_0 \text{ which are in the interval } I. \quad (6.105)$$

This is the proportion of the observations in the steady-state phase of the mth replication that are in the interval I. Now

$$E[\hat{p}_m] \approx p, \quad (6.106)$$

and the $\hat{p}_m$ are independent. Hence if we let

$$\hat{p} = \frac{1}{M} \sum_{m=1}^{M} \hat{p}_m \quad (6.107)$$

and

$$s^2(\hat{p}_m) = \frac{1}{M-1} \sum_{m=1}^{M} (\hat{p}_m - \hat{p})^2, \quad (6.108)$$

then as before,

$$\frac{\hat{p} - p}{s(\hat{p}_m)/M^{1/2}} \quad (6.109)$$

has approximately a t-distribution with $M - 1$ degrees of freedom. Again a confidence statement and interval is given by

$$\text{Prob}\{\hat{p} - t_{M-1}(1 - \alpha/2)s(\hat{p}_m)/M^{1/2} \leqslant p \leqslant \hat{p} + t_{M-1}(1 - \alpha/2)s(\hat{p}_m)/M^{1/2}\}$$
$$\approx 1 - \alpha \quad (6.110)$$

where $t_n(x)$ is the $100x$th percentile of the t-distribution with n degrees of freedom. Also, as before, it is best to keep M small, say 10, and increase $N - \hat{n}_0$ to decrease the size of the confidence interval.

c. Estimating a Percentile of a Steady-State Distribution

We next consider the estimation of a percentile of the steady-state distribution. The 100βth percentile x_β is the smallest value x such that

$$F(x) \geqslant \beta, \quad (6.111)$$

where $F(x)$ is the steady-state distribution function. We are interested in placing a confidence interval on x_β. Typically there is interest in the median, $x_{0.5}$, as a measure of the location of a distribution or in $x_{0.90}$ or $x_{0.95}$ as measures of the spread.

We let $F_n(x)$ be the distribution function of V_n and let $x_{\beta n}$ be the 100βth percentile of $F_n(x)$. Hence

$$\lim_{n \to \infty} x_{\beta n} = x_\beta. \quad (6.112)$$

We must generate an estimate $\hat{n}_0$ such that $x_{\beta n} \approx x_\beta$ for $n > \hat{n}_0$. Now if x_β is the median or a percentile near the center of the distribution then the best way to do this would be to generate estimates $\hat{\mu}_n$ of the transient mean and observe their convergence behavior as a function of n. However if x_β is near zero or one, e.g., the 95th percentile, then it would be best to obtain estimates $\hat{x}_{\beta n}$ and observe their convergence behavior as a function of n. This general problem is discussed in Section 6.3.2. For now we assume an $\hat{n}_0$ such that

$$x_{\beta n} \approx x_\beta \qquad \text{for} \quad n > \hat{n}_0. \tag{6.113}$$

Given $\hat{n}_0$ we follow the same steps described for estimating the mean and probability that the random variable lies in some interval. We generate M independent replications of the simulation. These generate the set $\{V_{mn} : m = 1, \ldots, M, n = 1, \ldots, N\}$ of observations described in Eq. (6.93). We assume $N \gg \hat{n}_0$. For each replication we generate the sample 100βth percentile $\hat{x}_{\beta m}$ of the $N - \hat{n}_0$ observations $V_{m, \hat{n}_0 + 1}, \ldots, V_{mN}$. Formally we let $Y_{m1}, \ldots, Y_{m, N - \hat{n}_0}$ be a reordering of $V_{m, \hat{n}_0 + 1}, \ldots, V_{mN}$ such that

$$Y_{mi} \leqslant Y_{m, i+1}. \tag{6.114}$$

We let $[y]$ equal the largest integer less than or equal to y. Then

$$\hat{x}_{\beta m} = \begin{cases} Y_{m, [(N - \hat{n}_0)\beta]} & \text{if} \quad (N - \hat{n}_0)\beta \text{ is an integer,} \\ Y_{m, [(N - \hat{n}_0)\beta] + 1} & \text{if} \quad (N - \hat{n}_0)\beta \text{ is not an integer.} \end{cases} \tag{6.115}$$

Now

$$E[\hat{x}_{\beta m}] \approx x_\beta, \tag{6.116}$$

and the $\hat{x}_{\beta m}$ are independent. Hence if we let

$$\hat{x}_\beta = \frac{1}{M} \sum_{m=1}^{M} \hat{x}_{\beta m} \tag{6.117}$$

and

$$s^2(\hat{x}_{\beta m}) = \frac{1}{M-1} \sum_{m=1}^{M} (\hat{x}_{\beta m} - \hat{x}_\beta)^2, \tag{6.118}$$

then as before,

$$\frac{\hat{x}_\beta - x_\beta}{s(\hat{x}_{\beta m})/M^{1/2}} \tag{6.119}$$

has approximately a t-distribution with $M - 1$ degrees of freedom. A confidence interval and statement paralleling Eqs. (6.99) and (6.110) can easily be supplied by the reader. Again it is best to keep M small, say about 10, and decrease the size of the confidence interval by increasing $N - \hat{n}_0$.

A few words of caution are in order with regard to percentile estimation. First, to estimate extreme percentiles, particular care has to be taken to make sure the individual runs are long enough for otherwise the estimates will be biased. See, e.g., Heidelberger and Lewis (1981). Second, sometimes a system performance specification is written as if requiring the estimation of a percentile when it can be recast in equivalent form where it requires only the estimate of a proportion, a generally simpler problem. For example, suppose a specification states that the 95th percentile of a response time distribution must be less than 3 s. This is *exactly* the same as the requirement that the probability that the response time is less than 3 s be greater than 0.95.

d. Estimating the Variance of a Steady-State Distribution

Finally we consider the estimation of the variance of the steady-state distribution using the method of independent replications. Again we assume an output sequence $\{V_n: n = 1, 2, \ldots\}$, where

$$\text{Prob}\{V_n \leqslant x\} = F_n(x) \to F(x). \tag{6.120}$$

We wish to obtain a point estimate and place a confidence interval on the variance σ^2 associated with $F(x)$. As before it is important to eliminate from consideration the early members of the sequence where $F_n(x)$ is not approximately equal to $F(x)$. This problem is discussed in Section 6.3.2. For our present purposes we assume an estimate $\hat{n}_0$ has been obtained and that for $n > \hat{n}_0$, $F_n(x) \approx F(x)$.

Given $\hat{n}_0$ we proceed, as before, by making M independent runs of the simulation of length N where $N \gg \hat{n}_0$. Hence again we have a set of observations $\{V_{mn}: m = 1, \ldots, M, n = 1, \ldots, N\}$ as described in Eq. (6.93). We begin by forming estimates

$$\hat{\mu}_m = \frac{1}{N - \hat{n}_0} \sum_{n = \hat{n}_0 + 1}^{N} V_{mn}, \qquad m = 1, \ldots, M, \tag{6.121}$$

of the mean from each of the M replications. We then form the overall estimate of the mean

$$\hat{\mu} = \frac{1}{M} \sum_{m = 1}^{M} \hat{\mu}_m. \tag{6.122}$$

Next for each replication we generate the variance estimate

$$s_m^2 = \frac{1}{N - \hat{n}_0} \sum_{n = \hat{n}_0 + 1}^{N} (V_{mn} - \hat{\mu})^2$$

$$= \frac{1}{N - \hat{n}_0} \left(\sum_{n = \hat{n}_0 + 1}^{N} V_{mn}^2 \right) - 2\hat{\mu}_m\hat{\mu} + (\hat{\mu})^2$$

$$= \hat{\gamma}_m^2 - 2\hat{\mu}_m\hat{\mu} + (\hat{\mu})^2, \tag{6.123}$$

where

$$\hat{\gamma}_m^2 = \frac{1}{N - \hat{n}_0} \sum_{n = \hat{n}_0 + 1}^{N} V_{mn}^2. \tag{6.124}$$

We use $\hat{\mu}$ in the first line of Eq. (6.123) rather than $\hat{\mu}_n$ to make s_m^2 less biased as an estimate of σ^2. As the point estimate of the variance we take the average of the s_m^2; i.e.,

$$\hat{\sigma}^2 = \frac{1}{M} \sum_{m=1}^{M} s_m^2 = \frac{1}{M} \sum_{m=1}^{M} \hat{\gamma}_m^2 - (\hat{\mu})^2 = \hat{\gamma}^2 - (\hat{\mu})^2, \tag{6.125}$$

where

$$\hat{\gamma}^2 = \frac{1}{M} \sum_{m=1}^{M} \hat{\gamma}_m^2. \tag{6.126}$$

Now this situation differs from the three discussed above in that the estimates derived from the M replications, the s_m^2, are not independent. They are all functions of the common quantity $\hat{\mu}$. Hence, the t-statistic cannot be used directly to obtain a confidence interval. However, a confidence interval can be obtained by jackknifing the estimator $\hat{\sigma}^2$ as was done in a different context in Section 6.2.4. We let $\hat{\sigma}_m^2$ be the estimate of σ^2 with the mth replication left out; i.e.,

$$\hat{\sigma}_m^2 = \frac{1}{M-1} \sum_{l \neq m} \hat{\gamma}_l^2 - \left(\frac{1}{M-1} \sum_{l \neq m} \hat{\mu}_l \right)^2, \tag{6.127}$$

and let

$$Z_m = M\hat{\sigma}^2 - (M-1)\hat{\sigma}_m^2. \tag{6.128}$$

Then if we let $\bar{Z}$ be the sample mean of the Z_m and s_z^2 the sample variance; i.e.,

$$\bar{Z} = \frac{1}{M} \sum_{m-1}^{M} Z_m \tag{6.129}$$

and

$$s_z^2 = \frac{1}{M-1} \sum_{m=1}^{M} (Z_m - \bar{Z})^2, \tag{6.130}$$

we have that

$$\frac{\bar{Z} - \sigma^2}{s_z / M^{1/2}} \tag{6.131}$$

has approximately a t-distribution with $M - 1$ degrees of freedom. Hence, we have an approximate confidence interval and statement

$$\text{Prob}\{\bar{Z} - t_{M-1}(1 - \alpha/2)s_z/M^{1/2} \leqslant \sigma^2 \leqslant \bar{Z} + t_{M-1}(1 - \alpha/2)s_z/M^{1/2}\} \approx 1 - \alpha.$$

$$(6.132)$$

Curves of $t_n(1 - \alpha/2)$ are given in Fig. 6.9 for $1 - \alpha = 0.9$ and $1 - \alpha = 0.95$.

6.3.4 The Dependent or Correlated Nature of Output Sequences

We let $V_n : n = 1, 2, \ldots$ denote a generic random output sequence which we assume to be in the steady state. We suppose we are interested in characteristics of the steady-state distribution function $F(x)$. Hence we have, from a single simulation run, a sequence of random variables all of which have approximately the probability distribution of interest. However, these random variables are not in general independent. In fact, they are frequently highly dependent. Hence, as we pointed out above the standard statistical procedures designed for independent observations do not directly apply.

The first method that we discussed in Section 6.3.3, circumvented this problem by generating independent sequences (of dependent random variables) via multiple independent replications of the simulation. An estimate was generated from each sequence and the mean of these independent estimates became the final estimate. Standard techniques based on the t-distribution were applied to obtain confidence intervals. The remaining three methods which we shall describe in the next three sections work on a single simulation run. For this reason they have two advantages over the method of independent replications. First, any residual effect of the initial transient is less, since the length of the single simulation run is much greater than the length of one of the multiple runs. Second, the simulation is more efficient, because the amount of data that must be thrown away to control the effect of the initial transient is substantially reduced. In fact, in the regenerative method no data is discarded.

The application of the method of batch means and the spectral method requires some understanding of the nature of the dependence in the output sequences. The purpose of this section is to provide that understanding. Suppose we have a pair of random variables, X and Y. We measure the dependence between X and Y in terms of a normalization of the covariance called the correlation. The covariance between X and Y is defined as

$$\text{Cov}[X, Y] = \text{Cov}[Y, X] = E[(X - E[X])(Y - E[Y])]. \quad (6.133)$$

If X and Y tend to vary together; i.e., if when X is greater than (less than) its expected value, Y tends to be greater than (less than) its expected value, the covariance is positive. If X and Y tend to vary oppositely, the covariance is negative. The correlation between X and Y is defined as

$$\text{Corr}[X, Y] = \text{Corr}[Y, X] = \frac{\text{Cov}[X, Y]}{(\text{Var}[X])^{1/2}(\text{Var}[Y])^{1/2}}. \tag{6.134}$$

The correlation has the same sign as the covariance but is independent of any origin or scale changes in the measurement of X and Y; i.e., for any constants a, b, c, and d

$$\text{Corr}[aX + b, cY + d] = \text{Corr}[X, Y]. \tag{6.135}$$

Furthermore,

$$-1 \leqslant \text{Corr}[X, Y] \leqslant 1. \tag{6.136}$$

If the correlation is equal to ± 1 the two random variables are linearly related.

For the system simulations of the type we have discussed in this handbook it is reasonable to model the output sequences in their steady-state phases as covariance stationary processes. What this means is that the degree of dependence or correlation which exists between random variables in the sequence is *not* a function of the absolute location of the random variables but only of the distance separating them. For example, if we consider some waiting time sequence $\{W_n\}$, then because of the perseverance of waiting lines, we would expect the correlation between adjacent waiting times to be large but we would expect it to be independent of location in the sequence. That is, W_{1000} and W_{1001} would be correlated as W_{1500} and W_{1501} or W_{2000} and W_{2001}. We now discuss this more formally.

We assume the generic sequence $V_n: n = 1, 2, \ldots,$ to be in the steady state. We let the common expectation be μ and the common variance be σ^2; i.e.,

$$E[V_n] = \mu \tag{6.137}$$

and

$$E[(V_n - \mu)^2] = \sigma^2. \tag{6.138}$$

We say such a sequence is a covariance stationary sequence if for any n and k

$$\text{Cov}[V_n, V_{n+k}] = \gamma(k); \tag{6.139}$$

i.e., the covariance is a function only of the separation between the random variables and not of their location in the sequence. The function $\gamma(k)$ is called the covariance function (sometimes the autocovariance function) and has the properties

$$\gamma(0) = \sigma^2, \tag{6.140}$$

$$\gamma(k) = \gamma(-k). \tag{6.141}$$

Equation (6.140) follows from Eqs. (6.138) and (6.139). Equation (6.141) follows from Eqs. (6.139) and (6.133).

The dependence in the sequence is best described by the correlation function (sometimes called the autocorrelation function). The correlation function $\rho(k)$ is the correlation between two members of the sequence with a separation of k units; i.e.,

$$\rho(k) = \text{Corr}[V_n, V_{n+k}]$$

$$= \frac{\text{Cov}[V_n, V_{n+k}]}{(\text{Var}[V_n])^{1/2}(\text{Var}[V_{n+k}])^{1/2}} = \frac{\gamma(k)}{\gamma(0)}. \tag{6.142}$$

The correlation function has the properties

$$\rho(0) = 1, \tag{6.143}$$

$$\rho(k) = \rho(-k), \tag{6.144}$$

$$-1 \leqslant \rho(k) \leqslant 1. \tag{6.145}$$

Generally, in the output processes of the models considered in this handbook, the correlation is positive; that is, the random variables in a sequence tend to vary together. Nearby members of the sequence are usually highly correlated. This correlation decreases with increasing distance and finally disappears for members widely separated. Formally

$$\lim_{|k| \to \infty} \rho(k) = 0. \tag{6.146}$$

The presence of this positive correlation tends to reduce the amount of information gained, per sample, concerning the steady-state probability distribution. If you know V_n, then V_{n+1} tends to provide relatively little additional information because of its positive correlation with V_n. As an illustration of this consider the problem of estimating the steady-state expectation μ. We suppose we have N samples $V_1, \ldots, V_N$ taken from the steady-state phase. A reasonable, unbiased estimate of μ is the sample mean

$$\bar{V} = \frac{1}{N} \sum_{n=1}^{N} V_n. \tag{6.147}$$

However, in this case, because of the correlation,

$$\text{Var}[\bar{V}] \neq \sigma^2/N. \tag{6.148}$$

(The equality would hold for uncorrelated observations.) We next derive the correct formula for $\text{Var}[\bar{V}]$. We saw in Section 2.1.3c of Chapter 2 that

$$\text{Var}[\bar{V}] = \frac{1}{N^2} \text{Var}\left[\sum_{n=1}^{N} V_n \right]$$

$$= \frac{1}{N^2} \left\{ \sum_{n=1}^{N} \text{Var}[V_n] + 2 \sum_{k=1}^{N-1} \sum_{j=k+1}^{N} \text{Cov}[V_j, V_k] \right\}. \tag{6.149}$$

Now substituting using Eqs. (6.139), (6.141), and (6.142), we have

$$\text{Var}[\bar{V}] = \frac{1}{N^2}\left[N\gamma(0) + 2\sum_{k=1}^{N-1}(N-k)\gamma(k) \right]$$

$$= \frac{1}{N^2}\left[\sum_{k=-(N-1)}^{N-1}(N-|k|)\gamma(k) \right]$$

$$= \frac{\gamma(0)}{N}\sum_{k=-(N-1)}^{N-1}\frac{N-|k|}{N}\rho(k)$$

$$= \frac{\sigma^2}{N}\sum_{k=-(N-1)}^{N-1}\frac{N-|k|}{N}\rho(k). \tag{6.150}$$

Furthermore, as we remarked, $\rho(k)$ goes to zero as k gets large and hence for large N from Eq. (6.150) we have the approximation

$$\text{Var}[\bar{V}] \approx \frac{\sigma^2}{N}\left[\sum_{k=-\infty}^{\infty}\rho(k) \right]. \tag{6.151}$$

Thus we see that, as with independent samples, the variance of the sample mean $\bar{V}$ falls off as $1/N$, but there is an additional factor approximately equal to the sum over the correlation function. Now, in most models of computer systems the correlation functions of output sequences are positive. Further, they can decrease very slowly with increasing k. Hence, this factor $\sum_{k=-\infty}^{\infty}\rho(k)$ can be very large, easily in the range 10 to 50. *This means that many correlated observations must be taken to give the variance reduction achieved by one independent observation.* In fact, the factor $\sum_{k=-\infty}^{\infty}\rho(k)$ is the number of correlated observations equivalent to one independent observation and $N/(\sum_{k=-\infty}^{\infty}\rho(k))$ is sometimes called the equivalent independent sample size.

Finally, we consider the problem of estimating the correlation function. The recommended estimate of the covariance function is the sample covariance function

$$\hat{\gamma}(k) = \frac{1}{N}\sum_{n=1}^{N-k}(\bar{V}_n - \bar{V})(V_{n+k} - \bar{V}), \qquad k \geq 0,$$

$$\hat{\gamma}(-k) = \hat{\gamma}(k). \tag{6.152}$$

The recommended estimate of the correlation function is the sample correlation function

$$\hat{\rho}(k) = \hat{\gamma}(k)/\hat{\gamma}(0). \tag{6.153}$$

The maximum lag for which the correlation function is estimated should be small compared to N, say $k \leq N/4$. For a detailed discussion of the estimation of the correlation function see Jenkins and Watts (1968, Section 5.3) and Box and Jenkins (1970, Sections 2.1.5 and 2.1.6).

As an example we have estimated the correlation function of the steady-state phase of the waiting time sequence $W_{2,n}$ as defined by Eq. (6.16). The first 100 observations were discarded and the next 1000 observations were used to generated the sample correlation function $\hat{\rho}(k)$ plotted in Fig. 6.13. From the appearance of $\hat{\rho}(k)$ one might conjecture that $\rho(k) \approx 0$ for $|k| > 30$. The distribution theory of the sample correlation function is difficult and complex.

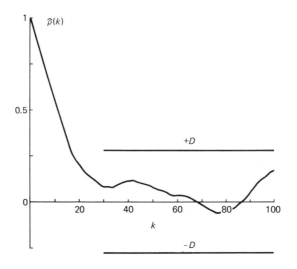

Fig. 6.13   A sample autocorrelation function for $W_{2,n}$.

Furthermore, the sample correlation function as a random process is more strongly correlated than the original process. Hence, great care has to be taken in interpreting it. However, if $\rho(k) = 0$ for $|k| > L$ then most (approximately 95%) of $\hat{\rho}(k)$ should lie between the limits $\pm D$ where

$$D = 2 \left(\sum_{k=-L}^{L} \frac{\hat{\rho}^2(k)}{N} \right)^{1/2}. \tag{6.154}$$

These limits are plotted in Fig. 6.13 for $L = 30$ and the fluctuations in $\hat{\rho}(k)$ for $k > 30$ are consistent with them. For more details see Box and Jenkins (1970, Sections 2.1.5 and 2.1.6).

We next discuss three additional methods for dealing with the correlation in the steady-state sequence. Two of these proceed, as did the method of independent replications, by forming a set of independent or approximately independent sequences. However, they form the sequences by partitioning a single simulation run into subsequences rather than making independent runs. The third method does not proceed via this partitioning approach but rather directly estimates the effect of the correlation using Eq. (6.151).

6.3.5　The Method of Batch Means

We now describe a method that exactly parallels the method of independent replications except that the sequences are adjacent, nonoverlapping subsequences of the output of a single simulation run. Once the subsequences are formed the procedure is identical to that described in Section 6.3.3.

We consider a generic output sequence of random variables which we again designate as V_n: $n = 1, 2, \ldots$. We saw in the previous section that the correlation in the steady-state phase of such an output sequence was characterized by a correlation function

$$\rho(k) = \text{Cor}[V_n, V_{n+k}]. \tag{6.155}$$

Further in the models under consideration in this handbook this correlation function goes to zero as k increases. Hence, the correlation in the sequence is "local" and for some sufficiently large positive integer L

$$\rho(k) \approx 0 \quad \text{for} \quad |k| > L. \tag{6.156}$$

Thus, elements in the output sequence greater than L units apart are approximately uncorrelated.

Let n_0 be a point beyond which the sequence V_n can be considered to be in the steady-state phase. Suppose we have a sample sequence of length $n_0 + N'$. Hence we have a steady-state sequence of duration N'. If we partition this steady-state sequence up into contiguous subsequences of length $N \gg L$ then estimates derived from these subsequences can be considered to be approximately independent and the method of independent replications of Section 6.3.3 can be applied to generate confidence intervals. To see that this is the case first consider any two nonadjacent subsequences. All the elements in one subsequence are uncorrelated with all the elements in the other subsequence, since the distance between all pairs of elements is greater than L. Hence, estimates derived from the two subsequences are uncorrelated. Next, consider two adjacent subsequences. Only the elements within a distance L of the endpoints connecting the two are correlated. Since the length of the subsequences N is much greater than L, most of the elements of each subsequence are uncorrelated with most of the elements of the other subsequence. Hence, estimates derived from the two subsequences are approximately uncorrelated. Thus, the set of subsequences have approximately the properties of the sequences obtained from independent runs of the simulation. We recommend that $N \geqslant 5L$.

Generally, the central problem in the application of this method is the estimation of L and the resulting choice of N. If N is not chosen large enough then the subsequence estimates are correlated enough to make the resulting confidence intervals invalid. Usually in this case, the confidence intervals are overly optimistic. They are too narrow and the probability that they cover the true value is less than the theoretical specification. We shall discuss the problems of estimating L and choosing N below. However, we first formalize the method.

We let n_0, L, N, and N' be defined as above. Further we assume that N divides N' and let

$$M = N'/N. \tag{6.157}$$

M is the number of subsequences. In Fig. 6.14 we have illustrated the

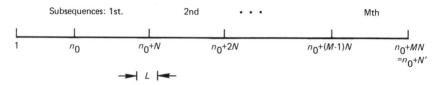

Fig. 6.14 The relationship between sequence lengths in the method of batch means.

relationship between n_0, L, N, N', and M. Paralleling the discussion in Section 6.3.3 and the definition given by (6.93) we define

$$V_{mn} = n\text{th member of the } m\text{th subsequence}$$

$$= V_{n_0 + (m-1)N + n}, \qquad m = 1, \dots, M, \quad n = 1, \dots, N. \tag{6.158}$$

Thereafter, the discussion parallels that given in Section 6.3.3 except that the n_0 elements in the transient phase need *not* be removed from each $V_{mn}: n = 1, 2, \dots$. They were removed once and for all from the single long sequence. Hence, paralleling Eq. (6.95)

$$\hat{\mu}_m = \frac{1}{N} \sum_{n=1}^{N} V_{mn} \tag{6.159}$$

paralleling Eqs. (6.104) and (6.105),

$$\hat{p}_m = v_m/N, \tag{6.160}$$

where

$$v_m = \text{number of } V_{mn} \text{ which are in the interval } I, \tag{6.161}$$

paralleling Eq. (6.115)

$$\hat{x}_{\beta m} = \text{sample } 100\beta\text{th percentile of } V_{mn}, \qquad n = 1, \dots, N, \tag{6.162}$$

and finally paralleling Eq. (6.123)

$$s_m^2 = \frac{1}{N} \sum_{n=1}^{N} (V_{mn} - \hat{\mu})^2. \tag{6.163}$$

Given these subsequence estimates the derivation of confidence intervals is exactly as in Section 6.3.3.

We let $\hat{L}$ be our estimate of L. If $N'/5\hat{L} > 10$; i.e., if letting $N = 5\hat{L}$ results in more than 10 subsequences, then it is best to increase N to $N'/10$ and have 10 subsequences. The risk in this method is that N will be too small and the assumption of approximate independence invalid. As long as $M \geqslant 10$ there is no significant disadvantage to a large N.

The central practical problem in this approach is how to estimate L, the point beyond which the correlation is approximately zero, and consequently N, the length of the subsequences. An estimate $\hat{L}$ of L can be obtained through the sample correlation function $\hat{\rho}(k)$ as defined by Eq. (6.153). This is not a simple judgment, however, because $\hat{\rho}(k)$ is a random sequence just like the output sequence V_n. Moreover, it is more strongly correlated than the sequence V_n from which it is derived. Hence, any particular realization of $\hat{\rho}(k)$ tends to generate more confidence in the accuracy of $\hat{L}$ than it deserves. In practice it is best, as we pointed out above, to be conservative in the choice of $\hat{L}$ and hence of N.

As a guide to interpreting the significance of fluctuations in the tail of the sample correlation function, the large lag limits cited in the previous section can be used. If $\rho(k) = 0$ for $k > \hat{L}$ then most (approximately 95%) of the sample values of $\hat{\rho}(k)$ for $k > \hat{L}$ should lie between the limits $\pm D$ where D is given by Eq. (6.154). If they do not, your $\hat{L}$ is not large enough.

For alternative methods for choosing the batch size N see Fishman (1978b) and Law and Carson (1979).

6.3.6 *The Regenerative Method*

We have so far discussed two methods for generating confidence intervals for characteristics of the steady-state distributions of the random output processes generated by simulations: the method of independent replications and the method of batch means. Both these methods as well as the method we shall discuss in this section generate, through an experimental protocol, independent or approximately independent sequences. The method of independent replications generates independent sequences through independent, repeated runs of the simulation. The method of batch means generates approximately independent sequences by breaking up the output sequence from one simulation run into contiguous subsequences which are long compared to the time extent of the correlation within the sequence. We shall now describe a third method that produces independent subsequences from a single run. This method cannot be applied to all output processes from all models because it requires a certain probabilistic structure which for some models and some output processes does not exist. However, it does apply to most output processes in a wide class of models.

The simulations of the models described in this handbook are discrete event simulations. This means that the simulation moves in time increments according to events marking changes in the state of the model: completion of service times, arrivals of customers from external sources, etc. We designate the sequence of times of these events by $\tau_1, \tau_2, \tau_3, \ldots$. Now we again consider a generic output sequence $\{V_n : n = 1, 2, \ldots\}$. Sometimes it is possible to define a subsequence $\tau_{k_1}, \tau_{k_2}, \tau_{k_3}, \ldots$ of the event time sequence such that this subsequence partitions the sequence $\{V_n\}$ up into independent, identically distributed segments. That is if we let

$$V_{n_1}, \ldots, V_{n_2-1} \quad \text{be the elements of } \{V_n\} \text{ occurring} \\ \text{in the interval} \quad \tau_{k_1} \leqslant \tau < \tau_{k_2},$$

$$V_{n_2}, \ldots, V_{n_3-1} \quad \text{be the elements of } \{V_n\} \text{ occurring} \\ \text{in the interval} \quad \tau_{k_2} \leqslant \tau < \tau_{k_3}, \quad\quad (6.164)$$
$$\vdots$$

then the subsequences $\{V_{n_1}, \ldots, V_{n_2-1}\}, \{V_{n_2}, \ldots, V_{n_3-1}\}, \ldots$ are independent, identically distributed subsequences. The sequence $\tau_{k_1}, \tau_{k_2}, \ldots$ is defined as the sequence of event times at which the model makes a particular change of state where a state of the model is defined in terms of the location of customers.

As an example, consider a simulation of the model described by Fig. 6.2. Again consider the output sequence

$$W_{2,n} = \text{waiting time of the } n\text{th departing customer from the} \\ \text{queue in front of the multiprogramming set.} \quad\quad (6.165)$$

We let the points $\tau_{k_1}, \tau_{k_2}, \ldots$ be defined as the points at which the model enters the state where all the customers are at the terminals, i.e., in Queue 1. Then since the terminal think times are exponential we have from the memoryless property of the exponential distribution [see Eq. (2.36)] that the process of departures is probabilistically identical following each time the model enters this state. Further, the first departure always sees the same empty system. Hence, once the model enters this state the probabilistic behavior of $W_{2,n}$ is exactly the same as the previous time it entered this state. The specific realization will be different each time but it will be driven in an independent fashion by the same probability mechanism. Such a state is called a regeneration state for the process $W_{2,n}$. Since in this model all of the service times are exponential we could, from the standpoint of the $W_{2,n}$, have chosen any state of the model, i.e., distribution of customers, as the regeneration state provided there were no customers in Queue 2. For example, we could have chosen the state defined by 20 customers at the terminals and 5 customers at Queue 3, in front of the processor. We could not choose a state where there were customers in Queue 2 since in that case the sequences would not be independent. For example, the waiting time of the first customer of each subsequence would depend upon the waiting time of the last customer of the previous subsequence. The problem of choosing a regeneration state to define the partitioning sequence $\tau_{k_1}, \tau_{k_2}, \ldots$ is a complex one and will be discussed at more length later.

The subsequences $\{V_{n_1}, \ldots, V_{n_2-1}\}, \{V_{n_2}, \ldots, V_{n_3-1}\}, \ldots$ are called tours. At the points n_k the process $\{V_n\}$ essentially regenerates or begins anew. The lengths of the tours $N_1 = n_2 - n_1$, $N_2 = n_3 - n_2, \ldots$ are random variables. Hence, we have partitioned our sequence (an output sequence from a single simulation run) up into *independent*, identically distributed subsequences of *random* lengths. Remember in the case of the method of batch means the subsequences were *approximately independent*, identically distributed subsequences of *constant* length.

In the practical application of the regenerative method the model is set initially in the regeneration state. Hence, $\tau_{k_1} = 0$ and $n_1 = 1$. Thus, the first tour begins with the first element V_1 of the sequence. Now since the first tour is probabilistically identical to all the other tours there is no reason to discard it or any part of it. Hence, no data need be discarded in the application of this method. The method also provides a ready answer to the question of what initial state to use.

In the application of this approach the simulation is started, as we mentioned above, in the regeneration state and is run for some fixed number, say M, of tours. Hence, we have M independent, identically distributed subsequences $\{V_1, \ldots, V_{n_2-1}\}, \ldots, \{V_{n_M}, \ldots, V_{n_{M+1}-1}\}$. Now the most direct procedure for generating a confidence interval would be to treat these subsequences the same as the subsequences generated by the method of batch means. Hence, for example, if we let V be a random variable with the steady-state distribution and we wish to generate a confidence interval on $E[V]$, we would form the subsequence averages,

$$\bar{V}_m = \frac{1}{n_{m+1} - n_m} \sum_{n=n_m}^{n_{m+1}-1} V_n, \qquad m = 1, \ldots, M, \qquad (6.166)$$

let $(1/M)\sum_{m=1}^{M} \bar{V}_m$ be our point estimate, and use standard methods based on the t-distribution to generated a confidence interval. The problem with this approach is that

$$E\left[\frac{1}{M} \sum_{m=1}^{M} \bar{V}_m\right] = E[\bar{V}_m] \neq E[V]. \qquad (6.167)$$

Because of the special way we have partitioned the sequence we have generated independent, identically distributed subsequences but the sample means of these subsequences are biased as an estimate of the steady-state mean. Hence, $(1/M)\sum_{m=1}^{M} \bar{V}_m$ has this same bias which remains constant, i.e., does not go to zero, with increasing M. Thus, we do not proceed in this fashion but rather more indirectly.

Again we consider the problem of generating a point estimate and a confidence interval on the steady-state mean $E[V]$. We let

$$Y_m = \sum_{n=n_m}^{n_{m+1}-1} V_n \tag{6.168}$$

and

$$N_m = n_{m+1} - n_m. \tag{6.169}$$

The quantity Y_m is the sum of V_n over the mth tour and the quantity N_m is the length of the mth tour. Hence, our partitioning generates M independent, identically distributed bivariate random variables $(Y_1, N_1), \ldots, (Y_M, N_M)$. The pairs of random variables (Y_m, N_m), (Y_l, N_l) are independent for $m \neq l$ but in general the individual Y_m and N_m are correlated; i.e.,

$$\text{Cov}[Y_m, N_m] \neq 0. \tag{6.170}$$

Now one can show (Crane and Lemoine, 1977; Iglehart, 1978) that the following result holds under very general conditions.

RESULT 1   *Let*

$$\text{Prob}\{V_n \leqslant x\} = F_n(x) \to F(x)$$

and let $E[V]$ be the steady state mean, i.e., the expectation associated with $F(x)$, then

$$E[V] = E[Y_m]/E[N_m] \tag{6.171}$$

where $E[Y_m]$ and $E[N_m]$ are the common expectations respectively of Y_m and N_m, $m = 1, \ldots, M$ as defined by Eqs. (6.168) and (6.169).

Hence, the problem of estimating $E[V]$ becomes the problem of estimating the ratio $E[Y_m]/E[N_m]$. That is, given independent, identically distributed pairs of observations $(Y_1, N_1), (Y_2, N_2), \ldots, (Y_M, N_M)$ how do we generate a point estimate and a confidence interval for the ratio of their expectations? This is a classical problem in statistics known as the problem of ratio estimation. We shall give recommended procedures, but first we generalize Result 1 to cover expectations of other functions of V, the steady-state random variable, and to cover continuous output processes.

We let $f(V)$ be any function of V whose expectation exists. Over each tour we let

$$Y_m = \sum_{n=n_m}^{n_{m+1}-1} f(V_n), \qquad m = 1, \ldots, M, \tag{6.172}$$

and let N_m be the length of the mth tour as defined by Eq. (6.169). Result 1 can be generalized as

RESULT 2 *With Y_m defined as in Eq. (6.172) and N_m defined as in Eq. (6.169) we have, for any function $f(V)$ whose expectation exists, that*

$$E[f(V)] = E[Y_m]/E[N_m].$$ (6.173)

The functions of typical interest would be V^k for $k = 1, 2$ and

$$f(V) = \begin{cases} 1 & \text{if} \quad V \in I, \\ 0 & \text{if} \quad V \notin I, \end{cases}$$ (6.174)

for the estimation of the probability that V was a member of some interval I. In this case

$$\text{Prob}\{V \in I\} = E[f(V)].$$ (6.175)

If we have a continuous parameter process such as a queue length process then, in the application of the regenerative method, this process would have regeneration points and we would partition the process at these regeneration points. We would form integrals of functions of the process over tours rather than over fixed periods of length δ as we did in the applications of the first two methods [see Eqs. (6.12) and (6.15)]. For example, consider the model of Fig. 6.2 and let

$$Q_3(t) = \text{queue length (number waiting and being served)}$$
at time t in Queue 3, the processor queue. (6.176)

Consider again the sequence of times $\tau_{k_1}, \tau_{k_2}, \ldots$ defined earlier; the times when the model enters the state defined by all the customers being at the terminals. This sequence is a sequence of regeneration times for the process $Q_3(t)$. The segments $\{Q_3(t): \tau_{k_1} \leqslant t < \tau_{k_2}\}, \{Q_3(t): \tau_{k_2} \leqslant t < \tau_{k_3}\}, \ldots$ are independent, identically distributed segments. Utilization processes, the other type of continuous process of interest, can be expressed as characteristics of queue length processes. For example, let

$$U_3(t) = \text{utilization of the processor at time } t,$$ (6.177)

then $U_3(t)$ can be expressed as

$$U_3(t) = \begin{cases} 1 & \text{if} \quad Q_3(t) \geqslant t, \\ 0 & \text{if} \quad Q_3(t) = 0, \end{cases}$$ (6.178)

and

$$E[U_3(t)] = \text{Prob}\{Q_3(t) \geqslant 1\}.$$ (6.179)

A result parallel to Result 2 can be obtained for continuous processes. Let $V(t)$ be a generic continuous output process and suppose $V(t)$ converges to a steady-state random variable V, i.e., let $F_t(x) = \text{Prob}\{V(t) \leqslant x\}$ and assume

$$\lim_{t \to \infty} F_t(x) = F(x),$$ (6.180)

where V has the distribution function $F(x)$. Let $\tau_{k_1}, \tau_{k_2}, \ldots$ be a set of regeneration points for $V(t)$, and let $f(V)$ be any function of V whose expectation exists. We define

$$Y_m = \int_{\tau_{k_m}}^{\tau_{k_m+1}} f(V(t)) \, dt \qquad (6.181)$$

and

$$T_m = \tau_{k_{m+1}} - \tau_{k_m}. \qquad (6.182)$$

We then have

RESULT 2′ *With Y_m and T_m defined as in Eqs. (6.181) and (6.182), respectively, we have, for any function $f(V)$ whose expectation exists, that*

$$E[f(V)] = E[Y_m]/E[T_m]. \qquad (6.183)$$

We see from Results 2 and 2′ that when we run the simulation for M tours we generate an independent, identically distributed sequence of bivariate random variables $(Y_m, \alpha_m): m = 1, \ldots, M$, and we are interested in generating a point estimate and a confidence interval for the ratio of their expectations

$$r = E[Y_m]/E[\alpha_m]. \qquad (6.184)$$

Here α_m is equal to either N_m or T_m depending upon whether the process is discrete or continuous. There are a number of procedures available for doing this. We now give the simplest and most direct.

We assume the simulation is begun in the regeneration state and run for a fixed number M of tours. As the point estimator of r we take the average of $f(V_n)$ or $f(V(t))$ over all the observations. This would be the usual point estimator of a steady-state quantity if no data were discarded to compensate for the initial transient. As we pointed out earlier, in the application of this method there is no reason to discard data. In the discrete case the estimator of r is given by

$$\hat{r} = \frac{1}{n_{M+1} - 1} \sum_{n=1}^{n_{m+1}-1} f(V_n)$$

$$= \left(\sum_{m=1}^{M} Y_m \right) \Big/ \left(\sum_{m=1}^{M} N_m \right)$$

$$= \left(\frac{1}{M} \sum_{m=1}^{M} Y_m \right) \Big/ \left(\frac{1}{M} \sum_{m=1}^{M} N_m \right)$$

$$= \bar{Y}/\bar{N} = \bar{Y}/\bar{\alpha}. \qquad (6.185)$$

In the continuous case it is given by

$$\hat{r} = \frac{1}{\tau_{k_{M+1}}} \int_0^{\tau_{k_M + i}} f(V(t)) \, dt$$

$$= \left(\sum_{m=1}^{M} Y_m \right) \bigg/ \left(\sum_{m=1}^{M} T_m \right)$$

$$= \left(\frac{1}{M} \sum_{m=1}^{M} Y_m \right) \bigg/ \left(\frac{1}{M} \sum_{m=1}^{M} T_m \right)$$

$$= \bar{Y}/\bar{T} = \bar{Y}/\bar{\alpha}. \tag{6.186}$$

Thus, in both cases $\hat{r} = \bar{Y}/\bar{\alpha}$. This estimate is biased but, unlike the estimator of Eq. (6.167), it is asymptotically unbiased; i.e.,

$$\lim_{M \to \infty} E[\hat{r}] = r. \tag{6.187}$$

To generate a confidence interval we consider the sequence of random variables

$$Z_m = Y_m - r\alpha_m, \qquad m = 1, \dots, M. \tag{6.188}$$

This is an independent, identically distributed sequence of random variables with

$$E[Z_m] = E[Y_m] - rE[\alpha_m] = 0 \tag{6.189}$$

and

$$\sigma_Z^2 = \text{Var}[Z_m] = \text{Var}[Y_m] - 2r \, \text{Cov}[Y_m, \alpha_m] + r^2 \text{Var}[\alpha_m]$$

$$= \sigma_y^2 - 2r\sigma_{y\alpha} + r^2\sigma_\alpha^2. \tag{6.190}$$

Hence, by the central limit theorem (see Chapter 2), as M becomes large the distribution of

$$\frac{\bar{Z} - E[Z_m]}{\sigma_Z/M^{1/2}} = \frac{\bar{Z}}{\sigma_Z/M^{1/2}}, \tag{6.191}$$

where

$$\bar{Z} = \frac{1}{M} \sum_{m=1}^{M} Z_m = \frac{1}{M} \sum_{m=1}^{M} Y_m - r \frac{1}{M} \sum_{m=1}^{M} \alpha_m$$

$$= \bar{Y} - r\bar{\alpha}, \tag{6.192}$$

converges to the unit normal distribution. The unit normal distribution is the normal distribution with zero mean and unit variance. Now

$$\frac{\bar{Z}}{\sigma_Z/M^{1/2}} = \frac{\bar{Y} - r\bar{\alpha}}{\sigma_Z/M^{1/2}} = \frac{(\bar{Y}/\bar{\alpha}) - r}{\sigma_Z/\bar{\alpha}M^{1/2}} = \frac{\hat{r} - r}{\sigma_Z/\bar{\alpha}M^{1/2}}. \tag{6.193}$$

Hence, the right-hand side of Eq. (6.193) has approximately the unit normal distribution for large M. This could be used to generate a confidence interval for r except that σ_Z^2 is unknown. However, it can be shown that the convergence to the unit normal distribution continues to hold when σ_Z^2 is estimated. Hence, for large M,

$$\frac{\hat{r} - r}{\hat{\sigma}_Z/\bar{\alpha}M^{1/2}} \qquad (6.194)$$

has approximately a unit normal distribution where

$$\hat{\sigma}_Z^2 = \hat{\sigma}_Y^2 - 2\hat{r}\hat{\sigma}_{Y\alpha} + \hat{r}^2\hat{\sigma}_\alpha^2, \qquad (6.195)$$

$$\hat{\sigma}_Y^2 = \frac{1}{M-1} \sum_{m=1}^{M} (Y_m - \bar{Y})^2, \qquad (6.196)$$

$$\hat{\sigma}_{Y\alpha} = \frac{1}{M-1} \sum_{m=1}^{M} (Y_m - \bar{Y})(\alpha_m - \bar{\alpha}), \qquad (6.197)$$

$$\hat{\sigma}_\alpha^2 = \frac{1}{M-1} \sum_{m=1}^{M} (\alpha_m - \bar{\alpha})^2. \qquad (6.198)$$

Thus, for large M, we have the approximate confidence statement and interval

$$\text{Prob}\{\hat{r} - \Phi(1 - \alpha/2)\hat{\sigma}_Z/\bar{\alpha}M^{1/2} \leqslant r \leqslant \hat{r} + \Phi(1 - \alpha/2)\hat{\sigma}_Z/\bar{\alpha}M^{1/2}\} \approx 1 - \alpha, \qquad (6.199)$$

where $\Phi(x)$ is the $100x$th percentile of the unit normal distribution. For $1 - \alpha = 0.9$, $\Phi(1 - \alpha/2) = 1.64$; for $1 - \alpha = 0.95$, $\Phi(1 - \alpha/2) = 1.96$.

Let V be a steady-state random variable, i.e., a random variable that has the steady-state distribution. To generate a point estimate and place a confidence interval on $E[V]$ or $\text{Prob}\{V \in I\}$ where I is some interval or set of possible outcomes, we would apply the above material directly. In the case of $\text{Prob}\{V \in I\}$, $f(V)$ would be given by Eq. (6.174). To generate a point estimate and place a confidence on the variance we would have to extend the arguments somewhat. Let

$$\mu_2 = E[V^2] \qquad (6.200)$$

and

$$\mu_1 = E[V], \qquad (6.201)$$

so that $\text{Var}[V] = \mu_2 - \mu_1^2$. Then using the above methods we could generate point estimates $\hat{\mu}_1$ and $\hat{\mu}_2$ and confidence statements

$$\text{Prob}\{L_1 \leqslant \mu_1 \leqslant U_1\} \approx \text{Prob}\{L_2 \leqslant \mu_2 \leqslant U_2\} \approx 1 - \alpha. \qquad (6.202)$$

The point estimate of the variance would be

$$\hat{\sigma}_V^2 = \hat{\mu}_2 - \hat{\mu}_1^2. \tag{6.203}$$

It can be shown [see the Bonferroni inequality, Eq. (6.86)] that the confidence intervals given by Eq. (6.202) hold jointly with a probability greater than or equal to $1 - 2\alpha$. Hence, we have

$$\text{Prob}\{L_1 \leqslant \mu_1 \leqslant U_1 \text{ and } L_2 \leqslant \mu_2 \leqslant U_2\} \geqslant 1 - 2\alpha. \tag{6.204}$$

From Eq. (6.204) we can infer

$$\text{Prob}\{L_2 - U_1^2 \leqslant \mu_2 - \mu_1^2 \leqslant U_2 - L_1^2\} \geqslant 1 - 2\alpha. \tag{6.205}$$

The inequality (6.205) gives a confidence statement and interval on the variance. The application of the regenerative method to the estimation of percentiles has been developed (see, e.g., Iglehart, 1976) but its discussion is beyond the scope of this handbook.

In the above discussion we assumed a set of regeneration points $\tau_{k_1}, \tau_{k_2}, \ldots$ was defined as the times when the model entered a *particular* state, called the regeneration state. A state of the model is defined in terms of the location of customers. A state is a regeneration state for an output process if the time points it defines partition the process into independent, identically distributed segments. These segments are called tours. The existence of regeneration states and the detail required in their definition are dependent upon the particular process and the particular model. It is a complex subject and a thorough treatment of it would be beyond the scope of this discussion. However, we now give some guidelines for a few special situations.

For a closed model or a stable, open, Poisson source model with the type of probabilistic routing discussed in Chapter 3, a single type of customer, and a set of queues with exponential service time distributions, any specific set of values for the queue lengths where all the customers are in the set of "exponential" queues constitutes a regeneration state for the following processes:

(1) all waiting times, queueing times, and subnetwork response times for queues and subnetworks which in the regeneration state have no customers, and
(2) for all queue lengths and hence all utilizations.

This is because of the memoryless property of the exponential distribution; i.e., the property that the distribution of the remaining service time of customers undergoing service does not change with time [see Eq. (2.36)].

As an example for the model of Fig. 6.2 and the waiting time sequence $W_{2,n}$ we could pick as a regeneration state *any* specific set of values for the queue lengths such that

$$Q_2 = 0, \quad \sum_{n=3}^{7} Q_n \leqslant 5, \quad \text{and} \quad Q_1 + \sum_{n=3}^{7} Q_n = 25. \quad (6.206)$$

A reasonable regeneration state is

$$Q_1 = 25, \quad Q_2 = \cdots = Q_7 = 0, \quad\quad\quad (6.207)$$

since this is a regeneration state not only for $W_{2,n}$ but for all the waiting times and the system response time.

For a model with probabilistic routing, *more* than one customer type, and a set of queues with exponential service time distributions that are either infinite server queues or follow a processor sharing service discipline, any *specific values* of queue lengths for each customer type, where all the customers are in this set of queues, constitutes a regeneration state for the processes that meet conditions (1) and (2) above.

As an example, many system models have the terminals represented as an infinite server, "exponential" queue (e.g., this is the case in the model of Fig. 6.2). In these cases all the customers at the terminals is a regeneration state for all waiting times, all queue lengths, and the response times in all subnetworks that do not contain the terminals.

For a stable, open model with Poisson sources, probabilistic routing, and either a single customer type or multiple customer types, the state where all the queue lengths are zero, i.e., where the network is empty, is a regeneration state for all the output processes. This is true even if the network contains no exponential queues.

If there is more than one regeneration state it is generally advisable to choose one which is frequently occurring since the method is a large sample method and becomes more valid as the number of tours increases. A priori, an experimenter does not know the frequency with which the various states occur. Hence, the choice is either a matter of judgement or can be based on some pilot experimentation.

The subject of the regenerative method is a complex one and the above discussion is very incomplete. For additional introductory discussion the reader should see Crane and Lemoine (1977), Iglehart (1978), and Fishman (1978a).

6.3.7 The Spectral Method

All three methods discussed above generate confidence intervals by creating independent or approximately independent sequences or sub-sequences and then applying standard statistical procedures to a set of "independent" statistics derived from these sequences. In this way they avoid the problem caused by the correlation. The method that we shall now describe does not proceed in this fashion. It directly estimates and corrects for the effect of the correlation.

Again we consider our generic output sequence $V_n: n = 1, 2, \ldots$. We assume an estimate $\hat{n}_0$ has been obtained of the extent of the transient phase and we consider the sequence $V_{n+\hat{n}_0}: n = 1, \ldots, N$. We first consider the problem of estimating μ, the steady-state mean. The standard point estimator of μ is

$$\bar{V} = \frac{1}{N} \sum_{n=1}^{N} V_{\hat{n}_0 + n}. \tag{6.208}$$

Now, for large N, $\bar{V}$ is approximately distributed as a normal random variable. Hence, we have for large N that

$$(\bar{V} - \mu)/\sigma_{\bar{V}} \tag{6.209}$$

is approximately distributed as a normal random variable with zero mean and unit variance. Thus, if a good estimator $\hat{\sigma}_{\bar{V}}$ of $\sigma_{\bar{V}}$ can be generated then we can use the normal distribution of (6.209) to generate the confidence statement and interval

$$\text{Prob}\{\bar{V} - \Phi(1 - \alpha/2)\hat{\sigma}_{\bar{V}} \leqslant \mu \leqslant \bar{V} + \Phi(1 - \alpha/2)\hat{\sigma}_{\bar{V}}\} \approx 1 - \alpha. \tag{6.210}$$

In the spectral approach to obtain this estimate $\hat{\sigma}_{\bar{V}}$ we return to Eq. (6.151). Extending it we have

$$\text{Var}[\bar{V}] = \sigma_{\bar{V}}^2 \approx \frac{\sigma^2}{N} \left[\sum_{k=-\infty}^{\infty} \rho(k) \right]. \tag{6.211}$$

Using Eqs. (6.140) and (6.142), this becomes

$$\sigma_{\bar{V}}^2 \approx \sum_{k=-\infty}^{\infty} \gamma(k). \tag{6.212}$$

Hence, to estimate $\sigma_{\bar{V}}^2$ we must estimate $\sum_{k=-\infty}^{\infty} \gamma(k)$, the area under the covariance function.

Now the dependence or correlation structure of a covariance stationary process can be characterized either in the time or frequency domain. In the frequency domain, under very general conditions, the process has a spectral density $p(f)$ which is related to $\gamma(k)$ by

$$p(f) = \sum_{k=-\infty}^{\infty} \gamma(k) \cos 2\pi f k. \tag{6.213}$$

There is also an inverse relationship

$$\gamma(k) = \int_{-1/2}^{1/2} p(f) \cos 2\pi f k \, df. \tag{6.214}$$

If we evaluate Eq. (6.213) at $f = 0$ we obtain

$$p(0) = \sum_{k=-\infty}^{\infty} \gamma(k). \tag{6.215}$$

Hence, combining Eqs. (6.212) and (6.215) we have

$$\sigma_{\bar{V}}^2 \approx p(0)/N, \tag{6.216}$$

and we see that to estimate $\sigma_{\bar{V}}^2$ we need only estimate the spectral density at zero frequency.

Two methods for estimating $p(0)$ have been proposed. In the first, an autoregressive time series model is fitted to the output sequence and $\hat{p}(0)$ is obtained from the estimated coefficients of this model. This is discussed in Fishman (1978a). In the second, regression techniques are applied to the log of the periodogram or sample spectrum. This is discussed in Heidelberger and Welch (1981a and b). Given $\hat{p}(0)$ a confidence statement and interval is obtained by substituting

$$\hat{\sigma}_{\bar{V}} = [\hat{p}(0)/N]^{1/2} \tag{6.217}$$

into Eq. (6.210).

The spectral method can also be applied directly to place a confidence interval on $\text{Prob}\{V \in I\}$ by working with the random sequence

$$Z_n = \begin{cases} 1 & \text{if} \quad V_n \in I, \\ 0 & \text{otherwise.} \end{cases} \tag{6.218}$$

This sequence is also a covariance stationary sequence and

$$E[Z_n] = \text{Prob}\{V_n \in I\}. \tag{6.219}$$

To place a confidence interval on the variance the method can be applied to the sequences V_n and V_n^2 and a confidence interval obtained by a procedure parallel to that described by Eqs. (6.200)–(6.205) for the regenerative method.

The spectral method cannot be directly applied to obtain confidence intervals for a percentile but it has been extended to cover this application (see Heidelberger and Lewis, 1981).

6.4 Achieving a Desired Accuracy: The Use of Pilot Experiments and Sequential Procedures

6.4.1 Introduction

In the discussion so far we have described how, given a specific experimental situation (a protocol and a set of output sequences), point estimates and confidence intervals can be generated for quantities of interest. Unfortunately, this does not directly satisfy the needs of an experimenter. The experimenter wants to know what specific simulation experiment he should conduct to get estimates of sufficient accuracy for his purposes. (He may modify his requirements in light of the cost of the experiment.)

This need cannot be satisfied a priori. Usually the accuracy requirement, as measured by the width of the confidence interval, is a function of the magnitude of the quantity to be estimated and generally there is little a priori information on this magnitude. Hence, the experimenter does not know what confidence interval width he requires. Further, he usually has no a priori knowledge as to what quantity of data (i.e., what number of sequences of what length) produces what confidence interval width. Hence, he does not know the confidence interval width he wants and would not know how to get it if he did know it.

The usual way of approaching this problem and making use of the material we have provided is to conduct a pilot experiment. This pilot experiment provides a rough estimate of the magnitude of the quantity of interest and a rough estimate of the relationship between the confidence interval width and the quantity of data processed. With these estimates a main experiment that will yield confidence intervals of approximately the desired width can be planned. An alternative approach is more directly sequential. The experiment is continued with periodic testing to see whether the confidence interval meets the requirement. The first time it does the experiment is stopped. We shall first discuss the application of these approaches to the estimation of transient characteristics.

6.4.2   The "Controlled" Estimation of Transient Characteristics

The *expected* width of the confidence intervals developed in Section 6.2 for characteristics of transient random variables are approximately proportional to $M^{-1/2}$ where M is the number of replications. The approximation becomes more accurate as M becomes large. Hence, for example, to halve the expected confidence interval width we would have to take four times as many replications and to reduce the expected confidence interval width by the factor $\frac{1}{10}$ we would have to take 100 times as many replications.

Suppose we are interested in a characteristic θ of a transient random variable. The quantity θ could be a mean, variance, probability, etc. Suppose in a pilot experiment we run M_1 replications. Suppose this pilot experiment generates a point estimate $\hat{\theta}_1$ and a confidence interval (L_1, U_1); i.e., after the pilot experiment

$$\text{Prob}\{L_1 \leqslant \theta \leqslant U_1\} \approx 1 - \alpha. \tag{6.220}$$

We let the width of the confidence interval be

$$\Delta_1 = U_1 - L_1. \tag{6.221}$$

Further, suppose we desire a confidence interval whose width is approximately 0.1 the value of the point estimate (i.e., $\pm 5\%$ of the estimated value). Now if $\Delta_1 \leqslant 0.1\hat{\theta}_1$ we would be finished. However, if $\Delta_1 > 0.1\hat{\theta}_1$, then we would conduct a main experiment of M_2 replications where

$$M_2 = [(\Delta_1/0.1\hat{\theta}_1)^2 M_1]^+ \tag{6.222}$$

with

$$[x]^+ = \text{smallest integer greater than or equal to } x.$$

From these M_2 replications we generate a point estimate $\hat{\theta}_2$ and a confidence interval with width Δ_2. Because of their random nature, $\hat{\theta}_2$ and Δ_2 will not be exactly as projected but they will approximately meet the requirement $\Delta_2 = 0.1\hat{\theta}_2$.

In the above discussion we have assumed that the data generated by the pilot experiment is not used in generating the final estimate and confidence interval. This would be the most statistically rigorous procedure and if $M_2 \gg M_1$ would not represent a serious inefficiency. However, it is common practice (with some theoretical support if M_2 is large) to combine the data from the pilot and main experiments to obtain the final estimate and confidence interval. In this case a main experiment of $M_2 - M_1$ replications would be conducted where M_2 is again given by Eq. (6.222). The two samples (of M_1 replications and $M_2 - M_1$ replications) would be combined as if they came from a *single* experiment, M_2 replications long. If this second confidence interval did not meet the requirement, this process could be repeated with the old pilot and main experiments combined as the new pilot experiment.

Alternatively, a purely sequential approach can be taken to the above problem. In this approach a number M^* is selected and the experiment is conducted sequentially by repeatedly adding M^* replications and testing whether the estimator and confidence interval (obtained from *all* the replications so far made) meet the requirement. Specifically, for the problem under discussion, we first generate M^* replications. From them we calculate a point estimator $\hat{\theta}_1$ and a confidence interval whose width we designate as Δ_1. If $\Delta_1 \leqslant 0.1\hat{\theta}_1$ we stop, otherwise we generate M^* more replications. A second point estimate $\hat{\theta}_2$ is obtained by combining the $2M^*$ replications as if they have all been obtained in one experiment. If the resulting confidence interval has a width Δ_2 such that $\Delta_2 \leqslant 0.1\hat{\theta}_2$ we stop. Otherwise we continue and make M^* more replications and so on. *At each stage we combine all the replications made so far and test them as if they had come from one large experiment.* We stop at the kth stage where for the first time $\Delta_k \leqslant 0.1\hat{\theta}_k$. If we designate this k by k^* then when we stop we will have made k^*M^* replications altogether.

This sequential approach tends to produce confidence intervals whose coverage is less than the theoretical confidence level. Hence, it is good practice to be conservative in the choice of the confidence level when using the method.

For example, one might generate 95% confidence intervals where normally one would settle for 90% confidence intervals. There is theoretical work showing that the actual coverage approaches the theoretical confidence level as k^*M^* becomes large or equivalently as the width of the confidence interval approaches zero. Hence, the method is best applied in these cases. For additional discussion and further references see Fishman (1978a, Section 2.9).

6.4.3   The "Controlled" Estimation of Steady-State Characteristics

a.   The Method of Independent Replications

In the method of independent replications, as applied to the estimation of steady-state characteristics, the expected widths of the confidence intervals are approximately proportional to $(MN)^{-1/2}$ where M is the number of replications and N is the number of samples in the steady-state phase of each replication.

We again consider the problem discussed in Section 6.4.2 in connection with the estimation of transient characteristics. Suppose we are interested in estimating a characteristic θ of a steady-state random variable. The quantity θ could be a mean, variance, percentile, etc. Suppose we want to have a confidence interval whose width is approximately 0.1 the value of the point estimate. Suppose we run a pilot experiment with $M_1 = 10$ replications and with N_1 samples in the steady-state phase of each replication. Suppose this pilot experiment yields a point estimate $\hat{\theta}_1$ with a confidence interval whose width is Δ_1. Then if $\Delta_1 \leqslant 0.1\hat{\theta}_1$, we are finished. If $\Delta_1 > 0.1\hat{\theta}_1$, we run a second, main experiment with $M_2 = 10$ replications and N_2 steady-state samples per replication where

$$N_2 = [(\Delta_1/0.1\hat{\theta}_1)^2 N_1]^+. \tag{6.223}$$

We choose $M_1 = M_2 = 10$ since this was the value recommended for M in Section 6.3.3. Because of the random nature of the estimates and confidence limits, the relationship between $\hat{\theta}_2$ and Δ_2, the point estimate and confidence interval width from the main experiment, will not be exactly as projected but will be approximately so.

In the above discussion we have assumed that the data generated by the pilot experiment is not used in generating the final estimate and confidence interval. This is the most statistically rigorous procedure and if $N_2 \gg N_1$ would not represent a serious inefficiency. If it were desired to combine the data from the pilot experiment and the main experiment to obtain the final estimate and confidence interval, then the most efficient approach would be to restart each of the 10 simulations at the point they had terminated and run them to achieve $N_2 - N_1$ more elements in each sequence. This would give $10N_2$ elements in all and would incorporate the pilot data in the most efficient manner. Estimates and confidence intervals would be generated assuming all the N_2 elements were combined in each sequence. The stopping and restarting of parallel simulations may, however, be difficult or impossible. In this case $M_2 = 10$ new independent simulations with steady-state phases of length $N_2 - N_1$ could be run. This would be somewhat less efficient because of the need again to discard the $10\hat{n}_0$ elements in the transient phases. As with the case where each sequence is extended, the new estimates and confidence intervals are obtained by assuming the 10 new sequences of length $N_2 - N_1$ are appended onto the end of the old sequences of length N_1 to form 10 sequences of length N_2. As we mentioned above this procedure will yield an estimate and confidence interval that approximately meets the design goal. If it is too far off, the process can be repeated with the first and second stages used to obtain the design for a third stage.

As an alternative in the method of independent replications, the experimenter could increase the number of replications and keep them the same length. That is, he could let $N_2 = N_1$, let

$$M_2 = [(\Delta_1/0.1\hat{\theta}_1)^2 M_1]^+, \tag{6.224}$$

where

$$M_1 = \text{number of replications in the pilot experiment,}$$

and run $M_2' = M_2 - M_1$ additional independent replications. If $M_2' < M_1$ this would be a more efficient procedure than running M_1 new simulations as described in the preceding paragraph since $M_2'\hat{n}_0 < M_1\hat{n}_0$; i.e., the amount of data discarded is less. In this case, i.e., $M_2' < M_1$, it would also result in longer sequences and hence reduce any residual effects of the transient phase. However, if $M_2' > M_1$ the other procedure would be more efficient and better from the standpoint of the reduction of the effects of the initial transient. If this procedure of adding replications of the same length were followed, the estimate and confidence limits would be obtained by combining the two sets of runs into one set of M_2 replications and using the methods outlined in Section 6.3.3.

Finally, a sequential approach could be pursued by selecting a number M^* and repeatedly adding M^* replications testing after the addition of each new batch whether or not the estimate and confidence interval meet the requirement. This procedure would be the exact parallel of the sequential procedure described for transient characteristics in Section 6.4.2, and the interested reader should see that discussion. The point estimate and confidence interval would be generated by combining all the replications made up to that time into a single set of replications and applying the methods of Section 6.3.3. Again, the coverage of the resulting confidence interval tends to be less than the predicted theoretical value. Hence, it is best, as with the sequential method for the transient case, to be conservative in the choice of a confidence level.

Additional care has to be taken with the method in this context since any bias due to the initial transient will remain constant and not approach zero as the total number of replications increases. This bias must be small relative to the desired confidence interval width or the coverage of the confidence interval will be further reduced. This latter is a problem that, fortunately, does not exist for the method when applied in the transient case or in the method of batch means and the regenerative method to be discussed below.

b. The Method of Batch Means

We now consider the case where the experimenter is using the method of batch means. Suppose he wishes to use the pilot experiment approach and suppose he faces the same requirements used in the examples above; i.e., he wishes a confidence interval whose width is 0.1 the value of the point estimate. He would conduct a pilot experiment consisting of a single simulation run with M_1 subsequences. From this he would generate a point estimate $\hat{\theta}_1$ and a confidence interval whose width we call Δ_1. Again, if $\Delta_1 \leqslant 0.1\hat{\theta}_1$ he is finished. If $\Delta_1 > 0.1\hat{\theta}_1$ then he would either obtain M_2 more subsequences where M_2 is given by Eq. (6.222) and generate a new point estimate and confidence interval without using the pilot data or he would obtain $M'_2 = M_2 - M_1$ more subsequences and use the pilot data. The additional subsequences could be obtained either by continuing the single simulation run or producing a second one.

The sequential approach could also be applied exactly as indicated above for the method of independent replications, only in this case the test would be conducted after each occurrence of M^* subsequences. Again, all the subsequences occurring up to each testing point would be used to obtain the point estimate and confidence interval. The cautions given earlier with regard to the sequential approach continue to apply.

c. The Regenerative Method

In the regenerative method the width of the confidence interval is approximately proportional to $M^{-1/2}$ where M *is the number of tours.* Hence, the pilot–main experiment approach and the sequential approach exactly parallel the corresponding approaches discussed in Section 6.4.2 for the transient case with tours replacing replications. The development and application of the sequential approach are discussed in Lavenberg and Sauer (1977).

d. The Spectral Method

In the spectral method the width of the confidence interval is approximately proportional to $N^{-1/2}$ where N is the number of elements in the steady-state portion of the run. Hence, again the pilot–main experiment approach and the sequential approach exactly parallel the corresponding approaches discussed in Section 6.4.2 with the number of elements in the sequence replacing the number of replications. A specific sequential approach is developed and evaluated in Heidelberger and Welch (1981).

6.5 Broader Statistical Questions

6.5.1 Introduction

We have been concerned exclusively in this chapter with the generation of confidence intervals for simulation model response characteristics. This is the simplest of the possible statistical problems facing a simulation experimenter. Other more complex statistical questions include the comparison of response characteristics from two models, the selection from a set of models of that one which is best with respect to the value of a certain response characteristic, and the estimation of the relationship between a model response characteristic and some other model parameter (or set of model parameters) such as work load mix, input rate, and device speed. The discussion of these questions is beyond the scope of this handbook and the reader is referred to Kleijnen (1974–1975, 1979, 1981), Fishman (1978a), and Law and Kelton (1981) for discussion and further references. However, we shall in the next section make a few brief remarks about a particularly important problem, the comparison of response characteristics from two different models, and its relationship to the confidence interval material we have presented.

6.5.2 The Comparison of Response Characteristics from Two Models

Suppose we estimate a common response characteristic θ for two simulation models which we call A and B. Let θ_A be the true value of the characteristic for Model A and θ_B be the true value for Model B. Suppose we are interested in comparing θ_A and θ_B; that is, we wish to place a confidence interval on $\theta_A - \theta_B$. This will provide information on the relative magnitude of θ_A and θ_B and provide a test of the hypothesis $\theta_A = \theta_B$. If zero does not lie in the confidence interval for $\theta_A - \theta_B$ then the hypothesis $\theta_A = \theta_B$ can be rejected at a significance level α where $1 - \alpha$ is the confidence level of the confidence interval. This means that the probability that the hypothesis $\theta_A = \theta_B$ will be rejected, when it is in fact true, is equal to α.

Standard statistical techniques can be applied to this problem if the experimenter is using the method of independent replications or batch means and if the experiments with the two models are independent. In this case the problem reduces to the comparison of two sets of independent observations which is discussed in almost all standard statistical texts [see, e.g., Hald (1952a, Chapter 15)].

If the methods of independent replications or batch means are used and the experiments with the two models are not independent (e.g., if common random number streams are used in the two experiments), then standard statistical techniques can still be applied if the number of replications (subsequences) in each experiment is the same. In this case let $\hat{\theta}_{A,m}: m = 1, \ldots, M$ and $\hat{\theta}_{B,m}: m = 1, \ldots, M$ be the estimates from the mth replications (subsequences) of the experiments with Models A and B, respectively. Then

$$v_m = \hat{\theta}_{A,m} - \hat{\theta}_{B,m}, \qquad m = 1, \ldots, M, \tag{6.225}$$

is a sequence of independent random variables with

$$E[v_m] = \theta_A - \theta_B, \tag{6.226}$$

and the standard technique based on the t-distribution which we applied extensively above [see, e.g., Eqs. (6.36)–(6.41)] can be used to place a confidence interval on $\theta_A - \theta_B$. This approach can also be applied if the two experiments are independent.

If the regenerative or spectral methods are used in the two experiments and if the two experiments are independent then a confidence interval on $\theta_A - \theta_B$ can be obtained by using the relationship

$$\sigma_{A-B}^2 = \sigma_A^2 + \sigma_B^2, \tag{6.227}$$

where

$$\sigma_{A-B}^2 = \text{Var}[\hat{\theta}_A - \hat{\theta}_B], \qquad \sigma_A^2 = \text{Var}[\hat{\theta}_A], \qquad \sigma_B^2 = \text{Var}[\hat{\theta}_B].$$

Both the regenerative and spectral methods yield estimates $\hat{\sigma}_A^2$ and $\hat{\sigma}_B^2$, and an estimate of σ_{A-B}^2 can be obtained as

$$\hat{\sigma}_{A-B}^2 = \hat{\sigma}_A^2 + \hat{\sigma}_B^2. \tag{6.228}$$

Hence, since $\hat{\theta}_A$ and $\hat{\theta}_B$ are approximately normally distributed with means θ_A and θ_B, respectively, $\hat{\theta}_A - \hat{\theta}_B$ is approximately normally distributed with mean $\theta_A - \theta_B$. Thus, we have the confidence statement and interval

$$\text{Prob}\{\hat{\theta}_A - \hat{\theta}_B - \Phi(1 - \alpha/2)\hat{\sigma}_{A-B} \leqslant \theta_A - \theta_B \leqslant \hat{\theta}_A - \hat{\theta}_B + \Phi(1 - \alpha/2)\hat{\sigma}_{A-B}\}$$

$$\approx 1 - \alpha, \tag{6.229}$$

where $\Phi(x)$ is the $100x$th percentile of the normal distribution with zero mean and unit variance.

Under completely general conditions we can obtain a confidence interval on $\theta_A - \theta_B$ from any pair of confidence intervals, one on θ_A and one on θ_B. If

$$\text{Prob}\{L_A \leqslant \theta_A \leqslant U_A\} = 1 - \alpha_A \qquad \text{and} \qquad \text{Prob}\{L_B \leqslant \theta_B \leqslant U_B\} = 1 - \alpha_B,$$

$$\tag{6.230}$$

then from the Bonferroni inequality, Eq. (6.86), we have the confidence statement and interval

$$\text{Prob}\{L_A - U_B \leqslant \theta_A - \theta_B \leqslant U_A - L_B\} \geqslant 1 - \alpha_A - \alpha_B. \qquad (6.231)$$

If the two confidence statements of Eq. (6.230) are independent then the slightly stronger statement

$$\text{Prob}\{L_A - U_B \leqslant \theta_A - \theta_B \leqslant U_A - L_B\} \geqslant 1 - \alpha_A - \alpha_B + \alpha_A\alpha_B \qquad (6.232)$$

can be made.

If we are testing the hypotheses $\theta_A = \theta_B$ then Eq. (6.231) has a simple interpretation. If the confidence intervals of θ_A and θ_B do not overlap then we can reject the hypothesis that $\theta_A = \theta_B$ at a significance level less than or equal to $\alpha_A + \alpha_B$. For example, if two 95% confidence intervals do not overlap, then we can reject the hypothesis that $\theta_A = \theta_B$ at the 10% level. Equation (6.232) has a similar interpretation.

References

Box, G. E. P., and Jenkins, G. M. (1970). "Time Series Analysis, Forecasting and Control." Holden Day, San Francisco, California.

Bradley, J. V. (1968). "Distributional Free Statistical Tests." Prentice-Hall, Englewood Cliffs, New Jersey.

Clopper, C. J., and Pearson, E. S. (1934). The use of confidence or fiducial limits illustrated in the case of the binomial. *Biometrica* **26**, 404–413.

Crane, M. A., and Lemoine, A. J. (1977). "An Introduction to the Regenerative Method for Simulation Analysis." Springer-Verlag, Berlin and New York.

Fishman, G. S. (1978a). "Principles of Discrete Event Digital Simulation." Wiley, New York.

Fishman, G. S. (1978b). Grouping observations in digital simulation. *Management Sci.* **24**, 510–521.

Hald, A. (1952a). "Statistical Theory with Engineering Applications." Wiley, New York.

Hald, A. (1952b). "Statistical Tables and Formulas." Wiley, New York.

Harvard Computation Laboratory (1955). "Tables of the Cumulative Binomial Probability Distribution." Harvard Univ. Press, Cambridge, Massachusetts.

Heidelberger, P., and Lewis, P. A. W. (1981). Quantile Estimation in Dependent Sequences. IBM Research Rep. RC 9087, IBM Research Center, Yorktown Heights, New York.

Heidelberger, P., and Welch, P. D. (1981a). A spectral method for confidence interval generation and run length control in simulations. *Comm. ACM* **24**, 233–245.

Heidelberger, P., and Welch, P. D. (1981b). Adaptive spectral methods for simulation output analysis. *IBM J. Res. Develop.* **25**, 860–876.

Iglehart, D. L. (1976). Simulating stable stochastic systems, VI: Quantile estimation, *J. Assoc. Comput. Mach.* **23**, 347–360.

Iglehart, D. L. (1978). The regenerative method of simulation analysis, *In* "Current Trends in Programming Methodology" (K. M. Chandy and R. T. Yeh, eds.), Vol. 3, "Software Modeling and Its Impact on Performance." Prentice-Hall, Englewood Cliffs, New Jersey.

Jenkins, G. M., and Watts, D. G. (1968). "Spectral Analysis and Its Applications." Holden Day, San Francisco, California.

Kelton, W. D. (1980). The Startup Problem in Discrete Event Simulation, Tech. Rep. 80-1. Dept. of Industrial Engineering, Univ. of Wisconsin, Madison, Wisconsin.

Kleijnen, J. P. C. (1974–1975). "Statistical Techniques in Simulation," Parts I and II. Dekker, New York.

Kleijnen, J. P. C. (1979). The role of statistical methodology in simulation, *In* "Methodology in Systems Modeling and Simulation" (B. Zeigler *et al.*, eds.). North Holland Publ., Amsterdam.

Kleijnen, J. P. C. (1981). Regression analysis for simulation practitioners. *J. Oper. Res. Soc.* **32**, 35–43.

Lavenberg, S. S., and Sauer, C. H. (1977). Sequential stopping rules for the regenerative method of simulation. *IBM J. Res. Develop.* **21**, 545–558.

Law, A. M., and Carson, J. S. (1979). A sequential procedure for determining the length of a steady state simulation. *Oper. Res.* **27**, 1011–1025.

Law, A. M., and Kelton, W. D. (1981). "Simulation Modeling and Analysis." McGraw-Hill, New York.

Miller, R. G. (1974). The jackknife – a review. *Biometrica* **61**, 1–15.

Parzen, E. (1960). "Modern Probability Theory and Its Applications." Wiley, New York.

Schruben, L. W. (1982). Detecting initialization bias in simulation output. *Oper. Res.* **30**, 569–590.

7

Simulator Design and Programming

Harry M. Markowitz

7.1 Introduction

Simulation analysis may be in order for dynamic, stochastic systems that are too complex for analytical or numerical solution by present-day techniques. In a simulation, a representation of a system is run through simulated time with pseudorandom numbers drawn to represent random delays or other random choices. One simulation run — with specific rules written into the program, specific data read as parameters, and specific initial "seeds" for the random number generators — produces a specific realization (a specific random draw) of the simulated system. If the logic and parameters are kept the same but new random seeds are introduced, then a new realization (i.e., new random draw of the simulated system as a whole) results. Further replication produces a sample of the population of possible outcomes for the simulation as a whole given its rules and parameters. Statistical analysis of these results may be required, since these are a sample rather than an entire population.

Variations in rules, as incorporated in the program, or variations in the parameters introduced as data, may be used to answer questions concerning the sensitivity of system performance to changes in rules and parameters.

Problems encountered in performing a simulation analysis include: the selection of the "right" problem, the timely development of the simulation program (or "simulator"), the collection of data of sufficient accuracy, the statistical analysis of output, the proper judgement of the significance of the results, and the effective implementation of conclusions. Our prime concern in the present chapter will be with the design and programming of the simulator. Statistical analysis of simulator results is discussed in Chapter 6.

The simulator programs discussed in this chapter are general purpose in one sense and special purpose in another sense. They are "general purpose" in that many specific systems can be represented with a particular simulator by varying input parameters such as the number of queues, number of servers per queue, rates at which customers arrive, etc. The simulators are special purpose, on the other hand, in that specific rules are programmed describing procedures (as distinguished from parameters) for such matters as how to generate customer arrivals, how to determine job routing, and so on.

The job of preparing a simulation run is much simplified if an existing simulator can be used, with appropriate input, rather than a new simulator written. An extremely wide range of systems can be simulated by means of one of the very general purpose "flow diagram processing" simulators such as GPSS (Gordon, 1975), Q-GERT (Pritsker 1977b), and APLOMB. GPSS was the first successful flow diagram simulator, and is probably the most widely used simulation package. The user describes a specific system to be simulated in terms of certain basic building blocks which generate jobs, queue jobs, randomly disperse jobs, etc. The GPSS user encodes this description in terms of GPSS input conventions. Experience has shown that a wide class of systems can be thus described to at least a satisfactory level of approximation. Q-GERT is a newer flow diagram processing simulator. APLOMB is the simulation portion of the RESearch Queueing package (RESQ), which is discussed in Chapter 8. APLOMB contains features particularly designed for the kinds of problems that are dealt with in this handbook.

But some problems for which simulation analysis is a suitable tool cannot be described in sufficient detail by any existing simulator, including GPSS or APLOMB. A new simulator must be written or an old one adapted. The present chapter is concerned with the design and programming of such simulators. In the following sections we consider programming first and design second, since fundamental considerations of the latter depend on details of the former.

One simulator design decision is the choice of programming language. We may distinguish three broad classes of languages: (1) general purpose languages without simulation capabilities such as FORTRAN, PL/I, or COBOL; (2) simulation packages such as GASP (Pritsker, 1974, 1977a) and SIMPL/1 (IBM, 1972a, b), which add a simulation capability to one of the former languages; and (3) languages such as SIMSCRIPT (Markowitz, 1979) and SIMULA (Birtwhistle *et al.*, 1973; Hills, 1973) which are self contained general purpose languages designed with simulation as either the primary, or one of the primary, application areas. We shall first illustrate simulation programming in terms of SIMSCRIPT II (Kiviat *et al.*, 1969), a language of the third type. This will allow us to ignore various programming details that are taken care of for us, and thereby see more immediately the overall structure of a simulator. Afterwards we shall describe programming techniques, needed when building a simulator with a language of type 1, and issues in selecting a language of type 2.

7.2 Simulation Programming

In the first instance we illustrate simulation programming by a "general purpose" SIMSCRIPT II network of queues simulator. But first we must discuss some basic concepts of SIMSCRIPT.

As of any instant in time a simulated system has a *status*. In SIMSCRIPT the status of a system is described in terms of how many of various types of *entities* exist; what are the values of their *attributes*; what *sets* do they belong to; and who are the members of the sets which they own.

The entities of a simulated computer system could include jobs, job steps, data requirements, channels, virtual machines, pages, I/O devices, etc. Attributes might include the expected CPU time required by a particular step, whether or not a channel is busy, etc. In high school algebra we learned to read $f(x)$ as f of x. Similarly in SIMSCRIPT we read TOT.VIRT.TM(VM) as TOT.VIRT.TM of VM, where VM refers to an entity (a virtual machine) and TOT.VIRT.TM refers to an attribute of this entity (total virtual CPU time used thus far). As of any instant in time a specific attribute of a specific individual entity has only one value. Multivalued attributes must be handled as sets.

Sets are collections of entities. For example, a simulation may distinguish the set of virtual machines waiting for CPU time, or the set of data requests waiting for a particular channel. We say that sets have owners and members.

For example, we say that channel 1 owns its set of data requests while channel 2 owns a different set of data requests. Data requests are the members of the set.

The system as a whole is referred to as an entity. It may have attributes and own sets, but it may not belong to a set. If there is only one set called LIST in a simulation, we say that LIST belongs to the system as a whole. If A and B are system attributes and LIST is a system set then we write A, B, and LIST rather than A(SYSTEM), B(SYSTEM), and LIST(SYSTEM). The treating of the system as a whole as an entity is particularly helpful when we speak of the attributes that an entity has by virtue of it being the owner or member of a set. In particular if LIST is a set owned by the system then first-in-list, last-in-list, and number-in-list are attributes of the system.

Status changes at points in time we shall call events. There are two ways in which events can occur: exogenously (caused from the outside) and endogenously (caused from within the simulated system). A deck of cards or a file of cardlike lines is prepared in advance of the simulation to indicate the times at which exogenous events are to occur, and to provide additional data to be read by the exogenous event routines. Endogenous events are caused by prior occurrences of endogenous or exogenous events.

An event — as decribed in an event routine, and in subroutines on which the event routine may call — may change status by creating or destroying an entity, by filing an entity into a set, by removing an entity from a set, or by changing an attribute value. It may do many such elemental actions, perhaps under the control of instructions such as FOR EACH DATA.REQUEST IN QUEUE(CHANNEL) DO ... or it may perform the elemental actions selectively as described by IF, GO TO or other control statements. SIMSCRIPT syntax is illustrated in an example to follow. The exact rules may be found in Kiviat *et al.* (1969); further discussion of basic concepts and other applications may be found in Markowitz (1979).

The example in the next subsection is written in the SIMSCRIPT II language. We must distinguish between three slightly different versions of SIMSCRIPT II. The first is the language as described in The RAND Corporation manual (Kiviat *et al.*, 1969). A second version is the language as implemented in the RAND produced SIMSCRIPT II translator, and available through SHARE at nominal cost. This version has most but not all of the features described in the manual. The omissions are described in a document supplied with the SHARE tape. The most serious omission is the ACCUMULATE and TALLY statements. The third version is the SIMSCRIPT II.5 (Johnson, 1974; Kiviat *et al.*, 1973) language and translator available commercially through CACI. This version contains almost the complete language as specified in the manual, plus additional features, not included in SIMSCRIPT II, such as an implementation of the process view as well as the event view of simulation timing (Russell, 1974).

7.2.1 A Network of Queues Simulator

Articles on simulation frequently include examples such as customers arriving at a grocery store with several places to pick up items before checking out, or customers arriving at banks where they must queue for service. The simplest of such examples are instances of single server or multi-server queueing models with one queue. More complex examples are instances of networks involving several queues. It is about as easy to build a "general purpose" network of a queues simulator as it is to build a specific simulator for a particular hypothetical grocery store. It is also more illustrative of recommended practice.

Figure 7.1 contains a slightly revised exercise which I have used in courses on simulation modeling and programming. [The original exercise is

Each job in the simulated network is of one or another "standard type." Jobs of the same standard type have the same routing and process time. For example, perhaps any job with standard type = 1 goes first to server group 3 and requires there 2.5 ms of processing, then goes (for example) to server group 17, etc. As of any moment in time the system may have any number of jobs of standard type = 1. These jobs may be at the same and/or at different steps of their routing. The same is true for any other standard type.

Write a simulation program with the following inputs:

    the number of server groups in the network;
    the number of servers in each server group;
    the number of standard types.
    For each standard type:
        the mean time between arrivals for jobs of this type.
    For each step in the routing of (any job with) the particular standard type:
        the server group required at this step;
        the process time required at this step;
        the priority of a job of this type at this step;
        the number of jobs of this type at this step in the system at the start of the simulation.

The model does the following:

For each standard type the model causes arrivals to occur randomly with an exponential distribution of interarrival times (and a mean interarrival time as read in above).

As a job routes through the network the model refers back to the standard routing for this type of job to determine server group and process time at each step of its routing.

Before filing a job into a queue the model sets the priority of the job equal to the priority associated with its type at the current step.

Queues are ranked by priority and, within priority, by arrival time of job. When a server needs a job, the job is taken from the front of the queue.

The output of the model should include the minimum, maximum, mean, and standard deviation of

    time in system, for each type of standard job, and for all jobs;
    queue size, by server group;
    number of idle servers, by server group.

Fig. 7.1 A network of queues exercise.

reproduced in Markowitz (1979).] Figure 7.1 asks the student to produce a simple but "general purpose" network of queues simulator in which the number of server groups (therefore the number of queues), the arrival rates of different types of jobs, and the routing of various standard types of jobs are input parameters. The exercise also specifies other matters, such as the dispatch rules used by the network and the outputs of a run.

Entity	Attribute	Owns	Belongs	Comment
SERV.GRP				Server group.
	FREE			Nr. servers in group now free.
		QUEUE		JOBs waiting to be processed.
JOB				Job to be serviced.
	JTYPE			Standard type of job.
	ARR.TM			Arrival time in system.
	JPRI			Priority of this job at this step.
	PLACE			Current STEP in ROUTING.
			QUEUE	See SERV.GRP.
STD.TYPE				A standard type of job.
	MT.BA			Mean time between arrivals.
		ROUTING		STEPs required by job of this type.
STEP				Step in the servicing of jobs of type.
	SG			Server group required at this step.
	PTIME			Process time required at this step.
	SPRI			Priority of jobs at this step.
			ROUTING	See STD.TYPE.

Fig. 7.2 Queueing network entities, attributes, and sets.

Before writing a simulator in SIMSCRIPT it is important to prepare oneself in two ways: one way is to have as complete a list as possible of the entities, attributes, and sets that are to appear in the simulated system; the other is to list the types of events to occur and a brief description of how each type of event changes status and causes other events. My current practice is to keep the description of entities, attributes, and sets in a computer file, and update this file before making any changes to the program. Figure 7.2 presents such a description of entities, attributes, and sets for the exercise network. It shows for example that the simulated system has entities such as SERV.GRP, JOB, and STD.TYPE; that a server group has as one of its attributes the number of free servers now available; that each server group owns a queue; and that jobs are members of queues. The program assumes that inputs will come from cards or cardlike lines in a file rather than be entered interactively. (The latter would require a larger program because of the prompting messages from the computer to the user).

A solution is presented in Fig. 7.3 written in SIMSCRIPT II as defined in the RAND Corporation manual (Kiviat *et al.*, 1969). Since at present I have a SHARE version translator at my disposal, and the latter does not have the ACCUMULATE and TALLY statements, I have not debugged the program in Fig. 7.3. I have debugged a longer SHARE version of the program.

```
01 PREAMBLE
02 NORMALLY MODE IS INTEGER
03 DEFINE A AS AN ALPHA VARIABLE
04 DEFINE ATIS AS A REAL VARIABLE
05   PERMANENT ENTITIES...
06 EVERY SERV.GRP HAS A FREE AND OWNS A QUEUE
07 EVERY STD.TYPE HAS A MT.BA, A TIS DUMMY AND OWNS A ROUTING
08 DEFINE MT.BA AND TIS AS REAL VARIABLES
09   TEMPORARY ENTITIES...
10 EVERY JOB HAS A JTYPE, A PLACE, A JPRI, AN ARR.TM AND BELONGS TO A QUEUE
11 DEFINE ARR.TM AS A REAL VARIABLE
12 DEFINE QUEUE AS A SET RANKED BY JPRI AND THEN BY ARR.TM
13 EVERY STEP HAS A SG, AN SPRI AND A PTIME AND BELONGS TO A ROUTING
14 DEFINE PTIME AS A REAL VARIABLE
15   EVENT NOTICES...
16 EVERY END.PROC HAS A MPROC AND A JPROC
17 EVERY SALE HAS A STYPE
18 EXTERNAL EVENT IS END.SIM
19 TALLY AMTIS=MEAN, ASTIS=STD.DEV, AMNTIS=MIN, AMXTIS=MAX OF ATIS
20 TALLY MTIS=MEAN, STIS=STD.DEV, MNTIS=MIN, MXTIS=MAX OF TIS
21 ACCUMULATE MQ=MEAN, SQ=STD.DEV, MNQ=MIN, MXQ=MAX OF N.QUEUE
22 ACCUMULATE MFR=MEAN, SFR=STD.DEV, MNFR=MIN, MXFR=MAX OF FREE
23 END
24 MAIN
25 READ N.SERV.GRP     CREATE EVERY SERV.GRP     READ FREE
26 READ N.STD.TYPE     CREATE EVERY STD.TYPE
27   FOR EACH STD.TYPE CALLED S DO THIS...
28     READ MT.BA(S)
29     CAUSE AN ARRIVL(S) AT EXPONENTIAL.F(MT.BA(S), 1)
30       UNTIL MODE IS ALPHA DO THIS...
31       CREATE A STEP CALLED P     FILE P IN ROUTING(S)
32       READ SG(P), PTIME(P), SPRI(P), N
33       ALSO FOR I=1 TO N, DO THIS...
34         CREATE A JOB     LET JTYPE(JOB)=S     LET PLACE(JOB)=P
35         CALL ALLOC(JOB)
36       LOOP     READ A
37   LOOP
38 START SIMULATION
39 END
40 EVENT ARRIVL(S) SAVING THE EVENT NOTICE
41 CAUSE THE "NEXT" ARRIVL AT TIME.V+EXPONENTIAL.F(MT.BA(S), 1)
42 CREATE A JOB
43 LET ARR.TM(JOB)=TIME.V     LET JTYPE(JOB)=S     LET PLACE(JOB)=F.ROUTING(S)
44 CALL ALLOC(JOB)
45 RETURN     END
46 ROUTINE TO ALLOC(J)
47 LET STEP=PLACE(J)     LET SERV.GRP=SG(STEP)
```

Fig. 7.3 Network of queues program.

```
48  IF FREE(SERV.GRP) > 0 SUBTRACT 1 FROM FREE(SERV.GRP)
49     CAUSE AN END.PROC(SERV.GRP,J) AT TIME.V + PTIME(STEP)
50     RETURN
51  ELSE LET JPRI(J) = SPRI(STEP)     FILE J IN QUEUE(SERV.GRP)
52  RETURN     END
53  EVENT END.PROC(M,J)
54  ADD 1 TO FREE(M)
55  IF S.ROUTING(PLACE(J)) = 0
56     LET ATIS = TIME.V-ARR.TM(J)
57     LET TIS(JTYPE(J)) = ATIS
58     DESTROY JOB CALLED J     GO TO A
59  ELSE     LET PLACE(J) = S.ROUTING(PLACE(J))     CALL ALLOC(J)
60  'A' IF QUEUE(M) IS EMPTY OR FREE(M) = 0     RETURN
61     ELSE REMOVE FIRST JOB FROM QUEUE(M)     SUBTRACT 1 FROM FREE(M)
62       CAUSE AN END.PROC(M,JOB) AT TIME.V + PTIME(PLACE(JOB))
63  RETURN     END
64  EVENT END.SIM
65  START NEW PAGE     SKIP 6 LINES     PRINT 1 LINE THUS...
66  TIME IN SYSTEM STATISTICS, BY TYPE OF JOB
67  SKIP 2 LINES     PRINT 2 LINES THUS...
68     JOB     AVERAGE     STANDARD
69     TYPE     T.I.S.     DEVIATION     MIN     MAX
70  FOR EACH STD.TYPE, PRINT 1 LINE WITH STD.TYPE, MTIS, STIS, MNTIS, MXTIS THUS
71     **     *.**     *.**     *.**     *.**
72  SKIP 1 LINE     PRINT 1 LINE WITH AMTIS, ASTIS, AMNTIS, AMXTIS THUS...
73     ALL     *.**     *.**     *.**     *.**
74  START NEW PAGE     SKIP 3 LINES     PRINT 1 LINE THUS...
75       QUEUE SIZE AND UTILIZATION STATISTICS BY SERVER GROUP
76  SKIP 2 LINES     PRINT 2 LINES THUS...
77     SERV     AVERAGE     STANDARD               AVERAGE     STANDARD
78     GROUP     QUEUE     DEVIATION     MIN     MAX     IDLE     DEVIATION     MIN     MAX
79  FOR EACH SERV.GRP PRINT 1 LINE WITH SERV.GRP, MQ, SQ, MNQ, MXQ, MFR, SFR,
80     MNFR, MXFR THUS...
81     **     *.**     *.**     ***     ***     *.**     *.**     ***     ***
82  STOP     END
```

Fig. 7.3   (continued)

Concerning the general style of SIMSCRIPT II syntax, note that one statement may appear on more than one line, or more than one statement may appear on a single line; that no punctuation marks are required between statements, although one or more periods may optionally appear at the end of any word. Comments begin with a pair of apostrophes and end either with another pair as on line 41, or at the end of the card. The line numbers are not part of the program but have been added here to facilitate discussion.

The definitions of entities, attributes and sets, and other global information, is contained between the PREAMBLE statement on line 1 and the END statement line on 23. For example the translator is told (please see line 6) that every server group has a free (number of servers) attribute and owns a queue. No further specification is needed, since in this example we let SIMSCRIPT II make the memory allocation decisions for us. In a similar manner the attributes, set memberships and set ownerships of standard types, steps in the routing of a standard type, and jobs are described elsewhere in the PREAMBLE.

The ACCUMULATE statement on line 22 of the program instructs SIMSCRIPT to maintain, for each server group, a time weighted total of FREE(SERV.GRP) thus:

$$S = \sum_{i=1}^{n} (t_i - t_{i-1})\text{FREE}_{i-1}, \tag{7.1}$$

where t_i is the value of time and FREE_{i-1} is the value of FREE(SERV.GRP) from t_{i-1} until t_i; t_0 is the last time that this sum was RESET; and t_n is the current time. In the present model the RESET command is not used; hence $t_0 = 0$. The ACCUMULATE statement on line 22 further instructs SIMSCRIPT to compute and return the time weighted mean of FREE(SERV.GRP)

$$\text{MFR} = S/(t_n - t_0), \tag{7.2}$$

whenever reference is made to the attribute MFR(SERV.GRP); and to compute SFR as the time weighted standard deviation, MNFR as the minimum, and MXFR as the maximum of FREE.

The MAIN routine, starting on line 24, is the first to receive control during the execution of any run. Its function here, as is usual, is to initialize the simulated system. It can also be used to set-up and initialize a series of simulations, accumulating statistics across these for an overall analysis. In the present case the MAIN routine reads the number of server groups for the present run (N.SERV.GRP), and creates this number of server groups with a CREATE EVERY statement. On lines 5 and 6 of the PREAMBLE, SERV.GRP is defined to be a permanent entity. SIMSCRIPT is thus told that server groups do not come and go during the course of a run. This implies that the CREATE EVERY statement is applicable, and that individual server groups are to be identified by their ordinal number, i.e., SERV.GRP = 1, or 2, or ..., N.SERV.GRP. MAIN next reads FREE for each server group. It reads the number of standard types and creates every standard type. For each standard type it reads the mean time between arrivals (MT.BA) attribute, CAUSEs the first occurrence of an arrival for this standard type (line 29), and does other initialization concerning standard types, such as creating steps (and reading their attributes) for each standard type and creating a specified number of jobs of the given type at a given step initially in the network.

The START SIMULATION statement on line 38 instructs SIMSCRIPT to call upon the timing routine to control the execution of the simulation. The timing routine will repeatedly ask which event is most imminent: one of the endogenous event occurrences now on the calendar, or the next (and only) occurrence of the exogenous event END.SIM. SIMSCRIPT II was told of these events on lines 15–18 of the PREAMBLE. Having determined the most imminent event, the timing routine updates its calendar, updates current TIME.V, and calls on the appropriate event routine. At the beginning of our illustrative simulation it will call on the most imminent ARRIVL. As described on lines 40–45, the ARRIVL event reschedules the next arrival for the same standard item reusing the same coming event notice as instructed on line 41 (and in the SAVING phrase of line 40). Thus each occurrence of an arrival for a particular standard type causes the next occurrence for this type to be placed on the calendar.

On lines 42–44 the arrival event creates a new job, notes its arrival time and type, notes that the current value of PLACE(JOB) is the step that is the first in the routing of the standard type, and calls upon the ALLOCate routine to dispose of the job. When ALLOC returns control to the ARRIVL event, the latter returns control to the timing routine, which again determines which is the most imminent event.

The ALLOC routine notes for its own use the step and the server group involved. If the number of free servers in the server group is greater than zero it decrements the number of free servers, and causes an end of processing event to occur on behalf of the given server group and job in PTIME(STEP) time units (lines 48 and 49). Otherwise, if there are no free servers in the server group, ALLOC notes the priority of the job at its present step, and files the job into queue (line 51). When the FILE statement is executed the job will be put into the appropriate position within the queue, as specified in the DEFINE SET statement in line 12 of the PREAMBLE.

When an END.PROC becomes the most imminent event, the END.PROC event routine is called with a server group and a job as its arguments. END.PROC increments the number of free servers of the server group. If the successor in routing attribute of the job's current step equals zero, i.e., if the job has reached the end of its routing, then END.PROC takes certain actions (lines 56 and 57) that, together with the TALLY statements on lines 19 and 20, will update the desired time-in-system statistics. (Incidentally, TIS is defined as a dummy attribute on line 7 to instruct SIMSCRIPT II not to store this attribute when assigned, as in line 57, but only TALLY its totals as specified on line 20.) Next, END.PROC destroys the completed job i.e., eliminates it from the simulation.

If the job is not at the end of its routing, END.PROC updates place of job and calls upon ALLOC to dispose of the job (line 59). In any case, whether the job was destroyed or sent to its next queue, the server is considered next. If the queue of the server group is empty, or the number of free servers in the server group is zero (because ALLOC happened to take what line 54 gave), then control is returned to the timing routine without further action (line 60). Otherwise the first job in the queue is removed, the number of free servers in the server group is decremented, and an end of processing for this server and job is caused to occur (lines 61 and 62). The three statements in lines 61 and 62 in effect start the processing of this job by this server.

The real action in this simulator takes place between the timing routine, the ARRIVL and END.PROC event routines, and the ALLOCate subroutine. The latter three create and destroy jobs, assign attribute values to jobs and server groups, file jobs into and remove them from queues, and schedule events to occur. The timing routine keeps asking which is the most imminent event, and transfers to the appropriate event routine, after updating TIME.V and its calendar of events.

When the exogenous END.SIM is more imminent than any endogenous event, the END.SIM event routine is called. This in turn displays the accumulated statistics in the manner pictured in lines 65–81. END.SIM then stops the execution of the program on line 82.

A SHARE version of the model, with about twice as many statements as in Fig. 7.3, requires about 16 s to translate and assemble on the IBM 370 Model 168. Of this about 6 s are spent for the routines generated by the PREAMBLE. To recompile, e.g., END.PROC takes about 2.75 s. For networks with short queues the object program will execute about 1500 to 2000 simulated events per CPU second. For networks with very large queues, where queues are "ranked" rather than LIFO or FIFO, execution performance will degrade unless one uses somewhat fancier programming. (A "ranked" set is ordered according to one or more attributes of its members.)

The same basic structure as in Fig. 7.3 underlies more complex network of queues simulators. For example, one way in which the APLOMB simulator (see Chapter 8) differs from the simple network of queues simulator presented here is APLOMB's "passive queues." We may imagine incorporating a similar feature in our illustrative network simulator as follows. In addition to the entity type SERV.GRP we can define an entity type called PASS.QU, with an attribute "number of available tokens" (AVAIL.TOKENS), and owning a set called PASQ. Each STEP in the routing of the job would indicate, by an attribute, whether the step requests processing time, requests a token of a passive queue, or returns a token of a passive queue. In the first case processing proceeds as in the existing solution. In the second case the program would test to see if a token were available; if available, the program would subtract one and proceed to the next step in the job's routing; if tokens were not available the job would be filed into the passive queue. In the third case the number of available tokens is incremented; the job proceeds to its next step; and the passive queue of jobs waiting for returned tokens is examined. These modifications to the program in Fig. 7.3 could be incorporated in an expanded ALLOCate routine. In addition the documentation file, the PREAMBLE, the MAIN routine, and END.SIM must be updated to document, define, initialize and report on the entity type PASS.QU.

Other reasonable exercises on modifying a basic queueing network model include: make job arrivals an exogenous event and have the routing of each job be part of the data for the specific arrival (see Kiviat *et al.*, 1969, regarding external inputs); or make routings and process times random.

Not all simulation models are queueing network models, although such models are found frequently in the simulation of computer systems.

7.2.2 A VM/370 Simulator

Figure 7.4 presents an extract from the file used to document the entities, attributes and sets of VSIM, a VM/370 simulator written in the SHARE version of SIMSCRIPT II. VSIM includes a detailed description of certain control program (CP) functions, particularly scheduling, dispatching, and paging. The purpose of VSIM is to test alternate decision rules or the settings of certain installation determined parameters.

The entities of VSIM include virtual machines (VMs), pages in the address space of virtual machines, direct access storage devices (DASD) on which pages are kept, and the system as a whole. Attributes include the log-on time (ARR.TM) of the VM, whether the VM is currently dispatchable, and so on. Sets include the set of nonshared pages which a VM has referred to but has not released, the set of VMs in the system's dispatch list, the set of pages in the system's user list, and so on. Figure 7.4 does not include all of the attributes and set memberships of the entities listed.

VSIM coding is illustrated in Fig. 7.5. This is a subroutine used within VSIM when simulated CP is required to find a page frame for a page demanded by an executing VM. Some background concerning the operation of the Control Program (CP) is required to make clear the operation of the routine.

VSIM, like the system is represents, maintains three sets of pages in main storage. One of these, called the free list (FR.LIST), consists of pages whose page frames may be given out without writing their current contents onto a paging drum or disk, because the contents have already been written out. The flush list (FL.LIST) consists of page frames whose contents have not been written to the paging DASD, but are to be given out before pages in the user list (USR.LIST). We shall not describe here what makes CP move a page from the user list to the flush list. VSIM also keeps a count of the page frames that are not occupied by any page. Before the STEAL.PG routine is called, VSIM checks to see whether a needed page is on the user list or can be reclaimed from the free or flush lists. If not, a page frame is needed and VSIM calls on STEAL.PG to find one.

STEAL.PG first attempts to obtain an unoccupied frame or a frame whose occupant is in the free list. If such is not available it takes a frame from the flush ist; and if this is not available it steals a page from the user list. In the last case

Entities	Attributes	Owns	Belongs	Comments
VM				Virtual machine.
	VM.TNR			Type number of machine's user program.
	ARR.TM			Time virt. mach. entered system.
	DSPABLE			Dispatchable: 0 ⇒ no; 1 ⇒ yes.
	INTRPD			= 1 ⇒ act interrupted; = 0 ⇒ not interrupted.
	TO.GO			Time to go on interrupted action.
	QU.NR			Queue number.
	WSPROJ			Nr. pages in projected "working set."
	LAST.WSPROJ			Previous WSPROJ.
	RES.PAGES			Nr. of resident pages.
	SUMRES.PAGES			Sum, over page reads, of resident pages.
	NU.RESPAGES			Nr. of updates to above tally.
	STEALS.QU			Nr. times pg wt entered for stolen pg.
	EPRIOR			Priority of VM in ELG.LIST.
	RPRIOR			Priority of VM in DSP.LIST.
	USR.FCTR			Factor used in EPRIOR calculation.
	PS.TIME			Time spent in problem state.
	CP.TIME			CP time spent on behalf of this VM.
	ETS.PS			Time slice will end if PS.TIME → ETS.PS.
	ETS.SS			Time slice will end if CP.TIME → ETS.SS.
	EQ.PS			Quantum will end if PS.TIME → EQ.PS
	EQ.SS			Quantum will end if CP.TIME → EQ.SS.
	CUR.STP.NR			Current step number.
	CUR.ACT			Current action.
	CUR.TYPE			Current (user, util., or CP) job type.
	ST.TIME			Time: state entered or last report.
		NBS		Pages needed but stolen.
		CPRS		Current page requirements (nonshared).
		SPRS		Shared page requirements.

Fig. 7.4 Extract from VSIM status.

Entities	Attributes	Owns	Belongs	Comments
		RSQD		Pages referenced since last qdrop.
			DSP.LIST	Dispatch list.
			ELG.LIST	Eligible list.
PAGE	SP.FLAG			= 0 (not a shared page).
	WHOSE			Virtual machine of page.
	NEEDED.BIT			= 1 ⇒ currently needed; = 0 otherwise.
	KEEP.BIT			= 1 ⇒ need persists beyond step; = 0 otherwise.
	LOCK.BIT			= 1 ⇒ Lock page when frame obtained.
	LOCKED.BIT			= 0 ⇒ page not locked; = 1 ⇒ page locked.
	MODIFY.BIT			= 1 ⇒ modify page when frame obtained.
	MODIFIED.BIT			= 0 ⇒ page not modified; = 1 ⇒ page modified.
	RFRNCD.BIT			→ 1 by use of page; → 0 by STEAL.PG routine.
	TAV.DRUM			Time of end trans. to paging drum or disk.
			FR.LIST	Free list, used by paging mngmnt rules.
			FL.LIST	Flush list, used by paging mngmnt rules.
			USR.LIST	User list, used by paging mngmnt rules.
			NBS	Needed but stolen.
			RSQD	Referenced since last queue drop.
THE SYSTEM	CUM.IDLE			Cumulative time, CPU idle.
	CUM.SOH			Cum CPU usage for system overhead.
	TOT.PROJWS			Sum of WSPROJs among VMs in DSP.LIST.
	EMPTY.FRAMES			Number of page frames without pages.
	CPUWORKING.FLAG			= 0 ⇒ CPU idle; = 1 ⇒ CPU working.
	EP.FCTR			Factor used in EPRIOR calc. in QDROP.
	RP.FCTR			Factor used in RPRIOR calc. in QDROP.
	DT.CUNP			
	PI.CUNP			

Fig. 7.4 (continued)

Entities	Attributes	Owns	Belongs	Comments
	P2.CUNP			Parameters for various distributions.
	DT.CURE			Each parameter name is of the form:
	P1.CURE			
	P2.CURE			$xx.yyzz$,
	DT.C1DC			
	P1.C1DC			where
	P2.C1DC			
	DT.TTDC			xx = "DT" means "distr. type"
	P1.TTDC			= "P1" means "parameter 1"
	P2.TTDC			= "P2" means "parameter 2",
	DT.C2DC			
	P1.C2DC			yy = "CU" means "CPU usage"
	P2.C2DC			= "C1" means "CPU before TT"
	DT.C1CD			= "TT" means "transmission"
	P1.C1CD			= "C2" means "CPU after TT",
	P2.C1CD			
	DT.TTCD			zz = "DC" means "drum to core"
	P1.TTCD			= "CD" means "core to drum"
	P2.TTCD			= "IO" means "nonpaging IO"
	DT.C2CD			= "WT" means "long wait."
	P1.C2CD			
	P2.C2CD			
	P2.C2CD			
	DT.C1IO			
	P1.C1IO			
	P2.C1IO			
	DT.C2IO			
	P1.C2IO			
	P2.C2IO			

Fig. 7.4 (continued)

Entities	Attributes	Owns	Belongs	Comments
	DT.C1WT			
	P1.C1WT			
	P2.C1WT			
	DT.C2WT			
	P1.C2WT			
	P2.C2WT			
	SPFR.CC			CPU tm rqd to steal page from FR.LIST.
	SPFL.CC			CPU tm rqd to steal page from FL.LIST.
	SPUS.AA			CPU tm to seek to stl pg from USR.LIST.
	SPUS.BB			Ditto – per page examined in USR.LIST.
		DSP.LIST		Dispatch list.
		USR.LIST		User list, used by paging mngr.
		FL.LIST		Flush list, used by paging mngr.
		FR.LIST		Free list, used by paging mngr.

Fig. 7.4 (continued)

```
ROUTINE TO STEAL.PG (REP)
    "OBTAINS PAGE FRAME.        REP = 1 = > REPLACEMENT FOR FREE LIST SOUGHT"
DEFINE PT AND PT2 AS REAL VARIABLES
    "IF O.K., OBTAIN PAGE FRAME FROM FREE LIST"
IF FR.LIST IS NOT EMPTY AND REP = 0 REMOVE FIRST PAGE FROM FR.LIST
    IF EMPTY.FRAMES + N.FR.LIST < = N.DSP.LIST CALL STEAL.PG(1) YIELDING PT2
    REGARDLESS...      RETURN.
    "OR, OBTAIN PAGE FROM FLUSH LIST"
ELSE IF FL.LIST IS NOT EMPTY REMOVE FIRST PAGE FROM FL.LIST      GO TO C
    "ELSE STEAL PAGE FROM USER LIST"
ELSE...
'A' FOR EACH PAGE IN USR.LIST DO...
    IF LOCKED.BIT(PAGE) = 1   GO TO B      ELSE
    IF RFRNCD.BIT(PAGE) = 0 GO TO FOUND      ELSE      LET RFRNCD.BIT(PAGE) = 0
'B' LOOP      IF SECOND.TIME = 0   LET SECOND.TIME = 1   GO TO A   ELSE CALL ERR(31)
'FOUND' REMOVE PAGE FROM USR.LIST
IF SP.FLAG(PAGE) = 0 AND NEEDED.BIT(PAGE) = 1 FILE PAGE IN NBS(WHOSE(PAGE))
    THEN IF WHOSE(PAGE) = VM      ADD 1 TO SELF.STEALS
    "PERHAPS TRANSMIT TO DASD."
'C' ELSE IF REP = 1 FILE PAGE IN FR.LIST      REGARDLESS
    IF MODIFIED.BIT(PAGE) = 0      RETURN      ELSE
    IF STORED.ON(PAGE) > 0 LET PGG.DASD = STORED.ON(PAGE)      GO TO D      ELSE
FOR PGG.DASD = 1 TO N.PGG.DASD WITH AVAIL.SLOTS(PGG.DASD) > 0   GO TO CC
                                                         ELSE CALL ERR(32)
'CC' SUBTRACT 1 FROM AVAIL.SLOTS(PGG.DASD)      LET STORED.ON(PAGE) = PGG.DASD
'D' ADD 1 TO NR.PG.WRITES
LET TAV.DASD(PAGE) = TIME +
                WAIT(DT.TTCD(PGG.DASD),P1.TTCD(PGG.DASD),P2.TTCD(PGG.DASD))
IF REP = 0      LET DSPABLE(VM) = 0      REGARDLESS      RETURN      END
```

Fig. 7.5   VSIM routine to steal page.

STEAL.PG, like the system it represents, seeks a page whose reference bit (RFRNC.BIT) equals zero. The reference bit is turned on, set to 1, by 370 hardware whenever a page is referenced. It is turned off, set to zero, by system software. In fact it is set to zero when each page with referenced bit equal one is encountered in examining the user list, until a page with reference bit equal to zero is reached. If the end of the user list is reached without encountering a page with reference bit equal to zero, then the user list is scanned once more, now usually encountering one of the pages whose reference bit has been set to zero. In seeking a page from the user list, STEAL.PG is not allowed to take a page frame marked as "locked." In case of the presumably rare but conceivable state in which every page frame is locked, VSIM stops with an error message.

If a page is selected from the flush list or the user list, the page may have to be transmitted to a paging drum or disk. This is unnecessary if the page has not been modified during its current stay in main storage. If the page has been modified its current copy will be written out to the particular slot on the particular DASD device from which its previous (now obsolete) copy was read. If the page has never been assigned a slot, then a slot will be assigned from the first paging device with a slot available.

When a page is removed from the free list (either when a page is reclaimed from the free list or when a page frame is taken for a new demand) if the free list is running low in a certain sense STEAL.PG is asked to find a page to be moved from the flush or user list to the free list. In this case STEAL.PG is signaled by an argument (REP = 1) that it is not to take a page from the free list, but must take one from the flush list, or failing that, from the user list. STEAL.PG calls itself recursively for this purpose.

The routine in Fig. 7.5 explains to the computer the same things that the above paragraphs explain to the reader. The routine in the figure has been simplified by deleting from the VSIM version some lines that accumulate certain simulated times, such as the time required to remove a page from the free list. WAIT, referred to on the next to the last line of the routine, is a function subprogram that takes a distribution type and two parameters as arguments and returns a perhaps random time increment.

7.3 Simulation Programming with a General Purpose Language

I recommend the following general procedure for programming a simulator using a general purpose language without simulation capabilities.

1. Make a first draft of the entities, attributes and sets of the simulated system as shown in Figs. 7.2 or 7.4. Also list the types of events that can occur together with a brief description, perhaps a paragraph for each event, of the ways in which each event changes status and causes subsequent event occurrences.

2. Next, make a more detailed description of the event routines, perhaps describing them at approximately the SIMSCRIPT level of detail without regard to SIMSCRIPT's syntax requirements. Update the status description insofar as the detailed event description reveals the need for new entities, attributes, or sets.

3. Inventory the programming conventions and utility programs needed to implement the system in 2.

4. Program and test the utility programs. Perhaps in parallel, program the event routines and subroutines. Test the latter when the utility routines are available.

Conventions and utility routines usually include a timing routine, random number generators for various distributions, conventions for the storing of attributes, routines for managing dynamic storage, and conventions and routines for managing sets. Methods for generating random numbers with various distributions are presented in Chapter 5. Below we discuss the various conventions and utility routines other than random number generation, postponing the discussion of event processing until after that of set processing.

There are alternate methods of solving the various implementation problems discussed below. Our objective here is not to survey the various alternatives. Rather our objective is to present at least one generally serviceable solution which the user may use as is, modify, or discard completely for some other solution, as his problem and tastes dictate.

7.3.1 Permanent Attributes and Arrays

In SIMSCRIPT the attributes of permanent entities are stored as arrays. Thus when the CREATE EVERY statement on line 25 of Fig. 7.3 is executed, the program reserves a FREE array, a F.QUEUE array (indicating the first in set for each server group), and so on. Each of these arrays consists of consecutive words of memory to store for example FREE(1), FREE(2),... FREE(N.SERV.GRP). In this manner the attribute of the ith server group, FREE(i), is quickly accessed as an array element.

More than for most other types of programming, flexibility is vital to simulation programming. Experimentation is a principal purpose of

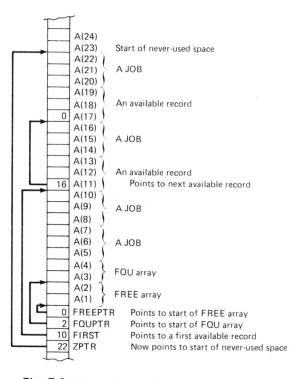

Fig. 7.6 Memory layout for a FORTRAN simulator.

simulation, including experimentation with alternate system configurations. For this reason it is usually essential to allow the number of a permanent entity to be determined at execute time. This may be done in PL/I by declaring arrays to be controlled. In FORTRAN the same effect may be accomplished by the following means, as illustrated in Fig. 7.6. Define a very large common array, denoted in Fig. 7.6 as $A(1)$, $A(2)$, ..., $A(N)$. The A-array is to fill the unused portion of the user's (virtual) memory and will be used both for arrays (such as are needed for storing the attributes of permanent entities) and for the space used by temporary entities such as JOBs. In addition to the A-array, common will include one word each for each of the various common variables (or "attributes of the system as a whole") used by the program. In addition it will include one word each for each array. In Fig. 7.6, FREEPTR is the name of this word in common associated with the array of FREE servers. The Ith element of the FREE array is stored at $A(FREEPTR + I)$; similarly the Ith element of FQU is stored at $A(FQUPTR + I)$.

Suppose that NSG is a common variable to be read during execution indicating the number of server groups. Suppose further that ZPTR is a variable that is initially 0, and is incremented by the amount of space assigned to any array within the A-array as space is allocated. Thus when NSG is determined we can assign the first NSG words in the A-array to the array of free servers by letting $FREEPTR = ZPTR$, and updating $ZPTR = ZPTR + NSG$; assign the next NSG words to the FQU-array by letting $FQUPTR = ZPTR$ and adding NSG to ZPTR; and so on for other arrays that are to be given space.

For the present discussion we shall assume that arrays are not released. For an application where arrays are to be reserved, released, and reserved again, perhaps the use of PL/I or SIMSCRIPT II should be considered.

7.3.2 Attributes of Temporary Entities

In PL/I the attributes of temporary entities can be stored as the fields of a based variable. In FORTRAN the attributes of temporary entities can be stored in the following manner. To begin, let us suppose that there is only one type of temporary entity, say with 3 attributes, each attribute occupying one word of memory. The 3 attributes of a given temporary entity will occupy 3 consecutive words of storage. In this case the create action may be accomplished by calling a routine which returns a location I in the A-array. The newly created entity will occupy $A(I + 1)$, $A(I + 2)$, $A(I + 3)$. It will continue to occupy these 3 words until the entity is no longer needed and is purged by a destroy action. In particular the filing of entities into sets and the removing of them from sets will not involve the physical movement of this individual from its 3 given words of the A-array. Whenever a specific individual is referenced it is referred to by a variable containing its location in the A-array. When referring to, for example, the second attribute of entity I one may write A(I + 2).

For simulations with a great deal of data it may be desirable to pack attributes into parts of words. This may be done by means of routines written in assembly language designed to pack and unpack attributes. For example, if the UP12 function routine unpacks the first half of a word we may refer to an attribute stored in the first half of the third word as UP12(A(I + 3)).

The first time a 3-word record is given out it starts at ZPTR, and the value of ZPTR is incremented by 3. This same procedure is repeated until a record is returned; i.e., an entity is destroyed. The first time this occurs an unsubscripted common variable (say, FIRST) is set equal to the space being returned; e.g., if the destroy routine is called with J as an argument, indicating that the 3 words following J are no longer needed, then the routine will assign FIRST = J. Subsequently (when FIRST is no longer zero) the destroy routine will maintain the last-in–first-out set illustrated in Fig. 7.6 by letting A(J + 1) = FIRST and FIRST = J. In this way J becomes the first in set, the former first in set becomes its successor, and any earlier members maintain their relative positions. In general when a new record is needed, if FIRST is zero the record is obtained by advancing ZPTR until ZPTR reaches the maximum dimension of A, at which point space is no longer available. If FIRST is not zero then the value of FIRST becomes the identification number of the newly created entity; and FIRST is assigned the value in A(FIRST + 1). A(FIRST + 1) will equal zero, in the natural course of things, when the last member of the LIFO set of the reusable space is encountered.

In the network example in Fig. 7.3 STEPs are created first (and never destroyed afterwards) before any JOBs are created and destroyed. In this case even if a step and a job require different numbers of words the above procedure can be applied with one size of increment to ZPTR until all steps are created, then another size used thereafter. Suppose however two or more sizes are to be created and destroyed at various times; e.g., records of size 3, 7, and 9. One way to proceed is as follows: Keep three separate LIFO sets, one each for records of size 3, 7, and 9, respectively. When an entity is destroyed return its space to the appropriate LIFO set. When an entity is created, first test to see if a record is available in the set of records of the desired size. If no record is available then make one by incrementing ZPTR. This procedure should be adequate if 3s, 7s, and 9s continue to be used in roughly the same proportions throughout the simulation, and if the maximum requirement for available space is not too close to the amount available.

7.3.3 Storing Sets

Sets are sometimes represented by storing entities (or pointers to entities) in a fixed number of consecutive words of memory. For example, we could allow each server group 20 words of storage in which to keep pointers to as many as 20 members of its queue. This method of storing sets usually proves to be inconvenient and inefficient for simulators. The comings and goings of members of sets, like jobs in queues, may fluctuate during the course of a simulation – sometimes one queue being larger, sometimes another. The maximum number in any one queue may vary considerably as we change the number of servers in each server group. We may average 5 jobs per queue, wasting an average of 15 words for unused slots, yet encounter a queue with a 21st member. This perhaps could be accommodated by an overflow region, but the searching of the overflow region can become costly.

A method of keeping track of sets that has generally proved simpler and more successful for simulation involves the use of pointers. We shall continue to refer to the owners and members of sets. A set may be held together and traced out if the owner of a set has a first-in-set attribute, and each member of the set has a next-in-set attribute. In this way the owner of the set knows which member is first, the first-in-set knows which is second, the second knows the third, etc. If the owner of the set is a permanent entity, such as the server groups in our exercise, then the first-in-set attribute is stored like any other attribute of a permanent entity. If the owner of the set is a temporary entity, such as a VM that owns the set NBS in Fig. 7.4, then first-in-set is stored like any other attribute of a temporary entity. If a set is owned by the system as a whole such as the USR.LIST in the VSIM example, then the owner attributes are unsubscripted global (or common) variables. The members of the set may be temporary entities or permanent entities. In both our illustrative programs the sets contained temporary entities; but cases do arise occasionally when permanent entities are filed into sets. If the member of the set is a temporary entity then the next-in-set attribute is stored like any other attribute of a temporary entity. If the member of the set is a permanent entity then the next-in-set attribute is stored like any other attribute of the permanent entity.

Since an entity (temporary or permanent) can have any number of attributes, it can have any number of first-in-set attributes, such as a first-in-queue, a first-in-list, a first-in-box. It may also have any number of next-in-set attributes, such as next-in-queue, next-in-string, next-in-stack. Consequently, an entity may own any number of sets, and belong to any number of sets as well as have any number of attributes.

Since next-in-set is an attribute of the member entity, and since an attribute can have only one value, it follows that a given individual can be in at most one set with a given name. For example, a job can be in only one queue and can be in the queue at most once at any one time. The job can be in sets with different names, such as a queue, a list, and a box, but in only one set at a time with a given name. Nevertheless, a situation in which there are overlapping sets – such as people who can belong to many clubs and clubs which can have many members – is routinely handled as follows: Define a new type of entity that we shall call a *membership card.* To enroll a new person as a member of a particular club we

CREATE A CARD
LET WHO(CARD) = PERSON
LET WHICH(CARD) = CLUB
FILE CARD IN WALLET(PERSON)
FILE CARD IN ROSTER(CLUB)

where "who" and "which" are attributes of card, wallet is a set owned by person, and roster is a set owned by club. The card may also have attributes such as the year in which the person first enrolled.

This mechanism can also be used when an entity can be in the same set more than once, as when a student can enroll more than once for a given course. In this case an enrollment entity may serve the roll of the membership card. A particular enrollment belongs to only one set owned by course and one set

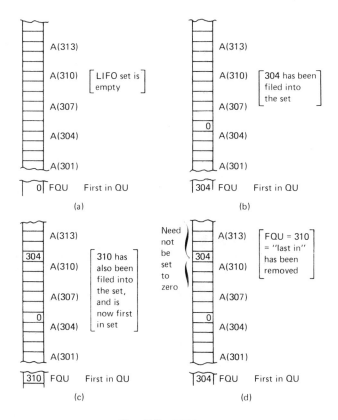

Fig. 7.7 LIFO sets.

owned by student. But more than one enrollment for a given student may belong to the set for the course.

In some cases it is desirable to have a last-in-set attribute of the owner entity as well as a first-in-set attribute. In some cases it is desirable to have a prior-in-set attribute of member as well as a next-in-set attribute. The need for last and prior attributes depend on the actions to be taken. For example, if a set is always to be treated last-in–first-out (i.e., if it is to be a LIFO or push-down–pop-up set) then only first-in-set and next-in-set attributes are required. Figure 7.7 shows how attributes are modified by file and remove actions for a LIFO set. In this example the set is named QU; it is owned by the system; and if I is a member of the set then $A(I + 1)$ contains its successor in QU. Figure 7.7b shows how the attributes of owners and members are affected when a first entity is filed into an empty set. Figure 7.7c shows how attributes are affected

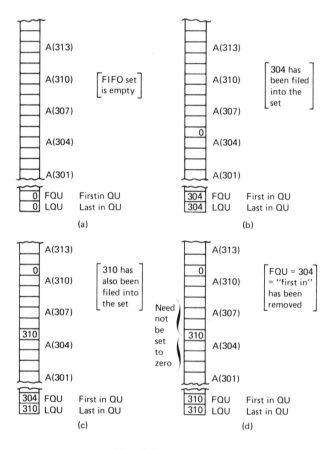

Fig. 7.8   FIFO sets.

when a subsequent member is filed into nonempty sets. Even if the set contains a large number of members, the file and remove actions only affect first-in-set, and the next-in-set attribute of one individual. The reader should also confirm that the individual who is removed by a remove action, as in 7.7d, is the remaining one which was filed most recently by a file action.

If a set is to be used as a first-in–first-out set, then a last-in-set pointer is essential for efficient operation. Figure 7.8 illustrates the file and the remove actions for a first-in–first-out set. Note that the individual removed with the remove action is indeed the earliest individual still remaining who was filed by a file action. Also notice that even if there are a large number of individuals in the set, the file action affects last-in-set (and first-in-set if the set is otherwise empty) and the next-in-set attributes of one individual. The remove action is also parsimonious in its references and actions.

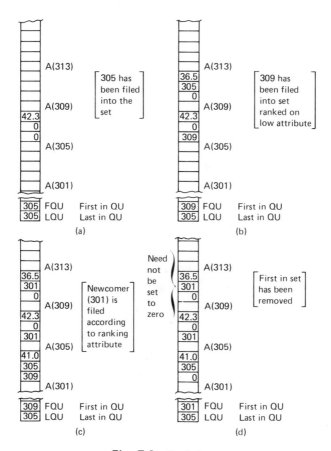

Fig. 7.9 Ranked sets.

Prior-in-set is needed to efficiently remove an arbitrary individual from a set, to insert an individual before or after some other individual at an arbitrary point in the set, or to maintain a set ordered according to some ranking attribute. Figure 7.9 illustrates the filing of an entity into a ranked set. The words at $A(J + 1)$, $A(J + 2)$, and $A(J + 3)$ represent, respectively, the next-in-set and prior-in-set attributes and the attribute according to which the set is ranked.

The filing and removing of members of LIFO and FIFO sets is not slowed by large sets. The filing of members into a ranked set will become slower (except under special circumstances) as the size of the set increases. Where the degradation in performance becomes of economic importance, a more elaborate method for storing ranked sets may be desirable.

7.3.4   The Timing Routine

In some simulations there is a natural time increment. In others, events can happen in arbitrarily small or large increments of time. For example, in a cash flow simulation for a large business it would be uneconomical to represent individual cash receipts and disbursements. Rather we would run the model on say a monthly cycle having one calculation represent monthly receipts and another represent disbursements.

In the simulation of other systems, however, individual events that can occur asynchronously are to be represented. My own recommendations under such circumstances is to represent time as a floating point (perhaps a double

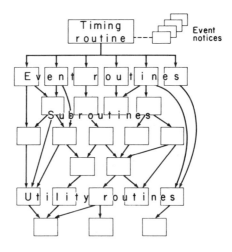

Fig. 7.10   Flow diagram for an asynchronous simulator.

precision floating point) variable and allow a timing routine to increment time to that of the most imminent event. We shall now consider how the timing routine is to keep track of such coming events.

Figure 7.10 presents a flow diagram applicable to most, if not all, asynchronous simulations. At the top is the timing routine which looks to a ranked set of *coming event notices* to determine which event is most imminent. One of the attributes of each notice is event type, another is time of occurrence. The timing routine calls upon one or another event routine according to the type of event that is most imminent. The event routines may call upon subroutines; and both the subroutines and the event routines may call on the utility routines which know how to create, destroy, file, remove, etc. The causing of an event is accomplished by creating a coming event notice, noting its event type, time of occurrence, and any information which is known at the time of causing and needs to be transferred to the time of happening. The timing routine gives the most imminent event routine the (pointer to its) coming event notice as an argument.

The set of coming events is ranked according to time of occurrence. In systems in which many events may be pending, the set of coming events may be subdivided in some appropriate manner, as is done in SIMSCRIPT's timing routines.

In a simulation language (such as SIMULA or SIMSCRIPT II.5), which allows "processes" as well as events, a routine may "suspend" itself (and the subroutines upon which it has called) – to be "resumed" later with all local variables still set as they were when the routine was suspended. The routine can be resumed after a time delay specified at the time it was suspended; or it may be resumed by another routine. In a general purpose programming language such as PL/I or FORTRAN (or in SIMSCRIPT II, without processes) the same effect may be achieved with greater difficulty by using attributes of the coming event notice in place of local variables, and placing the old coming event notice back on the calendar.

7.3.5 *The Accumulation of Performance Statistics*

As illustrated in Fig. 7.11, a time weighted mean of an attribute may be accumulated by computing a time weighted sum

$$S = \sum_{i=1}^{n} (t_i - t_{i-1})\text{FREE}_{i-1} \qquad (7.3)$$

as described for the queueing network example.

A time weighted variance may similarly be accumulated by accumulating the mean of the square of an attribute and then using the formula

$$\text{VARIANCE}(R) = \text{MEAN}(R^2) - (\text{MEAN } R)^2. \qquad (7.4)$$

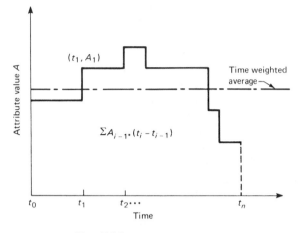

Fig. 7.11 Time weighted mean.

These formulas require actions only when the value of the specific attribute changes, and require one last update when the mean, variance, or standard deviation is to be reported. A minimum, a maximum, or even a time weighted histogram for an attribute may similarly be accumulated by actions taken only when the attributes change values, and perhaps when the statistic is about to be reported.

The program is generally more readable and easier to modify and debug if the statistical update procedures can be separated from the body of the simulation. One way to do this is by means of calls to statistical update routines. If the time required to call is objectionable, then the statistical update coding can be intermingled within the event routines and subroutines, with the statements that change status perhaps separated visually from them by some system of indentation.

7.4 Debugging

A simulator may be flexible, efficient, have convenient input and valuable outputs, but it is worth nothing if it cannot be debugged in a timely manner. Some programmers have trouble with debugging simulators, but a few good habits can be of great value. The first good habit for debugging concerns reading and rereading a simulator after it is written and before it is compiled. Read through the various subroutines and then the entire first draft of the source program, looking for design and/or coding errors. The first full readthrough reveals many errors. Once these are corrected a second readthrough reveals perhaps half as many errors. Once these in turn are corrected a third readthrough produces perhaps half again as many errors. It is my practice and strong recommendation that, in the programming of complex simulators, these readthroughs be continued until a careful readthrough reveals almost no bugs, e.g., one or two at most. For simpler programs it is a reasonable procedure to type a program into a terminal (or, in batch technology, manuscript and have it keypunched), read it through once, and then see how it works on the computer. But for programs of the complexity of a large systems simulator, bugs caught by reading (or "walk-throughs" with others) are found for much less labor, in much less elapsed time, not to mention computer costs, than bugs found by executing the program.

It is common to find during the programming and reading of a complex simulator that improvements can be made in its basic design. It is frequently found, for example, that a certain function, not originally recognized in the design, is being performed at several points in the program; that the program would be shorter and easier to grasp, and not perceptibly less efficient, if a subroutine were provided to perform this function. Later, once a substantial amount of time has been invested in debugging, one will hesitate to rewrite passages and move code just to improve the overall simulator design. But while still at the stage of finding bugs by reading, I find that design improvements pay for themselves in terms of easier subsequent readthroughs, easier debugging, easier documentation and easier subsequent modifications as new features are added.

Even if the simulator is programmed in a very high level language and has been read through a number of times until virtually no bugs can be found in this manner, debugging should procede on the assumption that bugs still exist. A *debugging strategy* should be followed to search for bugs systematically. In the debugging of a simulator of a complex system, the strategy of running the simulator against a realistic data case to see if the results are realistic is about the last step in the debugging task. A first step is to make sure that the initialization routines, which temselves are usually fairly complex, have set up initial status description correctly. For this purpose a subroutine should be written that displays, in at least a moderately readable manner, the status of the variables and data structures that are set up during initialization.

Once it appears that errors in initialization have been found and corrected, debugging can proceed to test cases whose detailed consequences can be computed by hand with such resources as are available to the project. The results of the hand calculations are compared with reports of the status of the system. These detailed status reports will not be part of the regular output of the completed simulation. Rather they will be removed or suppressed for production runs. During debugging however, they are much more informative than the summary statistics that constitute much of the eventual final output – particularly if the simulation ends abnormally before the final reports are reached.

7.5   Selection of a Type 2 Language

Languages like GÅSP (Pritsker, 1974; 1977a) and SIMPL/1 (IBM, 1972a, b) add a simulation capability to an existing general purpose language. For example GASP, the most widely cited and presumably the most widely used such language, uses an entity, attribute, and set view of simulation programming, and adds various simulation timing, filing, random number generator, and statistical accumulation capabilities to FORTRAN. It is limited, however, to one size of temporary entity in any given simulation, and temporary entities cannot own sets.

To evaluate the suitability of a language such as GASP, or SIMPL/1 which adds simulation capabilities to PL/1, proceed as if planning for the use of a general purpose language without simulation capabilities (as outlined above) through the step in which the need for conventions and utility routines have been inventoried. Then the choice of package can be made on the basis of needs versus facilities supplied, as well as on the basis of software cost, approximate execution speeds, and training requirements for each available language of all three types.

7.6   Simulator Design

The decisions made during the initial design, and subsequently during the detailed design, of a simulator affect subsequent implementation, utilization, and modification. Design decisions should be made with these affects in mind.

Figure 7.12 presents a broad flow diagram of the major tasks of a simulation project. Each of the major tasks appearing in Fig. 7.12 itself consists of many subtasks. The heavy lines connecting the major tasks represent general precedences as to which major tasks must be (mostly) done before another major task can start in earnest. The dotted lines represent feedback in which the experience of one major task alters some of the products of prior tasks. Tasks are numbered in the figure for ease of reference.

1. *The decision to simulate.*   The first major task is to decide whether or not the building of a proposed simulation model is the best use of the resources required. In performing this task the decision maker, or decision making team, must look forward to the final product and its applications. It must ask: What kinds of questions will be asked of the model? What will be required in the way of computer space and time when run for interesting cases? Where will we get the data? What types of real world objects and events need be programmed into the simulator, and approximately how much information (and roughly what kind of information) is needed about these objects as far the simulation is concerned? How long will it take to design, program, and

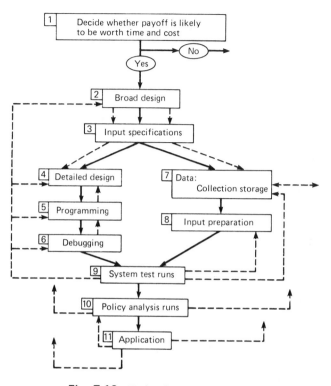

Fig. 7.12 Tasks of a simulation project.

debug the simulator, collect the required data, and test the model? Will there be uses for the model, or easily made variations of the model, beyond its initial area of application? The raising of such questions leads to the subtasks required to assess the feasibility, costs, and benefits of the proposed simulator development.

To estimate computer time requirements roughly, in order to see at least that the simulation will not be prohibitive economically, a rough estimate is required of the number of event occurrences in a typical large run. This estimate is divided by a planning factor whose dimensions are events per CPU second. In SIMSCRIPT II, for example, with programs such as the queueing network and VM/370 simulator examples discussed earlier (in which there are many asynchronous event occurrences, but each event involves a relatively small thread of actual computations), a planning factor of 1000 events per second usually proves to be reasonably conservative. Thus a simulation (of this sort) which generates 10,000 event occurrences per interesting length of run may be expected to take less than 10 s of CPU time; whereas one that generates 10,000,000 event occurrences per run (times several runs per simulation analysis) is likely to be uneconomical for most potential applications. Almost without exception, the reason why a simulation programmer is unpleasantly surprised by the slowness of his simulator is *not* that his planning factors are too rough, but that he did not try to make the estimate at all.

For large computers such as the 370 Model 168, the size of the simulator program is rarely a serious constraint. If memory is a problem it is usually because there are too many hundreds of thousands of individuals of some entity type, or some array is too large. Where main storage is possibly a bottleneck, estimates should be made of the maximum number of individual entities in the system, times the number of bytes of attributes per individual, plus the bytes occupied by any substantial arrays. Usually a rough calculation of such space requirements is quite adequate to establish whether memory is a limiting factor.

Thus the feasibility of the simulation in terms of space and time can usually be established fairly firmly by a rough calculation. No professional simulation analyst or programmer would proceed with a substantial model without such a calculation – by definition of "professional." The estimation of how long it will take to build a simulator is more difficult, since it can vary considerably with the skill and experience of the programmer(s) as well as the complexity of the model and the language chosen. Estimation of the economic value of the final product depends on the substance of the specific model rather than the state-of-the-art of simulator building, and thus is beyond the scope of this chapter.

2. *Broad design of the simulator.*   The next major task has two principal products:

(a)   a more complete list (than developed in task 1) of the types of entities to appear in the simulated world, and the properties of these objects required to characterize them during the course of the simulation. These decisions concerning simulated system status can be documented by a first draft of a file such as in Fig. 7.2 or 7.4.

(b)   a more complete list of the types of events that will occur in the simulated world, and a general description of how each type of event changes the state of the simulated world and causes further event occurrences. One paragraph per event should be sufficient.

After (a) and (b) have been completed, the rough calculations of speed and space should be made again. The object still is to produce rough numbers for general feasibility and desirability considerations, but now more information about the model is available.

When broad design decisions are documented for management, or for potential users not already familiar with simulation, it is customary to include an overall flow diagram of the simulation. If the simulation is asynchronous then the flow diagram will probably look like Fig. 7.10, except with specific event routines and subroutines appearing. This "all-purpose" flow diagram can be omitted when organizing the team's work or communicating to persons already familiar with the handling of asynchronous simulators.

3. *Input specification.* Frequently in large simulation projects a different team is responsible for collecting the inputs than is responsible for programming the simulator. Before the data team and the simulator development team go their separate ways, however, it is essential that parameters, to be presented later to the model, and the probable format by which the model will accept them, be specified in advance. This task of input specification is frequently the first time that the modelers and the substantive experts come to an understanding, at the level of detail and rigor needed before programming or data collection can begin, of the precise features that the substantive experts desire or are willing to live with. The input specifications also serve to document the agreement between the data team and the simulator team. Even when the data team and the simulator team are one in the same, it is recommended that input specifications be laid out before coding begins.

Thus a first draft of status description, a good draft of input specifications, and at least a rough draft of the functions of the various types of events should be written down before detailed simulator design begins. A sketch of possible output is sometimes produced in conjunction with tasks 1 and 2, but is not as critical a prerequisite for starting programming as is the other documentation listed above. There are two reasons for the asymmetry between the need for input and output specifications at this point. First, the input includes a complete characterization of the system as of an instant in time (namely the initial conditions). An understanding of status as of an instant is essential to, and usually a large percentage of, the understanding of a model. Second, the final outputs are not needed until a late stage of debugging (as discussed under *debugging*), and then frequently are obtained by accumulating statistics for a few crucial attributes. Thus programming cannot start without essentially knowing how to characterize initial conditions at the least, whereas output specifications are desirable but not mandatory.

4. *Detailed simulator design.* The choice of programming language must be made at this point, if it has not been made already. If a standard language without a simulation capability is to be used, it is advisable at this time to consider in detail how certain basic functions (such as storing attributes and sets) are to be handled.

In addition to providing for basic simulation capabilities, e.g., by choice of simulation language or design of utility routines, a detailed description of the program is advisable at this stage. My own practice is to write out much of the simulator in a semi-SIMSCRIPT: specifying the actions to be taken by the various events of the simulation without worrying about the syntax requirements of the language to be used. These are notes from me to the programmer(s), perhaps from me to me, which are intended to make clear the simulated actions to be taken. Each line of these notes can be replaced, in task 5, by one or more lines of code in the syntax of the chosen language.

Other tasks shown in Fig. 7.12 include programming and debugging discussed previously, data collection and preparation, and runs to test and draw conclusions from the model. It is the essence of simulation that these tasks will suggest changes in the model. A viable model must be capable of being modified gracefully; hence the value, emphasized elsewhere in this chapter, of a clean structure, dimensioning at execute time rather than compile time, the separation of analysis from physical system description, and good, up-to-date documentation.

7.7 Summary

The design of a simulation project includes, as one of its major parts, the design of its simulator. The design of the simulator, in the first instance, consists of deciding the entities, attributes, and sets to be represented within the simulated system and the events which change status. If a general purpose programming language without simulation capabilities is used, then when the event routines are spelled out in some detail (but before programming begins) a survey should be made of the fundamental simulation utilities needed particularly for timing and filing; and the basic conventions should be designed.

The thorough reading and rereading of the program should be considered a part of both final design, efficient programming, and the beginning of easy debugging. A divide and conquer approach facilitates debugging generally. The initial design of the simulation project should take into account the space and time requirements of the final simulator, the interface between the user and the simulator, and the need for flexibility as the simulator evolves with usage.

A story with many applications goes as follows: A young violinist on his way to his first recital at Carnegie Hall becomes hopelessly lost in the New York subway system. In desperation he rushes up to an old man sitting on a station bench and asks "How do I get to Carnegie Hall?" The old man stares intently at the yound man, raises a finger, and says "Practice!"

To quickly build good, flexible simulators:

(a)   take all my advice very seriously;

(b)   do it your own way;

(c)   practice!

References

Birtwhistle, G. M., Dahl, O., Myhrhaug, B., and Nygaard, K. (1973). "SIMULA BEGIN."
Auerbach, Princeton, New Jersey.

Gordon, G. (1975). "The Application of GPSS V to Discrete Systems Simulation." Prentice-Hall, Englewood Cliffs, New Jersey.

Hills, P. R. (1973). An Introduction to Simulation Using SIMULA, Publ. No. S55. Norwegian Computing Center, Oslo.

IBM (1972a). SIMPL/1 Operations Guide, SH 19-5038-0, New York.

IBM (1972b). SIMPL/1 Program Reference Manual, SH 19-5060-0, New York.

Johnson, G. D. (1974). SIMSCRIPT II.5 User's Manual: S/360-370 Version, Release 8. CACI, Los Angeles, California.

Kiviat, P. J., Villanueva, R., and Markowitz, H. M. (1969). "The SIMSCRIPT II Programming Language." Prentice-Hall, Englewood Cliffs, New Jersey.

Kiviat, P. J., Villanueva, R., and Markowitz, H. M. (1973). SIMSCRIPT II.5 Programming Language (E. C. Russell, ed.). CACI, Los Angeles, California.

Markowitz, H. M. (1979). SIMSCRIPT, "Encyclopedia of Computer Science and Technology" (J. Belzer, A. G. Holzman, and A. Kent, eds.), Vol. 13. Dekker, New York.

Pritsker, A. A. B. (1974). "The GASP IV Simulation Language." Wiley, New York.

Pritsker, A. A. B. (1977a). GASP, "Encyclopedia of Computer Science and Technology" (J. Belzer, A. G. Holzman, and A. Kent, eds.), Vol. 8. Dekker, New York.

Pritsker, A. A. B. (1977b). "Modeling and Analysis Using Q-GERT Networks." Wiley, New York.

Russell, E. C. (1974). Simulating with Processes and Resources in SIMSCRIPT II.5. CACI, Los Angeles, California.

8

Extended Queueing Network Models

Charles H. Sauer and Edward A. MacNair

8.1 Introduction

Extended Queueing Networks. In analyzing the performance of computing and communication systems, one often finds the dominant factor to be contention for resources such as processors, memory, secondary storage, communication links, etc. Queueing network models have been very successfully used to characterize this contention and estimate system performance. This success is evident in the discussions in Chapters 1, 3, and 4 and the case studies in Sauer and Chandy (1981).

We have previously discussed in Chapters 3 and 4 the assumptions made in queueing network models in order to obtain exact numerical solutions. These assumptions are with respect to characteristics such as arrival and service distributions, queueing (scheduling) disciplines, simultaneous possession by a job of several resources, and simultaneous activities by a job (e.g., CPU–I/O overlap in a computer system or packetizing of messages in a communication system). This chapter will discuss extensions to queueing network models that allow explicit consideration of these and other system characteristics.

These extended queueing network models are primarily intended for simulation solutions and are designed to allow use of the regenerative method of simulation output analysis to obtain confidence intervals. [See Chapter 6, Chapter 7 of Sauer and Chandy (1981), Crane and Lemoine (1977), and Iglehart (1978) for discussion of the regenerative method.] However, exact numerical (Chapter 3) or approximate numerical (Chapter 4) solutions are sometimes possible, as will be illustrated by some of our examples.

Solutions for the examples were obtained using the RESearch Queueing package (RESQ) a program package developed at IBM Research for defining and solving extended queueing network models such as these. RESQ provides a numerical solution component, QNET4, using the convolution algorithm for product form networks (see Sections 3.5–3.7) and a simulation component, APLOMB. See Sauer and MacNair (1979) and Sauer *et al.* (1982) for general discussion of RESQ. [The extended queueing networks we use in our examples are a subset of those allowed by RESQ. These models could also be solved using other queueing network software packages. See Sauer and MacNair (1979), Merle *et al.* (1978), and Information Research Associates (1981) for further discussion of queueing network software.]

In our discussion of extended queueing networks we use the terminology used with RESQ. This terminology is similar to, but not the same as, that used in Chapters 3 and 4. The elements of our extended queueing networks include:

1. *A population of jobs.* (Jobs were called "customers" in Chapters 3 and 4.) Each job has an attached variable that can be used to retain job attributes.

2. *A set of queues.* There are two types of queues, *active* and *passive*. Active queues are queues in the traditional sense and consist of servers and waiting areas, called *classes*. (Active queues correspond to the "service centers" of Chapters 3 and 4.) The classes have unlimited room for jobs. Passive queues consist of a pool of tokens and nodes for allocating, releasing, destroying, and creating tokens. A job belongs to a passive queue whenever it possesses or is waiting for tokens of that queue. One difficulty with conventional queueing models is that jobs may possess only one resource at a time. Often the modeled system's analogue of a job requires several resources at a time, e.g., a computer program must possess memory before it can use a processor. Jobs may belong to one active queue and several passive queues simultaneously. The terms "active queue" and "passive queue" are intended to

indicate the nature of the queue's effect on a job's use of a server or token, respectively. With an' active queue the length of time a job holds a server is entirely determined by the characteristics of that queue and the jobs at that queue. With a passive queue the length of time a job holds a token is determined entirely by events at other queues.

3. *A set of nodes.* Some types of nodes, e.g., classes, are parts of queues. Other nodes are used for auxiliary functions such as creation of jobs or changing the value of a job's variable.

4. *A set of routing rules.* These rules allow probabilistic and logical routing of jobs among the nodes of the network.

The remainder of this chapter consists of three sections. Section 8.2 is intended to be an informal definition of the extended queueing networks. Section 8.3 consists of a series of examples of models using extended queueing networks. The purpose of these examples is to show that complex system features can be represented by extended queueing network models and that it is feasible to construct and solve such models. In particular, the examples contradict the common belief that interesting system models are not regenerative. These models are of hypothetical systems; there is no attempt made to compare the model solutions with measurements of actual systems. However, some of the models are based upon previous efforts that included model validation with system measurements (see the case studies in Sauer and Chandy, 1981, for examples). Section 8.4 defines the branching Erlang distribution used in all of the simulation examples and explains why this distribution was chosen.

8.2 Extended Queueing Network Elements

8.2.1 *Active Queues*

An *active queue* consists of a set of servers, a set of waiting areas for jobs requesting or receiving service from one of the servers, and a control mechanism for allocating the servers to the jobs.

The waiting areas of the queue are nodes called *classes*. (These classes are local to the queue and are to be distinguished from the global "classes" sometimes used in queueing literature.) As described in Section 8.2.9, a job is routed to one of these classes and joins the queue. Upon arrival the work demanded by the job is determined as follows: First, a sample is taken from the work demand distribution (called "service demand distribution" in Chapters 3 and 4) associated with the job's class. The work demand distribution may be a function of the job variable. (Thus if the job represents a message and the job variable contains the message length, the work demand may be dependent on the message length.)

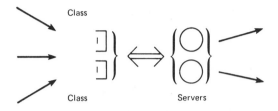

Fig. 8.1 Active queue with two classes and two servers.

Once placed in the waiting area, the job remains there until all of the work demanded is completed. When all of the job's work is complete, the job instantaneously departs from the queue. The server chooses which job to serve, if any, according to the queueing discipline. The effective rate of the server may be a function of the number of jobs at the queue.

The following queueing disciplines are allowed:

1. First Come First Served (FCFS).
2. Priority (PRTY). Each class has a positive integer assigned as its priority level. Highest priority is given to the first priority level, lower priority is given to the second priority level, etc. The priority levels are not necessarily numbered consecutively. Preemptions are not allowed.
3. Priority with Preemption (PRTYPR). This discipline is similar to PRTY. If a higher priority job arrives during the service of another job's work demand, preemption may occur. The decision of whether or not to preempt is based on the numerical difference between the priorities of the two jobs. If the magnitude of this difference is greater than or equal to the *preemption distance* associated with the queue, then preemption occurs. (Note that a preemption distance of one will always cause a higher priority job to preempt; a sufficiently large preemption distance will exclude preemption.)
4. Processor Sharing (PS). The processor is able to share itself equally among all of the jobs at the queue. (See Section 3.3.3c for further discussion.)
5. Last-Come-First-Served Preemptive Resume (LCFS). (See Section 3.3.3d for further discussion.)

8.2.2 Passive Queues

A basic problem with many queueing models is that a job may contend for only one resource at a time when in the system being modeled several resources may be required simultaneously. The primary purpose of passive queues is to allow a job to possess several resources simultaneously.

A passive queue consists of a pool of tokens, a set of waiting areas for jobs requesting or possessing tokens, possibly sets of other nodes for actions on the queue, and a control mechanism for allocating tokens to the jobs. The tokens of the passive queue are analogous to the servers of an active queue. The waiting areas are called *allocate nodes.* There are three other types of nodes that may be associated with a passive queue: *release nodes, destroy nodes,* and *create nodes.*

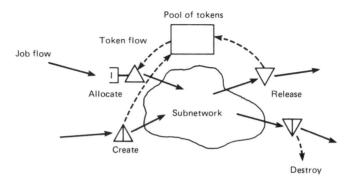

Fig. 8.2 Passive queue and associated nodes.

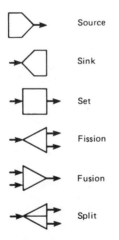

Fig. 8.3 Diagram symbols for other node types.

Allocate Nodes. A job arriving at an allocate node requests possession of a number of the queue's tokens. The number requested is determined by sampling from a positive integer valued distribution. As soon as the tokens are allocated, the job is allowed to visit other nodes of the network. However, as long as the job waits for or possesses tokens of a given passive queue, it is considered to be part of that queue. Thus a single job may be a member of one or more passive queues and one active queue simultaneously. If the tokens requested by a job are available at the time of arrival at an allocate node, then the tokens are allocated instantaneously. Otherwise the job must wait until sufficient tokens become available and are allocated to the job. Tokens may become available through the action of a release node, through the action of a create node, through a job leaving the network, or through a job being absorbed by a parent job at a fusion node (see Section 8.2.6). Tokens are allocated to jobs waiting for tokens according to the queueing discipline. The following queueing disciplines are allowed:

1. First Come First Served (FCFS).
2. First Fit (FF). First fit assigns tokens to jobs in first-come-first-served order wherever possible. However, if the request of the job that has been waiting the longest cannot be satisfied but there are other jobs with satisfiable requests, tokens will be assigned to these jobs in first-come-first-served order.
3. Priority (PRTY). PRTY assigns positive integer priority levels to each allocate node of a passive queue with several allocate nodes. Higher priority is given to smaller numbers. Within a priority level, assignment of tokens is on a first-come-first-served basis. Preemptions are not allowed.

Release Nodes.   When a job visits a release node associated with a queue that the job is a part of, the job instantaneously returns to the pool all its tokens belonging to the queue; then the job is no longer part of the queue. When a job visits a release node associated with a queue that the job is not a part of, there is no effect on the job or the queue. In either case the job's visit to the release node is instantaneous and the job proceeds without delay.

Destroy Nodes.   When a job visits a destroy node associated with a queue that the job is a part of, the job instantaneously destroys all its tokens belonging to the queue; then the job is no longer part of the queue. When a job visits a destroy node associated with a queue that the job is not a part of, there is no effect on the job or the queue. In either case the job's visit to the destroy node is instantaneous and the job proceeds without delay.

Create Nodes.   A job visiting a create node adds new tokens to the pool of its associated queue. The number added is determined by sampling from a positive integer valued distribution associated with the node. There is no effect on the job; its visit is instantaneous and it proceeds without delay. It does not join the queue.

8.2.3   Sources

A source emits jobs one at a time. The time between a given arrival from a source and the next arrival from a source is determined by a sample from a continuous distribution associated with the source. The sample is divided by the current value of the chain variable. Chain variables are associated with routing chains (see Section 8.2.9). This is useful in representing complex arrival processes, e.g., time dependent arrival rates, as illustrated in the final example. The chain variable is initially set to one. The job variable is set to zero when the job is emitted.

8.2.4   Sinks

Sinks are nodes that allow jobs to exit from the network. A job exiting from the network releases all tokens held, if any, and returns them to the appropriate pools. The exiting process is instantaneous.

8.2.5   Set Nodes

A set node is used to affect the value of a job variable, a chain variable, or a global variable. Job variables are associated with individual jobs. In addition to the message length example above, job variables are useful for controlling routing, e.g., to keep a count of the number of times a job has visited a given subnetwork. Chain variables are associated with routing chains (see Section 8.2.9). Global variables are independent of individual jobs and chains; they may be used in the same manner as programming language variables. A job visiting a set node executes an assignment statement corresponding to assignment statements in programming languages. The left-hand side of the assignment statement indicates the job variable, chain variable, or global variable to be affected. The right-hand side of the assignment statement may be an arbitrary scalar expression involving job variables, chain variables, global variables, distribution values, etc. A job's visit to a set node is instantaneous.

8.2.6   Fission and Fusion Nodes

A job arriving at a fission node generates one or more additional jobs. This is useful in communication system models where a message may be divided into several packets and in computer system models where a program may create tasks to perform input/output operations while processing continues.

The generating job is referred to as the *parent* and the generated jobs are referred to as *offspring*. A parent job and its offspring are considered to be *related* and know the identities of each other. Each of these jobs has a separate routing path from the fission node. The visit of the parent job is instantaneous; the offspring depart from the node immediately after generation. The offspring do not possess any tokens; their job variables have the same values as the parent job.

A fusion node provides a waiting area for related jobs. A fusion node has no effect on a job that has no relatives; such a job proceeds through a fusion node without delay. A job that has relatives waits at a fusion node at least until another job of its family arrives at that fusion node or all jobs of its family leave the network through sinks. In this latter case the job leaves the fusion node as soon as the last job of its family leaves the network. In the former case there are now two jobs of the same family at the fusion node. A fusion node will never allow more than one job of a family to remain at the fusion node. If one is the parent, then the offspring is destroyed, and any tokens possessed are returned to the appropriate pools. In this subcase the parent would remain at the fusion node if it still has offspring; otherwise it leaves the node instantaneously. If both of the related jobs are offspring, then the one which was generated first is destroyed, and any tokens it possesses are returned to the appropriate pools. The other job remains at the node if it still has relatives; otherwise it leaves the node instantaneously. For jobs generated at the same simulated time, the order of generation is determined as follows: (1) If the two jobs were generated on separate visits to a fission node, then the job generated on the first visit is considered to have been generated first. (2) If the two jobs were generated on the same visit to a fission node, then the one with the earlier specified routing path (in RESQ notation) is considered to have been generated first.

8.2.7 Split Nodes

Split nodes are like fission nodes with the difference that the generating job and the generated jobs are independent of each other; they are not considered to be related. This is useful in communication system models where a message arrival may trigger an acknowledgment or other reply.

8.2.8 Dummy Nodes

Dummy nodes have no effect on a visiting job or any other part of the network. They are used primarily to simplify routing definitions when fission and split nodes are used (see the following).

8.2.9 Routing

When a job leaves a node it is instantaneously routed to another node. All nodes except fission nodes, split nodes, and sinks may have several alternate destination nodes (for jobs leaving the node). Fission and split nodes have separate fixed destination nodes for the creating job and each created job. (Dummy nodes may be used with fission or split nodes to provide alternate routing paths for jobs leaving those nodes.) A node with alternate destination nodes has a list of possible destination nodes. The selection of the destination node may be probabilistic or may be deterministic based on predicates tested at the time a node is to be chosen.

Predicates. In addition to the probabilistic routing rules usually found in queueing network models, we allow predicates, i.e., functions with Boolean (true or false) values, which can be used to represent complex routing decision mechanisms. Status functions are provided for use in predicates to test for tokens available at passive queues, to test queue lengths, to test whether a job has relatives, to test values of job variables, etc.

Chains. The nodes of a network are separated into one or more disjoint sets called *chains*. A chain is defined as a subset of nodes such that none of the nodes of the chain are connected to nodes of another chain. *Open* chains are those that include sources and/or sinks. All other chains are *closed*.

8.3 Examples

In this section we will give a series of examples of models of a hypothetical computer communication system. The examples will begin with a model that considers very few system characteristics. Subsequent examples will include additional system characteristics and exclude characteristics considered in previous models. Since these are hypothetical systems there are no measurements to validate the models. We shall point out the effects or lack of effects of the system features considered. The figures and text should be considered complete definitions of the models.

The examples presented will of necessity be simplified and ignore features that may be significant in actual systems. Except as noted, it will be assumed that all users of the modeled systems have the same characteristics, that all continuous distributions have an exponential form, and that all nonconstant discrete distributions have a geometric form. These restrictions can be removed in extended queueing network models in a straightforward manner but would obscure more interesting features in the examples. (Removal of some of these restrictions may preclude application of the regenerative method or make application of the method more complex.)

Computing System Models. The hypothetical system to be modeled has a small computer which primarily services interactive terminals. There is a CPU with an effective rate of 0.2 MIPS (million instructions per second) and four memory partitions. The CPU scheduling algorithm is a low overhead round robin discipline which can be considered to be equivalent to processor sharing. The two I/O devices, a floppy disk and a hard disk, share a common channel.

The floppy disk has a mean seek plus rotational delay of 170 ms and a mean
data transfer time of 50 ms. The hard disk has a mean seek plus rotational delay
of 16.122 ms and a mean data transfer time of 2.878 ms. The mean number of
instructions executed per terminal interaction, including supervisor overhead,
is 80000. The mean number of instructions between I/O accesses is 10000. Ten
percent of the accesses are to the floppy disk, the remainder to the hard disk.

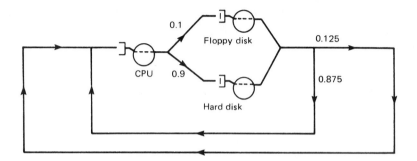

Fig. 8.4   Central server model (solved with QNET4).

```
MODEL:csm
  METHOD:qnet4
  NUMERIC PARAMETERS:deg_m_p
  NUMERIC IDENTIFIERS:floppytime disktime cputime
    FLOPPYTIME:.22
    DISKTIME:.019
    CPUTIME:.05
  QUEUE:floppyq
    TYPE:fcfs
    CLASS LIST:floppy
      WORK DEMANDS:floppytime
  QUEUE:diskq
    TYPE:fcfs
    CLASS LIST:disk
      WORK DEMANDS:disktime
  QUEUE:cpuq
    TYPE:ps
    CLASS LIST:cpu
      WORK DEMANDS:cputime
  CHAIN:multi_prog
    TYPE:closed
    POPULATION:deg_m_p
    :cpu→floppy disk;.1 .9
    :floppy disk→cpu
END
```

Fig. 8.5   RESQ definition of central server model.

First we are interested in estimating the utilizations of the CPU and I/O devices and the system throughput when all four partitions are in use. The first model considered is a central server model (see Section 3.4). It assumes that each of the memory partitions is always in use and thus should provide the desired estimates of maximum values. See Fig. 8.4. There are 4 jobs, one for each memory partition. There are three active queues: Queue 1 represents the CPU and has service rate 0.2 and mean work demand 0.01 (million instructions) yielding mean service time 0.05 s. Queue 2 represents the floppy disk and has mean service time $0.170 + 0.050 = 0.220$ s. Queue 3 represents the hard disk and has mean service time $0.016122 + 0.002878 = 0.019$ s. It is most convenient to assume the number of CPU–I/O cycles per interaction has a

```
eval2 csm
RESQ2 VERSION DATE: JUNE 17, 1981
DEG_M_P:4
NO QNET4 ERRORS DETECTED.
WHAT:ut

ELEMENT        UTILIZATION
FLOPPYQ        0.41965
DISKQ          0.32618
CPUQ           0.95375
WHAT:tp(cpuq)

ELEMENT        THROUGHPUT
CPUQ           19.07506
WHAT:
DEG_M_P:3
NO QNET4 ERRORS DETECTED.
WHAT:tp(cpuq)

ELEMENT        THROUGHPUT
CPUQ           18.04608
WHAT:
DEG_M_P:2
NO QNET4 ERRORS DETECTED.
WHAT:tp(cpuq)

ELEMENT        THROUGHPUT
CPUQ           15.88912
WHAT:
DEG_M_P:1
NO QNET4 ERRORS DETECTED.
WHAT:tp(cpuq)

ELEMENT        THROUGHPUT
CPUQ           11.22334
WHAT:
DEG_M_P:
```

Fig. 8.6 RESQ output for central server model.

geometric distribution starting at one (see Section 2.1.2b). The mean number of cycles is $80000/10000 = 8$. Since the geometric distribution with parameter p has mean $1/(1 - p)$, we choose $p = 1 - \frac{1}{8} = 0.875$. Thus the probability that the service of an interaction is complete after a disk service is 0.125.

Figure 8.5 shows a possible RESQ definition of this model (see Sauer *et al.*, 1980), and Fig. 8.6 shows the result of solving this model with RESQ for several degrees of multiprogramming, using QNET4, the numerical solution portion of RESQ. At the maximum degree of multiprogramming, four, we estimate that the utilizations are 95%, 42%, and 33% for the CPU, floppy disk, and hard disk, respectively, and the CPU throughput is 19.08 jobs per second. To estimate the system throughput, divide the CPU throughput by the mean number of I/O accesses $(80000/10000 = 8)$ and obtain 2.385 terminal interactions per second. We can estimate the mean memory residence time using Little's formula (see Section 2.3). Here $L = 4$, $\lambda = 2.385$, so $R = 4/2.385 = 1.677$ seconds per terminal interaction.

Response Time and Memory Contention. The basic central server model is not sufficient to estimate response times seen by terminal users. It is possible to estimate the time spent resident in memory, but not the time spent waiting for a memory partition. Figure 8.7 shows an extended central server model which includes terminals and memory contention. (We have considered similar models in Section 4.3.) The terminals are represented by an active queue, and the memory is represented by a passive queue with each token representing a partition sufficient for one job's activity. The active queue representing the terminals has as many servers as there are jobs in the network; i.e., it is an "infinite server" queue.

We assume that there are 30 terminals and the user "think time," including keying time, has a mean of 10 s. There are 30 jobs in the model, one per

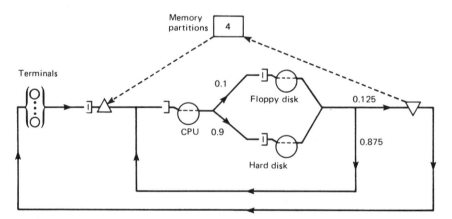

Fig. 8.7 Central server model with terminals and memory (solved with APLOMB)

terminal. A job spends a think time at the terminal queue and then requests memory. After receiving a token representing a partition, it traverses the central server model an average of 8 times, releases the token, and has another think time.

It would be possible to construct a similar model without the passive queue and solve it numerically with QNET4 (i.e., using the methods of Section 3.5.2). Such a model computes the utilizations as 93%, 41%, and 32% for the CPU, floppy disk, and hard disk, respectively, the system throughput as 2.324 jobs per second, and the mean response time as 2.911 s. However, it also computes the *mean* number of jobs at the CPU and disk queues as 6.764. Since memory contention in the actual system will limit this number to 4, one must question these results.

The decomposition approximations discussed in Section 4.3 are appropriate for the model with memory partitions. The composite queue of Fig. 4.9 will have service rates for queue lengths one, two, and three equal to the outer loop throughput of Fig. 8.4 for populations one, two, and three, respectively. For queue lengths four and larger, the service rate will be equal to the outer loop throughput of Fig. 8.4 for population four. Thus the service rate for queue length one will be $11.22/8 = 1.403$, the service rate for queue length two will be $15.89/8 = 1.986$, the service rate for queue length three will be $18.05/8 = 2.256$, and the service rate for queue length four or more will be $19.08/8 = 2.385$. Then we compute the utilizations as 91%, 40%, and 31% for the CPU, floppy disk, and hard disk, respectively, the system throughput as 2.270 jobs per second, and the mean response time as 3.217 s.

In order to confirm the approximation results, we can simulate this model using the simulation portion of RESQ (APLOMB). The regenerative method is used to obtain confidence intervals. (All confidence intervals given in this chapter will be at a 90% level.) To do so one specifies a system state such that the system regenerates when it enters that state. In other words, the system "restarts" and its behavior is independent of past behavior when the system enters the regeneration state. The periods between visits to this state are called *regeneration cycles* or *tours*. (See Section 6.3.6 for more details.) A sequential stopping rule (Lavenberg and Sauer, 1977) is used to run the simulation until the results seem satisfactory.

The APLOMB solution uses a regeneration state of all jobs at the terminals. The model run had a simulated time of 5397 s using 94 s of CPU time on an IBM 3033. (All simulations we discuss were run on a 3033.) In this time 303 regeneration cycles occurred.

The utilization point estimates were 90%, 41%, and 31%, respectively, with confidence intervals (89.8%, 91.2%), (39.6%, 41.8%), and (30.8%, 31.3%), respectively. The system throughput estimate was 2.279 with a confidence interval of (2.25, 2.31) and the mean response time estimate (the mean queueing time at the memory queue) was 3.12 with a confidence interval of

(2.97, 3.28). Thus we can say that the approximate results and the simulation results are in agreement for this model. The mean memory residence time estimate was 1.58 s. We conclude that queueing for memory is a significant portion of the response time.

The simulation solution also provides estimates for values not obtainable with the approximate solution. Especially interesting is the response time distribution. Following are estimates given by RESQ for specified points on the distribution:

t	$F_r(t)$	Confidence interval
1	0.191	(0.173, 0.210)
2	0.374	(0.346, 0.402)
3	0.554	(0.525, 0.584)
4	0.706	(0.681, 0.731)
5	0.811	(0.791, 0.832)
6	0.886	(0.870, 0.901)
7	0.931	(0.921, 0.943)
8	0.959	(0.951, 0.967)

The columns, in order, are a queueing time value, the point estimate for the cumulative distribution for that value, and a confidence interval.

Batch Work Load.   Let us assume that this system also supports a small batch work load and that we would like to estimate the effect of this load on utilization and response time. Because the load is light and the interactive commands are given priority both for memory (nonpreemptive) and for processor time (preemptive), it is expected that the effect will be small. The batch jobs have a mean interarrival time of 200 s, a mean number of

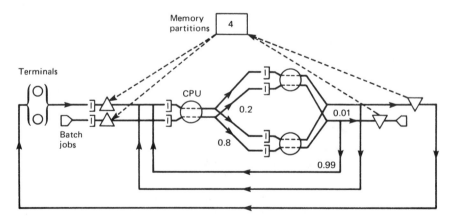

Fig. 8.8   Central server model with terminals, memory, and batch load (APLOMB).

instructions executed per job of 1,500,000, and a mean number of instructions between I/O accesses of 15,000. Twenty percent of the batch I/O accesses are to the floppy disk and 80% to the hard disk.

Figure 8.8 illustrates this model with batch work load. There is a second routing chain for batch jobs which is similar to the chain for interactive jobs, but there is a source for arrivals of batch jobs and a sink for completed jobs. The memory partition passive queue has a PRTY discipline with priority given to the allocate node for the interactive commands. The CPU queue has a preemptive priority discipline (PRTYPR) with priority given to the interactive commands and preemption distance 1.

The simulation of this model used a regeneration state of all interactive jobs at the terminals and the system empty of batch jobs. Then 586 regeneration cycles were observed in a run of 18847 simulated seconds using 285 CPU seconds. The estimates for utilization were 93%, 42%, and 30% for the CPU, floppy disk, and hard disk, respectively, with the batch contributing 4%, 2%, and 0.8%, respectively. The mean response time estimate was 3.619 s [confidence interval (3.47, 3.77)], with 47% of response times not exceeding 3 s and 90% not exceeding 7 s. The mean batch turn around time was 104 s, with 81% of the turn around times not exceeding 160 s. We conclude that the batch work load has a small effect on the interactive terminals, as we expected.

Channel Contention. One potential problem with the basic central server model is that it ignores contention for the channel. A job using a disk must briefly have the channel to initiate positioning (seek and latency). It will need the channel again later for the transfer. If the channel is not available at that time, there will be an additional delay incurred for the disk to rotate to the proper sector again. See Section 4.4 for a detailed discussion of disk systems.

Since the utilization estimates for the disks are low, there is probably little contention between them for the channel. However, we shall be more careful and construct a model which explicitly considers the channel contention. This model is the original central server model with the channel added. See Fig. 8.9. For each disk, there is both a passive and an active queue. The passive queue represents contention for the device among jobs, and the active queue represents the timing – there will never be more than one job at the floppy disk or hard disk active queues, as we discuss in detail below.

Along with the channel representation, it is appropriate to consider the physical positioning and timing of the disks in more detail. We use simulation global variables to keep track of the current cylinder position and the destination cylinder position (for when the arm moves) for each disk. We assume that with probability $\frac{2}{3}$ that a disk access will be to the current cylinder and with probability $\frac{1}{3}$ that a disk access will be to a different cylinder. [See Lynch (1972) and Wilhelm (1976) for discussion of this assumption.] When the arm must move, it is assumed that every cylinder (except the current one) is

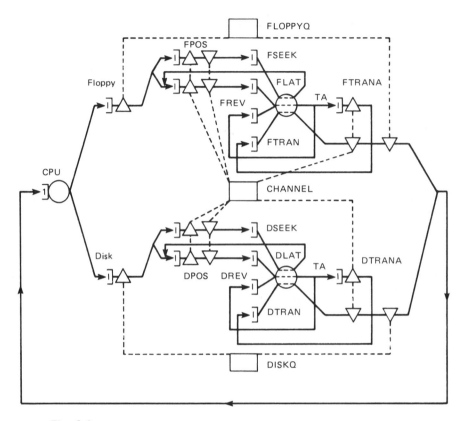

Fig. 8.9 Central server model with channel contention (solved with APLOMB).

equally likely as a destination. The set nodes for manipulating the global variables are not shown in Fig. 8.9 to keep the figure from being cluttered. There is a set node just before the class representing the seek time (FSEEK and DSEEK, for the floppy disk and hard disk, respectively), to determine the destination cylinder, and a set node just after the class representing the seek time, to record the destination cylinder in the current cylinder variable.

The floppy disk has 76 cylinders. We assume it takes 3.333 ms to start and stop moving the floppy disk arm and 10 ms per cylinder moved. (The class FSEEK service time is determined from these values and the number of cylinders traveled.) A full rotation of the floppy disk takes 166.7 ms; the latency (rotational positioning time) is assumed uniform from 0 to one revolution. The data transfer size is assumed fixed, so the transfer time is assumed constant at 50 ms. The hard disk has 400 cylinders. We assume it takes 10 ms to start and stop moving the hard disk arm and 0.1 ms per cylinder moved. (The class DSEEK service time is determined from these values and the number of cylinders traveled.) A full rotation of the hard disk takes 16.67 ms; the latency (rotational positioning time) is assumed uniform from 0 to one revolution. The data transfer size is assumed fixed, so the transfer time is assumed constant at 2.878 ms.

A job using the floppy disk first is allocated (the token representing) the floppy disk (allocate node marked FLOPPY). A routing decision (a Bernoulli trial) is made to determine whether a seek is required or not. Then the job acquires (the token representing) the channel (allocate node marked FPOS), initiates positioning (holding the channel for a negligible time), and releases the channel. If a seek was required, then these steps are repeated for latency. After service time(s) representing positioning delay, it tries to reacquire the channel. The "token available" (TA) predicate is used to test whether the channel token is available. If not, then the job experiences a service time representing a full rotation (class FREV). Eventually the job will acquire the channel (allocate node FTRANA), experience a service time representing the transfer (class FTRAN), release the channel, and release the floppy disk. A similar sequence occurs for jobs using the hard disk.

The APLOMB solution used a "regeneration" state of all jobs at the CPU. To strictly define a regeneration state we would also have to consider the values of the global variables, but this was not done. (Each global variable was initialized to represent having the disk arm at the middle cylinder of the disk.) The simulated time for the run was 1041 s and the run required 95 s of CPU time. During this run 7505 regeneration cycles occurred. The point estimates for utilization for the CPU, floppy disk, and hard disk were 96%, 44%, and 38% [confidence intervals (95.5%, 96.3%), (40.0%, 48.3%), and (37.0%, 38.1%)], respectively, and the CPU throughput estimate is 19.20 jobs per second. The channel utilization estimate is 14.5% [confidence interval (14.2%, 14.8%)], the estimate of the floppy disk utilization in lost rotations is 2%, and the estimate of the hard disk utilization in lost rotations is also 2%. We conclude that channel contention has little effect on this particular system.

Printer Spooling. Another potential problem with the basic central server model is that it ignores spooling of disk files to slower speed input/output devices. Let us assume that there is a 300 line per minute printer supported by this computer system and that there are two tasks constantly present which handle the spooling. One task fills buffers from the hard disk for the printer and the other dumps the buffers to the printer. There are two buffers for the printer and each buffer contains 30 lines. Thus the transfer time for one buffer is 6 s [30/(300/60)].

To represent the printer spooling in the central server model we add two chains, one for each task, and two passive queues, one for full buffers and one for empty buffers. The passive queues will be used, in part, to represent communication between the tasks, corresponding to the use of semaphores

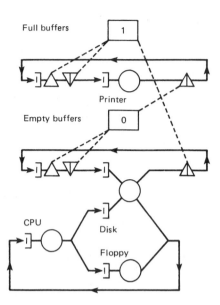

Fig. 8.10 Central server model with printer spooling (solved with APLOMB).

and similar process communication primitives in operating systems. The number of tokens of each pool will fluctuate between zero and two, because of create and destroy nodes, and the total number of tokens will usually be less than two. See Fig. 8.10. The task that empties the buffers (top chain in the figure) acquires a token representing a full buffer, destroys it, transfers the buffer contents to the printer, and creates a token of the pool representing empty buffers. Similarly the task that fills the buffers (middle chain in the figure) acquires an "empty buffer" token, destroys it, transfers from the hard disk to the buffer, and creates a token of the "full buffer" pool. The buffer emptying task waits at the allocate node in the top chain when no full buffers are available, and the buffer filling task waits at the allocate node in the middle chain when no empty buffers are available.

The numbers of tokens in the figure are for the initial and regeneration state. This state has the buffer emptying task emptying one buffer (thus it has acquired and destroyed a "full buffer" token), one additional full buffer ready to be printed, and the buffer filling task waiting at the allocate node in the middle chain. The "regeneration" state used also has all four user jobs at the CPU. This model is not strictly regenerative because constant service times are used at the queue representing the printer, and there is a service time in progress in the chosen state. The simulated time for the run was 1055 s using 32 s of CPU time. There were 8317 regeneration cycles.

The utilization estimates were 96%, 41%, and 32% for the CPU, floppy disk, and hard disk, respectively, and the CPU throughput estimate was 18.95 jobs per second. The confidence intervals contained the values from the basic central server model. The estimate of hard disk utilization by the spooling task was 0.3%, and the printer utilization was 100%. We conclude that printer spooling has little effect on this system.

Communication Systems. We have assumed so far that all terminals are local to the computer and that communication times are negligible. Suppose that this is not the case, that the terminals are in three groups of ten, one group of which is local to the computer and the other two remote. The two remote terminal groups are connected to the computer by a 2400 baud full-duplex line. The messages sent to the computer system have a mean length of 600 bits and the responses have a mean length of 1200 bits. In addition to the values already estimated, we would like to estimate the utilization of both the inbound and outbound portions of the communication line.

Figure 8.11 shows a model of this system. The computer system is represented as a single queue with queue dependent rates. The rates are the ones we previously computed for the model of Fig. 8.7. The active queues representing the communication lines have FCFS queueing disciplines. A message from a remote terminal group is sent on the inbound portion of the line and goes to the computer system. The response goes on the outbound portion of the line to the terminals. The mean service time at the inbound line

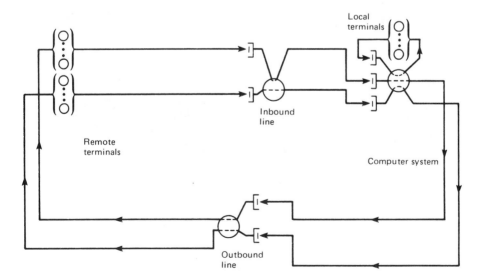

Fig. 8.11 Computer communication system (solved with QNET4).

will be $600/2400 = 0.25$ s and the mean service time at the outbound line will be $1200/2400 = 0.5$ s.

This model has a product form solution and can be solved with QNET4. The mean response time is 2.668 s for the local terminals and 4.447 s for the remote terminals. (The remote terminal mean response time includes 0.373 s at the inbound line, 2.719 s at the computer system and 1.355 s at the outbound line.) The line utilizations are 35% for the inbound and 69% for the outbound. The computer system throughput is 2.174 jobs per second. CPU, floppy disk, and hard disk utilizations could also be determined, as discussed in Section 4.3.

Polling of Terminal Groups. Polling of the two terminal groups was ignored in the above model. In an actual system, each terminal group controller would only send messages on the inbound line when *polled* by the communication line. Otherwise, the two terminal groups might attempt simultaneous transmission and interfere with each other. Assume that the two remote terminal groups are polled alternately. A polling message of 20 bits is sent to a terminal. Only then may the polled group transmit all messages that it has to send. After all messages have been exhausted at that group, it sends a 20 bit reply to that effect and the other group is polled.

This polling mechanism may be represented using passive queues (Fig. 8.12). Figures 8.12 and 8.13 are based on Fig. 8.11, but add new detail. Some of the labeling from lower numbered figures is omitted in higher numbered figures so that the added detail will be more easily understood. A passive queue has been added to obtain response time estimates other than the mean. (RESQ simulations allow distributions to be gathered for queueing times at passive queues, i.e., times from a job's arrival at an allocate node to its departure from the queue via a release node, destroy node, or sink. A passive queue with an "infinite" supply of tokens can be used solely for measuring response times, as in this model.) There is also a passive queue for each terminal group where messages wait (at allocate nodes POLLWAIT1 and POLLWAIT2) until the group is polled. Initially there are no tokens in either passive queue. A special polling message will create a token (nodes POLL1 and POLL2) for the passive queue. These passive queues have priority disciplines (PRTY) with higher priority given to allocate nodes used by terminal messages and lower priority given to allocate nodes used by the polling message. When the polling message creates a token, a message waiting for transmission obtains the token, is transmitted, and releases the token so that other messages can be sent. The polling message waits at an allocate node with lower priority until all messages from a terminal group have been sent. The polling message obtains the token, destroys it, is sent on the inbound line, and then is sent on the outbound line to poll the other group. The polling message is given priority on the outbound line. The service time for the polling messages on the line is $20/2400 = 0.083$ s.

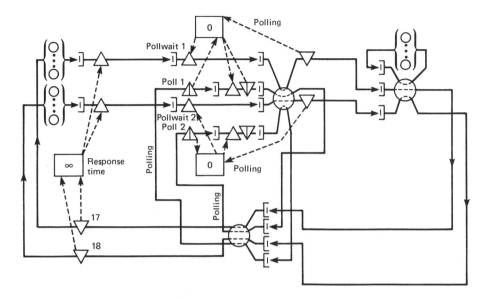

Fig. 8.12 Computer communication system with polling (solved with APLOMB).

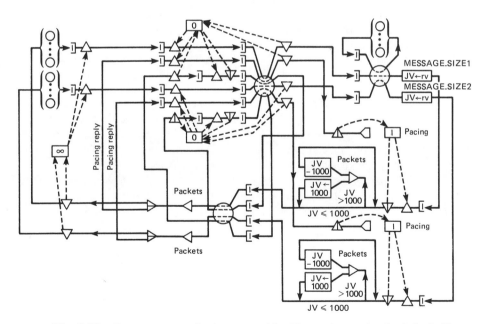

Fig. 8.13 Computer communication system with polling, packets, and pacing (solved with APLOMB).

To run the simulation, a "regeneration" state of all jobs at the terminals and the polling message being sent to group 1 on the outbound line was used. This is not strictly a regeneration state because of the constant service time for the transmission of the polling message. The model ran for 3046 s of simulated time, requiring 57 s of processor time. Here 192 regeneration cycles were observed.

The estimates for mean response time were 2.650 [confidence interval (2.527, 2.772)] and 4.849 [confidence interval (4.735, 4.963)] for the local and remote groups, respectively. The remote group response time was estimated not to exceed 3 s 17% of the time and not to exceed 7 s 87% of the time. The line utilization estimates were 43% and 76% for the inbound and outbound portions, respectively.

Other Communication Characteristics. Suppose that all messages longer than 1000 bits on the outbound line are divided into *packets* of at most 1000 bits. This would hopefully reduce response times, especially if long messages are preventing polling messages from being sent. Suppose also that a *pacing* mechanism is used to prevent a terminal group from being flooded with outbound messages. After each message sent to a group the computer system must receive a pacing reply before it can send another message to that group. The pacing mechanism is likely to increase response time.

These characteristics can be represented by using set nodes, fission and fusion nodes, passive queues, and split nodes. See Fig. 8.13.

Packet Representation. A message being sent to a remote terminal has a random value, representing its length in bits, assigned to its job variable (at set MESSAGE_SIZE1 and MESSAGE_SIZE2). The service time at the outbound line will be constant at 1/2400 s times the message length found in the job variable. Before a message reaches the outbound line, the value of its job variable will be tested by a routing predicate. If the job variable is greater than 1000, then the job (message) will go to a fission node where it will create a related job (a packet); otherwise it goes directly to the outbound line. The created job (packet) will have a value of 1000 assigned to its job variable and go to the outbound line. The creating job will have its job variable decremented by 1000 and again test the value of the variable. If the value is still greater than 1000, then another job (packet) will be created. When the job variable is less than or equal to 1000 the job goes to the outbound line. After leaving the outbound line, the packets wait at a fusion node until all packets have arrived and the job representing a reassembled message can proceed.

Pacing Representation. Pacing is represented by a passive queue for each terminal group. Before a message can be sent on the outbound line, it must acquire a token. It then destroys the token and proceeds. When it reaches the terminal group, it goes to a split node where it creates a pacing reply which goes back through the inbound line. The allocate node (of the polling passive queue) used by the pacing reply at the inbound line has highest priority. The length of the pacing reply is assumed constant at 20 bits. After going through the inbound line and releasing the polling token, the pacing reply creates a new token for the pacing queue for that terminal group and leaves through a sink.

The same "regeneration" state was used as with the polling model. The run lasted 4166 simulated seconds, requiring 90 processor seconds. Here 257 regeneration cycles were observed. The mean response time estimates were 2.603 s [confidence interval (2.501, 2.705)] for the local terminals and 5.015 s [confidence interval (4.880, 5.150)] for the remote terminals. The remote response time was estimated not to exceed 3 s 17% of the time and 7 s 83% of the time. Though the polling, packetizing, and pacing may be having compensating effects, it seems that the original model was underestimating the response time.

There are many other communication network characteristics that could be incorporated in a similar manner. Additional communications processors, buffers, acknowledgments, retransmission, slowdown mechanisms, etc., might be included. See Sauer (1978) for additional discussion.

Time-Dependent Arrival Rates. All of the models in this chapter have restricted attention to closed networks, except for the model that considered batch workload (Fig. 8.8). In systems where external arrivals should be represented, it is often the case that the arrival process depends on the system state or on some external condition, for example, the time of day. Extended queueing networks can be easily used to represent such arrival processes. The final example will again assume all terminals are local to the computer system

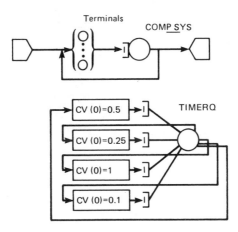

Fig. 8.14 Computer system model with time-dependent arrival rates (solved with APLOMB).

and will consider performance as the number of terminals in use varies. The previous models have assumed that the number of terminals in use was fixed at 30. It is more likely that the demand for terminals fluctuates throughout the day, according to the schedules of the terminal users. We assume Poisson arrivals of users at the computing facility, with the mean interarrival time varying with the time of day. The mean time between arrival of users is 200 s from 9 A.M. to noon, the mean interarrival time is 400 s from 12 to 1 P.M., the mean interarrival time is 100 s from 1 to 5 P.M. and the mean interarrival time is 1000 s from 5 to 9 P.M. The mean number of interactions per user is 200. See Fig. 8.14. The terminal's queue is represented as before, and the queue labeled "COMP_SYS" represents the memory, CPU and disks, and has queue-dependent rates (computed as with the network of Fig. 8.7).

So far we have described one of two disjoint subchains of this model. (Note that our definition of "chains" in Section 8.2.9 allows the nodes to form disjoint subchains.) The second subchain consists solely of set nodes used to change the chain variable. The fluctuating arrival rate is effected by these changes to the chain variable (see Section 8.2.3). The unscaled user interarrival time is 100 s. A single job is initialized at the set node labeled "CV(0) = 0.5," so the scaled user interarrival time is 200 s initially. That job goes on to the class at "TIMERQ" where it has a service time of 10,800 s, representing the period 9 to 12. After that service, the job goes to the set node labeled "CV(0) = 0.25" making the scaled interarrival time of users 400 s, goes on to "TIMERQ," and proceeds similarly to the remaining set nodes and classes.

We are examining transient, not equilibrium, behavior with this model, so it is not appropriate to use the regenerative method for confidence intervals. However, the method of independent replications is ideally suited to estimating transient behavior (see Section 6.2). Twenty-five replications were made of the simulated period from 9 A.M. to 5 P.M. This required 693 s. It was estimated that the mean number of terminals in use was 14.72. It was estimated that the mean time spent at a terminal was 2302 s. The mean response time during this period was estimated to be 1.695 s. Ninety percent of the observed response times were less than 4 s.

8.4 The Branching Erlang Distribution

The exponential, Erlang, and hyperexponential distributions were described in Chapter 2. These distributions are all members of a class of distributions defined by the *method of* (*exponential*) *stages*. The branching Erlang distribution is also a member of this class originally defined by Cox (1955). Cox showed that if we allow the artifice of complex "probabilities" and rate parameters, then there is a branching Erlang distribution equivalent to any other distribution which has a rational Laplace transform (see Section 2.1.4b).

It is readily apparent from the definition below that the exponential and Erlang distributions are special cases of the branching Erlang distribution without this artifice. (Though we may take advantage of this artifice in numerical solutions, we have no way to deal with complex "probabilities" in simulation.) Sauer showed that, without this artifice, there is a branching Erlang distribution equivalent to any hyperexponential distribution (Sauer and Chandy, 1981).

Let X_1 and X_2 be statistically independent (see Section 2.1.3a) exponential random variables which have rate parameters λ_1 and λ_2, respectively. Let Y be a Bernoulli random variable which is statistically independent of X_1 and X_2 and which has probability distribution

$$\text{Prob}\{Y = 1\} = q, \qquad \text{Prob}\{Y = 2\} = 1 - q. \tag{8.1}$$

The random variable X, defined by

$$X = \begin{cases} X_1 & \text{if } Y = 1, \\ X_1 + X_2 & \text{if } Y = 2, \end{cases} \tag{8.2}$$

is a branching Erlang random variable with $k = 2$ "stages" and parameters q, λ_1, and λ_2. In other words, X is equal to X_1 with probability q and X is equal to $X_1 + X_2$ with probability $1 - q$. The probability density function and probability distribution function of X are given by

$$f_X(t) = \begin{cases} 0 & \text{if } t < 0, \\ q\lambda e^{-\lambda t} + (1 - q)\lambda^2 t e^{-\lambda t} & \text{if } t \geqslant 0, \quad \lambda_1 = \lambda_2 = \lambda, \\ q\lambda_1 e^{-\lambda_1 t} + (1 - q)\lambda_1\lambda_2(e^{-\lambda_1 t} - e^{-\lambda_2 t})/(\lambda_2 - \lambda_1) & \text{if } t \geqslant 0, \quad \lambda_1 \neq \lambda_2, \end{cases} \tag{8.3}$$

$$F_X(t) = \begin{cases} 0 & \text{if } t < 0, \\ 1 - e^{-\lambda t} - (1 - q)\lambda t e^{-\lambda t} & \text{if } t \geqslant 0, \quad \lambda_1 = \lambda_2 = \lambda, \\ 1 - q e^{-\lambda_1 t} - (1 - q)(\lambda_1 e^{-\lambda_2 t} - \lambda_2 e^{-\lambda_1 t})/(\lambda_1 - \lambda_2) & \text{if } t \geqslant 0, \quad \lambda_1 \neq \lambda_2. \end{cases} \tag{8.4}$$

If H is a hyperexponential random variable with parameters p, λ_1, and λ_2 [whose probability density function and probability distribution function are given by Eqs. (2.45) and (2.46)] such that $\lambda_1 > \lambda_2$, then X is equivalent to H for

$$q = p + (1 - p)\lambda_2/\lambda_1. \tag{8.5}$$

We can define the branching Erlang distribution similarly for $k > 2$ stages. In that case X would be X_1 with probability q_1, the sum of X_1 and X_2 with probability $(1 - q_1)q_2$, the sum of X_1, X_2, and X_3 with probability $(1 - q_1)(1 - q_2)q_3$, etc. The mean and second moment are given by

$$E[X] = \sum_{i=1}^{k} (1 - q_1)(1 - q_2) \cdots (1 - q_{i-1})q_i \sum_{j=1}^{i} \lambda_j^{-1}, \tag{8.6}$$

$$E[X^2] = \sum_{i=1}^{k} (1 - q_1)(1 - q_2) \cdots (1 - q_{i-1})q_i \left[\sum_{j=1}^{i} \lambda_j^{-2} + \left(\sum_{j=1}^{i} \lambda_j^{-1} \right)^2 \right]. \tag{8.7}$$

The great generality of the branching Erlang distribution makes it especially appropriate for use in a simulation program (or in a numerical program such as the ones mentioned in Section 4.3.3a) so that we may have fewer forms to deal with both for the user and the program. RESQ uses the branching Erlang distribution exclusively for representing distributions defined by the method of stages. In using the regenerative method for confidence intervals it will often be necessary to represent some (or all) distributions by the method of stages in order to have a regeneration state. Notice that a simulation program does not have to obtain X_1 and X_2 simultaneously but can first obtain only X_1 and schedule an event accordingly. When that event occurs, with probability q the service time is complete, and with probability $1 - q$ the value of X_2 is obtained and another event is scheduled. We can define the regeneration state partly by whether any jobs at a given class have sampled more than the first value (stage). The branching Erlang has two additional advantages with respect to some alternative forms of the method of stages, e.g., the hyperexponential. First, a job will always use a value from the first stage as (part of) its service time. Second, for some systems the regeneration state will occur more frequently if the branching Erlang is used rather than the hyperexponential.

The price of this generality is additional complexity, as is evident from expressions (8.6) and (8.7). (Recall that the expressions for the hyperexponential distribution in Table 2.2 are also complex.) In defining a model one would usually not wish to directly specify all of the parameters. Thus one would usually make arbitrary restrictions such as limiting the number of stages k. RESQ provides standardized (but arbitrary) forms defined entirely by $E[X]$ and $C[X]$, the coefficient of variation of X, according to the following rules: If $C[X] \leqslant 1$, then

$$k = \text{ceil}(C[X]^{-2}) \tag{8.8}$$

(where "ceil" is the integer ceiling function, i.e., it returns the smallest integer greater than or equal to its argument),

$$q_1 = \frac{2kC[X]^2 + k - 2 - (k^2 + 4 - 4kC[X]^2)^{1/2}}{(k - 1)2(C[X]^2 + 1)}, \tag{8.9}$$

$$q_2 = q_3 = \cdots = q_{k-1} = 0, \qquad q_k = 1, \tag{8.10}$$

$$\lambda_1 = \lambda_2 = \cdots = \lambda_k = [k - q_1(k - 1)]/E[X]. \tag{8.11}$$

If $C[X] > 1$, then $k = 2$ and

$$q = C[X]^2 \left[1 - \left(1 - \frac{2}{1 + C[X]^2}\right)^{1/2}\right], \tag{8.12}$$

$$\lambda_1 = \frac{1 + [1 - 2/(1 + C[X]^2)]^{1/2}}{E[X]}, \tag{8.13}$$

$$\lambda_2 = \frac{1 - [1 - 2/(1 + C[X]^2)]^{1/2}}{E[X]}. \tag{8.14}$$

The choice for $C[X] \leqslant 1$ is primarily defined by the arbitrary constraint that all of the rates be equal. The choice for $C[X] > 1$ is primarily defined by the arbitrary constraint that both stages contribute equally to the mean.

References

Cox, D. R. (1955). A use of complex probabilities in the theory of stochastic processes, *Proc. Cambridge Philos. Soc.* **51**, 313–319.

Crane, M. A., and Lemoine, A. J. (1977). "An Introduction to the Regenerative Method for Simulation Analysis." Springer-Verlag, Berlin and New York.

Iglehart, D. L. (1978). The regenerative method for simulation analysis, In "Current Trends in Programming Methodology, Vol. III, Software Modeling and Its Impact on Performance." (K. M. Chandy and R. T. Yeh, eds.). Prentice Hall, Englewood Cliffs, New Jersey.

Information Research Associates (1981). PAWS – Performance Analyst's Workbench System: Introduction and Technical Summary. I.R.A., Austin, Texas.

Lavenberg, S. S., and Sauer, C. H. (1977). Sequential stopping rules for the regenerative method of simulation, *IBM J. Res. Develop.* **21**, 5.

Lynch, W. L. (1972). Do disk arms move? *Perform. Eval. Rev.* **1**, 3–16.

Merle, D., Potier, D., and Veran, M. (1978). A tool for computer system performance analysis, In "Performance of Computer Installations" (D. Ferrari, ed.). North-Holland Publ., Amsterdam.

Sauer, C. H. (1978). Passive queue models of computer networks, *Comput. Network. Symp., Gaithersburg, Maryland* (IEEE Catalog no. 78CH1400-1).

Sauer, C. H., and Chandy, K. M. (1981). "Computer Systems Performance Modeling. " Prentice-Hall, Englewood Cliffs, New Jersey.

Sauer, C. H., and MacNair, E. A. (1979). Queueing network software for systems modeling, *Software – Practice Exp.* **9**, 5.

Sauer, C. H., MacNair, E. A., and Kurose, J. F. (1982). The research queueing package: past, present, and future. *Proc. 1982 Nat. Computer Conf.* AFEPS, Arlington, Virginia.

Wilhelm, N. C. (1976). An anomaly in disk scheduling: A comparison of FCFS and SSTF seek scheduling using an empirical model for disk access, *Comm. ACM* **19**, 13–17.

Index

A

Active queue, 368, 369
Aggregation, *see* Decomposition
Allocate node, 371
APLOMB, 332, 334, 368
Approximate analysis, 173–175, 187–190
  closed product form queueing network, 175–183
  closed queueing network without product form, 183–186, 197–207
  open queueing network without product form, 208–220
Arrival process, 46, 255, *see also* Source
Arrival rate, *see also* Arrival process
  dependent on number of customers, 88, 157
  time-dependent, 389
Attribute, 333, 349–351
Autocorrelation function, *see* Correlation function
Autocovariance function, *see* Covariance function

B

Batch means, 307–309, 325, 327
Bernoulli random variable, 16
  random number generation, 231
Beta random variable, random number generation, 241–242
Binomial random variable, 17
  random number generation, 234
Bonferroni inequality, 293
Branching Erlang random variable, 390–393
Branching Poisson process, 262–263
  sample path generation, 264

C

Capacity function, 123, 165
Cauchy random variable, random number generation, 244

Central limit theorem, 42
Central server model, 112–119, 377
Chain variable, 373, 390
Chandy–Herzog–Woo theorem, 190–193, 204
Characterization method, for random number generation, 238–242
Chebyshev's inequality, 22, 34
Class, 368, 369
Closed product form queueing network, 119
  multiple chain, 143–151, 175–183
  single chain, 120–142
Closed queueing network without product form, 183–207
  multiple chain, 204–207
  numerical solution, 187–190
  single chain, 197–204
Coefficient of variation, 22, 34
  table, 21, 35
Communication system model, example, 152, 156, 176, 385–389
Comparison method, for random number generation, 246
Composition method, for random number generation, 233–235
Computational algorithm, for product form network, 124–126, 145, 161, *see also* Convolution; Local balance algorithm for normalizing constants; Mean value analysis
  programmable calculator implementation, 141
Computer system model, example, 4–6, 107–111, 113, 116–119, 121, 122, 131, 143, 151, 152, 160, 162–164, 175, 375–378, 381–385, 389
  with memory contention, 6, 202, 207, 269, 378–381
Conditional probability, 39

395

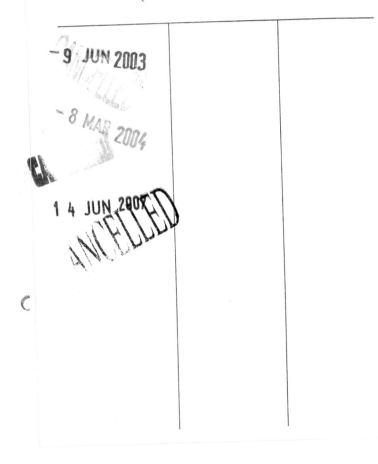